THE THATCHER EFFECT

THE
THATCHER EFFECT

EDITED BY
DENNIS KAVANAGH
and
ANTHONY SELDON

CLARENDON PRESS · OXFORD
1989

Oxford University Press, Walton Street, Oxford OX2 6DP

Oxford New York Toronto
Delhi Bombay Calcutta Madras Karachi
Petaling Jaya Singapore Hong Kong Tokyo
Nairobi Dar es Salaam Cape Town
Melbourne Auckland

and associated companies in
Berlin Ibadan

Oxford is a trade mark of Oxford University Press

Published in the United States
by Oxford University Press, New York

British Library Cataloguing in Publication Data
The Thatcher effect: a decade of change.
1. Great Britain. Politics, history
I. Kavanagh, Dennis   II. Seldon, Anthony
320.941
ISBN 0–19–827745–8
ISBN 0–19–827746–6 (pbk)

Library of Congress Cataloging in Publication Data
Data available

Set by Wyvern Typesetting Ltd, Bristol
Printed in Great Britain
by the Guernsey Press Co. Ltd,
Channel Islands

Preface

THERE have been many books on Mrs Thatcher, her life, political career, and government. The volumes and programmes have grown apace as her years in office have lengthened and commentators have accepted that she is a politically significant figure. She is, as is now well known, the only post-war Prime Minister to have lent herself to a political doctrine and style—Thatcherism—the only Prime Minister to have won three successive general elections in this century, and the longest serving Prime Minister for over a century. There is no doubt of her importance in post-war British politics.

This book differs from most others. Rather than concentrating on the governmental or political record, we have tried to examine the change, or lack of change, in a wide number of areas over the past ten years—from the arts to welfare. In commissioning the essays we asked our contributors to address two themes. What have been the main changes during the decade 1979–1989, and to what extent have the changes been produced by the initiatives of the government? Alternatively, did the trends pre-date 1979 and were similar changes discernible abroad? (In other words, to what extent might they have occurred without Mrs Thatcher?) We need to resist the temptation to explain too much in terms of her dominating personality.

Our contributors arrive at strikingly different conclusions. Samuel Brittan argues that there have been substantive changes to the economy. In contrast, Professor Ivor Crewe, in his study of public opinion and values, argues that there has been very little change, which suggests that Thatcherism has been 'a revolution that failed'. Some, like Professor John Tomlinson, a former Director of Education in Cheshire, think that the changes in schools have been significant and largely fuelled by the government. But Peter Hennessy is sceptical about the enduring impact of change on the Civil Service. Our authors reveal how uneven has been the Thatcher 'revolution': indeed, they call into question the whole validity of a Thatcher revolution. The government's impact has been tangential, major, insignificant, or catalytic, depending on the subject under review, and indeed the predilections of the author.

The Institute of Contemporary British History is aware of the pitfalls and risks of writing the history of events as recent as those described in this book, the full effect of the events being impossible, as yet, to tell. It is also aware that no authors can be value-free in their judgements, and especially not when writing about the day before yesterday. It nevertheless believes that the dangers of *not* tackling the study of the recent past are greater than abandoning the task to those for whom objective fact-finding and reasoned analysis are not the prime guiding factors.

This book constitutes one of the most difficult of the ICBH's assignments. The authors are not, of course, neutral; neither did we ask them to be. But we did seek a balance among the twenty-five authors of government supporters and critics, of left and right, in the hope that taken as a whole the book will constitute a reasonably balanced portrait of Britain in the 1980s. The authors do, of course, speak for themselves, and in no sense do they express the views of the Institute.

Finally, we would like to thank Stephanie Maggin and April Pidgeon for their help in putting the book together in the very tight deadlines available.

D.K.
A.S.

April 1989

Notes on Contributors

BRYAN APPLEYARD is a freelance writer, contributing primarily to *The Times* and *The Sunday Times Magazine*. He has written three books: *The Pleasure of Peace: Art and Imagination in Postwar Britain* (1979), *The Culture Club* (1984), and *Richard Rogers: A Biography* (1986). He was General Feature Writer of the Year in the British Press Awards 1986.

VERNON BOGDANOR is a Fellow of Brasenose College, Oxford. His most recent book is *Constitutions in Democratic Politics* (1988). He is at present working on a book on the comparative government of modern democracies.

GEORGE BOYCE is a Reader at the Department of Political Theory and Government, University College, Swansea. His most recent publication is *The Irish Question and British Politics 1868–1986* (1988).

SAMUEL BRITTAN is an assistant editor of the *Financial Times*. His most recent book is *A Restatement of Economic Liberalism* (1988). He was a member of the Peacock Committee on the Finance of the BBC. He is an Honorary Fellow of Jesus College, Cambridge, and Honorary Professor of Politics at Warwick. He has been awarded an Honorary Doctor of Letters by Heriot-Watt University, Edinburgh, and is a winner of the George Orwell and Harold Wincott Prizes. He has been a Visiting Professor at the Chicago Law School and a Visiting Fellow of Nuffield College, Oxford.

IVOR CREWE is Professor of Government, University of Essex, and co-editor of the *British Journal of Political Science*. He was Director of the SSRC Data Archive 1974–82 and co-Director of the British Election Study 1974–81. His recent books include *Decade of Dealignment* (1983; with Bo Sarlvik), *Electoral Change in Western Democracies* (1985; with David Denver) and *Political Communica-*

tions: The General Election of 1983 (1986; with Martin Harrop). He is currently completing a book on the rise and fall of the SDP. He regularly comments on electoral and political matters for the BBC.

LAWRENCE FREEDMAN is Professor and Head of the Department of War Studies, King's College, London. He writes regularly on defence matters for the *Independent*. His most recent books are *The Price of Peace* (1986) and *Britain and the Falklands War* (1988).

LESLIE HANNAH is Professor of Business History in the Department of Economic History at the LSE.

PETER HENNESSEY is co-Director of the Institute of Contemporary British History, author of *Cabinet* (1986), and Whitehall columnist on the *Independent*.

ALASTAIR HETHERINGTON is Emeritus Professor of Media Studies, University of Stirling. He was the editor of the *Guardian* 1956–75, Controller, BBC Scotland 1976–8, research Professor of Media Studies, Stirling 1982–7, and chairman of Scott Trust (owner of the *Guardian* and *Manchester Evening Newspapers plc*) 1984–9. His books include *Guardian Year* (1982), *News, Newspapers and Television* (1985), *News in the Regions* (1989), and *Perthshire in Trust* (1988).

DENNIS KAVANAGH is Professor and Head of the Politics Department at the University of Nottingham. His most recent publications are *The British General Election of 1987* (1988; with David Butler), and *Consensus Politics from Attlee to Thatcher* (1989; with Peter Morris).

DAVID MARTIN is Emeritus Professor of Sociology at the London School of Economics; from 1975–83 he was President of the International Conference of the Sociology of Religion. He is currently producing a book on Protestantism in Latin America.

ALAN MURIE is a senior lecturer in the School for Advanced Urban Studies at the University of Bristol. He is editor of the journal *Housing Studies* and the author of a range of publications, including *Selling the Welfare State* (1988; with R. Forrest) and *Housing Policy and Practice* (1987; with P. Malpass).

SIR ANTHONY PARSONS is a retired British diplomat. He served in FCO (Assistant Under Secretary 1971–4), Baghdad, Ankara, Amman, Cairo, Khartoum, Bahrain (Political Agent 1965–9). Ambassador to Iran 1974–9. Permanent Representative to UN, New York 1979–82. Adviser on foreign policy to the Prime Minister 1982–3. Research Fellow, University of Exeter. Publications: *The Pride and the Fall—Iran 1974–79* (1984), *They Say the Lion: Britain's Legacy to the Arabs* (1986).

J. ENOCH POWELL. Fellow of Trinity College, Cambridge 1934–8, Professor of Greek, Sydney University 1937–9, MP for Wolverhampton SW 1950–74, Down South 1974–83, South Down 1983–7, Minister of Health 1960–3. Hon. Brigadier, formerly R. Warwickshire Regt. Author (joint) *History of the House of Lords in the Middle Ages* (1968).

MARGARET REID is a financial journalist and author. Once a Treasury Official, she has worked for the *Financial Times* and the *Investors Chronicle* (of which she was Finance Editor), and has been Journalist Research Fellow at Nuffield College, Oxford. Her latest book, *All Change in the City: The Revolution in Britain's Financial Sector*, was published in 1988.

PETER RIDDELL is currently US Editor of the *Financial Times*, having previously been its Political Editor from 1981 until 1988. His book *The Thatcher Government* appeared in 1983.

BEN ROBERTS is Emeritus Professor of Industrial Relations at the LSE. He is the founder and editor of the *British Journal of Industrial Relations* 1963–89, the former

President of the British Universities Industrial Relations Association, 1962–5, the first President of the International Industrial Relations Association 1965–73, and the author of many books and articles on industrial relations.

RICHARD ROSE is Director of the CSPP at the University of Strathclyde and has been studying the territorial dimension and the politics of the United Kingdom for more than a quarter-century. His books include: *Governing Without Consensus: An Irish Perspective* (1971), *United Kingdom Facts* (1982), and *Politics in England* (fifth edition, 1989).

PETER SCOTT is editor of *The Times Higher Education Supplement*. Before that he worked on *The Times*. He is the author of *The Crisis of the University*, published in 1984.

ANTHONY SELDON is co-Director of the Institute of Contemporary British History and editor of *Contemporary Record* and *Modern History Review*. He has co-edited *Ruling Performance* (1987) and written *Churchill's Indian Summer* (1981).

JOHN TOMLINSON is Director of the Institute of Education at Warwick University. He was founder-Chairman of the Further Education Unit 1976–8, Chairman of the Schools Council 1978–82, and President of the Society of Education Officers 1982–3. He is a Vice-President and Chairman-elect of the Royal Society of Arts. His most recent publications include: *The Changing Government of Education* (edited with Stewart Ranson, 1986) and *Assessing the Impact on Local Education Authorities of Current Reforms* (1989).

CHARLES WEBSTER is a Senior Research Fellow of All Souls College, Oxford. He is author of *Problems of Health Care: The British National Health Service before 1957* (1988), which is the first volume of the Official History of the National Health Service.

TOM WILKIE is science correspondent for the *Independent*.

DAVID WILLETTS is Director of Studies at the Centre for Policy Studies.

KEN YOUNG is Professor and Director of Local Government Studies at the Institute of Local Government Studies, University of Birmingham, and Visiting Professor at the Bartlett School of Architecture and Town Planning, University College, London. He is the author of a number of books on local government, economic development, and race and community relations.

GRAHAM ZELLICK is Drapers' Professor of Law and Head of the Department of Law at Queen Mary College, University of London. He was formerly Professor of Public Law and editor of *Public Law*. He has also been Dean of the Faculty of Laws of Queen Mary College and of the University of London. He is currently Chairman of the Committee of Heads of University Law Schools.

Contents

List of Figures   xv
List of Tables   xvi

1. The Thatcher Government's Economic Policy   1
   Samuel Brittan

2. Mrs Thatcher, Capital-Basher?   38
   Leslie Hannah

3. Mrs Thatcher and the City   49
   Margaret Reid

4. Trade Unions   64
   B. C. Roberts

5. The Conservative Party   80
   J. Enoch Powell

6. The Changing Political Opposition   89
   Dennis Kavanagh

7. Cabinet and Parliament   101
   Peter Riddell

8. The Civil Service   114
   Peter Hennessy

9. Local Government   124
   Ken Young

10. The Constitution   133
    Vernon Bogdanor

11. Thatcherism and Defence   143
    Lawrence Freedman

12. Britain and the World   154
    Sir Anthony Parsons

13. The Health Service   166
      Charles Webster

14. The Schools   183
      J. R. G. Tomlinson

15. Higher Education   198
      Peter Scott

16. Housing and the Environment   213
      Alan Murie

17. The Irish Connection   226
      D. George Boyce

18. Values: The Crusade that Failed   239
      Ivor Crewe

19. Divisions That Unite Britain   251
      Richard Rose

20. The Family   262
      David Willetts

21. The Law   274
      Graham Zellick

22. The Mass Media   290
      Alastair Hetherington

23. The Arts   305
      Bryan Appleyard

24. The Thatcher Effect in Science   316
      Tom Wilkie

25. The Churches: Pink Bishops and the Iron Lady   330
      David Martin

    Index   343

List of Figures

1.1. Oil prices and world inflation · 10

1.2. Companies' real rates of return · 14

1.3. Share of UK exports in total world trade in manufactures · 17

1.4. Share of imports of goods (excluding oil) in total domestic demand · 18

1.5. Sterling against the D-Mark · 22

1.6. Sterling index · 22

1.7. RPI inflation: percentage changes on a year earlier · 32

16.1. Public sector housing: sales and new building (1977–1988) · 218

22.1. National morning newspapers (quality): average daily sales · 293

22.2. National morning newspapers (popular): average daily sales · 294

List of Tables

1.1. UK growth rates: annual average percentage changes 12

1.2. International growth comparisons: annual percentage changes in real GDP 14

1.3. UK current account 15

1.4. Comparative productivity: using purchasing power parity exchange rates 19

1.5. Unemployment 23

2.1. The major privatizations 43

2.2. Total factor productivity increases of privatized companies 43

6.1. Conservative–Labour shares of votes in post-war elections 89

13.1. Resources available for services 1980/1–1986/7 170

13.2. Increase in NHS staff and output 1980–1986 172

16.1. Principal housing and related legislation of the Conservative governments 1979–1989 215

16.2. Elements of housing activity in England 1979 and 1989 217

16.3. Proceeds from housing and other privatization 1979–1989 219

16.4. Council house sales: local authorities in England reporting sales of 30% and over between 1979 and June 1988 220

18.1. Socialist v. Thatcherist values 242

18.2. Thatcherism's economic priorities: taxes v. social services 246

18.3. The standing of the trade unions 248

18.4. Nationalization and privatization 249

19.1. Regional differences in GDP per head 254

19.2. Changes in electoral support in Britain,
1964–1987 259

20.1. People in households in Great Britain: by type of
household and family in which they live 263

22.1. TV audiences: average reach and viewing 304

24.1. Expenditure on R. & D. by departments 318

24.2. Government funding of R. & D. as a percentage
of GDP 320

24.3. Manpower engaged on R. & D. (degree or
equivalent) 325

The Thatcher Government's Economic Policy

SAMUEL BRITTAN

INTRODUCTION AND OVERVIEW

A very conscientious economic historian, Professor Nick Crafts of Warwick, has identified the problems of the British economy as 'weak management, poor industrial relations, ineffective research and development, and low levels of vocational training'.[1] Moreover, overmanning for a long time reduced the benefits from new technology. This is familiar and unsensational. It was the refrain of the post-war Anglo-American productivity teams, and could probably have been applied at any time over the last century.

Unfortunately, and quoting Professor Crafts once again, both Labour and Conservative governments were 'seduced into ill-advised dashes for growth, supporting declining industries, over-enthusiastic encouragement of mergers, and subsidies to investment'. The Thatcher government deserve two cheers for avoiding some of these traps, and for starting to reduce the difference in performance between Britain and her main trading partners.

I use the term 'Thatcher government' not to give support to the cult of personality but as a term of convenience. For there have been two Chancellors and seven Secretaries of State for Industry since the present government came to office in 1979; and I want to discuss the underlying trends of the decade rather than the problems of curtailing demand current in early 1989 and which may be quite different from the problems a year hence.

The judgement that the government has had some success in improving Britain's relative growth rate is based on the experience of the whole decade since 1979 and would not be materially affected even if the tighter policies introduced in 1988 to reduce inflation and contain the payments deficit resulted in a growth recession.

The sources of economic growth do not lie with government. The Thatcher administration did, however, do something to create the conditions in which Britain could start to catch up with its partners and competitors. But paradoxes abound. For instance, the source of the success of the first attack on inflation— and the roots of the productivity upsurge—lay in the *failure* of the intended gradualist anti-inflation programme and the administration of a short sharp shock via the exchange rate in 1979–81, which was unintended and due to policy errors.

The growth achievement had its underside in rates of unemployment, which remained very high even after the recovery from the 1986 peak. Moreover, if the poor did not become poorer in an absolute sense, there was certainly a major relative shift against them in the distribution of income and wealth.

Even on the mainstream achievement there remain lingering doubts, in particular about how fundamental the reform of management and industrial relations has really been. The public sector (which excluding privatized or still nationalized industries continues to employ a fifth of the labour force) is still strongly attuned to national wage bargaining, which pays quite inadequate regard to local or occupational differences in the scarcity of labour. This major rigidity, which also affects in lesser degree some of the larger privately owned firms, is a much more fundamental obstacle to continued and satisfactory growth than the financial headline issues such as interest rates, budgets, and the balance of payments.

THE INTERNATIONAL CONTEXT

Before going any further it is necessary to ask: how far has there been an international convergence around so-called Thatcherite policies such as cutting subsidies to loss-making industries and privatization? And how far was Britain (or the US under President Ronald Reagan) out on a limb?

David Henderson, head of Economics at the OECD, has enumerated the general movement of Western governments in a market-orientated direction[2]—a movement which international officials prefer to call 'structural adjustment' to minimize political argument.

He dates this shift to roughly 1979, but believes that it is not associated with a shift of power towards conservative governments. It is also evident for instance in Australasia, Spain, Sweden, and France, which have been under left-wing rule for most of the period—although even the most revisionist of British Labour leaders have continued to oppose many of the key elements of the platform.

Henderson lists four main areas. First, there is taxation, where there have been reductions in high marginal rates of personal tax, a shift towards taxing consumption, and—less clearly—attempts to reduce exemptions and privileges. Secondly, in product markets many countries have engaged not only in privatization, but in deregulation, especially in transport and telecommunications. There has also been at least a *desire* to phase out industrial subsidies. Thirdly, labour markets have been shaken up by the removal of controls and a shift away from centralized collective bargaining, as well as by reductions of the disincentive effect of the social security system—usually by the not very subtle means of limiting benefits. Fourthly and most conspicuously, there has been the freeing of capital markets, including measures such as the abolition of credit controls and interest ceilings, and allowing greater participation by foreign enterprise.

British efforts do seem in some areas greater in scope than those at least in the rest of Europe, not only in privatization, deregulation, but in the rolling back of union power. I would also highlight the phasing out of industrial subsidies. Industrial support is the one area where public spending in Britain has been cut drastically, even in nominal terms. Although part of the cut-back reflects privatization or classification changes, that is by no means the whole story. Nothing like it has been seen, for instance, in Germany, where regional and industrial interests have triumphed over the Federal Republic's theoretical commitment to the social market economy.

A less desirable difference is that the shift to freer markets in Britain has involved greater tensions and been associated with a blitz on intermediate sources of authority between the state and the individual not seen in other countries. The blitz has covered not only unions, but local authorities, employers' associations, universities, and even the Church. This centralization of state power is hardly necessary to eliminate corporatism. Much of it is incompatible with the dispersion of authority and influence, which is just as much part of a wider liberalism as free markets themselves.

A different point stressed by Henderson is how patchy the supposed triumph of economic liberalism really is throughout Western Europe. An obvious gap occurs with housing, which in many countries is still highly regulated, controlled, or subsidized.

The most conspicuous omission, however, occurs with trade in goods and services. In Henderson's view, trade regimes are on balance less liberal than they were ten or twenty years ago, despite successive GATT summits and the current EC drive to the Single Market by 1992.

The protectionist measures, which may have more than outweighed these initiatives have been *ad hoc* and industry-specific. Three categories have been especially important: subsidies or preferences for domestic producers; discriminatory import restrictions, many of them of a supposedly voluntary kind; and—increasingly—countervailing or anti-dumping duties.

All these measures discriminate between countries and products; they reduce the scope for competition and freedom of entry; above all they turn what could be low-level transactions between people and businesses into subjects of official negotiation between governments.

LEADING IDEAS

Enough has been said to warn the unsuspecting against using the advent of the Thatcher government as a pretext for an essay on the virtues and drawbacks of market economics, or even of the philosophic individualism which is said to lie behind it.[3]

To do so would be to exaggerate the influence of both long-dead and still-living political philosophers and economists. It would be to underplay the influence of specific events and pressures, particularly the mistakes believed to have been made by the government's predecessors. It would also be to flatten into a bogus consistency the disparate elements which enter into any government's thinking and policy, both because of the personalities of the leaders and because of the need to build a winning coalition from supporters with different values as well as different material interests.

Moreover, it is all too easy to forget that the post-war consensus had already been fractured before the Thatcher government came to office. Both unemployment and inflation had been getting worse in each successive economic cycle. Attempts to use incomes policy to secure stable prices without accelerating inflation had ended in spectacular failure, not only when Prime Minister Edward Heath was beaten by the miners' strike in 1974, but also when Labour's incomes policies subsequently collapsed in the Winter of Discontent in 1979. Nevertheless, partly in order to obtain union support for wage restraint, union power had become more strongly entrenched both legally and de facto. The desire to secure union support also contributed to the seemingly inexorable rise in the share of public spending in the national income.

It is often forgotten how long incomes policy retained support among Conservative leaders. The 1978 Right Road for Britain and the 1979 Conservative manifesto still contained hints about a possible national pay forum under the slogan of 'responsible pay bargaining'. But, because of events such as the Winter of Discontent, it was not in the end too difficult for the Thatcher wing of the Conservative Party to generate both scepticism about incomes policy in general and the thought that there was nothing in it for a Conservative government in particular.

Mrs Thatcher has clearly learned the lesson of not biting off more than she can chew. Professor Patrick Minford[4] reminds us that the Thatcherite ministers concentrated on three limited economic objectives—mastering inflation, union reform, and privatization—in carefully selected and cautious order. What would strike a Martian who had only read New Right literature was how little she has done to dismantle the post-war settlement, for instance in the NHS, social benefits, or the state provision of education, despite numerous and even draconian administrative changes.

Contrary to widespread belief Mrs Thatcher has not made many speeches outlining the case for relying on market forces, Manchester liberalism, the views of Milton Friedman, or anything else as ambitious. During the Conservative period in opposition Sir Keith (now Lord) Joseph had made a number of notable speeches setting out what he then called the social market economy. But in 1981 Joseph was switched from the Department of Industry to that of Education, and in 1986 he retired from the government altogether. The Chancellor Nigel Lawson did give a few addresses on policy principles, but in fairly general terms.[5] There is no Thatcherite equivalent to the detailed analytical account of Reagan policies by advocates who are also professional economists in the final Report of Beryl Sprinkel's Council of Economic Advisers.

The few ministers with an interest in economic ideas, such as Mr Lawson, and their advisers, were a good deal less intellectually interested in the micro-side than in the macro-side. Their general attitude was that, whatever some textbooks might say, intervention was more often the cause than the cure of malfunctioning markets. Their approach, although not their remedies, was akin to that of the US public choice theorists and allied writers who emphasized the threatened overload on governments, the effects of interest group pressures, the dangers of bureaucratic power, the potentially unlimited nature of so-called economic rights, and the distortions imposed by the political market-place, which could be worse than those of the commercial variety.[6]

But innocence of the economic analysis of externalities, public goods, and the like exacted its price. For the government's choice of where to pull back and where to continue to intervene has been based on the strength of political resistance. For instance privatization was hardly mentioned in the 1979 Conservative manifesto, except for shipbuilding, aerospace, and National Freight. But it became a major thread when it was found easier to carry out than many other Conservative aspirations. One reason why training was neglected and underfinanced for most of the government's first decade was the ignoring of the externality or spillover aspect. In other words, the incentives to individual firms to act as free riders on the training efforts of others in the absence of corrective policies were disregarded.

MACRO-ECONOMIC POLICY

Little of this innocence was to be found in macro-economic policy, where the major efforts of analysis were concentrated. The Medium Term Financial Strategy introduced in 1980 was a notable innovation likely to survive changes of government. Nevertheless many of its sentiments and even sentences were foreshadowed in the Letter to the IMF written in December 1976 by the Labour Chancellor Denis Healey. The rejection of the belief that governments could spend their way into full employment came under Prime Minister James Callaghan.[7] The IMF was the scapegoat for, not the cause of, the turn-round. Money supply objectives, targets for reduced government borrowing, and attempts to stabilize the share of public spending in GNP all date from 1975 or 1976. Indeed the words 'New Realism' were first used by Peter Jay to describe the Callaghan policies when he was ambassador in the USA in the following years.

One can speculate how far the Labour government, if it had been returned, would have retained its commitment to sound finance after 1979 in the face of the unemployment explosion that would have faced any new administration. Nevertheless, the new (or reformulated old) principles were in fact followed by socialist governments in, for instance, Australia, New Zealand, and France (after the initial Mitterand experiment) as well as by centrist and coalition governments in Europe. The main odd man out, on the fiscal although not the monetary side, was the Reagan administration, which gave higher priority to low taxes than to balanced Budgets.

In Britain, Conservative Chancellors were, of course, more explicit about the meaning of sound money than the previous Labour government had been. The essential principles of the new financial approach were succinctly stated by Nigel Lawson in an introduction to a book on Keynes.[8] 'The recipe for economic success is the greatest practicable market freedom within an overall framework of firm financial discipline—precisely how that financial discipline is best applied being essentially a second-order question though clearly one of considerable practical and operational importance.'

In his Mais lecture,[9] Lawson had taken the apparently radical step of reversing the traditional assignment of instruments and objectives. He assigned 'microeconomic (or supply side)' policies the job of promoting conditions favourable to growth and employment and 'macroeconomic policy' (what others would still call demand management) the task of suppressing inflation. This reversal was old hat, if still controversial, to those who had been following the international debate, but the British economic establishment seems to have an endless capacity for astonishment, as its reaction to the Mais lecture showed.

In fact Lawson was not a complete follower of his own doctrines. If he had not believed that macro-economic policy had some effect on output and employment—at least in the short term—he would surely have embarked on a quick anti-inflationary kill when he became Chancellor in 1983, instead of returning to the policy of gradualism that the government had unintentionally departed from under Sir Geoffrey Howe. One disadvantage of gradualism is that any policy error is likely to stall or even temporarily reverse the whole disinflation effort. Ironically enough, real growth performed much better during most of Lawson's reign than did inflation, which, even abstracting from the 1988–9 resurgence, stopped coming down and fluctuated around a higher level than in most competitor countries—a disappointment for the government's sound money supporters.

Some of the policy errors which led to a stalling of the anti-inflation effort in the mid- and late 1980s were in the realm of what Lawson rightly called second-order problems, but which nevertheless have their importance. The choice of intermediate objectives indeed troubled Thatcher Chancellors—as it did overseas authorities—for the whole period. No less than five different sets of monetary targets were announced,[10] and there were many changes of emphasis between targeting money, targeting the exchange rate, and aiming directly at total spending or income (measured by the statisticians as Nominal GDP): and there were public differences about the role of sterling between Mrs Thatcher and Nigel Lawson.

Because of these problems the Medium Term Financial Strategy was more significant for the general idea than for the detailed monetary numbers. The MTFS projections which did attain some credibility were on the fiscal side, where performance was 'better' than expected.

Both Conservative Chancellors had an instinctive suspicion of making short-term adjustments in spending and taxation for demand management purposes. Hence the same establishment economists who criticized the government for too tight a fiscal policy in the 1980–1 recession censured it for too loose a policy in the 1988 boom.

The thrust of fiscal policy was first to reduce the government borrowing and—when the fiscal outlook improved—to balance the Budget over an economic cycle, excluding the proceeds of privatization. The controversial 1981 fiscal clamp-down was justified as a move towards balance in the longer term. That-cherite Chancellors and their advisers used a bewildering variety of theories to rationalize a policy which reflected a mixture of instinct, reading of history, and opportunist taking advantage of unexpectedly high tax revenues. The rapid shift from one ration-alization to another no more than mirrored the academic debate.

HISTORICAL BACKGROUND

It is high time to move from ideas and principles to the govern-ment's actual record. Those who are prepared to take the statist-ical detail as read may want to skip ahead to the section 'The Sterling Shock'. But those who want to investigate further must go back much earlier, to 1973, which was a threshold year for the whole world economy. It was also the year of the Arab–Israeli Yom Kippur War, when OPEC, the oil producers' cartel, suc-ceeded in raising the price of oil by a factor of five.

The first oil price explosion marked the end of the post-war Golden Age of growth and full employment. Growth rates

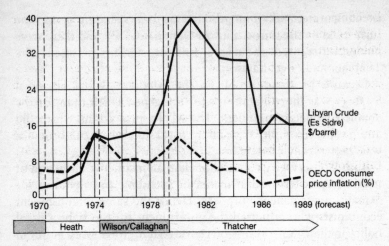

Source: Shearson Lehman Hutton Securities.

FIG. 1.1. Oil prices and world inflation

subsequently fell a great deal throughout the industrial world, including Japan. Creeping inflation also gave way to that ugly combination of slow growth and high inflation known as stagflation.

The rise in oil prices was probably more a trigger than a cause. The partial collapse of oil prices in the mid-1980s certainly did not restore earlier conditions of trouble-free growth. The sense that the post-war Golden Age was over was one factor behind the Western economic summits inaugurated by President Giscard d'Estaing; and the Organisation for Economic Co-operation and Development (OECD) marked the new mood with an inconclusive report by the specially appointed McCracken Group.[11]

Students of British history are more inclined to remember 1974, which saw the Three Day Week, the defeat of the Heath government by the miners' strike, and the well-publicized view of senior civil servants and centrist politicians that Britain had become ungovernable.

Nevertheless it was the leap in the international price of energy which strengthened the miners and weakened Mr Heath. And subsequent events, such as the initial success of the Wilson–Callaghan pay policies and their collapse in the 1978–9 Winter of

Discontent, as well as the shift of the Labour government to a form of monetarism, were a British version of a drama which was being played out on a world scale.

Then in 1979–80 there came the second oil explosion associated with the deposition of the Shah of Iran, which set off a further burst of world-wide stagflation. But this time the response was different. Nearly all major countries—and not just Germany and Japan—gave early priority to sound money policies; and inflation soon fell back from double digit to low single figures. But growth did not return to pre-Golden Age rates. Unemployment continued to rise in Europe, although not in the US and Japan.

THE THATCHER GROWTH RECORD

The second post-Golden Age cycle coincided with the arrival of the Thatcher government in 1979. Those commentators who take all the post-war years as a single period, or who start from the 1960s, see nothing very special about the Thatcher performance.[12] For them what should require comment (but rarely receives it) is the slow-down of 1973–9 under Labour. But those who take the years after 1973 as a new phase, as is suggested by the evidence, will come to a different conclusion.

Comparisons are best made for whole economic cycles: and the best available basis is the 1973–9 cycle compared with that of 1979–88. The earlier cycle started in the Heath period and encompassed the whole of the succeeding Labour governments of Harold Wilson and James Callaghan. The subsequent period of 1979–88 includes the severe recession at the beginning of the Thatcher government's terms of office and nearly all the subsequent recovery, which is surely near its peak.

Over this last cycle output per head in manufacturing has risen at an average annual rate of $4\frac{1}{4}$ per cent (Table 1.1). Not only is this increase much faster than the near zero average recorded during the 1973–9 cycle, it is faster even than the $3\frac{3}{4}$ per cent recorded in the Golden Age before the first oil price explosion.

The whole economy is much more difficult to measure, but, of course, more important. Service output has always been difficult

TABLE 1.1.   *UK growth rates: annual average percentage changes*

	1964–73	1973–9	1979–88
Real GDP[a]	2·7	1·3	2·2
Output per head[b]			
Manufacturing	3·75	0·75	4·2
Whole economy	2·75	1·0	1·9
Non-North Sea economy	2·75	0·5	1·8

[a] Based on output measure.
[b] Of the employed labour force, based on output measure.

Source: Treasury Autumn Statement (HMSO, 1988), CSO.

to quantify; and all the national income estimates have been undermined by the notorious discrepancies which became especially important in 1988. The estimates, for what they are worth, suggest that the average annual growth of real GDP per worker increased from $\frac{1}{2}$ per cent in 1973–9, to nearly 2 per cent in 1979–88.[13] This is a major improvement, but not quite enough to return to Golden Age productivity growth. Indeed no major country has returned to these growth rates.

For many of the Thatcher years the improvement in productivity was not reflected in the growth rate of total output, because it was running to waste in higher unemployment. But that ceased to be true by the end of the first Thatcher decade.

We can now see an improvement not merely in output per head, but in the growth rate of total output. Taking the whole period since 1979, it has averaged just over 2 per cent per annum. This is almost certainly too low because of the statistical weaknesses mentioned. Yet even the official estimate is nearly twice as high as that recorded in the previous economic cycle, and is at long last up to the European average, after many decades in which it was much lower.

I have stuck to estimates for the whole period after 1979 for the sake of caution. Nevertheless there is evidence that the more rapid increases in productivity of the later Thatcher years were not just a temporary recovery phenomenon but a more lasting change. Independent estimates of the underlying rate of economic growth sustainable in the longer term now range from 3 to $3\frac{1}{2}$ per cent per annum.[14] (They would be $\frac{1}{4}$ per cent higher without the gradual decline of North Sea oil output.)

The question is sometimes asked whether the British productivity improvement is a special case or has parallels in other countries, where governments have also gone in for deregulation, and privatization and other supply-side policies. Sticking strictly to the official estimates for 1979–88, Britain has done about as well as the Continental average; and the growth gap has come to an end mainly as a result of a slow-down on the European side. But if one is allowed to look at the evidence for the long post-1981 upturn, the picture is of British growth faster than that of Germany and France.

The most clear-cut evidence of the supply-side improvement of the UK economy is the sharp recovery in profitability from the depressed level of the late 1970s and early 1980s. Excluding North Sea oil, the real net rate of return achieved by industrial and commercial companies soared to 11 per cent by 1988, far higher than during the peak of the last economic cycle in 1978–9 and indeed a level not seen since the early 1960s.

Some downturn from these peaks was likely as the government tried to squeeze inflationary pressures from the economy, and perhaps too as a result of completion in the European Community Single Market programme. But the corporate sector had become more resilient; and nothing like the depressed rates of return of the late 1970s was likely. This was so whether the government succeeded in inducing a 'soft landing' or whether a few quarters of low growth or contraction were to occur.

THE BALANCE OF PAYMENTS

How far did the emergence of a record current balance of payments deficit of nearly £14.7bn. in 1988 qualify the general picture of improvement? The deficit was almost certainly overstated. It was for instance smaller than the unrecorded *inflows*, initially estimated at over £15bn. Many of the inflows were of a capital nature; and there is no need to quibble about the emergence of current deficit which even on a truer estimate probably still exceeded £10bn., or 2 per cent of GDP.

TABLE 1.2. *International growth comparisons: annual percentage changes in real GDP*

	OECD Europe	USA	Japan	UK[a]
1964–73	4·5	3·7	8·9	3·1
1973–9	2·4	2·6	3·6	1·4
1979–88	2·1	2·7	4·9	2·1

[a] Based on average measure.
Source: OECD, CSO.

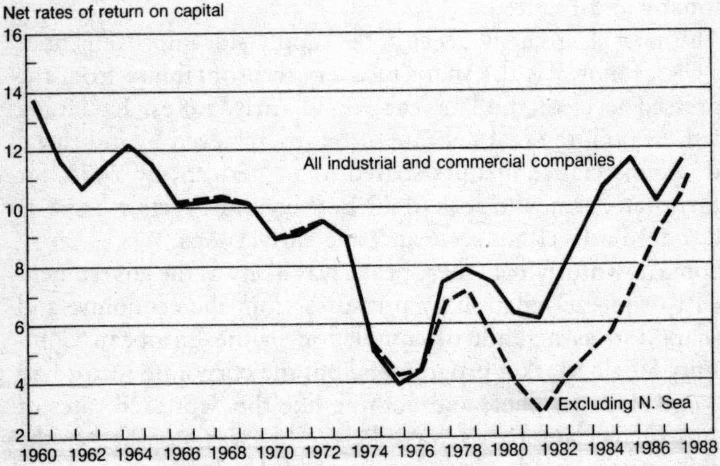

Source: *Treasury Autumn Statement* (HMSO, 1988).

FIG. 1.2. Companies' real rates of return

The horror with which it was greeted by commentators who had lived for a generation and a half with post-war payments crises was understandable but misplaced. One big difference compared with the earlier periods was the emergence of a unified and liberalized world capital market. Investors in surplus countries such as Japan, Germany, and the Far Eastern newly industrializing countries (NICs) needed external outlets for their

TABLE 1.3.   *UK current account* (£bn.)

	As published	Balancing item	Official reserves ($bn.)
1979	−0·5	+1·0	22·5
1980	+3·1	+0·6	27·5
1981	+6·9	+0·3	23·3
1982	+4·7	−2·4	17·0
1983	+3·8	+0·5	17·8
1984	+2·0	+5·6	15·7
1985	+3·3	+5·6	15·5
1986	−0·2	+14·6	21·9
1987	−3·0	+12·5	44·3
1988	−14.7	+15·0	51·7

Source: CSO.

savings and were short of creditworthy borrowers. There was no need for Britain or any other major Western country to go 'cap in hand' to the IMF or to other governments in search of official finance, so long as their own creditworthiness was maintained.

Another difference was that the British current account deficit reflected private sector borrowing rather than Budget deficits. This distinction, much stressed by the British Treasury, fell on sceptical ears. But it still remains true (*a*) that the private sector— unlike the government—cannot default on its obligations by inflation or currency depreciation, and (*b*) that the growth of private sector borrowing must eventually level off when some prudential debt-to-income ratio is reached.

Of course the levelling-off might take several years, and the forebearance of the financial markets could run out before then. But there were underlying reasons for the markets to exercise patience. The UK had built up net external assets over the 1980s amounting by late 1988 to around £100bn. or a fifth of GDP, a higher ratio than that of any other major country, even including Japan. The US by contrast had net liabilities of around £500bn. or 10 per cent of its own GDP.

It is quite true that the overseas assets belonged to private investors and were not available to the British authorities, except for war-type emergencies. But they were beginning to generate a rapidly rising stream of earnings which would add to UK invisibles in the years ahead.

Moreover, contrary to widespread belief, only about half the asset accumulation reflected directly the balance of payments surpluses built up in the oil-rich early 1980s. The other half was due to capital gains of various kinds, reflecting portfolio appreciation, currency gains, and a limited revaluation of direct investments. So, although capital gains cannot be guaranteed in any particular year, there was no need for a zero balance to maintain the British external position.

More fundamentally, the emergence of the UK payments deficit was not due to a fall in savings. (The aggregate of all savings, including corporate and public sector as well as private savings, remained remarkably stable in the 1980s.) It was due rather to a very sharp rise in investment, much of which occurred in 1988 itself, and which it was legitimate, on the most cautious criteria, to finance from overseas.

The basic problem was that this investment boom, superimposed on a rising consumption trend, led to an inflationary increase in demand, part of which was deflected into imports or on to exportable goods.

This could not continue much longer and the basic problem at the end of 1988 and in the first few months of 1989 was not the balance of payments itself, but the inflationary rise in demand of which it was a symptom. That demand could be curbed by interest rate policy, designed both to maintain a strong pound and discourage domestic lending, provided that the policy was maintained long enough and firmly enough in the face of political unpopularity.

No policy could guarantee a 'soft landing', while the economy returned to non-inflationary rates of capital and labour utilization and resources shifted out of the domestic sector. Meanwhile, the balance of payments will take care of itself, but if, and only if, the government succeeds in reversing the inflationary tide and putting a severe limit to any depreciation of sterling.

The stability of the UK share of world net exports of manufac-

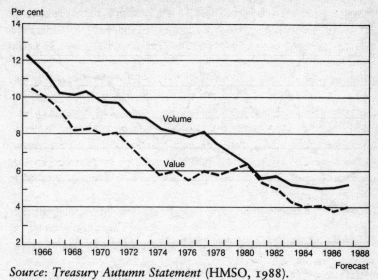

Source: *Treasury Autumn Statement* (HMSO, 1988).

FIG. 1.3.   Share of UK exports in total world trade in manufactures

turing since the early 1980s was prima-facie evidence that the UK industry was reasonably competitive under conditions of normal demand. So was the slowing down in the rise of import penetration before the 1987–8 boom.[15]

In any case a policy of systematic sterling depreciation would be more likely to be eroded in rapid inflation than to lead to any lasting improvement in competitiveness. Even in the pre-Thatcher period, it is very doubtful if there really was a balance of payments constraint on growth, except as a symptom of supply-side failures and the rigidity of wages in the face of market pressures.

NORTH SEA OIL

The improvement in British growth and productivity cannot be explained away by North Sea oil. Oil had a useful effect in the 1980s in maintaining real incomes in the face of the recession and industrial shake-out. But at its peak in 1985, it amounted to under $5\frac{1}{2}$ per cent of GNP. By 1988 it had fallen to $1\frac{1}{2}$ per cent, more because of the fall in prices than because of that in

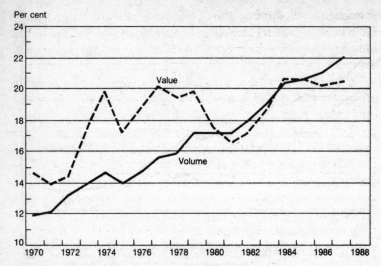

Source: *Treasury Autumn Statement* (HMSO, 1988).

FIG. 1.4.   Share of imports of goods (excluding oil) in total domestic demand

production. Since 1985, the North Sea has subtracted about half a per cent per annum from the annual growth of output. North Sea receipts now account for only 2 per cent of public sector revenues.

Nor is it true that North Sea revenues were wasted. They were, for instance, an important—but as we have seen not the only—factor in the UK accumulation of external assets. Of the recorded deterioration in the UK balance of payments of nearly £15bn. since 1986 less than £2bn. reflected the change in the net balance in oil.

REMAINING GAP

The level or growth of real output per head is not, of course, a measure of happiness nor even of economic well-being. There are plenty of bads, such as pollution or congestion or destruction of pleasant vistas, which are not measured in GDP figures—just as there are plenty of goods such as fresh air or favourable overspills which equally escape measurement. Attempts to correct these distortions still show positive, if slower, growth rates. A high GDP is usually better than a low one, although it is far from the only or necessarily the most important criterion for judging the state of society or the success of its government.

To keep the growth improvement in perspective we need to remember that the UK started the 1980s with a very substantial output and productivity gap compared with its leading trading partners. Figures of absolute levels of performance are much more difficult to estimate than growth rates; and to be meaningful it is important to compare different countries' output at exchange rates which equalize purchasing power rather than at market exchange rates—a precaution not always taken.

There are many estimates in circulation which either understate or exaggerate international productivity gaps. For instance GDP per head figures tend to underestimate the gap because Britain has a comparatively high proportion of its population at work. A less misleading comparison is between output per worker, which shows France and Germany some 14 to 21 per cent ahead of Britain, even in 1987, and the US over 40 per cent ahead.

TABLE 1.4. *Comparative productivity: using purchasing power parity exchange rates* (UK=100)

	GDP per capita (1987)[a]	GDP per worker (1987)[b]	Manufacturing, output per worker (1985)
France	104	121	127
Germany	108	114	122
Italy	99	121	117
Japan	107	97	116
USA	149	141	167

[a] Whole economy GDP at current prices divided by total population.
[b] Whole economy GDP divided by total civilian employment (including self-employed).

Sources: OECD National Accounts vol. ii, OECD Quarterly Labour Statistics, and NEDO.

As for manufacturing productivity, the estimates in Table 1.4, which are derived by the National Economic Development Office from OECD data are about the best available. They show German and French productivity (in 1985) about 25 per cent higher than British, and US productivity 65 to 70 per cent higher. Again the comparisons do not allow for working hours.

It is, however, the very gap between British productivity and productivity overseas—the culmination of a century of comparatively slow growth—which has created the opportunity to catch up. There is no economic miracle in reducing the distance between the UK and richer countries employing best-practice technology; the opportunity increases with the size of the gap. The UK has at last begun to take that opportunity.

THE STERLING SHOCK

For the origins of the British productivity improvement as of most other things, good or bad, in the Thatcher government's economic policies, we have to go back to its first two painful years, from its inauguration in 1979, up to and after the 1981 Budget, which led to the famous protest of the 364 economists.

The incoming Thatcher administration presided over a wage explosion. The annual increase in earnings rose in 1980 to the astonishingly high rate of 20 per cent before subsiding to the $7\frac{1}{2}$ to 9 per cent average, where it subsequently remained. The wage explosion was partly due to the knock-on effect of the second oil price shock on the Retail Price Index. It was also a backlash from the collapse of the Labour government's pay policies and reflected too the contagious effects of the awards of the Clegg Commission, set up by the outgoing government to terminate the public sector strikes in 1979, but which both main political parties were pledged to honour.

The new government stoked up the explosion by the near doubling of VAT in its first Budget. Whatever the pros and cons of such a move, this was the worst possible time for it. The net result of all the various knock-on factors was a recorded rate of inflation of 18 per cent in 1980, which fed back into pay awards despite the gathering depression.

But this was not all. For at the very same time when British costs were exploding anyway, there was a sharp rise in the pound, which, at its peak in 1981, was (in terms of the index) 25 per cent higher than two years before. The real exchange rate, which takes into account international cost movements, rose by nearly twice as much.

The 1979–80 rise in sterling was largely an international portfolio movement due to confidence in Britain as an oil producer at a time of world-wide worries about oil supplies, reinforced by the effects of the 'Thatcher factor'. It was responsible for the rapid fall in inflation which took both the government's critics and the official forecasters by surprise.

But it was also the proximate cause of one of the unhappiest experiences of the Thatcher period. Manufacturing employment, which had been contracting even in the 1970s, fell by over 2 million from its 1979 level, mostly in the early years of the Thatcher government.

The number of jobs created outside manufacturing was not, initially, sufficient to prevent unemployment (adults seasonally adjusted) trebling from 1.1 million in 1979 to a peak of 3.2 million in 1986. Again most of the rise came in a single burst in the 1980–1 recession; but even after that it continued to creep upwards.[16]

The pay explosion, the severe recession, and the unemployment leap of the early Thatcher years were three interrelated phenomena—almost aspects of each other. The government's great mistake, especially given its gradualist approach to union reform, was to underrate the perversities of the British labour market: the attachment to 'going rates', the distaste for market-related pay, the extreme rapidity with which even temporary price explosions fed into pay, and the dominant power of 'insiders' with jobs in fixing remuneration over outsiders without. The result was that the government underestimated both the job losses in tackling inflation solely from the demand side and the underlying forces making for high unemployment.

It is now also well known that the Thatcher government was misled about the severity of the demand squeeze in its initial couple of years because it did not take the sterling exchange rate

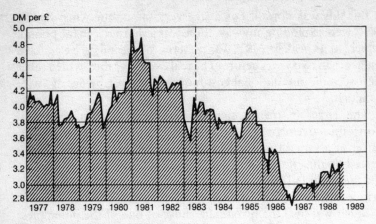

DM per £

FIG. 1.5. Sterling against the D-Mark

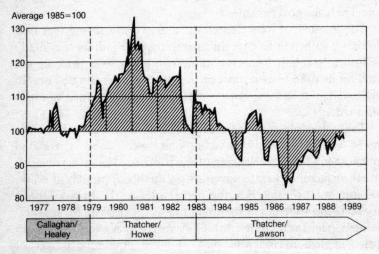

Average 1985=100

| Callaghan/ Healey | Thatcher/ Howe | Thatcher/ Lawson |

FIG. 1.6. Sterling index
Source: Bank of England.

sufficiently into account, and because it did not adjust its monet-ary targets to take account of structural changes in the desire to hold money—including changes brought about by its own actions such as the abolition of exchange controls and the

TABLE 1.5.   *Unemployment (% of total labour force)*

	UK DE	UK OECD	EEC[a]	USA	Japan
1973	2·1	3·0	2·9	4·8	1·3
1976	4·5	5·6	5·0	7·6	2·0
1977	4·8	6·1	5·4	6·9	2·0
1979	4·3	5·0	5·7	5·8	2·1
1982	9·8	11·3	9·6	9·5	2·4
1986	11·4	11·2	10·9	6·9	2·8
1987	10·2	10·3	10·7	6·1	2·8
1988	8·1	8·3	10·2	5·4	2·5
1989 (Jan.)	6·8[b]	—	9·8	5·4	—

[a] EEC figures cover Belgium, France, Germany, Netherlands, Spain, and UK.
[b] February.
Source: OECD figures, partially standardized.

removal of the direct limit on the growth of bank deposits known as the 'corset'.

The exchange rate squeeze was doubly unintended. It arose out of monetary policy mistakes, which transformed an intended gradual disinflation into a sharp shock. Yet it had a silver lining. For the resulting pressure on profit margins led to a blitz on overmanning and a productivity spurt in industry.

The unforeseen result was that what was meant to be a financial policy to reduce inflation became a highly successful, if accidental, industrial strategy. In other words the benefits flowed from mistakes. As Professor Geoffrey Maynard has said:[17] 'By refusing to accommodate rising costs and poor productivity with exchange rate depreciation, macro-policy imposed pressure on industry to raise productivity, lower costs, and generally move its product up market. Many firms whose managements were often vociferous in their criticism of government exchange rate policy subsequently achieved productivity improvements and product upgrading' to an almost revolutionary degree.

The overvalued pound began to decline from early 1981 onwards. This was partly due to international changes. For from that time Reagan's America began to replace Thatcher's Britain as the main magnet for footloose funds. Internally the British government, fortified by the controversially tough Budget of 1981, which raised taxes despite the recession, began to worry less about the overshoot of its original target monetary aggregate (Sterling M3) and began a staged reduction of interest rates, with some temporary reversals when sterling fell 'too quickly'.

The combination of a continued world upturn, an easing of UK monetary and exchange rate policies, and structural policies to improve the British labour market eventually resulted in a turn-round in unemployment. But the enhanced training and job search programmes, and attempts to move away from national pay bargaining and going rates in the public sector, hardly began until near the end of the second Thatcher government—perhaps with the realization that ministers could hardly fight a second election (that of 1987) with unemployment still rising.

It was from the second half of 1986 that the unemployed claimant total started to fall. It did so fairly rapidly, but was in the winter of 1988–9 not far below 2 million or nearly twice as high as when the government took office. Most seriously of all, this level of unemployment coincided with severe labour shortages, especially, but not only, of skilled workers, in many parts of the country, and widespread anxiety about inflationary overheating. The level of registered vacancies came back to where it was when the Thatcher government arrived in office, suggesting an increase in 'mismatch' between vacancies and unemployment.

The claimant count was affected by a series of programmes and procedures which have discouraged marginal claimants from registering. How much of the 1.2 million drop in unemployment in the two and a half years after mid-1986 represented such pressures is highly controversial.[18] The 1988 Labour Force survey suggests, however, that most of the unemployment drop—at least up to the spring of that year—was also observable under interna-tional survey definitions.[19]

The UK unemployment percentage remained higher than that of the US and much higher than that of Japan, although lower than the European Community average.

SPENDING AND TAXES

The exchange rate shock and demand squeeze gave the initial impetus to the supply-side improvement. But they cannot explain why the improvement persisted. In the words of the OECD Report on the UK, 'the persistence of high rates of output and productivity growth throughout an exceptionally long recovery phase, judged by past performance and that of other countries, suggests that the improvements on supply side performance is more than a transitory cyclical phenomenon.'[20]

What were these supply-side policies? The government has received both praise and blame for public spending cuts and giving priority to tax reductions. Both are largely misplaced. In the early Thatcher years the public spending ratio actually increased, under the influence of recession, increased demands on the social security system and electoral pledges on defence and police spending.

The public expenditure ratio reached its peak in 1982–3; but it was not until 1987–8, the Thatcher government's ninth year of office, that the ratio dipped decisively below that of 1978–9, the last year of the Callaghan government. By 1988–9 the ratio had fallen to 39¾ per cent (excluding privatization proceeds), the lowest since 1963–4.[21] It was projected to fall further and dip below 39 per cent in the early 1990s. But continued success in reducing this ratio could not be taken for granted once the period of boom growth and rapidly falling unemployment came to an end.

More fundamentally, the Thatcher government had not after nearly two and a half terms in office reduced the range of its responsibilities for social security, health, or any of the large spending areas. The result was that, because of changing needs and technology (e.g. in the health service), it had to be as tight-fisted as possible simply to contain spending increase. Thus the defenders of the Welfare State saw meanness and cheese-paring all round, while the Radical Right felt it had been betrayed. Indeed, by 1989 there were already signs that one key element in the government's public expenditure policy—the linking of benefits to inflation rather than incomes—was coming under strain.

Partly because the public sector balance had moved from deficit to surplus, the total UK tax burden had not come down at the end of the first decade. Tax revenues, excluding those from the North Sea, still amounted in 1988–9 to a higher proportion of GDP than before the government took office. While the headlines concentrated on the reductions in the basic rate of income tax, these were more than offset by the increase in VAT and employers' contributions in the early Thatcher years and later by the automatic effects of rising real income in bringing more and more taxpayers into higher tax zones in the later years ('Real fiscal drag').

The tax rate which counts from the point of view of incentives is the marginal tax on each pound earned. Taking National Insurance and consumer taxes properly into account, this still amounted in 1988–9 to approximately 50 to 58 per cent, depending on family status, and only slightly less than in 1979.[22]

There has been of course a much bigger cut in the top marginal rate, which on a similar basis was approximately 60 per cent for a salaried employee compared to over 85 per cent when the government took office. These very high marginal rates brought in little or even negative revenue and produced all manner of distortions not imagined by those who sneered at the incentives case. It is surely better that a country should attract high earners rather than push them into tax exile.[23]

Penal marginal rates unfortunately still remain at the bottom of the income scale, in the shape of the poverty and unemployment traps—which would be extremely expensive to tackle without reducing the standards of those who depend entirely on benefit. That difficulty is, however, no reason for restoring penal rates at the top, which would be a concession to envy and do nothing to alleviate the poverty trap.

UK NO MARKET PARADISE

Greater use of competition and markets is not the same thing as reducing public spending. Many interest group privileges—for instance the pension funds, mortgage holders, or farmers—appear as tax reliefs. Other anti-market policies, such as quotas

on textiles or Japanese cars, or so-called EC anti-dumping provisions against the Far East, do not cost the Exchequer a single
penny. And the biggest burden of the Common Agricultural
Policy is not the tax transfer to Brussels but the inflation of food
prices above world levels.

The Thatcher government has been far from a single-minded
promoter of competitive markets. British Rover was sold to an
aerospace company not because of industrial logic, but because
of a political veto on an overseas purchaser. Quotas have pro-
liferated on 'high-tech.' and 'low-tech.' imports alike, whether
they come from Japan or the newly industrializing countries.
Inside the European Community the British stand has been more
protectionist than anyone would suppose from public denunci-
ations of 'Fortress Europe'.

In the UK tax subsidies to home ownership, rigid restrictions
on land use, and pension fund privileges remain: and their
harmful effects have been magnified by financial liberalization, in
itself desirable. Rent controls have been tackled only in the late
1980s—with what effectiveness remains to be seen.

On some of these issues, such as the motor car industry, Mrs
Thatcher was overruled by her colleagues. On others, such as
mortgage privileges, she has herself been the main perverse
driving force.

Too many of the Prime Minister's radical urges have been
wasted on peripheral issues such as the abolition of the Greater
London Council and attempts to eliminate domestic rates,
despite the fact that houses are already over-subsidized and
undertaxed compared to other assets. No one seems to have been
able to convince her that all these subsidies and privileges do not
in the end benefit the young suburban couple of Tory fantasy, but
spill over into high land prices and interest rates. The combination has been too often one of strident rhetoric and irrelevant
action.

SUPPLY-SIDE POLICIES

Something, however, must have gone right. Because supply-side
policies consist of thousands of different acts, many of them not

thought of as part of economic policy and certainly not as part of one great strategy, it is extremely difficult to summarize them, let alone assess their relative weight.

The most controversial such policy has, of course, been privatization. Its importance has been overrated by Conservative politicians but underrated by academic economists on the grounds that not enough has been done to introduce competition into denationalized concerns. This assessment ignores the intractable problems of government relations with the nationalized industries which helped to trigger off privatization and accounted for its international popularity.

It ignores, too, fundamental political economy. Such activity and interest as there has been in deregulation, franchising, and contracting out, and prospects for more in future are largely an outcrop of the privatization debate. Privatization has stirred up many corners of the British economy—less effectively than truly radical policies such as unilateral free trade would have done, but more effectively than anything else that was on the political agenda of the late 1980s.

The main effect of privatization to date has been efficiency improvements induced by the drive to sell off state industries. Impressive productivity gains have emerged in a study by Bishop and Kay of firms which were publicly owned in 1979. But these findings are grudgingly reported on the grounds that 'these are changes in management culture associated with clearer commercial objectives'—as if these objectives had nothing to do with privatization.[24]

A near-unmentionable hope is the opportunity privatization provides for the gradual erosion of union influence in a sector hitherto 100 per cent unionized—starting probably in the smaller and peripheral enterprises, out of the spotlight of publicity. Simply taking labour issues out of the political arena is a much underrated weapon on the side of common sense and market-based pay settlements.

Among other supply-side policies the OECD mentions deregulation, ranging from the financial markets to express coaches and opticians to competitive tendering for local authority and hospital services—like all things in life, subject to abuse. The

Lord Chancellor has tried to reduce restrictive practices even among lawyers. The OECD mentions housing and education initiatives. But many of these came very late and another government might have done more, earlier. It also mentions measures to decontrol rents and fresh encouragement in the 1988 Budget for companies building to let. The general level of distortion in the housing and land markets remains, however, dismal.

An underrated reform has been the corporation tax changes in the 1984 Budget. These reduced or abolished many of the special allowances, which in the OECD's words 'encouraged purely tax motivated investment', and replaced them by a lower overall tax rate. The reform removed the pre-1984 subsidization of machinery, especially machinery financed by debt.

Strong labour productivity growth has been less clearly linked than in the past to investment, which at least before the top of the recent boom 'remained lower relative to GDP than in earlier recovery periods'. It seems linked instead 'to changes in organisation, with inflexibility and outdated job demarcation giving way to more rational allocations' (*OECD Survey*, p. 79).

FUNDAMENTALS

More important than any single policy may have been, quoting the OECD again, the 'abandoning of traditional objectives of macroeconomic policy', including the commitment to secure full employment by boosting demand or bailing out loss-making firms. The rundown in subsidies to industries such as aerospace, shipbuilding, and steel may have had some parallel in other countries. But by personifying the slogan, 'The world does not owe us a living', the Prime Minister succeeded in convincing industry that the government was less likely than its predecessors or opposite numbers abroad to bail out firms or individuals from their economic difficulties.

If I were to single out two supply-side policies from the mass of detail, they would be the abolition of exchange control in 1979, at the beginning of the government's term, and union reform. The first coincided with globalization and increased efficiency of financial markets. The combination made it impossible for firms to survive with a rate of return below the going international average. In the words of one industrial economist: 'A consequence has been the growth in mergers, acquisitions, demergers, sell-offs, management buyouts and contracting out. Perhaps most important of all has been the increase of self-confidence. There has been both pressure to improve, and a massacre of 1970s excuses.'[25]

The same economist argues that even the 'short termism' of financial markets has its advantages. For 'the short term results provide the financial strength to support the longer term strategy'.

The second fundamental change was the weakening of union power, encouraged by the Acts of 1980, 1982, and 1984 covering union law. These withdrew some legal immunities (especially for secondary strikes and picketing), made union officials more accountable (e.g. by secret ballots), weakened the closed shop, and put union funds at stake in case of breaches of the law.

The union legislation contributed, with other factors, to a blitz on restrictive practices. There is little sign yet of a reduction in the market power of unions to price workers out of jobs as measured by the wage differential between unionized and non-unionized sectors. Yet that might be in the pipeline. It is only recently that employers have become at all confident about using the new legislation.

But the greatest success came from the handling of the miners' strike of 1984-5. The spectre of Britain being ungovernable without union consent which terrified some of the more reflective Labour ministers, as well as the Civil Service, when Labour returned to office after the Heath government's defeat, may at last have been banished. The victory over militant violence—repeated by Rupert Murdoch in Wapping—was quite as important as any economic result. The victory owed nothing to the talking classes, who insisted on endless discussions of the personality of Margaret Thatcher when the real issue was Arthur Scargill's conduct of the coal dispute.

THE GOD THAT FAILED

One disappointing aspect of economic performance under the Thatcher government was that the underlying rate of inflation stopped falling in the middle of the 1980s. British inflation rose faster than in other major countries up to its 1980 peak after the second oil price explosion, but then indeed fell more quickly. Yet the inflation decline came to a halt in about 1983, and from then the underlying rate fluctuated at around 5 per cent. The UK was overtaken on the anti-inflation front by the other summit countries, including a traditionally high-inflation country like France, whose inflation rate was down by 1988–9 to 3 per cent.

An underlying British inflation rate of 5 per cent means that it will fluctuate between around 3 per cent in good periods and 7 to 8 per cent in bad periods. The peculiar way in which mortgage interest enters the Retail Price Index magnifies these fluctuations and makes them more erratic.

The reason why inflation has got stuck at too high a level is that total spending in money terms has still been rising too quickly.[26] The main significance of the 'trade gap' and the current payments deficit, which generate so much hysteria, is that they provide a safety valve for excess domestic demand—if they did not exist inflation would have been much higher.

The interesting question is why total spending increased so quickly in the later 1980s. The short answer is that a sharp fall in the personal (although not the national) savings ratio boosted consumption; and from 1987 onwards an investment boom added to demand pressures.

The fall in the personal savings ratio and the boom in house prices and construction were, in their turn, linked to rapidly expanding credit at a time of high but stable income growth. The boom could itself be linked to liberalization of financial markets—for example the removal of most of the remaining constraints on the lending of banks and building societies, who began to compete fiercely to lend money.

But this explanation only puts the search back a stage. Surely one thing that monetarism was supposed to do was to give a signal when too much cash was being injected into the economy

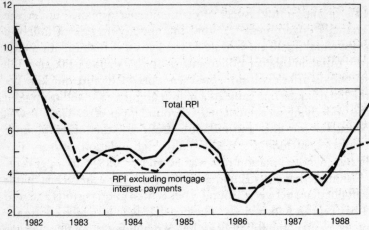

Source: *Treasury Autumn Statement* (HMSO, 1988).

FIG. 1.7.   RPI inflation: percentage changes on a year earlier

so that the Bank of England could raise interest rates in time. It has been a case of the god that failed.

I have already touched on the sharp acceleration of the officially targeted broad measure of the money supply in 1980–1, when the economy was suffering an unprecedented recession. Thus when the broad measure of money again started rising in 1985–6, Treasury economists were understandably sceptical that it meant more inflation—just as the boy who has falsely cried 'wolf' is not believed on the next occasion. The very narrow measure of money which the Treasury came to prefer ('Mo'), consisting mainly of cash circulation, provided a false sense of security until well into 1988.

LOST EMS OPPORTUNITY

One signal, however, could have prevented the inflationary resurgence if the government had been prepared to heed it. There is a well-established expedient for a country whose monetary indicators are erratic and unreliable. That is to link its currency with that of a country with unimpeachable credentials for price stability, such as West Germany, and keep interest rates high until the policy becomes credible.

The opportunity was lost in 1985 when Mrs Thatcher—who is not a Thatcherite—vetoed the only serious Treasury attempt to take Britain into the European Monetary System. At one time this looked like a merciful deliverance. For when the oil price collapsed in 1986, sterling was allowed to depreciate further without immediate visible inflationary effect, thus giving British industry a temporary competitive advantage and stoking up the boom over the election period.

But with hindsight it became clear the UK would have been better off without that depreciation, which was purchased at the expense of higher inflation. If sterling had joined the EMS at just above DM3.5 in late 1985, the right signals would have been given in time to tighten domestic financial policy. To be sure the growth of output might have been less than during the hectic 1987–8 boom period, but it would also have been more durable and less plagued with doubts. The opportunity to lock Britain into a low German-type rate of inflation was thus thrown away and the fall in UK inflation came to a halt and reversed at a higher level than in the other main European countries.

By the time the Chancellor embarked on his personal policy of shadowing the Mark—roughly the year up to March 1988—it was too late. The policy started too far on in the economic cycle, was maintained for too short a period, and was embarked upon at too low a rate for sterling.

Both Thatcher's Foreign Secretaries and her Chancellors of the Exchequer favoured joining the exchange rate mechanism of the European Monetary System. The failure to do so was almost entirely due to the Prime Minister's personal veto. She offered a bewildering variety of rationalizations for her attitude. First there was the threat of a run on sterling in the approach to the 1987 general election. Then we were told on successive occasions that a link with the D-Mark would be too deflationary and too inflationary. The justification current at the time of writing is that the EMS will collapse with the freeing of capital movements due by 1990. Clearly it was the sacrifice of independence that most affected her. She wanted to be free to decide whether to allow the

exchange rate or interest rates to move in the face of currency
pressures—a view held with a passion only comparable to Harold
Wilson's determination not to devalue in 1964–7, until events
forced the decision upon him.

DISTRIBUTIONAL EFFECTS

It would be wrong to end this chapter on questions of monetary
management, even ones going to the roots of the Prime Minister's
personal determination to be in control, so often forgotten by
economist observers.

We must before finishing at least glance at the broader question
of domestic winners and losers from the changes of the Thatcher
decade, 'glance at', for it would be impossible to cover distribu-
tional changes properly at the end of an already long chapter.

But it takes no special investigation to see that pre-tax income
differentials increased greatly, a trend which started well before
the Thatcher government, reflecting a world-wide change in
labour markets—a change which was enhanced in the UK by the
ending of the attempts at pay control and government approval
of market-based differentials. More remarkable is the extent of
the widening of differentials even after tax and social security.

It is easier to attach rough magnitudes to the process for those
mainly dependent on earnings than for those dependent on the
social security system. If we compare the eight Thatcher years for
which there are estimates, 1979–87, with the preceding eight year
period, 1971–9, the increase in net pay for the median earner was
very similar—some 13 to 13½ per cent after tax, National
Insurance contributions, and child benefit.

But in view of the deliberate Thatcherite policy of reducing
personal marginal tax rates at the top, as well as the general
economic forces just mentioned, it is not surprising that the top
10 per cent of earners gained far more in the eight Thatcher years
than in the earlier period—28 per cent compared to 8 per cent.

We are dealing with far too short a period to expect any
evidence of 'trickle down' to those at the bottom. But it is
worrying that the least well-off should have fared as badly as they
did. For the official estimates already cited showed that the
bottom 10 per cent of earners received net gains of only 5 per cent

in 1979–87 compared with 8 per cent in the previous eight years.[27] The least well-off thus did badly in relation both to past performance and to the general run of income earners. Even in absolute terms they made only modest gains—which would have vanished or become losses for those individuals who faced particularly severe changes in personal circumstances.

This impression of near standstill for the poor is reinforced by the social security changes. The government's stated policy was to link the main benefits to inflation rather than earnings. (The statutory link with earnings for retirement pensions was severed in 1980.) The intention was to combine a near freeze on most universal benefits—which spilled over into the middle and higher income brackets—with greater selectivity towards those with greatest need.

In principle, given sufficient generosity by the government on behalf of the mass of taxpayers and adequate take-up, this approach could have helped the least well-off. And benefit for one-parent families and invalids did indeed rise in real terms.

But the most important example of greater attempted select-ivity was the shift from child benefit which, unlike other benefits, increased by much less than inflation to the more selective Family Credit. The problem of take-up remained however, unsolved. Even on an expenditure basis that remained at only 65 per cent. By and large the impression gained from social security as well as earnings changes is that the poor did little better on average than maintain their absolute positions.

But even this uninspiring picture seems difficult to reconcile with the evidence of our eyes—for instance the great increase in the number of people sleeping under the arches or in the streets and the growth in the number of down-and-outs of all ages. The official statistics cover only households. The homeless and people in institutions are excluded. There are all sorts of problems related to the under-class on the margins of society which national aggregate or conventional income distribution statistics hardly touch.

The more general question confronting the political economist is: could the poor have fared better without endangering the supply-side improvements?

The tentative conclusion I reach in a recent book[28] is 'Yes'. But it could not be done by soaking the rich or raising marginal tax rates in the middle. To improve the position of the poor in a well-functioning market economy would require an onslaught on what has been called 'the middle class welfare state'. Redistribution and incentive alike would be satisfied by a combination of more selective, but also more generous, benefits paid through the tax system. Something like the present income tax rates and VAT rates could be combined with more redistribution, if there were an onslaught on fiscal privileges, for example for pension funds, home owners, and landowners.

The difficulties in the way of forming a political coalition in favour of such a radical social market programme are obvious. But even the masses of middle income voters who would bear the impact of the change would ultimately gain from the combination of greater incentives and a quieter conscience.

Continuing in the pre-Thatcher way was not an attractive option or even possible. The task now is to remedy the black spots, while keeping the achievements.

Notes

1. Nick Crafts, *British Economic Growth before and after 1979* (Centre for Economic Policy Research, 1989), p. 27.
2. 'Perestroika in the West', in John Nieuwenhuysen (ed.), *Towards Freer Trade Between Nations* (Oxford University Press, forthcoming 1989).
3. For a full discussion of these subjects, see S. Brittan, *A Restatement of Economic Liberalism* (Macmillan, 1988).
4. Chapter in Robert Skidelsky (ed.), *Thatcherism* (Chatto & Windus, 1988).
5. e.g. *The State of the Market* (Institute of Economic Affairs, 1988). See also *Economic Report of the President* (US Government Printing Office, Jan. 1989).
6. Interestingly enough the different strands in the New Right critique of social and economic engineering have been more often brought together by revisionist writers on the left than by anyone on the New Right side. For a recent example see K. Hoover and R. Plant, *Conservative Capitalism in Britain and the United States* (Routledge & Kegan Paul, 1988).
7. The full text of the relevant passages of Mr Callaghan's famous speech to the 1976 Labour Party Conference can be found in S. Brittan, *The Role and Limits of Government* (2nd impression, Wildwood House, 1987), p. 185.
8. W. Eltis and P. Sinclair (eds.), *Keynes and Economic Policy* (Macmillan, 1988), p. xvi.
9. N. Lawson, 'The British Experiment', Fifth Mais Lecture, Centre for

Banking and International Finance, City University Business School, London (1984).

10. 1979–82: Sterling M3; 1982–4: Sterling M3, M1, PSL2; 1984–7: MO, Sterling M3; 1986: MO, raised Sterling M3 target; 1987– : MO.

11. *Towards Full Employment and Price Stability* (OECD, Jan. 1977).

12. Sir Donald MacDougall, 'Fifty Years On: Some Personal Reflections', 17th Keynes Lecture in Economics, British Academy (1988).

13. Excluding North Sea oil.

14. This is the range suggested, for instance, by Gavyn Davies and Mark Brown in their work for Goldman Sachs and Phillips and Drew respectively.

15. For an econometric attempt to demonstrate that the world income elasticity of demand for British goods has risen from 0.65 to unity in the course of the 1980s—so that the British share of world exports of manufactures might expect to remain stable—see M. Landesmann and A. Snell. 'The Consequences of Mrs Thatcher for UK Manufacturing Exports', *Economic Journal* (Mar. 1989).

16. Manufacturing employment fell from 8.1 million in 1971 to 7.3 million in 1979 and 5.4 million in 1983. It then continued to creep gradually downwards to reach a low point of 5.1 million in 1987, after which it began a slow recovery.

17. Geoffrey Maynard in *The Economy under Mrs. Thatcher* (Basil Blackwell, 1988).

18. The unemployment fall is not, however, as sometimes asserted, the result of changes in definitions. For the official statisticians have adjusted the figures for several years back to take account of definitional changes—most of which were in any case made well before 1986.

19. Preliminary Results from the 1988 Labour Force Survey (Dept. of Unemployment, Mar. 1989).

20. *OECD Economic Survey: UK* (HMSO, 1988), p. 84.

21. General government expenditure (excluding privatization proceeds) as a percentage of GDP at market prices (*Treasury Autumn Statement* (HMSO, 1988)).

22. Information supplied to author by Institute for Fiscal Studies on basis of its tax model.

23. A good analysis is provided by Assar Lindbeck, *The Limits of the Welfare State* (1988) (obtainable from the Dept. of Economics, Birkbeck College, London). Lindbeck, who is chairman of the Economic Nobel Prize Committee, is far from having a New Right background.

24. M. Bishop and J. Kay, *Does Privatization Work?* (London Business School, 1988).

25. D. McWilliams, Inaugural Lecture, Kingston Business School (1988).

26. When the current balance is changing, total domestic spending in nominal terms, which rose by about 13% in 1988, gives a better idea of demand pressure than Nominal GDP.

27. Figures for a married man with two children (*Social Trends* (1988), Chart 5.1, and *Social Trends* (1989), 5.14).

28. op. cit. n. 3 above.

2

Mrs Thatcher, Capital-Basher?

LESLIE HANNAH

Transatlantic analysts of Britain's economic decline, like Mancur Olson, have stressed the sclerosis of British business, its cosy, restrictive commercial practices, and the laconic dominance of giant firms as chronic sources of British economic weakness, paralleling her union problems and reinforced by them. Yet what *has* Mrs Thatcher done to British business to prod it into more vigorous competitive behaviour?

Mrs Thatcher's credentials as a union-basher are generally considered to be impeccable. The further suggestion that she is attacking the vested interests of capital is viewed with scepticism or, on the left, with outright disbelief. Yet Mrs Thatcher's disdain for the views of the old Establishment, her petty bourgeois instincts, and her admiration of the independent, competitive businessman make her status as an impartial capital-basher— promoting competition and attacking vested interests—less fanciful than might at first sight appear.

As with union-bashing, the key element in capital-bashing was the government-inspired recession of 1979–81. The collapse of markets both at home and overseas left firms with little choice but to retrench and become more efficient. That the penalties of failing to do so were as real for firms as for workers is shown as directly in the rising bankruptcy statistics as it is in the rise in unemployment and the catastrophic decline in union membership. By 1981 the real rate of return on the capital of non-oil companies in the UK fell to a post-war low of 3 per cent, and new investment also fell to its lowest level for two decades. The squeals of business were, for a time, almost as loud as those of the unions.

The impact on manufacturing industry was particularly traumatic, and differentiates Britain from its main OECD competitors. Whilst almost all these countries have seen a decline in their manufacturing work-force since 1973, Britain's decline started in the mid 1960s and has in the 1980s become even more precipitate. From a peak of 8.4 million manufacturing workers in 1966, there were only 7.1 million workers in British manufacturing by 1979, and by the last quarter of 1988 the total was only 5 million. Britain's manufacturing output as a proportion of GDP is still on a par with most other OECD countries (though well below the leaders, Germany and Japan), but the speed and trajectory of the adjustment from the former high level of manufacturing intensity has made the change more traumatic.

A good deal of the change can be traced to Britain's increasing comparative advantage in the non-manufacturing sector. The striking expansion in the same period of high-wage industries such as financial services and low-wage ones such as tourism, suggests a more than average competence in these fields. Between 1982 and 1987, for example, employment in the hotel and catering industry rose from 1.7 to 2.4 million. But overwhelmingly in the 1980s, the pressure for structural change has come from the coincidence of full-scale output of North Sea oil and gas with the OPEC oil-price rises. Japan and Germany desperately needed to increase their exports of manufactured goods if they were to pay for the greatly increased costs of energy inputs. Britain, by contrast, by 1983, had oil exports equivalent to 20 per cent of her merchandise exports, and was the only major western economy to be self-sufficient in oil.

There were, of course, those who hoped that Britain could both become Europe's Texas *and* export more manufactures, taking the double benefit in higher living-standards all round. Yet if this had happened, sterling would have gone even higher than it in fact did, and the squeeze on profit margins would have been all the greater. For this to have been successfully and sustainably overcome, productivity in manufacturing would have had to have been even greater than it was.

The idea that Britain's manufacturing productivity in the 1980s might have grown faster than in fact it did stretches credibility. For a hundred years, British manufacturing productivity has been growing significantly less than in the other OECD countries; yet in the squeeze of 1979–86, British productivity growth—both in manufacturing and in the economy overall—was half as high again as in the other six major industrialized nations. This was already a remarkable turn-round; the increase in manufacturing productivity in the last decade has been faster even than that achieved by Japan.

Those who are sceptical of a British industrial renaissance suggest that the short-run figures substantially overstate the case, either because the improvement is merely a cyclical recovery from an extremely sharp recession, or because it has been achieved at the cost of losing manufacturing output by simply shutting down the least efficient plant, leaving a small rump of high-productivity factories. Both explanations look increasingly implausible. The cyclical recovery has been exceptionally long-lived, and even a recession in 1989 would still leave Britain well on the way to closing the productivity gap. Whereas output per manufacturing employee in West Germany was 39 per cent above Britain's in 1979 it was only 13 per cent above Britain's by 1987. Moreover, research at the National Institute of Economic and Social Research has demonstrated that the improvement cannot simply be traced to the closing-down of inefficient plants. The precise sources of productivity gain remain controversial, but the most plausible candidates for the 1980s look like restructuring (with a substantial growth in industries like pharmaceuticals in which Britain appears to have a newly created competitive advantage) and a generally improved climate of labour relations leading to the elimination of many restrictive practices and the more effective use of both labour and capital.

The troubles of British industry are none the less far from over. Whatever one's conclusion from current doubts about the trade deficit and the sustainability of recent rates of expansion, there remain severe structural problems. Import propensities remain high; export propensities remain constrained by problems of quality, marketing and reputation. Competition both from newly industrializing countries and from high-tech sophisticates remains intense, and Britain's share in the market for technology-intensive products continues to decline as others overtake our spending on long-run investments in Research and Development or in training. What has changed is that, for the first time in a long time, British industrialists whose firms have survived can feel that they have got somewhere faster than the competition, and the broader problems can now be addressed from an optimism born at least as much from experience as from hope.

It is, then, not surprising that the survivors of the 1979–82 recession have a confidence born of their triumph in the winnowing process which borders on the ecstatic. Workers still in jobs are rapidly improving their real take-home pay, but business is now profiting even more handsomely from the new atmosphere. In 1980–1, gross trading profits (net of stock appreciation) were about 11 per cent of gross domestic product; their share is now rising above 18 per cent. The rate of return on non-oil companies has risen from 3 per cent to 11 per cent. After the temporary setback of last year, the Stock Exchange boom has resumed. Some of the new prosperity of the 1980s is due to a shift in the tax system to give the well-off more at the expense of the poor, but this is not true of corporate profits. Indeed, in 1987/8, the £15.7 billion of tax paid in corporation tax amounted to 24 per cent of all taxes collected by the Inland Revenue. Ten years earlier, the figure had been only £3.3 billion: only 15 per cent of the Revenue's total take.

But do higher profits arise simply because British business is now cosseted and protected in other less obvious ways? Or has British business been bashed out of its comfortable sclerosis into a more competitive, market-orientated future where it earns its profits and they will be sustainable? Has the government's long-run structural policy laid the foundations for continued productivity growth or for a relapse into old sclerotic ways when the invigorating effects of the cold bath of 1979–81 wear off? That is the long-run test that Thatcherism has to face. And if I hear current business leaders' views right, they *do* believe there has been a fundamental change. Certainly they now feel, more than at any time I can remember, that if their businesses are going awry, the buck stops with them rather than with the government of the day.

Nowhere is this more clear than in the industries which, in

1979, were in the public sector. For this, the radical impetus of the privatization programme (see Table 2.1)—which has galvanized all public corporations whether privatized or not—is largely responsible. More than £15 billion have been raised by council house sales and more than £24 billion from sales of the public sector assets such as Rolls-Royce, British Airways, the Rover Group, and British Petroleum: mainly at bargain-basement prices. In some cases this has led to increased competition by freeing firms of government investment restraints. In housing, competition has come from direct encouragement of new supplies of rented housing and new options for tenants. But, in general, the effects on increasing competition have been slight. Indeed, in the two largest privatizations so far—British Gas and British Telecom—the government shied away from the opportunity to create a more competitive industry structure.

The somewhat paradoxical experience of the 1980s has been that Mrs Thatcher is the most effective manager the nationalized industries have ever had. Indeed, any socialist who still believed with Herbert Morrison that nationalized industries led to efficient management would have been proud of the figures in Table 2.2. Most of these increases in productivity occurred *before* privatization, but it is reasonable to conclude that the carrots and sticks of imminent exposure to the private sector, with increasingly parsimonious Treasury control, combined to induce them. What is less clear is whether they will be sustainable after privatization. The increases in, for example, British Steel productivity are historically unprecedented and are unlikely to be sustainable now basic inefficiencies have been squeezed out, at least without a quantum leap in technical sophistication. But at least steel has the spur of competition with other European and overseas enterprises to keep it on its toes in the private sector. In most other sectors, the picture is far more bleak.

The heavily discounted share sales undoubtedly gave a great boost to popular capitalism, but the structural problems created by their hurried sale as unitary organizations are already coming home to roost. The government was rightly criticized for being more wedded to the ideology of private enterprise than it was to creating the conditions of competition which would improve industry's

TABLE 2.1. *The major privatizations*

Date	Company	Price (£m.)
Nov. 1982	Britoil (51%)	549
Nov. 1984	British Telecom (51%)	3,916
Dec. 1986	British Gas	5,434
Feb. 1987	British Airways	900
May 1987	Rolls-Royce	1,363
July 1987	British Airports	1,225
Oct. 1987	BP (remaining government holding)	5,727

Source: Matthew Bishop and John Kay, *Does Privatization Work? Lessons from the UK* (Centre for Business Strategy, London Business School, 1988).

TABLE 2.2. *Total factor productivity increases of privatized companies (% p.a.)*

Company	1979–83	1983–8
British Airports Authority	0·0	2·8
British Gas	−0·2	6·2
British Steel	8·4	12·4
British Telecom	2·0	2·5
Electricity Supply	−1·6	4·0

Source: Matthew Bishop and John Kay, *Does Privatization Work? Lessons from the UK* (Centre for Business Strategy, London Business School, 1988).

performance. To its credit, however, the government has not buried its head in the sand. British Gas, for example, has been forced to make its industrial pricing policy more transparent, after it became apparent that the competition the government mistakenly hoped would discipline the corporation was ineffective.

In the biggest and probably most important new privatization now being planned, there are further signs of a change of heart. The nettle of a radical long-run, structural solution, which Peter Walker flunked with British Gas, has been firmly grasped by Cecil Parkinson, his successor as Secretary of State for Energy. His planned privatization of electricity proposes the break-up of the CEGB into competing organizations, and new entry into generation is being actively encouraged. The short-term political difficulties of implementing this radical policy are being squarely faced. Optimists can, then, see the commitment of Thatcherism to a permanent revolution of creative business challenges turning the initially disappointing privatization programme around. What was initially no more than a PR campaign for private ownership with giveaway incentives may become a serious policy for encouraging competition in sclerotic backwaters which now have huge potential for stimulating future growth.

In the private sector the record is equally mixed, though a trend towards virtue is harder to discern. The Thatcher government has continued to benefit from the substantial increase in competitive forces unleashed by our entry into the Common Market, and by the reinforcement of those pressures in the EEC's 1992 initiative. In many industries it is no longer appropriate to think of Britain as the relevant market when judging competition, and the Office of Fair Trading and Monopolies Commission are increasingly reflecting this view. Meanwhile, both Leon Brittan in the EEC and Lord Young at the Department of Trade wrestle with the difficulties this creates for merger policy.

The government's rhetoric clearly favours competitive solutions and deregulation. A few concrete policy initiatives suggest this may become a real commitment. Airline deregulation has proceeded with the sale of British Airways and—far more important—with the opening-up of routes to competition, at least where other governments will agree. The solicitors' statutory monopoly on conveyancing has already been unceremoniously withdrawn, and Lord Mackay's Green Papers threaten some remaining restrictive practices of solicitors and barristers. The restrictive regulation of opticians no longer inhibits competition on price. Restrictions on advertising by professionals are steadily being eroded.

In all of these areas the slogans of competition work in a relatively trouble-free way: vested interests sheltering inefficiently behind them have been exposed. Yet things are not always so easy, and in some respects government regulation has increased. The financial services sector is now not subject to the simple old restrictions, like the separation of jobbing and broking, but it has a vastly greater and expensive web of regulatory bodies controlling its conduct in far greater detail. It remains to be seen whether this will ultimately redound to the benefit of the consumer.

It is certainly the case that the capital markets are now a source of greater competitive pressure on firms. Even the largest firms can now fall prey to take-over bids, or management buy-outs, in a way that would have been unthinkable ten years ago. Yet it remains unclear whether capital markets work efficiently in these areas, and suspicion remains that these are, at best, expensive ways of compelling increased managerial efficiency, at worst merely legal expropriation of shareholder value by managers exploiting insider information. Life for the large quoted company is certainly more complex and more dangerous today, but in some respects the competitive pressures in these markets are patently not geared to promoting long-run performance improvement. In general, however, except where there is a serious threat to competition, the government has given the market a free hand.

Elsewhere, the government's stance has been only ambiguously, if at all, pro-competitive. The Common Market Agricultural Policy remains as one of the strongest restrictions on competition, with British farmers retaining their position as strong and effective lobbyists, despite their weak voting power. The EEC also shows an increasing tendency to the covert protectionism of 'Fortress Europe' *vis-à-vis* the rest of the world, and the British government has not been able (and, in some cases, has not been willing) to hold this in check.

Instead we have had the hype of the 1992 initiative, on which Sir John Hoskyns recently poured cold water. In some areas like electrical engineering and wholesale financial services, 1992 looks set to have a real impact. The directives already accepted by the Community and the ones with a realistic chance of passing over the next few years have a genuine possibility of reducing the barriers which at present prevent competition: barriers such as public purchasing policies or regulatory controls. For much of

British manufacturing industry, however, firms are fully exposed to the vagaries of competition already (with, in some cases, devastating results given Britain's clear competitive disadvantages against German firms and others). Many of those that are not can expect very few changes after 1992 since they will continue to operate in national markets segmented by factors like consumer tastes or high transport costs in ways that will be little affected by 1992.

The government's policy for the private sector has been more clearly pro-competitive in the encouragement of enterprise. It is easy to criticize the workings of the Loan Guarantee Scheme for small businesses. It is easy to dismiss the Business Expansion Scheme as merely another free tax hand-out distorting the venture capital market. Yet, the changed culture in which business operates is palpably clear. Lord Young has carried the banner of enterprise and deregulation into the heartland of the Department of Industry. The rise in the number of self-employed or of new businesses formed; the quadrupling in value of British venture capital funds; the special enterprise zones; the increased market share of small- and medium-sized firms at the expense of large firms in many industries: all point to a new competitive upsurge from below (or, the sceptic might retort, to the power of unemployment to change career choices). In a Britain in which, for decades, small firms had been declining at such a rate that commentators began to suspect that entrepreneurial opportunity had been snuffed out, these changes must surely have improved the competitive edge, not only of the newcomers but of the established firms who have been sharpened by the new challengers. Entrepreneurial culture is difficult to define, but it has gained the ultimate accolade of acceptance by the Opposition. The more disciplined and focused approach of the local enterprise boards still controlled by some Labour authorities in the 1980s would surely not have emerged as easily under a Labour government. We all favour enterprise now.

What the Thatcher government has *refused* to do is arguably just as important as what it *has* done in central areas of industrial policy. The government's insistence that businesses on the verge of bankruptcy will not be rescued has been a tremendous source of realism and creative response in business. While in the 1960s and 1970s most large firms knew they were too big for the government to allow them to go bust, now they are all equally clear that whether they go bust or not is largely their own business. Subsidies from Whitehall are harder to win these days and more focused. The DTI budget which peaked at £3.2 billion in 1981/2, is already below £1.56 billion and forecast to fall further.

Yet, in key areas, the 'hands-off' approach of a government content to exhort industrialists to solve their own problems has ignored the fundamental lesson of our economic decline rooted in market failure and requiring constructive government intervention.

In industrial training, for example, we have the worst of all possible worlds. Individuals in Britain will not invest in their own training as readily as they do in the US, either because skill differentials are still too low to provide an incentive or because the market is not equipped to provide the loans. Equally, firms will not invest in training as they do in Germany or Japan if employees are more mobile here and competitors can hijack their training for nothing. The government, while removing employers' rights to 'handcuff' their employees with non-portable pensions, has had little new to offer to promote training. It has been long on exhortation, short on the public money required: the recent moves to expand training are only the first, hesitant steps on what will be a long and expensive process. Meanwhile, overseas competitors have sensibly seen training as a fundamental area in which governments can oil the wheels and have been doing so generously. Skill shortages could well be the major bottle-neck in continued recovery.

The balance sheet of Thatcherism in business and industry will be judged over decades, not over the remarkable years we have just experienced. Britain has been a failing business nation for some time; its troubles were deep-rooted; only some of them have so far been effectively tackled. The government has unequivocally turned the British economy towards a more competitive, market-orientated approach to its salvation, but it still has a long way to go.

Yet it already has no equal in the advanced industrial world, and the rewards are clearly visible. The UK record of recent productivity improvement in manufacturing industry is now superior to that of all of the OECD countries, even Japan. Competitive pressures—whether from recession or from the industrial policy changes we have described—have compelled British firms to face up to and remedy their weaknesses. *Laissez-faire* rhetoric has, under Mrs Thatcher, become reality far more than we have been used to expect from politicians generally. Reagan, despite similar words, became the most protectionist US president for decades and quite failed to maintain the impetus of deregulation. Germany, despite the ideology of its leaders, has not faced up to the reduction of public subsidies to its failing industries.

The capitalism that has emerged in Britain is now a healthier, more self-confident, and more efficient capitalism than we have known for many decades. Capitalists have to work a little harder, and they can earn a lot more. British policies, it is true, have their parallel in other countries, even where left-leaning governments have been in power, as in Spain, France, or Australia. These policies perhaps in part derive from the international pressures of the oil crisis and from the collapse of confidence in the efficacy of interventionism world-wide. Yet everywhere the pressures of vested interests have limited change.

Nowhere has the impetus of policy shifts towards *laissez-faire* and competitive enterprise been so great as in Britain. Nowhere else are they so securely grounded in subjective perceptions of success as to have a sporting chance of becoming a permanent revolution. If the capitalist, communist, and Third worlds are all experiencing a free-market revival, Britain can certainly make a strong claim to spiritual leadership of the western flank on its performance so far.

3

Mrs Thatcher and the City

MARGARET REID

The City of London votes Conservative almost to a man. Yet it is not, by all accounts, a constituency with which Mrs Margaret Thatcher feels notably at home. People observing her often claim she instinctively prefers enterprises which manufacture things to those which make money from money.

The City—spanning banks, stock market, insurance, and much more—multiplied its net foreign earnings from £1.5bn. to £9.4bn. in the ten years to 1987 and has boosted its jobs total too.[1] But it has also thrown up some events—the scandals at Lloyd's insurance market and elsewhere—which have angered the Prime Minister and had key sequels in new watchdog systems.

The ten years of Mrs Thatcher's premiership have witnessed the greatest City shake-up this century, the Big Bang revolution in the stock market's workings, and its virtually total take-over by large banks. But this transformation was not a long-planned Conservative initiative, though its deregulation theme mirrored Thatcherite principles.

Again, although the City contains some of the most enthusiastic contributors to Tory funds—among the entrepreneurial merchant banks, not the more institutional high street banks—it gets only scant allocations of Honours. Within its narrow borders are some of the Prime Minister's warmest admirers, but one of its most judicious personalities roundly says: 'She's not a friend of the City.'

These paradoxes are perhaps not surprising considering that the City's Square Mile has often seemed alien terrain to governments—and that the woman who has dominated her administration for a decade is a law and science, not a financial, specialist. As a senior banker remarks: 'All Tory governments tend to rub with the City because each thinks the other should be on their side and they aren't. The City is an independent power centre in its own right and has been for centuries.'

Although not associated with the financial sector through her early working life or parental connections, Mrs Thatcher, from her assumption of the Tory Party leadership in 1975, took a close interest in the City. Her bent for housekeeping prudence, which reputedly inclines her against borrowing and credit cards, her faith in competition in services in the fight against inflation, and her basic aim of curbing the latter all led her to focus on the economy. And with this in turn came detailed attention to the levers of economic management and the centres of financial power. Notable among these last is the state-owned Bank of England, the development of the Thatcher government's relations with which is a saga in itself.

From the mid-1970s, the future Prime Minister consulted various academic and City advisers, generally those regarding the size of money supply as *the* quantity to be regulated for economic health. A consequent stress on squeezing money supply then predominated in the economically troubled early 1979–80 days of the Thatcher government, when jumps in interest rates and in the pound–dollar rate to $2.40 burdened industry and triggered the 1980–2 recession. It was following the Premier's intense personal attention to these matters, and her arbitration among conflicting views on them, that the rigour of the squeeze was—in line with the opinion of her new economic adviser Professor Sir Alan Walters—abated later in the winter of 1980–1.

Among the government's earliest economic decisions, and one much in tune with its leader's free-market thinking, was the total scrapping in October 1979 of Britain's forty-year-old exchange control system, which liberated money to be switched abroad. The move can be considered prescient, given the technology revolution which now allows information and cash to be switched world-wide at the touch of an electronic button and so has partly outmoded financial frontiers.

While Mrs Thatcher has often sought opinions from City personalities—she several times consulted Mr Robin Leigh-Pemberton, chairman of the National Westminster Bank, before

appointing him Governor of the Bank of England from 1983—
she has another whose views are more constantly at hand. This is
her husband Denis, a former director of Burmah Oil and a
wealthy man, whose influence on the Premier's thinking those
well placed to know rate high. 'She has enormous respect for his
judgments on business and financial matters', says one. Nor are
Mr Thatcher's views hesitantly expressed: 'Denis always delivers
his judgments in strong black and white, never in shades of grey.'

One subject on which the couple's views seem to have been
strong is that of the early 1980s scandals at Lloyd's. In some cases
outright fraud was alleged, while in others there was protest at
certain controversial management and reinsurance practices,
held to be to the detriment of some of the 30,000 underwriting
'names'—those well-off people whose capital backs the insurance
operations. Some recall business manœuvres by certain operators
at the time being described, in conversations with the Thatchers,
as 'stealing from their friends'. Much spring-cleaning ensued in
the market, involving the creation of a new governing Council of
Lloyd's and the institution of a post of the market's chief
executive.

Lloyd's 'names' were among the Thatchers' friends and
acquaintances and the resultant feelings of anger would hardly
have burnished the City's reputation in the Prime Minister's eyes,
confined though the malpractice no doubt was. 'Lloyd's scandals
were most traumatic for her—a sign of national degeneration and
corruption', is how one observer vividly characterizes their
impact.

Another blow was the later whiff of scandal within the merchant bank Morgan Grenfell, where one senior executive was
convicted of insider trading and another faced charges in connection with the take-over by a client, Guinness, of Distillers, the
subject of a lengthy official probe. The authorities, via the Bank of
England, exacted a top management shake-up at the bank as a
mark of their concern.

As it happened, while the crisis on this subject was publicly
escalating in January 1987, the first night took place at the Royal
Opera House, Covent Garden, on the fourteenth, of Verdi's
Otello, which was sponsored by none other than Morgan Gren-

fell, in line with the Conservative government's very policy of encouraging commercial sponsorship of the arts. Mrs Thatcher was present, sitting in the royal box, for the occasion. But it was noticed that during the evening the Prime Minister did not seem keen to meet Morgan Grenfell representatives. The widely held interpretation of her attitude was that she felt the sort of thing that had been going on let her and the City down.

The significance of these occurrences and the Prime Minister's reaction to them was another seeming paradox—that they encouraged the creation of a relatively tough watchdog system for the City's stock markets, which was not the obviously predictable aim of a government cherishing free-market principles. The resultant complex procedures, under the Financial Services Act 1986, are widely called 're-regulation' to balance the 'deregulation', a more familiar Thatcherite phenomenon—seen during the past decade in many financial sectors but most of all, through Big Bang, in the greatly transformed securities market.

By no means all of the changes have been the planned result of actions by Mrs Thatcher and her government. The technological revolution, which has brought world stock markets closer together and so much fostered the electronic transmission of facts and payments, has been a powerful independent force blurring geographical and sector divides in various parts of the money world.

Quite apart from the revolutionary Big Bang stock market shifts, the decade has seen major developments, which should be briefly noted, in other parts of the UK financial industry. For instance, the banks have not only broken, in a quite new way, into the home loans field as lending rivals to the building societies but have also greatly raised their advances to individuals, directly and through credit cards. One factor in this credit boom has been the government's abandonment, from mid-1980, of the former 'corset' control[2] which, through penalties, had restricted the banks' freedom to lend. Following this piece of deregulation, the government was left with interest rate and fiscal measures as instruments for guiding the economy, rather than the more extensive armoury of controls and persuasions formerly used.

In the ten years to November 1988, banks in the UK raised their non-housing loans by 600 per cent, from £4bn. to £28bn., while their home loans outstanding multiplied by over ten times, from £6bn. to £63bn., as the new mortgage business developed.[3] Whether these were excessive rises can be debated: individuals may before have been undergeared. But the loan expansion allowed by the 'corset' deregulation has been on a scale that has shifted the balance of the big banks' business, as well as probably contributing to the recent inflationary upswing and the house price surge.

Another 1980s trend has been a widening of share ownership, a cause long on the agenda of the Tories and Mrs Thatcher, who have been keen to add the share owning to the house owning habit, doubtless partly to cement loyalty to the established order of things and to the Conservative Party. To date, though, the change here has been less than appears at first sight. For, while the proportion of individuals owning shares has trebled to 21 per cent[4] in the past decade, most new holders have such tiny investments (such as a few hundred British Telecom or British Gas shares) that the balance of shareholding between institutions, wealthy individuals, and new small holders has not changed in the latter's favour.

There are considerable City, as well as political, dimensions to the wider share ownership issue. Much of the supply which has gone to the fresh investors has arisen through another key development of the Thatcher years—the string of privatization issues, whose management has given major tasks to City merchant banks like Kleinworts and N. M. Rothschild, as well as to brokers. And the billions of pounds of proceeds which have flowed to the Exchequer from selling off what the late Earl of Stockton called 'the family silver' have greatly affected, perhaps distorted, Budget-making and the government bond—gilts—market. One consequence has been that for the first time this century some National Debt is being repaid.

But the major City event of the 1980s—though the government's changing, turbulent relationship with the Bank of England, discussed below, is also a key area—has undoubtedly been the stock market Big Bang in 1986. This deregulated the trading system of the somewhat insular UK Stock Exchange, making dealing commissions competitive and abolishing the old split between brokers (the investor's agents) and market-makers (wholesalers trading from their own books). It opened up the ownership of Exchange firms to newcomers, with the dramatic result that almost all stock market firms of any size became offshoots of big banks, UK or foreign. This drastic competitive shake-up, which was fostered by the Bank of England, with the government's blessing, was aimed at entrenching the City's securities market as the main European time-zone site in a troika of stock market centres, with Tokyo and New York. The moves followed the New York Stock Exchange's deregulation of commissions in May 1975 and have in turn been echoed, in the increasingly technologically open world markets, in Canada, France, and other centres.

The scale of the purchasing banks' commitment to the stock market was huge since, as the present writer has estimated,[5] these buyers laid out at least £3bn. on their Big Bang investment. Some £1.5bn. was spent on taking over the goodwill of the Exchange firms bought out, and as much again (by now more) used to endow them with new equipment and capital. Since the first £1.5bn. was withdrawn from the market and went into the selling partners' pockets, the acquiring firms face a formidable task in making their £3bn.-plus investment pay. So far from earning the aggregate annual £450m. a year that would be needed to service £3bn. at 15 per cent, the market was authoritatively calculated in early 1989 to be losing £500m. a year.[6] Thus Big Bang's start, which has also been attended by controversy over 'telephone number salaries' to 'yuppie' recruits, and squabbles over dealing rules, has not been trouble-free. A brighter stock market climate would, however, help much and it will only be possible over time to judge the venture's success.

Dramatic as was the Big Bang revolution, nothing of the kind was on the Tory programme when Mrs Thatcher came to power in 1979 or indeed for some years afterwards. There is not a hint of the changes in either the 1979 or the 1983 Tory election manifestos.

In fact, the whole shake-up grew out of a competition case against the Stock Exchange rulebook launched some years earlier by the Director General of Fair Trading, Sir Gordon Borrie, under the Restrictive Practices legislation. But before mid-1983 the Bank of England and the government were worried at how unpredictable this case's outcome was and resolved to take a firmer grip in moulding events. The conjuncture of world developments—with US and other groups building strong securities houses in more liberated markets—was judged to have set the right context for new departures. And so, in a pact of July 1983 between Mr Cecil Parkinson, the Trade and Industry Secretary, and Sir Nicholas Goodison, the Stock Exchange chairman, the government arranged to call the case off,[7] on condition the Exchange dismantled its fixed commission structure within some three years and made other changes.

Decisions by the Exchange to abolish the broker–jobber divide and to remodel its trading on to a screen-based competing market-maker system came next. The Bank of England followed up by actively encouraging the giant take-over operation by which the banks bought up the stock market industry. The whole revolution[8] was seen as the means of making Britain's under-capitalized stock market better fitted to compete in a world securities arena which the new technology had rendered a 'global village'. This aim was in harmony with the Bank's familiar policy of promoting the City as the world's financial centre, in this instance through encouragement for a more international stock market to grow up alongside the existing huge 'offshore' banking operations, foreign exchange, and Eurobond markets, and many more activities.

The Big Bang revolution exhibits certain authentic Thatcherite features, despite its partly fortuitous origins. New competition has roughly halved the dealing costs of the big investing institutions though, worryingly, it has allowed those of many small investors to rise.[9] The competition theme was also evident in the Bank of England's ready admittance of all suitable market-maker applicants to the reshaped gilt-edged arena, even though the initial twenty-seven participants (twenty-two now) were widely regarded as too many for the business volume and substantial aggregate losses have in fact been incurred.[10] Also, the enlarged City securities industry is (even after some cut-backs) a classic instance of the type of modern service industry to which the government looks for economic growth. Mrs Thatcher herself, though not closely involved in Big Bang's planning, took an interest in it and even telephoned the Governor of the Bank of England just before Big Bang day, 27 October 1986, to ask if all systems were working well.

Since Big Bang was deregulating and, by encouraging the formation of investment banks which combined advisory and dealing services, created possible conflicts between the interests of clients and the groups, a need for some balancing new controls was perceived. These took the shape of the elaborate watchdog system for the securities markets whose creation, under the Financial Services Act 1986 (FSA), has been another major landmark of the Thatcher years.

The addition by a free-market-minded government of this extensive piece of legally backed re-regulation to the Big Bang exercise in deregulation could be thought surprising. But it was very characteristic of the Thatcher government, which detects no inconsistency between giving greater play to what are seen as benign market forces and at the same time seeking to clamp down sharply on malpractice. A parallel development followed in the field of the building societies, which were permitted to expand into fresh areas like consumer lending, and even to convert into bank-type public companies, but were also subjected to new regulation. And in the early 1980s insider trading (misuse of privileged information for personal gain) had been outlawed with all-party support, through a law later as severely enforced as were prohibitions on multiple applications for privatization issues.

The designing of the new investor protection regulation system, which is run under the FSA by the Securities and Investments Board (SIB) top watchdog and five satellite-sector self-regulating organizations (SROs), was no easy task. The creation of a governmental regulation agency like the US Securities and Exchange Commission (SEC) would have been too 'official' for the Thatcher administration, which yet wanted to safeguard investors from rip-off risks and was ready to provide some legal teeth. So the outcome was the hybrid structure of SIB, a City-financed private company, but one to which government powers under the FSA have been devolved, and with, in its turn, a certain authority over the SROs. The pattern is often described as one of practitioner-cum-legal regulation.

Not surprisingly, given its hybrid nature, this watchdog system—introduced some time after Big Bang, from 1988—has been attacked as unexpectedly legalistic and its rules as over-complex. One outraged senior foreign banker, used to the Bank of England's familiar supervisory techniques, complained the addition of the FSA structure (covering his bank's dealing and advisory activities) had meant a regulatory system 'of many arms like an Indian god'. Some City people think the design strains can only be resolved by SIB's one day becoming an official SEC-type body, and not just the private operator of devolved legal powers. But now efforts are being made to ease the problems otherwise. Indeed it was the Bank of England which, while pursuing its own task of bank supervision, in practice extended its influence over the field of securities regulation in 1988. It then, in agreement with the government, put in its own director, Mr David Walker, as SIB chairman with a remit to simplify enough to make the investor protection system workable.

The Bank's role of helping to sort out the SIB worries is a reminder of its position as the City's top authority and of the significance of its changing relationship over the past ten years with Mrs Thatcher's government. This relationship, which the present writer has discussed at length elsewhere,[11] started with tension as the new administration, attempting in 1979–80 to impose a highly money supply-orientated policy, began striving to assert its authority over the state-owned central bank. This latter process, in which Mr Nigel Lawson, Financial Secretary to the Treasury in 1979–81 and from 1983 Chancellor of the Exchequer, played a not unimportant part, continued for some years.

In the first, 1979–83, Thatcher government, the Bank's Governor was Lord Richardson, an internationally respected central banker but, as one who had worked with the Heath administration and with Labour governments, not viewed in 10 Downing Street as 'one of us'. When his second term drew to a close, Mrs Thatcher—who, in the unkind words of a close observer, 'did not want an English gnome of Zurich'—decided on a change. As his successor she picked Mr Robin Leigh-Pemberton (whom she knew and liked), who was chairman of the National Westminster Bank but had not been a career-long banker.

Mr Leigh-Pemberton's early days at the Bank were marred by the crisis over Johnson Matthey Bankers (JMB), in which this gold bank, which had expanded its lending unwisely, tottered, facing large losses, and was taken over by the Bank of England in a rescue move to avoid knock-on harm to the City. Although the Bank's costs were eventually recouped and the bulk of JMB resold, the affair triggered an outburst of polemics that was surprising considering the discreet peacefulness of earlier bank rescues.[12] Mr Lawson, by then Chancellor of the Exchequer, broke with tradition by publicly berating the Bank's supervision of JMB.[13]

Various improvements to the Bank's supervisory system and to the Banking Act 1979 were proposed in the report[14] of a Joint Bank–Treasury committee chaired by Mr Leigh-Pemberton and including the influential Permanent Secretary to the Treasury Sir Peter Middleton. However, so great did the prevailing atmosphere of opposition to the Bank briefly become that in July 1985, when the affair was most inflamed, it was even suggested in Whitehall that the Governor's chances of survival in his post were only 'a stingy better than evens'.[15] But Mr Leigh-Pemberton stood his ground and from the summer holidays of 1985 the situation rapidly calmed down.

Mrs Thatcher's own feeling over JMB appears to have been one of initial annoyance with the Bank, but later of desire to ease the crisis. She opined at a summer meeting that Whitehall would do better to see protesting left-wing Labour MPs as the adversary, rather than the Bank of England. She also sided with the Governor in opposing as unnecessary a proposal that there should be an official Companies Act investigation into JMB.[16]

A significant instance of the Prime Minister's not infrequent arbitration role in matters financial can be revealed here. Following the Leigh-Pemberton Report, the Chancellor Mr Lawson who had been so critical of the Bank over the JMB affair, saw merit in changes which would, to a degree, have divorced responsibility for bank supervision from the central bank, somewhat on the French model. This would have been a further blow to the prestige of the Bank.

The matter was settled by a form of compromise which essentially favoured the Bank. It was decided the latter should retain the watchdog role, but that a new advisory Board of Banking Supervision (BBS), headed by the Governor, though with a majority of outside members, should be added. Any differences between the three Bank members of the Board and the six independents were to be reported to the Chancellor.

The timing of this compromise can be clearly dated to the autumn of 1985. The proposal for the BBS was unveiled in the government's final plans for bank supervision reforms in a White Paper of December 1985,[17] whereas there had been no sign of it in the Leigh-Pemberton Report from the Bank–Treasury committee six months earlier. (The White Paper outlined arguments which could be advanced for a supervisory authority separate from the Bank, but went on to say that the government had decided against such a radical change.)

Significantly the formula which settled the issue arose soon after the appointment in September 1985 as future Deputy Governor of a very experienced hand at bank supervision, Sir George Blunden, who was probably the architect of this solution. But quite as great interest attaches to the fact that, in accepting it, Mrs Thatcher came down on the Bank's, rather than the Chancellor's, side. This avoided the need for the Bank of England to dilute its bank supervision task, an outcome which would have left that organization bereft of a major arm and humiliated.

From late 1985 the heat went out of the JMB affair and relations between government and Bank improved, not least because, with Sir George Blunden as Deputy Governor, the Thatcher administration had got its own appointees in both the Bank's top posts. The Bank's revived say in policy formation has since become steadily more apparent. That it can on occasion prevail over the Chancellor was demonstrated when, in March 1988, Mrs Thatcher opted to let the pound float above the informal DM3.00 peg, on the ground that 'you can't buck the market'.

Mr Leigh-Pemberton's reappointment for a second five-year term from mid-1988 further enhanced his authority. And the top team he forms with Sir George—who, as chairman of key Bank committees, can be regarded as the nearest a Deputy Governor has yet come to being the Bank's chief executive—is an effective partnership, working harmoniously with the government. Two assessments by senior City people in early 1989 were: 'The Bank has made a big comeback' and 'Robin [Leigh-Pemberton] is in an undisputed position now'.

The City retains a continuing fascination for Mrs Thatcher, even if it is the fascination of the slightly alien, the imperfectly understood, even the occasionally shocking generator of scandals. With this has gone a persistent preoccupation with the City as the site of the financial markets so intimately linked with monetary conditions, perceived as so closely associated with the key anti-inflation aim.

In her early (partly pre-prime ministerial) days, Mrs Thatcher listened to various monetarist gurus. She then, as Premier, at first involved herself in intense debates in the fraught latter part of 1980 on monetary policy and even in the intricacies of certain schemes for monetary base control.[18] Yet she approved the rejection of the radical form of these latter.[19] Thereafter, she relied quite heavily on the advice of Professor Sir Alan Walters, who returns to 10 Downing Street in 1989 after an earlier spell in the Prime Minister's office. With money supply targets now cast (partly because of the more open world markets) for a much reduced role,[20] the Premier is still sometimes called her government's last remaining monetarist. But if this is so, it is with less zeal than ten years ago.

None the less, the PM retains a love of occasionally handling the levers of monetary power: it is said that if the Chancellor is abroad at a time of money market turmoil it is Mrs Thatcher, not a Treasury minister, who acts as his deputy. Some subjects

specially take her fancy. Her eyes glistened when she was told—
however visionary the forecast—that the £180 bn. National Debt
could be wiped out before the twenty-first century at the present
rate of repayment from Budget surpluses. She also concerned
herself with the tangled tale of the Tin Council crisis in 1985–6.

Mrs Thatcher has taken trouble to get to know people in the
City, where she has her particular likes. Mr Leigh-Pemberton has
become a familiar acquaintance and another friend is Mr Michael
Richardson, the acute corporate finance specialist who is a
managing director of N. M. Rothschild and who handled the
privatization of British Gas and the far trickier BP share sale in the
1987 share crash.

Sir Hector Laing, the industrialist who heads United Biscuits
and has since 1981 been a non-executive director of the Bank of
England is another valued friend, while Sir David Scholey,
chairman of S. G. Warburg, the independent investment bank, is
among others the PM sometimes sees. Within the public sector,
Sir Peter Middleton, the Treasury chief, is a close adviser, while at
the Bank of England Mrs Thatcher is well acquainted with Sir
George Blunden and Mr Eddie George, the monetary side
director.

The Premier's preference is clearly for the cheerful, extrovert
type of City personality and she can like both the traditional
landowner type, such as Mr Leigh-Pemberton, and the successful
new entrepreneur, for example, Mr John Gunn, head of the
British & Commonwealth financial group. She has less natural
affinity with the quieter, scholarly thinkers among the City's top
people, such as Sir Jeremy Morse and Sir Kit McMahon.
However, the range of those she meets, or entertains at
10 Downing Street or Chequers, is quite wide, so there is an
opportunity for her to hear various views, though mostly from
those at least sympathetically disposed to understand the PM's
own viewpoint. Often, too, when she hosts informal gatherings
of social-and-financial flavour, the Premier seeks to get her own
opinions across, as when, at a Chequers lunch in the autumn of
1988, she voiced concern at the credit boom and also urged the
need for cheap, quick, and simple dealing procedures for small
investors.

Altogether, these contacts have helped broaden the Prime Minister's knowledge of the City down the years—if not her admiration of it. For there remains an evident reserve about the City's complex of markets and institutions, which have not invariably proved quite malleable to prime ministerial wishes.

With the big high street clearing banks, mutual understanding has not always been great. Nor was it enhanced when a £400m. 'one-off' tax was slapped on in 1981, perhaps partly because the clearers had, from good earnings, given generous pay rises judged in Whitehall as likely to encourage Civil Service claims. (A stockbroker challenged a government minister at the time, asking whether a special tax on a successful company like Marks and Spencer—a Thatcher favourite—would also be thought a suitable sequel to a profits rise.)

The scandals occasionally cropping up in the City and mentioned above are probably considerably to blame for the fact that the Thatcher government has been notably stingy over conferring Honours on City people. A careful study of the Honours lists under Mrs Thatcher's and earlier regimes shows roughly a halving in the number of City knighthoods and other awards. Where these are given, it is often after a longer wait than had been customary. For instance, although Sir Peter Miller oversaw much regulatory tightening at Lloyd's as chairman from 1982 to 1986, the knighthood that has invariably been conferred on Lloyd's chairmen was not awarded to him until after he had left the post. Allocations of this form of recognition elsewhere in the financial world have also been scant or slow.

All of which would seem to suggest that the verdict on the City of the woman who has unprecedentedly sat in the headmistress's chair for Britain a whole decade is 'could do better'. For its own part, the Square Mile remains rather short of 100 per cent willing to be told what to do.

Notes

Where no reference is given the statement is either the one about information widely known or, alternatively, is the result of private information. *BEQB* = *Bank of England Quarterly Bulletin*.

  1. British Invisible Exports Council, *Annual Report and Accounts, 1987–1988*, pp. 17–18.

2. *Announced in Monetary Policy*, Cmnd. 7858 (1980), p. 5.
3. *BEQB* (Dec. 1980), Table 5 and (Feb. 1989), Table 5.
4. The Treasury, *Economic Progress Report* (Apr. 1988).
5. The estimates here are in Margaret Reid's *All-Change in the City* (Macmillan, 1988), pp. 66–8.
6. Remarks of Mr Andrew Hugh Smith, chairman of the International Stock Exchange, *Financial Times*, 24 Feb. 1989.
7. This was done by legislation, the Restrictive Practices (Stock Exchange) Act 1984.
8. Described in more detail in Reid, op. cit., chs. 2–5.
9. *BEQB* (Feb. 1987), 54–65, and various issues of the International Stock Exchange's *Quality of Markets* journal from 1987.
10. *BEQB* (Feb. 1989), 49–57.
11. Reid, op. cit., ch. 10.
12. See Margaret Reid, *The Secondary Banking Crisis, 1973–75* (Macmillan, 1982).
13. HC Deb., vol. 81, 20 June 1985, cols. 454–65.
14. *Report of the Committee set up to Consider the System of Banking Supervision*, Cmnd. 9550 (1985).
15. *The Economist*, 27 July 1985, p. 69.
16. Reid, op. cit. 6 above, p. 231.
17. *Bank Supervision*, Cmnd. 9695 (1985).
18. As in Cmnd. 7858 (see n. 3 above).
19. As appeared in *BEQB* (Dec. 1980), 428–9.
20. See in particular Bank of England Governor's speech at Loughborough University, *BEQB* (Dec. 1986), 499–507.

4

Trade Unions

B. C. ROBERTS

The Thatcher years have seen a number of radical changes in the British industrial relations system. The nature of these changes and what their effect has been are analysed in this chapter. A question of crucial importance is whether they are likely to be permanent or merely temporary. Would the passing of Mrs Thatcher bring a rapid return to the pattern of industrial relations which prevailed before the 1980s? It will be argued that there are substantial reasons for believing that whoever succeeds Mrs Thatcher, whichever party is in power in the 1990s, and beyond, it is unlikely that a complete reversal will occur. In short the 1980s will be historically significant as a period in which Mrs Thatcher's government brought about a fundamental change in the British industrial relations system, which affected the power and status of the trade unions in particular.

MRS THATCHER'S INHERITANCE

When Mrs Thatcher came to office as Prime Minister in 1979 it was in the immediate aftermath of the humiliation of Mr Callaghan and the Labour government by the shameful events of the 'Winter of Discontent'. The defeat of the Labour government, to which the public service unions had signally contributed, was not the first time in the post-war period that the trade unions had played a major part in the overthrow of a government. Their hostility to government policies was also a factor in the downfall of Mr Attlee's Labour government in 1951; and when he sought to curb the abuse of union power to resist change and to destabilize the economy by strikes and inflationary pay demands, Harold Wilson's Labour government was made to suffer, in

1970. The unions had also been largely responsible for the defeat of Mr Edward Heath's government in 1974, aborting a more far-reaching attempt to reform them. Ironically it was this painful defeat of Heath by the miners that opened the door for the election of Margaret Thatcher as leader of the Conservative Party, and eventually Prime Minister of a government which has substantially removed the public policy support for the unions first established by Disraeli and Gladstone over a century ago.

On taking office for the first time Margaret Thatcher was principally concerned to tackle the problem of soaring inflation by a vigorous monetary policy. She would have nothing to do with the kind of incomes policy which the Labour Party had tried and failed to make effective. She accepted Milton Friedman's view that inflation was not directly caused by the unions, but believed that they were an incubus that sat heavily on British industry and that they ought to be cut down to a size which would reduce the pernicious effects they had on efficiency and on the climate of industrial relations. Having no wish to invite the fate of her predecessor she chose to proceed cautiously. Almost certainly there was no worked-out long-term plan as to exactly how the industrial relations system should be reshaped, except, in very general terms, to reduce the power of the unions. Proceeding stage by stage she showed remarkable determination and great political skill in bringing about a fundamental reorganization of the industrial relations system without provoking, with the exception of the miners, the kind of union resistance and political crisis that brought previous attempts to naught. This has been all the more impressive in the light of the half-hearted support each Bill was to receive from employers' organizations, with the exception of the Institute of Directors.

MRS THATCHER'S NEW LAWS

Her first Secretary of State for Employment, Jim Prior, was hardly the man for an all-out attack on union power. He was in the Macmillan tradition, and had little inclination for a serious conflict with the unions. This undoubtedly came as a relief to the senior officials of the Department of Employment, steeped in the conciliation traditions of its forerunner, the Ministry of Labour, whose retired members quickly informed the press of the folly of any departure from the classic pattern of total union autonomy and the unwisdom of any new form of legal regulation.

The first of the six Acts passed during Mrs Thatcher's decade of office, in 1980, was aimed at bringing about a fairer balance between the rights and duties of the trade unions, their members, and employers. Cleverly designed to appeal to the union rank and file it encouraged the wider use of the secret ballot in union elections and on such issues as industrial action. It gave the Secretary of State power to issue codes of good industrial relations practice, but no more special power to intervene in industrial disputes than had always existed. The Act removed the immunity of union members and officials from legal action through the courts by an employer who was not a party to the dispute, but it left the immunity of the union as such intact. In addition the Act made secondary picketing unlawful by restricting picketing to union members at their own place of work.

In repealing the sections of the Employment Protection Act which enabled a union to seek the aid of the Advisory Conciliation and Arbitration Service to secure recognition by imposing sanctions, the government indicated that unlike the previous Labour government it was not prepared to strengthen the unions by putting statutory pressure on employers.

The 1980 Act was inevitably harshly criticized by the unions, though it placed relatively little restriction on their activities. Employers were far from enthusiastic; many had doubts that it would do much to curb abuses of bargaining power. They disliked the obligation it placed upon them to take action in the courts if they wished to deter unions from unlawful strikes and picketing, since it was feared this would antagonize the unions. Another view, which was certainly shared by the Prime Minister, was that the Act did not go far enough. This was apparently not the view of James Prior, who was replaced soon after the Act was passed by Norman Tebbit, who had no inhibition in taking the reform of the law considerably further. He had the aid of a new Permanent Secretary, appointed by Mrs Thatcher from outside of the Department of Employment, who had made a reputation as an exceptionally able and determined administrator.

The second Thatcher Employment Act, which became law in October 1982, firmly grasped the nettle of trade union immunity from liability for damages for unlawful actions. It struck a further blow against sympathetic strikes by narrowing the definition of a lawful strike to one wholly or mainly between workers and their own employer. It further strengthened the position of employers in relation to dismissals for collective breaches of conduct, by allowing them to re-engage, after a period of three months, employees they were not anxious to lose, without having to face claims for unfair dismissals from those they wanted to be rid of. The Act also weakened the power of the unions to compel employers to deal only with unionized firms when sub-contracting.

THE MINERS' STRIKE

The full impact of making union funds subject to awards for damages and court orders for breach of the law became clear during the prolonged miners' strike in 1984–5.

The government was determined to reduce the enormous losses incurred by the massively overmanned nationalized industries. The largest loss-maker was the mining industry, but it was also the most strategic in terms of the effect of a major coal strike on the electricity supply industry, and on the political future of the Prime Minister and her government.

When the government started to put pressure on the industry Mrs Thatcher was in an extremely strong political position, having won an election with a large majority in the aftermath of her Falklands victory. In addition to making changes in the law which could be used against the NUM, should this prove neces-sary, she had, in Sir Ian Macgregor as chairman of the Coal Board, appointed a man who was every bit as tough as Arthur Scargill, and as determined to defeat the miners' leader as Scargill was to destroy him. Mrs Thatcher had also taken the precaution of creating a central police co-ordination authority which could mobilize police forces from all over the country to ensure that mass picketing and violence did not have the same results as

Scargill had achieved against Heath a decade earlier. Having made a tactical retreat in 1982 when faced by a confrontation with the miners, when the challenge came in 1984 Mrs Thatcher was fully ready to meet it and to defeat it.

There were many faint hearts who believed during the miners' strike that Mrs Thatcher had gone too far in her unflinching support for the police, who played a crucial role in preventing mass violence from triumphing. At times in the course of the strike defeat seemed perilously close, but Scargill was never able to cut off the supply of coal to the main power stations, from the mines that continued to work, or imports transported from the docks by unionized drivers who did not support the NUM.

Although the TUC and most of the unions gave support to the NUM they were mostly reluctant to give much more than token help in case they ran foul of the law and the hostility of their members for supporting an unpopular strike. Moreover from the outset of the strike Scargill had split the union and undermined his position by the devious way in which he had manipulated the constitution of the NUM to avoid having a national ballot he feared he might lose.

The defeat of the miners provided the government with a powerful endorsement of its policies to contain this type of exercise of union power which had brought disaster for Heath. It was a defeat not only for the miners, but also for the unions generally in their opposition to the restructuring of industry which the government was determined to achieve.

DEMOCRATIZING THE UNIONS

The refusal of Scargill to hold a ballot before calling the strike and his election as President for life added justification to the government's Employment Act of 1984. This Act made a secret ballot a legal requirement for the election of voting members to the executive council of the unions, at intervals not greater than five years; for all those who might be called upon to take official industrial action before doing so; and for setting up or retaining an existing political fund. A subsidy provided by the government to help cover the costs of ballots split the unions, but those who were opposed to taking this money have in the end come round to accepting it.

The results of the ballots required for the establishment of political funds disappointed the government, which had hoped that a majority of union members might vote in favour of abolishing them. Where political funds existed, in every case the retention of these funds was approved by comfortable majorities. Although there has been press speculation from time to time that the government had under consideration reverting to the 'contracting in' system, which was a legal requirement under the 1927 Trade Union Act, repealed in 1945, instead of the current practice of 'contracting out', no indication has been given by the government that this is likely. The government seems ready to accept that union political allegiance still leans to the Labour Party and that it is best to allow this to erode under the influence of social and political change as there are some signs of it doing.

In addition to the revision of the laws relating to collective actions of the unions and their legal implications the Thatcher governments have made considerable revisions of the laws relating to employee rights. These have been concerned, *inter alia*, with aspects of unfair dismissal; maternity leave; the introduction of the principle of equal pay for work of equal value; and minimum wages. Under the Wages Act 1986 three changes were made. One related to the manner in which it was lawful to pay wages; one to the amount of deductions that could be made; another restricted Wages Councils to setting a single minimum hourly rate and an overtime rate and limited their application only to those over the age of 21.

The object of these changes was to reduce the administrative burden of these schemes, especially on small firms, and to permit a greater degree of flexibility in determining pay levels and conditions of employment in response to changing market conditions and social needs.

THE DECLINE OF UNION MEMBERSHIP

The decline in the membership of the unions has been one of the most remarkable features of the Thatcher years. In 1979 union membership in Great Britain stood at 13.5 million; 57 per cent of potential union membership.[1] In 1986 union membership was 10.5 million; 43 per cent of potential union membership. Since 1986 membership has continued to fall, but at a much slower rate.

The dramatic fall in union membership since 1979 was initially due to the impact of recession, brought on in 1980 by the turndown in world economic activity. The rapid rise in unemployment after 1980 was aggravated by the government's determination to reduce the rate of inflation. This brought an unforeseen bonus, since the increase in unemployment was largely concentrated in the heavily unionized manufacturing industries, mining, construction, docks, and railways. Between 1979 and 1986 membership in the NUM fell by 72 per cent, in the TGWU by 34 per cent, in the AEU by 34 per cent, in the EETPU by 24 per cent, and in the GMBU by 16 per cent.

The reduction in union membership was also influenced by structural changes in the pattern of employment. In the 1980s there has been, as a result of changes in technology and labour requirements, a considerable increase in employment in sectors which unions have traditionally found difficult to organize, namely the services. There has been in particular in these sectors a considerable increase in part-time workers, female employees, employment in subcontracting, and self-employment. There has also been a growth of small-scale enterprises which have usually been much less well organized than large-scale enterprises. Many of these newer enterprises have been located on greenfield sites in small towns and rural areas where unions have often been absent.

There are some sectors of employment where union membership has held up, and even increased. These have been in parts of the public sector, such as the health services, and in the private sector in financial services, especially banks. There has also been a growth of professional organizations such as the Royal College of Nursing at the expense of the unions.

Part of the decline in union membership was due to a failure to mount effective recruitment campaigns, made more difficult by the fact that union membership had come to depend to a large degree on the support of public policy and the co-operation of private employers, through the closed shop and the collection of union subscriptions by means of the check-off. The closed shop has been made unlawful, but *de facto* union membership is still made a condition of employment in many enterprises, though it cannot be legally enforced, and it is especially important in those occupations where union membership is a condition of entry.

Unlike the United States, British employers have not in the last decade launched a massive anti-union campaign. However there is evidence that a small but growing number in the private sector are resisting unionization. In some cases where unions continue to be recognized traditional collective bargaining procedures have been modified or abandoned.

There is also evidence that many employers have questioned their need to have as many shop stewards as the unions have had in the past and have insisted on changes, but these often seem to have been of a minor kind. There is a growing feeling among employers that the cost of financing union representation is too great and that the multi-union representation based on sectional interests is outdated. The 1989 Employment Bill, when it becomes law, will, *inter alia*, reduce the time for which an employer can be called upon by statute to release a union member for union duties and training at the employer's expense.

The conclusion can be drawn that there is unlikely to be a sudden collapse of union membership unless there is a catastrophic slump and a massive rise in unemployment, or a radical change in employer attitudes, and this looks unlikely in the immediate future. It is equally unlikely that there will be a rapid increase in union membership unless the government permits inflation to run away, as happened in the 1970s, and this hardly seems likely.

NEW MODELS IN INDUSTRIAL RELATIONS

There have been some changes in the patterns of industrial relations which may have radical consequences if they become more widespread. The two most significant have been those associated with the advent of Japanese companies into Britain and, also originating abroad (in the USA), human resource management.

Some Japanese companies have sought to avoid recognizing unions at all, but the larger companies, especially those which have established manufacturing facilities on greenfield sites, decided they must avoid the traditional features of Britain's conflictual industrial relations without alienating their employees and public opinion by bypassing the unions altogether. They have succeeded in achieving this goal by confining union recognition to a single organization; entering into strike-avoidance agreements with final-offer arbitration in place of strikes; reducing the role of shop stewards by the establishment of a company council based on employee representatives regardless of union membership. The underlying philosophy of these agreements is paternalistic; the company is perceived as analogous to a family. The pattern of industrial relations it is sought to achieve is based upon the notion that all sections of the company's employees must be mutually supportive. The traditional British concept of adversarial relations between management and workers, the two sides locked in a never-ending conflict, mitigated from time to time by a truce that is never more than a temporary respite, is rejected in favour of continuous co-operation. As in any family there will be quarrels, but the aim is to resolve these within a framework which promotes mutuality of interest. The concept of mutuality is continuously reinforced by a style of management which is authoritative, but also participative and egalitarian. This is symbolized by all employees, from top to bottom, wearing the same style of company dress and starting the day with exercises in which everybody takes part.

Although these ideas are alien to British trade union traditions they have been well received by employees, but they have only been taken up by the EETPU with whole-hearted enthusiasm as a manifestation of the kind of industrial relations that are likely to become the dominant form in advanced industrial societies. A majority of unions in the TUC, led by those on the left, apparently believe that the Japanese model is inimical to the interests of trade unionism in a society which they see as dominated by class divisions and a rapacious capitalist system.

The opposition to the Japanese model, especially to the concept of single unionism and final-offer arbitration in place of strikes, culminated in the expulsion of the EETPU from the TUC when it refused to withdraw from an agreement which was deemed by the TUC to have broken the rules protecting the interests of unions claiming prior bargaining rights. A number of other unions have signed similar agreements, but have done so with tongue in cheek, regretting in public the need to do so, but not willing to forego the advantage of signing.

Perhaps of greater significance than the advent of the Japanese model during the Thatcher years has been the emergence of the concept of human resource management as an alternative strategy to the classic model of authoritarian management tempered by the pressures exerted by trade unions. Encouraged by the new climate of industrial relations human resource management, which had its origins in the United States (where union membership has shrunk to 16 per cent of the labour force), puts stress on the importance of the individual, on planning the most effective utilization of every individual employed in relation to their personal development and to the achievement of the targets of the enterprise, and doing this through consultation rather than by the adversarial collective negotiations, often followed by some form of industrial action, that are extremely costly to both employees and the enterprise. Human resource management is compatible with recognition of unions, but, if it is to succeed, it requires a similar change in their response to that which they have been called upon to make in the case of the Japanese model.

Faced by these developments EETPU was one of the first unions to recognize that it must develop a new role and a new image which would appeal to employees as individuals rather than as members of large, bureaucratic organizations concerned primarily with achieving collectivist goals. The EETPU now offers not only convalescent homes, and a limited range of friendly benefits, but a whole package of services, including individual and family legal advice, extensive technical training facilities aimed at improving career development, and a 'moneywise' package of financial services which provides members with professional advice on house purchase, personal motor, accident, and house insurance, and unit trust and financial counselling. The union's training programmes are now so good they are being bought by employers who are short of skilled labour. The GMB and the AEU and a number of other unions, without going as far as the EETPU, are beginning to think on similar lines.

The TUC has tentatively endorsed some of these developments and there has been talk of the TUC itself taking a lead in organizing comprehensive financial services for the generality of union members. The unions in the United States have been in the vanguard of such developments and they increasingly see the union as an organization to protect the interest of members not merely as producers, but also as consumers. These concepts of the new role of the unions will probably gather pace, but it is too soon to come to any firm conclusion that this will happen. There is little evidence that the unions, except perhaps the EETPU, have clearly thought through the implications for their traditional collective bargaining role and their support for politically imposed collectivism, which is unlikely to be reconcilable with an emphasis on individualism without a radical adjustment to their philosophies.

Competition for membership is leading the unions to seek mergers and amalgamations. The merging of the ASTMS with the TASS to become the Manufacturing, Science and Finance Union, with over 600,000 members, is a clear pointer to the direction in which most union leaders are convinced unions will have to go in the future. The decision of the NUM, once one of the largest and most powerful unions, to open merger discussions with the TGWU has underlined the steps unions are being compelled to take to survive.

ESTATE OF THE REALM

One of the most significant changes that have occurred during the Thatcher years has been the decline in the political status of the TUC. By the end of the First World War the TUC had achieved the distinction of being described as an estate of the realm. The general strike of 1926, which was perceived by leaders of the

Conservative Party as an act of grave disloyalty to the state, surprisingly did not significantly diminish the standing of the TUC for more than a very brief period. At the end of the Second World War the TUC had 'established a towering presence in the world of British pressure groups at large'.[2]

Over the period from 1945 to 1979 the authority of the TUC grew. It was seen by all governments as the legitimate representative of working people. It was accepted as the proper body to nominate to such tripartite organizations as ACAS, NEDC, and to dozens of other quangos and official committees.

Until Mrs Thatcher took office the TUC regarded access to the Prime Minister, on matters it saw as important, as a right that it was entitled to exercise whenever it thought necessary. This policy has not been followed by Mrs Thatcher. It was made clear, early in Mrs Thatcher's occupancy of No. 10, that the door would not any longer always be open.

Surprisingly, until January 1989 there was no effort made by ministers to bypass the TUC in the appointment of trade unionists to official bodies. In that month it was announced by the Secretary of State for Employment that henceforth he would open nominations to government-appointed bodies to a wider constituency than the TUC and the CBI.

It is unlikely that the TUC will regain its past monopoly of representing working people. It is even possible that it may face a rival central organization if the division which has opened up between it and EETPU and UDM is not closed and these organizations can come together with the large professional associations to pursue common interests.

IS THE IMPACT OF THE THATCHER YEARS LIKELY TO BE PERMANENT?

The number of strikes and man days lost has declined to the lowest levels since the 1950s, but it would be ridiculous to suggest that the trade unions, with over nine million members, have entirely lost their clout and become an enfeebled body that will in a short space of time disappear. Yet there is a growing feeling that the impact of the changes during the Thatcher years has raised the question of the continued relevance of unions and that unless they can find a more positive role their continued decline and possible ultimate demise is conceivable. This prediction may be countered by a number of arguments. One which is advanced strongly by trade unionists is that, when Mrs Thatcher's government is replaced by a government of the left, the laws curbing the unions and the economic policies which have weakened them will be replaced with laws and policies which will encourage their growth and restore their power.

The election of a government of the left may not be as imminent as supporters of the unions wish, but even if a Labour government were elected in the early 1990s it is extremely unlikely that it would sweep away all the legal changes made by Mrs Thatcher and try to return to the 1970s. In spite of the fact that the Labour Party and the TUC are committed to this goal, in practice the reality of politics would make it difficult to achieve, and certainly if the next government were a coalition of Labour with the SLD and SDP it would be impossible.

It is clear that a government of the left, if it is to be successful in achieving its aims to raise real incomes and secure a return to full employment, will find it necessary to control union bargaining power; if it fails it will be as vulnerable as Labour governments were in the past. It will therefore need to keep the unions relatively weak. The promise that has been made by Mr Kinnock that the Labour Party will break with the traditional block vote to move towards an electorally more acceptable party mainly consisting of individual members has far-reaching political implications for both the unions and the party.

The truth of the matter is that democratic societies cannot, any more than socialist societies, enjoy both high levels of economic growth and powerful, autonomous, adversarial unions. Unions therefore have to be curbed either in the Conservative way, by the imposition of legal limits to the exercise of their bargaining power, by restricting the scope of strikes, picketing, and other forms of disruption that inflict severe damage on society (by giving employers rights of redress through the courts), or by bureaucratic socialist administrative methods, such as incomes policies that reduce flexibility, increase inefficiency, and bring political instability. Or they have to change their role fundament-ally, as the EETPU seems to have begun to recognize.

The problem of the role of the unions in Britain is likely to be compounded in the future by the development of the European Economic Community. Mrs Thatcher has clearly perceived that the Delors' proposals, which have been welcomed by the TUC, to impose minimum wages, health, and safety standards, union rights to representation on company boards and unrestricted access to confidential company information, and the encourage-ment of European-wide collective bargaining, have threatening implications. Deregulation would be reversed, union power would be greatly strengthened, and a bureaucratic layer of intervention would be imposed on company flexibility, which would lead to a substantial increase in costs.

The Delors' concept of a European-wide industrial relations system would inevitably bring about a return to the two-tier system of industrial relations condemned by the Donovan Com-mission as a prime cause of the inefficiencies of the British system in the 1960s and 1970s. Industry-wide bargaining has virtually disappeared in Britain; industrial relations are now almost entirely focused on the plant or enterprise. This permits manage-ment and employees to secure the maximum advantages in terms of flexibility, greater efficiency, and improved standards of work and rewards. The prime beneficiaries of the Delors' proposals would be the unions as institutions, rather than the relation between workers and managers, which experience has shown is best achieved if this is not mediated through strong unions. British employers believe strongly that Mrs Thatcher is correct to see the dangers in the policies advocated by the Commission, which reflect the views of the European countries which have a different type of trade unionism, one that is much weaker in the workplace, and which have long had much more legally regulated patterns of industrial relations in which collective bargaining has a less damaging effect on economic performance than in this country.

CONCLUSIONS

The reform of industrial relations and the results that have followed must rank as one of Mrs Thatcher's greatest achievements. Government policies made effective by the length of her office, together with the effects of economic, social, and technological changes, have resulted in a significant reduction in union power, which has brought considerable benefits to all sections of society. Industrial conflict is at its lowest level since the war, productivity is the highest in Europe, profits have sharply increased and induced a much needed upsurge in investment. These improvements in the performance of industry have been accompanied by an increase in real incomes to an all-time high. Direct taxes have been reduced substantially and public finance is in an extremely healthy state. More new jobs have been created than at any time in recent history and unemployment is falling steadily. However, inflation has not been brought down to Mrs Thatcher's stated aim, zero; Britain has a serious balance of payments problem, and, in spite of the large increase in real income per head, still lags behind a number of other countries; but the gap is closing.

On the past record it is extremely unlikely that these achievements could have been made without the reform of industrial relations. However, trade union power is still able to push up wages and salaries at a rate which is a major cause of inflation running at 5–8 per cent in early 1989; and union resistance still continues to be a drag on the improvement of productivity. It may take a considerable period to consolidate the change in the industrial relations system achieved in the 1980s and to ensure that the role of the unions will not revert to the pattern which had such a baleful effect on the performance of the economy during the war[3] and in the three decades that followed. After such enormous gains, it would be extraordinarily perverse if the British public were to be willing to return to the discredited model of the past.

Notes

1. G. S. Bain (ed.), *Industrial Relations in Britain* (Basil Blackwell, 1983).
2. R. M. Martin, *TUC: The Growth of a Pressure Group, 1868–1976* (Clarendon Press, 1980).
3. Correlli Barnett, *The Audit of War* (Macmillan, 1986).

5

The Conservative Party

J. ENOCH POWELL

Having ceased in February 1974 to belong to the Conservative Party I have no direct knowledge of events or movements of opinion within that party after Mrs Thatcher was elected leader a year later. There is nothing more invisible than the inner realities of a political party to those outside it. What I have endeavoured to do therefore in what follows is to trace in the period before 1974 what seemed to me the antecedents of tendencies and changes in government policy which have become publicly manifest during the years of her premiership.

After declining to join Sir Alec Home's government in October 1963, and even more after the Conservative Party went into opposition in October 1964, I enjoyed greater freedom than for some years previously to formulate views upon policies which proved to be dominant themes during the following twenty years. This freedom of expression was not seriously reduced by serving on the opposition front bench as spokesman on transport in 1964–5, particularly as the late Iain Macleod and I agreed expressly with Sir Alec Home as leader of the Opposition that we would not be deemed to be restricted to our 'Shadow' portfolios. On becoming opposition spokesman on defence after Edward Heath's election as party leader in July 1965, I did not at first feel increased inhibition, because I assumed a similarity or identity of view between us; but unease and friction tended to increase as time went by, until in April 1968 my freedom of expression was fully restored, and indeed enlarged, by my being dropped from Heath's Shadow Cabinet with the clear intimation that I would not be invited to join any future government of his.

By far the most important for subsequent developments in

politics and for the course of Conservative government after 1979 amongst the themes which, by no means alone, I was exploring after 1963 was that of the cause and remedy of inflation, which continued to dominate and bedevil the experience of successive administrations.

In 1957–8 Chancellor of the Exchequer Peter Thorneycroft (later Lord Thorneycroft) was led to conclude that inflation was being generated by the level of government expenditure and the increase in money supply which government borrowing to cover the excess of expenditure over the receipts was causing. This assertion, which was later to be known as 'monetarism', until that term became debased to denote anything associated with government policy after 1979, was closely relevant to two other themes: the exchange rate of the pound sterling, and the immunities and economic power of the trade unions.

Successive governments, convinced that an exchange rate fixed and controlled in accordance with the Bretton Woods Agreement of 1944 was indispensable, found themselves effectively enslaved by the obligation to borrow from other national banks and from international institutions the massive sums necessary to maintain a particular parity of the pound sterling in terms of the gold equivalent of the dollar. Until the dollar 'came off gold' in 1968 and subsequently the exchange rates of the major currencies were allowed in 1971 to 'float' on the exchanges, I devoted much speech and writing to ridiculing the desirability, let alone the inevitability, of governments committing themselves to maintain an internationally agreed or indeed any particular exchange rate between their national currencies.

Although this heresy became, in practice if not in theory, the prevailing orthodoxy as early as 1971, familiarity with the intellectual attractions and justification of a 'floating pound' undoubtedly fortified the Conservative government of 1979 in dismantling the last vestiges of control over capital movements into and out of sterling, and contemplating with equanimity and determination of the sterling exchange rate by market forces irrespective of substantial fluctuations. The Prime Minister, if not the Chancellors of the Exchequer, remained resistant to contrary pressures either from the United States, which persistently

wanted to 'window dress' the dollar rate, or from national
banks, particularly the Bank of England, which continued
privately to fiddle the exchange rates and aspired to do so on a
grander scale. This was the cause of the severe quarrel between
Mrs Thatcher and other ministers in 1988—as indeed earlier in
1978 between Mr Callaghan and the Labour Party's back-
benchers—over Britain's continued refusal to join the exchange
rate regime of the European Monetary System.

Consequently, despite suspicions of the extent to which the
cost of exchange rate fudging helped to fuel the recrudescence of
inflation in 1988, Mrs Thatcher's government has continued to
reap the benefits of 'floating' on both the national and the
international scene. Sterling remains—what other currencies
used to be called in the past—a 'strong currency'.

Much more important, however, than has been appreciated is
the strength which the post-1979 Conservative government drew
from the first corollary of monetarism—that if governments
alone cause inflation, the employers and the trade unions therefore cannot and do not.

The 1960s were marked by a sharp rise in public criticism of
the legal privileges of the trade unions; but it was around their
ability to exercise coercion upon individuals that the criticism
centred. A legalized power to victimize individuals increasingly
appeared incompatible with the rule of law. Nevertheless the
prevalent assumption remained intact that trade union activity
upon the whole was beneficial to the real remuneration of
unionized workers and that, as their monopoly power made them
decisive in causing or refraining from causing inflation, they had
to be conciliated as far as was humanly possible and that any
serious attempt to curtail their legal entrenchment must be
politically disastrous.

This assumption appeared to be confirmed by the ignominious
fiasco of the Heath–Carr Industrial Relations Act of 1971. What
was not understood was that the Act had attempted two totally
distinct objectives—to reduce the incompatibility between trade
union privilege and the rule of law, and at the same time to place
in the hands of government new authority to restrain the supposedly inflationary exertion of trade union power. When in

1972 the Heath government took its plunge into a prices-and-incomes policy incompatible with monetarist theory, the industrial relations legislation was doomed to destruction at the hands of its own authors.

To an extent that I admit having underestimated at the time, it was the monetarist philosophy which enabled the Conservative government after 1979 to legislate into existence without serious disturbance and with complete self-confidence a new statutory framework for trade unions. Monetarism was doubly the key to this. It destroyed the myth that co-operation from the trade unions was indispensable to any government for controlling inflation; and by pointing to public expenditure and government borrowing as the true causes of monetary expansion it placed the trade unions in a situation of impotence which could not long be concealed from their own members. The downfall of Arthur Scargill and the NUM and the re-education of the trade union movement in 1984–6 were the result of this. Perhaps the most lasting consequence of the period of Conservative government 1979–89 will prove to have been the elimination of the factor of collective trade union power from the political scene and the removal of the awe with which that power was previously hedged about. The change cannot be unconnected with the collapse in the internal morale of the Labour Party, a morale which throughout its history had centred around the strength and public status of trade unionism. What brought this change about was not so much the critique of privileged collective action—'conspiracy' was the old-fashioned term—and not so much the libertarian and individualist objection to private and privileged coercion, as the espousal by government of an economic theory which bereft the trade unions of a role in political power.

It was in 1968, on the fringe of the Conservative Party's annual conference at Blackpool, that I produced an alternative Budget under the title 'Income Tax at 4 shillings and 3 pence in the £'. The currency terminology is now of course out of date, but the standard rate of income tax fixed in the Budget of 1988 came closer to the equivalent of 4s. 3d. than anyone—including myself—would have been willing to predict in 1968. The principal intellectual tool which 'Income Tax at 4 shillings and

3 pence in the £' employed and illustrated was the market mechanism, which was being explored with widening enthusiasm in the Conservative Party from the mid-1950s on. No account of that exploration would be well balanced which underestimated the effectiveness of the work of the Institute of Economic Affairs and its proselytizing influence in the Conservative Party. It challenged head-on the prevailing orthodoxies of natural—and therefore presumably irreversible—public monopoly and of the use of collective action—from government planning through to private cartels—as an instrument for the allocation of resources. 'If the market will take the decisions, why use any other mechanism?' was the question which threw governments and political parties on to the defensive.

Denationalization—in the widest sense of the term—was the means by which the balance of public and private finance was decisively shifted between 1979 and 1989, to produce a 3 per cent level of inflation, a negative public sector borrowing requirement, and a prospect of decline in the fraction of the national income earmarked for the state. The received wisdom that nothing can be denationalized was replaced by a new wisdom that anything, not excluding water supply and coal mines, can—and should—be denationalized and the ownership and therefore the management of the assets transferred to boards of management responsible to shareholders. Like the sale of monastic lands and property by Henry VIII, the transfer of ownership and control of industries and services to a wide public gave to Conservative government precisely the sense of irreversibility which is daunting to political opponents.

Mrs Thatcher has denationalized her way through Britain and the British economy at an undiminished rate since 1979; but the intellectual conviction and moral preparation necessary for her doing so was the breakthrough which market theory achieved in the mid-1970s in the Conservative Party and among the public at large. Commonly a breakthrough of this kind is accompanied by savage counter-attacks from the defeated theory: the death throes of a dying philosophy can be formidable. As in the context of monetarism, so in the context of market economics, the fatal U-turns of the Heath administration provide convenient benchmarks. In 1971 I was the only Conservative MP to denounce the nationalization of Rolls-Royce, as in 1972 I was among the few to denounce the reintroduction of prices-and-incomes policy. By the fall of Heath in 1974 the Conservative Party had made up its mind, 'Never again!' A party which had just tested state intervention to the miserable point of destruction had by 1975 become a party unafraid of the consequences of capitalist competition and free-market allocation of resources.

The delightful discovery that sale of shares in publicly owned industries and utilities was equivalent to raising huge inflation-free loans from the public commended on budgetary grounds what the logic of market economics had prescribed. I have lived not only to see 'Income Tax at 4 shillings and 3 pence in the £' as a fact and not a piece of political satire. I have lived also to watch the massive denationalization by which that adventurous Budget was underpinned. They hang together.

Nothing in life is 100 per cent. All government is a business of compromise and trade-off. The thesis that monetarism and market economics made possible between 1979 and 1989 a consistency in administration which the electorate twice sealed with its approval, as in the mid-nineteenth century it had sealed the consistencies of free trade and tariff abolition, is not refuted by drawing attention to whole areas of government untouched with the prevailing enlightenment and impeccably inconsistent with it. It so happens that these grand inconsistencies too can be argued to have demonstrable common roots, like the grand consistencies derived from monetarism and market economics. They are to be found flourishing in the external policies of the United Kingdom.

From the debris of the Heath administration, amid whose ruins the Conservative leadership and Party of 1979–89 sprang up, one survival has remained standing. Britain's membership of the European Community is still sustained by a grudging conviction of its inevitability, such that the Labour Party, after duly and formally resolving to disengage, fled terrified of its own temerity from the field of battle, such, indeed, that a prediction of British exit from the EEC before AD 2000 is even now found as incredible—well, as incredible as a prediction of income tax at 4/3 in the pound or of a free-floating pound sterling on the exchanges!

Quite apart from other considerations, like national independence and parliamentary sovereignty, the EEC is inherently on the side of dirigism in economic policy. It represents the aspiration towards a customs union within which production and investment are bureaucratically regulated but which does not participate in international free trade externally. While free trade in general is concerned with the international division of labour, a customs union is concerned with common economic regulation, the seed-bed of political unity. There has nevertheless been until very recently no critique from the Conservative government of the principle of UK membership of the EEC. Market economics and—except so far as the EMS exchange rate regime and the project of a European central bank are concerned—monetarism have stopped short of application to the EEC.

The contradiction cannot be dismissed as the result of previous commitment. In all other directions too Mrs Thatcher had been an uncomplaining member of Heath's Cabinet, which would no more have inhibited dissociation from his European than from his economic policy. The explanation of the inconsistency lies, I believe, at a deeper level—the congeniality to the Conservative Party and its leader of being aligned with the United States, misunderstood as the working model of a free-market capitalist economy and miscast as the indispensable safeguard of the United Kingdom and of something called (in American terminology) the 'free world'. Britain had adopted since 1957 in the wake of the Suez expedition fiasco a severe retrenchment of defence expenditure and the doctrine of the nuclear deterrent, primarily an American deterrent but one in which Britain purported to retain a junior share. This became the core of British defence and foreign policy, defining the position of this country in the East–West bisection of the globe.

Critique of the pro-American axiom and of the nuclear deterrent which underpinned it was not lacking in the 1960s and 1970s; but it was not developed so long or so intensively as the critique of the planned and state-regulated economy, nor was it at all closely connected with the Conservative débâcle in 1974. Thus the foreign policy, unlike the economic policies, of the Conservative Party was not in the 1970s a field in which the demand or the preparation for a decisive shift prevailed. In Europe, where the EEC's aspiration for political unity is for America the counterpart of the North Atlantic Alliance, and outside Europe, where the consequences of Suez continued to reverberate, the United Kingdom remained after 1979 the uncritical satellite of the United States, reproducing American ideology and vocabulary and unquestioningly conforming with American proceedings in the Mediterranean (Libya), in the Middle East (Palestine and the Gulf), and in the Far East, and representing the United States as having been more helpful and supportive to Britain in the recapture of the Falkland Islands than the facts justified.

The contrast between the outburst of innovative activity in home and economic affairs and the conservative adherence to conventional policies in defence and foreign affairs ought not to surprise. For governments, as for individuals, there is only so much energy available. The tactic of 'taking one thing at a time' imposes itself unsought. It is by no means to be assumed however that from 1989 onwards the Conservative government will run on the same tramlines as since 1979. Not only is the outside world drastically altering in a manner which calls into question the forty-year-old American hegemony. The Reagan years are over. The Conservative government has unfinished business elsewhere than in regions where market economics and monetary theory underpinned its achievements between 1979 and 1988. There is even a positive attraction in shifting public attention away from past achievements, which can be taken for granted and left, so to speak, to look after themselves. A government which looks forward—whether prophetically or not, we cannot know—to governing for the rest of this century is a government that needs and wants to 'move on'.

It would be a purblind observer who imagined that Mrs Thatcher and her Cabinet interpret what is happening in Central Europe and in the European Community in terms of the conventional formulae which it remains convenient meanwhile to continue to repeat. In the 'Europe without the Americans' which 1988 ushered in, there is plenty of scope for the United Kingdom to exert itself, and the Conservative Party does not lack cards to play. It was by no coincidence that, as 1988 drew to a close, the Prime Minister delivered at Bruges a carefully prepared oration reviving the ideas of national independence and parliamentary sovereignty, or that an ex-member of her Cabinet was heard talking about a non-nuclear defence policy. The 1980s were the decade of economics. The 1990s could be the decade of foreign policy. There have been such decades before, and to the Conservative Party they have not proved uncongenial—or unfavourable.

6

The Changing Political Opposition

DENNIS KAVANAGH

Between 1945 and 1979 the British party system was more competitive than at any other time in the twentieth century. In general elections between 1945 and October 1974 the Conservatives averaged 43.6 per cent of the vote and Labour 44.5 per cent, and each party was in office for seventeen years. The decade since 1979 has radically changed the picture (Table 6.1). From a

TABLE 6.1. *Conservative–Labour shares of votes in post-war elections* (%)

	Labour (av.)	Conservative (av.)	Labour lead
1945– Oct. 1974	44·5	43·6	0·9
1979–87	31·8	43·0	−11·2

position of virtual parity in shares of the vote, Labour in the last three elections has trailed the Conservatives by an average of 11 per cent. Between 1950 and 1979 neither Conservative nor Labour ever had as much as 55 per cent of the combined Lab.–Con. (two-party) vote. In 1983, however, the Conservatives won 60.6 per cent of the two-party vote, in 1987, 58 per cent.

Labour's electoral problem is conveyed by the following figures: In 1979 its vote was 6.9 per cent behind the Conservatives, in 1987 it was 11.5 per cent; in 1979 its vote was 23.2 per cent ahead of the third-placed Liberals, in 1987 it was just 8.2 per cent ahead of the Alliance.

In historical perspective it was the frequent turnover of government in the 1960s and 1970s that was unusual. A pattern of lengthy Conservative rule has been more characteristic of British politics than the so-called swing of the pendulum. The post-war period has seen two lengthy periods of single-party rule, both Conservative, between 1951 and 1964 and again since 1979. Although Labour was in office for all but three and a half years in the period 1964–79, only for the years 1966–70 did it have an assured working majority in Parliament.

In our study of *The British General Election of 1979* (Macmillan, 1980) David Butler and I expressed doubts that that election signalled the renewed dominance of the Conservative Party; that would only be decided by the results of subsequent general elections. It was clear, however, that the much discussed post-war political consensus was already weakening. By the mid-1970s it appeared to have resulted in overweening trade unions, inflationary Keynesianism, a lack of social discipline, and a growing sense that parts of the Welfare State undermined economic efficiency. In 1976 Labour executed a U-turn in its economic policies and elements of what came to be called Thatcherism—monetarism, privatization, tax cuts, and a squeeze on public spending—were introduced. This change—when the policies and some of the vocabulary of one party were appropriated by the other—betokened more significant and enduring shifts in the political agenda.

It is worth remembering the background to the exit of the last Labour government and the rise of Mrs Thatcher. Her election in 1979 was part of a reaction (found in other Western states) against high inflation, high taxes, and a growing public sector. The onset of economic recession and the slow-down of economic growth made it difficult to fund public spending without squeezing take-home pay. In Britain the reaction was strengthened by long-term economic uncompetitiveness, slow economic growth, and the drag of unreformed industrial relations. Above all there was the Winter of Discontent, which appeared to mark the death throes of a political tradition and style of political management.

OPPOSITION TURBULENCE

In many respects, the past decades have seen more dramatic changes in the opposition parties than in the Conservatives. The following events amount to a picture of instability:

1979   Labour trails Conservatives by 7 per cent in election;
1981   Split in Labour Party and creation of SDP by leading Labour right-wingers;
1982   Creation of Alliance between Liberals and SDP for election;
1983   Labour trails Conservatives by 14.8 per cent in election;
1987   Labour trails Conservatives by 11.5 per cent in election;
1988   SDP split;
       End of Liberal Party;
       Formation of Social Liberal Democrats, from Liberals and majority of SDP.

One should resist the temptation to explain too much about the record of the opposition parties in terms of the influence of the Thatcher government. Labour's shift to the left after 1979 and its constitutional changes in 1981 were a reaction to the record of the previous Labour government. The departure of Labour right-wingers was due to internal party politics, not to Thatcherism. The creation of the Alliance, its collapse in 1987, and the creation of the SLD in 1988 were based on calculations of electoral advance. There is also good survey evidence to suggest that Labour's electoral decline was already well under way in the 1970s.

In many ways what has *not* happened has been significant. The trade unions have declined in membership and influence and, apart from the NUM's year-long struggle in 1984 and 1985, have not mounted a sustained battle against government policies. Some left-wing local authorities attempted a concerted campaign against government spending policies but, in the end, were divided and defeated. The Labour leadership did not support either campaign. After three decisive electoral reverses, Mr Kinnock has undertaken a review of policies, as Gaitskell did in similar circumstances after the 1959 defeat. Equally notable has been the lack of a serious and sustained challenge to the Labour leadership. Kinnock has also managed to dominate the party machine to a greater extent than any party leader since Harold Wilson in the 1960s. The efforts of the centre parties, some

Labour MPs, *Samizdat*, Charter 88, and others to promote constitutional change, electoral reform, and electoral accommodations with the Democrats are designed in part to mobilize an anti-Thatcher coalition. They also represent a sense of defeatism that Labour can win again on its own.

For a time in 1981 the new Alliance seemed poised to smash the two-party system and perhaps bring multi-party politics and coalition government to Britain. Shirley Williams captured the safe Tory seat of Crosby in November 1981 (pushing up the previous Liberal share of the vote by 35 per cent). Other successes followed. There was talk of 'breaking the mould' of two-party politics and forcing a realignment of the parties. In spite of gaining in 1983 and 1987 the largest third-party shares of the vote in over fifty years and making spectacular by-election gains, the Alliance was frustrated by the electoral system. It will be for historians to decide how near the mould was to being broken.

The opposition parties have changed considerably since 1979. Labour's constitutional changes, giving the trade unions and local parties the major role in the election of the leader and the mandatory reselection of MPs, gave greater power to the activists, at a time when they were increasingly unrepresentative of ordinary Labour voters. The changes also had the effect of driving a score of right-wingers from the political party. After 1979 Labour moved sharply left. Its 1983 manifesto promised the abolition of the House of Lords, an end to Britain's nuclear defence, withdrawal from the European Community, an end to the sale of council houses, repeal of the government's trade union legislation, and renationalization of recently privatized industries as well as an extension of public ownership. In the 1987 manifesto, however, there was some reversal. The party accepted Britain's membership of the European Community, sale of council houses to tenants, retention of Cruise while the United States and the USSR talks continued, and, although it proposed taking some of the privatized industries back into 'social ownership', this was not a priority. Further changes seem to be likely, including the abandonment of unilateralism.

Mr Callaghan gave way as party leader to Mr Foot in 1980 and he in turn was replaced by Mr Kinnock in 1983. By the end of

1989 he will have been opposition leader for over six years and only Hugh Gaitskell (1955–63) will have had a longer continuous spell as a leader of the Opposition in the twentieth century. Mr Kinnock was the first Labour leader to be elected by the new electoral college, which gave 70 per cent of the vote to affiliated trade unions (40 per cent) and constituency parties (30 per cent). The party consciously turned to a younger generation. His rise was a mark of the split between the so-called 'soft' and 'hard' left, organized around Kinnock and Benn respectively (it was notable that Benn and Heffer were sexagenarians challenging Mr Kinnock twenty years their junior for the leadership in 1988). Mr Kinnock was a new face, indeed he had no experience in government. He came from a bastion of socialism, South Wales, was good on television, and seemed dedicated to winning. As leader he has hammered the hard left represented by Mr Benn, Mr Scargill, Militant, and Ken Livingstone.

Among Labour's collective leadership there has also been a great turnover. Compared to the elections among Labour MPs held in June 1979 for the twelve members of Labour's Shadow Cabinet, only two were elected in 1988, Roy Hattersley and John Smith. Of the others, Owen and Rodgers have left the party, Mason, Varley, Booth, and Silkin are no longer in the House of Commons, and Healey, Orme, and Rees are regarded as *passé*. Only two (Hattersley and Smith) of the present front bench have had Cabinent experience. Many observers are impressed by the parliamentary performances of the young front-benchers—Cook, Straw, Brown, Blair, and Cunningham.

MUST LABOUR LOSE?

The facts of electoral decline (set out in Table 6.1) are not in dispute. Discussion centres on whether and to what extent it is reversible; whether Labour is likely ever to form a government again in its own right.

Optimists claim that Labour has been here before. In 1959 Labour had lost a third successive election and its vote had fallen from 49 per cent in 1951 to 44 per cent. The party had done badly among the affluent working class. Then, as now, many commentators regarded Labour's continued electoral decline as largely inevitable. The contraction of the working class, increase in home ownership, and spread of the symbols of affluence (such as televisions, washing machines, cars, and foreign holidays) appeared to weaken the sense of working-class loyalty. Of course Labour went on to win four of the next five general elections. Under Harold Wilson, in 1964 and, much more, 1966, Labour looked like a natural party of government and was able to present itself as the party of modernization. History, the optimists say, is on our side.

Optimists can also point to the climate of opinion. There was certainly a move to the right before 1979. But surveys suggest (see Ivor Crewe) that there has not been any further movement since. Indeed, on attitudes to further privatization, many social issues, the death penalty, women's rights, and choosing between increased spending on social services or tax cuts there has been a shift to the left. It is often said that Thatcherism has won the wallets but not the hearts and minds of the British people. 1987 was a pocket-book election in which people rewarded the government for the increase in prosperity. At the next election Labour may perhaps gain from the mood of 'time for a change'.

Optimists further argue that it is misleading to lump the three successive election defeats together. Each defeat they claim was the product of a unique set of circumstances; in 1979 the Winter of Discontent and the minute improvement in living standards delivered by the Wilson and Callaghan governments; in 1983, the weak leadership of Michael Foot, the divisive Benn–Healey contest over the deputy leadership, the Falklands, the split in the party in 1981, and the creation of the Social Democrats all worked against it; and in 1987 the Conservatives won on a prosperity ticket. Such analysis argues that Labour has been unlucky in each of the elections and that one should not extrapolate from them about the party's future. Part of Labour's decline may have social causes, but part also has been the product of the party's mistakes on policy and strategy. Academic studies suggest that some 6 per cent to 8 per cent of Labour's decline since 1964 may be due to changes in the social structure. That party's vote has fallen 13.3 per cent.

The pessimists, on the other hand, observe that the social trends identified in the study *Must Labour Lose?* (1960) after the 1959 election have been consolidated. In 1959 the manual working class was two-thirds of the electorate. Now it is less than half. In 1959, 62 per cent of the working class voted Labour, in 1987 the figure fell to 42 per cent. Where 40 per cent were home owners in 1959 the figure is now 64 per cent. The so-called 'new working class'—manual workers who work in the South, are home owners, work in the private sector, and are not members of trade unions—was heavily Conservative in 1987. It is worth noting that some of these adverse social and economic trends— notably the growth of self-employment and private home owner- ship, decline of employment in manufacturing and the public corporations, and fall in trade union membership—have been encouraged by Conservative government policies. Because three- quarters of Labour's 229 MPs already sit for seats in North Britain and Wales, Labour has to reach out to seats in the Midlands and the South, areas of prosperity. Even in 1989 it is still not doing so.

A second reason for pessimism lies in the fragmentation of the non-Conservative vote in the last two elections. With the rise of the Alliance, Labour was no longer the sole beneficiary of anti- Conservative sentiment. In the last two general elections the Alliance was particularly successful in making inroads among middle-class public sector workers (teachers, further education lecturers, and local government administrators). Labour's polit- ical fortunes have been, and are likely to remain, tied to the progress of the successors to the Alliance, now the Democrats and the SDP. In 1987 the Alliance finished second in two-thirds of Conservative seats.

Finally, pessimists note that Labour's image contains a number of deeply unfavourable features. The party is widely regarded as incompetent on the economy, unsound on defence, too respectful of the unions, and soft on law and order. Many of these images have been around for at least a decade now and may be difficult to remove.

Comparison with the fortunes of the left in Western Europe are encouraging for Labour, but also chastening. In the recessionary

1970s most governments were turned out at elections or saw their share of electoral support fall. The misery index (the combined percentages of unemployment and inflation) reached new heights. The 1980s have seen some shift to the political right in the United States and West Germany. But the socialist share of the vote has hardly changed over the two decades in Austria, Scandinavia, West Germany, and Italy. It has increased substantially in France and Spain, and Labour governments have been re-elected in New Zealand and Australia. Only in Britain has the fall in popular support for the left been substantial. Indeed the scale of decline for such a major party is virtually unparalled in any other state in post-war Western Europe.

The good news for Labour from a comparative survey is that such features as wider home ownership, affluence, and the *embourgeoisement* of the working class are not necessarily electorally adverse. Democratic socialist parties can still thrive in prosperous societies as the example of France proves. It is worth adding that, compared to some other socialist parties, Labour has not been handicapped by the opposition or suspicion of a powerful Catholic Church (as in some West European states), or divided by a powerful communist movement in party politics and in trade unions (as in France and Italy). Moreover, because of the first-past-the-post electoral system and the predominantly two-party system, it has been almost uniquely able to form a government on its own. Elsewhere socialist parties have had to compete in multi-party and proportional electoral systems and usually share power in government. The question that such analysis then suggests is; why has Labour done so badly? Perhaps other parties, simply because they have lacked the British Labour Party's advantages, have necessarily had to be more adaptable and willing to make alliances. Left governments in Australia, New Zealand, France, and Spain have had to pursue a series of economic and social policies that are not too dissimilar to those that Mrs Thatcher's government has pursued since 1979.

In the 1980s significant political opposition to the government has come from within the Conservative Party, from 'wet' Conservatives, usually on social issues, from right-wingers resisting the harmonization of policies with the EEC and calling for a more

'Thatcherite' line for the economy and the trade unions, and from the House of Lords. Outside Parliament, the Churches, the BBC, universities, and the professions have been lobbies resisting the government's policies. Labour has been handicapped in Parliament in the 1980s by the irregular attendance of many MPs, in-fighting (most notably the Benn–Healey deputy leadership contest in 1981 and then the Kinnock–Benn leadership contest in 1988), and the failure of first Foot and then Kinnock to be commanding at the dispatch-box. Until 1989 the party also suffered from having too many indifferent front-bench performers. The Alliance and now the centre parties have had too few MPs to make a mark in Parliament, although David Owen spoke with authority at the time of the Falklands conflict and in the last Parliament. In all, the opposition in Parliament from the non-government benches has been ineffective.

Yet Labour remains the only effective vehicle in the foreseeable future for displacing the Conservatives. The combination of the electoral system and Labour's many safe seats in Scotland and northern cities means it will remain a substantial force in Parliament even if its popular vote declines even further. The split of the Alliance after the 1987 election and the eclipse of the Democrats and the SDP has given Labour its best chance since 1981 to present itself as the sole alternative to Thatcherism.

But does a Labour recovery mean that socialism has a future? The political commentator Peter Jenkins has talked of Britain now entering a post-socialist era, and the American Irving Kristol claims that the outstanding feature of the twentieth century has been the death of socialism. The Bennite left regards the success of Thatcherism as a reverse example of what a socialist Labour government could do, given sufficient commitment and political will. This wing calls for greater state ownership of economic enterprises, more economic planning, and a complete reversal of the post-1979 policies on taxation, privatization, public spending, and trade union legislation.

For the 'revisionists' (although they would reject the term) on the other side of the party, markets, wealth creation, and decentralization are in; they want to make capitalism work more efficiently, and combine it with policies to provide greater social justice. For Mr Hattersley and Mr Gould it is a matter of updating policies (not principles, they hasten to add) in the light of changing circumstances. They want to emulate what R. A. Butler did for the Conservatives after 1945. But Butler's achievement consisted largely in persuading the party to accept what the 1945 Labour government had done. After 1951 the Conservatives substantially consolidated and adapted, but did not reverse, policies on full employment, the trade unions, the National Health Service, welfare, and public ownership.

Labour's problems may be more fundamental than those envisaged by the revisionists. If we leave aside the social changes already mentioned, and whose effects have not fully worked through, and Labour's negative image, the party still has to come to terms with the legacy of Thatcherism. Labour is now likely to accept pre-strike ballots, abandon blanket renationalization, not restore top tax rates to the 1979 levels, and abandon unilateralism. Can Labour, even after the recent policy review, credibly defend low taxes as well as good public services, support consumers over producers, profitable firms over nationalized industries, and an efficient market over economic *dirigisme*? At some future date the climate of opinion will change, but not necessarily back to that of 1945 or the mid-1960s.

Mrs Thatcher has reversed what Sir Keith Joseph called the socialist ratchet and Labour almost certainly will have to fight on new ground. The political agenda in the next two decades is likely to be more responsive to so-called *post-materialist* issues like the environment, public services, citizenship rights and duties, and women's rights. These are precisely the ideas which left of centre parties in France, Italy, and West Germany are making their own—with great effect. There are few votes in the 1990s in a return to the politics of the 1970s.

AN ANTI-THATCHER MAJORITY?

There is much loose or wishful talk about the anti-Thatcherite majority. By aggregating the Alliance and Labour votes at the 1987 general election it is possible to arrive at a 54 : 42 per cent anti-Conservative majority. Perhaps only on defence and electoral reform are the Labour and the centre parties far apart and this may narrow as the next general election approaches. But the single-minded rejection of Thatcherism is hardly the basis for a coalition, electoral pact, or even accommodation. David Owen favours some arrangements between the centre and Labour parties. The official Labour and Democratic leaderships are not interested in such arrangements, certainly this side of an election. Mr Ashdown would like the Owenites belatedly to merge with his Democratic Party and in 1988 was talking of replacing Labour. Labour's ambition is to form a government on its own. Some Labour front-benchers, notably John Cunningham and Robin Cook, appear to discount the possibility of the party getting a majority at the next election, and, by implication, raise the need for an electoral pact. *Marxism Today*, *Samizdat*, and a number of MPs and strategists in the non-Conservative parties favour it. Yet for the Labour leadership this is the thought that dare not speak its name. Electoral pacts or even the introduction of proportional representation could be used in the future against a Labour Party. It is, moreover, very doubtful that the party leaders, even if they wished, could deliver their local parties to such an agreement.

Before 1987 it was said that another bad defeat for Labour would require the parties of the centre and left to come together. Now it is said that such a move will be on the cards only after another bad defeat. Paradoxically, for the non-Thatcherite majority to be mobilized, Labour leaders will first have to recognize the existence of an even larger non-Labour majority. Certainly, if three-party politics are here to stay, and Labour's ceiling percentage among voters is in the middle to high 30s, and two or even three parties divide the non-Conservative 60 per cent of the electorate, it is difficult to see Mrs Thatcher being defeated.

In spite of so much that has happened since the creation of the SDP in 1981—the pact with the Liberals, Alliance, split, and then incomplete merger—there is still a considerable centre vote. There is, however, no *one* centre party. Paddy Ashdown's task, once the doctor and his SDP group refused to join the new Democrats, was to kill off the SDP. As the by-elections in Epping (1988) and Richmond (1989) show, he has failed. Comparing Crosby in 1981 with the centre parties' large but divided vote in

Richmond in 1989 shows that in terms of forging a credible third force the centre has gone backwards. The decade has been one of spectacular by-election successes and much media hype.

The existence of a strong opposition is important in presenting a meaningful choice to voters, posing an alternative government, and providing effective and coherent criticism of the government of the day. The institution of legitimate organized political opposition is important in any political system, particularly in Britain, where the government faces so few formal political checks and balances. Other Western countries, which have coalition governments or levels of significant local and state government, can provide executive experience for members of the opposition or other parties. In the British system, particularly with a weakened role for local government, the *total* exclusion of the opposition has its disadvantages. The dominance of Mrs Thatcher's government was not inevitable; a large part of the explanation is to be found in the sheer disarray of the opposition parties.

7

Cabinet and Parliament

PETER RIDDELL

Mrs Margaret Thatcher has changed the structure of the British political system—in Cabinet and Parliament—much less than she has the rest of Britain.

She has enjoyed such a personal dominance over both bodies that it is difficult to assess how permanent have been the changes since 1979. It is tempting, though misleading, to project into the long term what have in practice been aspects of her personal rule. It is necessary to distinguish between institutional and behavioural aspects—the framework and how it is used.

Mrs Thatcher has been reluctant to alter the machinery of government, at least at the centre—merely merging the odd ministry here or there, and on a considerably smaller scale than most of her predecessors. She has left the basic structure at the heart of Whitehall decision-making intact, unlike the periphery and local government which have been shaken up (and down) to an extent not seen since the 1940s.

In particular, Mrs Thatcher has resisted the idea of creating a prime minister's department—unlike, say, parallel parliamentary systems in Australia and Canada. But she has strengthened the personal policy advice at her disposal in Downing Street, with the expansion of the Policy Unit, though only up to about ten or a dozen, and with the recruitment of occasional *ad hoc* advisers. These have included both her personal economic adviser Professor Sir Alan Walters, with two Downing Street stints and in regular contact in between from Washington, as well as foreign affairs advisers like Sir Anthony Parsons and Sir Percy Cradock.

However, the numbers of Downing Street staff still remain small by comparison with other Whitehall departments or the offices of other heads of government. There have been extensions to the Cabinet Office machinery, notably the scrutiny work of the efficiency unit set up by Lord Rayner, and the existence of an enterprise unit for a year in its offices after Lord Young's entry into the Cabinet in 1984. On the other hand, the Central Policy Review Staff, or think-tank, was abolished in 1983, to the regret more of civil servants and advisers than of politicians. But these are grafts on to, and cuts from, a familiar framework rather than revolutionary changes.

Similarly, Mrs Thatcher has been a conservative about Parliament—a reluctant, rather than enthusiastic, supporter of select committees and an opponent of televising the proceedings of the Commons. She has also been the first prime minister in twenty years to recommend hereditary peerages—along the way showing no interest in ideas for reforming the House of Lords or any other kind of constitutional change.

Mrs Thatcher has used these familiar structures in a highly individual way. Yet there is sometimes a conflict between the myth of the dominant personality brooking no dissent—the conviction Prime Minister—and the frequently agonized and lengthy debates before decisions are reached. Mrs Thatcher may have adopted a more presidential—even at times quasi-monarchical—style than her predecessors, but collective decision-making has not been totally pushed aside.

The full Cabinet still meets every Thursday morning outside holidays and there remains an extensive framework of committees—even though the former meets less frequently than before and there is a simplified structure of the latter than under some previous prime ministers. One of the few facts about the Cabinet to emerge via the Downing Street briefings of Parliamentary Lobby journalists is the length of such Thursday meetings. Unfortunately no one seems to have kept a record, though in my experience the meetings were seldom said to have lasted for more than an hour or ninety minutes and were often preceded or followed by a meeting of a Cabinet committee.

Mrs Thatcher rarely uses the Cabinet to discuss major issues, but treats it more as a reporting session on decisions taken earlier by ministerial committees or for routine briefings from the Foreign Secretary, the Chief Whip, and so on. Only rarely in the late 1980s have there been major discussions in the full Cabinet according to the comments of senior ministers. Exceptions are where an issue suddenly flares up and concern is expressed by ministers round the Cabinet table. For instance, protests by constituents over the impact of the April 1988 social security and housing benefit changes on retired people were raised by ministers, leading to a package of help for those worst hit. But these are exceptions.

The treatment of the full Cabinet as a dignified rather than efficient part of the constitution contrasts with the practice of Labour administrations and Mrs Thatcher herself in her first two years in office. The delicate political balance in Labour administrations, with a powerful left always threatening action, forced both Lords Wilson and Callaghan to thrash out major issues in the full Cabinet. This was classically shown during the lengthy deliberations by the full Cabinet over the International Monetary Fund stand-by credit in the autumn of 1976, as vividly recalled in Joel Barnett's memoirs.

Similarly, Mrs Thatcher still had many powerful sceptics and senior figures from the Heath era in her own Cabinet when she took office in May 1979. There was a collegiate structure at this stage, albeit a divided one in the manner of a C. P. Snow novel. This was the period of bitter Cabinet arguments over economic policy as well as regular leaks by ministerial dissidents to their Fleet Street friends; the proper Sir Geoffrey Howe was never so skilful in such manœuvring.

All this changed from the autumn of 1981 onwards. First, the Cabinet reshuffle of that year led to the dropping of several doubters about the economic strategy, such as Sir Ian Gilmour, Mark Carlisle, and Lord Soames, the exiling of James Prior to Belfast, and the promotion to the Cabinet of loyalist believers such as Norman Tebbit, Cecil Parkinson, and Nigel Lawson. Second, Mrs Thatcher's successful leadership during the Falklands War in the late spring and early summer of 1982 made her own position unassailable, as it has remained ever since apart from a few days during the Westland Affair in early 1986.

The result of these two changes was to enable Mrs Thatcher to pursue her conviction politics with less internal opposition and with like-minded allies. It was from the end of her first term onwards that there developed her distinctive style of operating, her preference for convening small groups of ministers, civil servants, and special advisers to examine problems rather than to discuss them through more broad-based committees. Critics have argued that this has meant prejudging the conclusions. But Mrs Thatcher has had clearly defined instincts which she has brought to bear on problems and it was for this reason that she believed that the Central Policy Review Staff had outlived its usefulness, and why she preferred instead the more committed advice of her own Policy Unit. This is also why she has had little patience with free-standing Royal Commission-type inquiries. Within this framework there has, however, often been plenty of discussion about the policies to be adopted. Mrs Thatcher, and the Treasury, have generally had their way in the end, though with arguments along familiar inter-departmental lines.

This approach was seen, for instance, in the review of health provision during 1988–9. In response to a wave of protests Mrs Thatcher set up a small group of ministers, consisting of herself, two Treasury ministers, and relevant departmental ministers, serviced by civil servants, special advisers and her own Downing Street Policy Unit. There was not only no direct public input—though a wide range of views was expressed in the newspapers and in pamphlets during the period of the review—but other ministers had little chance to participate directly.

Defenders of the traditional view of the Cabinet as a deliberative body, often ministers whom she has dismissed, have argued that Mrs Thatcher has in this way devalued collective decision-making. They argue that Mrs Thatcher has shifted towards a presidential style in which she and her allies reach decisions rather than the Cabinet as a whole. There is something in this view but it should not be exaggerated.

First, all prime ministers have used *ad hoc* groups on particularly sensitive issues, such as the exchange rate or nuclear defence; Mrs Thatcher has just applied this practice more widely. Indeed, she has sometimes delighted in not using the formal committee structure. For instance, she has regarded it as a victory when the annual public spending round can be completed without bringing in the Star Chamber arbitration committee. Second, her dominant style is still dependent in the end on the support of colleagues. On big issues she has always been careful to inform the Cabinet and to obtain its approval, even if at times only after cursory discussion by ministers generally.

This was illustrated in the two great tests, and apparent breakdowns, of collective decision-making, the Falklands War and the Westland Affair. The failure to take appropriate action to deter the Argentine invasion of the Falklands in April 1982 reflected not only shortcomings in intelligence appreciation but also the unwillingness of the Foreign Office to confront either other ministers or Parliament with what was happening. The Franks Report noted that government policy towards Argentina and the Falkland Islands was never formally discussed outside the Foreign Office between the start of 1981 and the invasion crisis fifteen months later. It was not a priority compared with pressing domestic economic and social issues. Yet, following the invasion, a small 'War Cabinet'—formally known as Overseas and Defence (South Atlantic) Committee—was created with a balanced political membership to handle operational matters, though the full Cabinet was involved on major decisions. In times of crisis, collective decision-making was reasserted.

The Westland Affair is more controversial since Michael Heseltine and Mrs Thatcher and her allies present diametrically opposed versions. To Mr Heseltine, the affair was 'an affront to the constitution', a culmination of breaches by the Prime Minister of long-established procedure on collective Cabinet decision-making. To Mrs Thatcher, as she explained on the 'Face the Press' programme at the height of the crisis, 'there was a period when the Cabinet did not seem and, in fact, was not acting with collective responsibility, because one person was not playing as a member of the team'.

Again the issue was initially one that did not appear very important—the fate of a small helicopter company based in Yeovil. At first, the matter was discussed in *ad hoc* groups of interested ministers, then taken to a meeting of the Cabinet's economic strategy committee, all in the first half of December 1985. Mr Heseltine then claims, with some evidence to back him, that a further meeting was arranged, then cancelled, and Mrs Thatcher stopped further discussion. In his words, 'from the moment that decision was taken to cancel the opportunity for a collective judgement to be taken, I knew that something very wrong had happened'.

There then followed a period of extraordinary briefing and counter-briefing—leaked letters and accounts of meetings—before Mrs Thatcher attempted to restore order by insisting that future statements on Westland would have to be cleared by the Cabinet Office. Mr Heseltine said he then told the Cabinet that 'I could not accept that the traditional basis for collective responsibility had been established. In these circumstances, on a constitutional matter, I was obliged to leave the Cabinet.' And so he walked out in the most dramatic manner since Joseph Chamberlain left Gladstone's third administration almost a century earlier.

Fellow ministers at the time did not think that there had been any great constitutional impropriety. Indeed, that traditionalist Lord Whitelaw was even more furious than Mrs Thatcher with Mr Heseltine. A common view among Mr Heseltine's friends was that frustrations with Mrs Thatcher's style which had slowly built up had finally snapped, and that everybody involved, including Mrs Thatcher's close Downing Street staff, had behaved badly on a minor matter. Afterwards, there was much wringing of hands about the need to restore Cabinet government, and Mrs Thatcher was for a time less than her usual confident self. She had to back down two months later over the proposed sale of Land Rover to General Motors in face of a threatened revolt and possible resignations by one or two ministers.

Moreover, while Mrs Thatcher removed many of her critics (often previous allies like John Biffen) in a series of reshuffles—leaving only three survivors of her original Cabinet by mid-1989—this did not mean she had a Cabinet of like-minded clones. She operated rather like a strong-minded headmistress promoting on merit and respecting hierarchy. Thus, former close supporters of Edward Heath like Douglas Hurd and Kenneth Baker, and mainstream Tories like Kenneth Clarke and Malcolm Rifkind, entered the Cabinet, while strongly Thatcherite middle-ranking ministers like Sir Rhodes Boyson and Sir Geoffrey Pattie were dropped, never having made the grade. In the same way as former prime ministers, Mrs Thatcher has had to work with the talent that is available.

What Mrs Thatcher has done is to use and mould the Cabinet structure as she has found it, rather than to create a new one. Her force of personality and will have been sufficient to change the direction of Whitehall. There may at times have been only lip-service to the forms of collective decision-making by the Cabinet, but at least it has been lip-service. She has in the end to be obeyed, but others also have a say. Mrs Thatcher has been faced with open Cabinet dissent on issues like Britain's membership of the European Monetary System and the development of the Community. This has at times produced the extraordinary situation when she has distanced herself semi-publicly from other ministers. While Mrs Thatcher may have adopted a somewhat presidential style in her handling of colleagues and of meetings, the familiar Cabinet structure remains largely as it was when she came to power.

The changes in Parliament during the 1980s have owed less to Mrs Thatcher because she has had less direct control. The most notable features of the period have been the creation of the departmentally related select committees and the associated strengthening of scrutiny of expenditure (highlighted by the creation of a National Audit Office directly accountable to Parliament), the series of back-bench revolts, the repeated votes in favour of increases in MPs' pay and allowances for secretaries and research staff, the vote in early 1988 in favour of the experimental televising of the Commons, and the election in June 1983 of Mr Bernard Weatherill as Speaker. In each case Mrs Thatcher was either lukewarm, or in the latter three examples strongly opposed to what happened.

The Lords, itself televised from 1985 onwards (thanks to the strong support of its then leader, Lord Whitelaw), has proved to be a regular irritant in the side of government. Their lordships, whose virtues and independence have been more trumpeted than real, have inflicted regular, generally minor, defeats on Mrs Thatcher's legislation. The government lost more than 120 times between 1979 and the end of the 1987–8 session. But most of these have been fairly minor, detailed, provisions rather than central clauses. None the less, it has required all the ingenuity of Chief Whip Lord Denham to summon Tory peers to their duty in large numbers from time to time to avoid defeat on larger issues. Such set-backs have generally been avoided, as in the summer of 1988, when, in what appeared like an audition for Iolanthe, the shires and the City boardrooms produced the second highest turn-out ever to defeat a proposal to introduce a progressive element into the flat-rate poll-tax.

In most cases the bark of the Lords has been worse than its bite. This is partly because threatened revolts have fizzled out and also, in particular, because there is a difference between those who speak and those who vote. The speakers are notably life peers— former MPs or representatives of the professions which Mrs Thatcher so much delights in offending, such as university vice-chancellors and professors, lawyers, and, of course, the bench of bishops. Debates in the Lords have often been dominated by the voice of the offended, and ageing, Establishment of the 1960s and 1970s. The criticisms have attracted more attention since January 1985 when the Lords began to be televised on an experimental basis, made permanent in 1986—including a memorable swan-song from the Earl of Stockton. But the active speakers have often been unrepresentative of those who vote. Even though the Tories do not have a majority of all regularly attending peers, they do represent by far the largest single block in face of the divided forces of Labour and the centre parties. So with the addition of occasional hereditary peers on big occasions, as well as many cross-benchers, the Tories have generally been able to win through.

The number of government defeats may have been large but its scope has been limited. There is cross-party support in the Lords for issues affecting the disabled, charities, housing, the universities, rural areas, pensioners, and the constitution. When a matter affects two or more of these overlapping groups, such as charitable housing for the elderly and disabled, the Lords can be insistent. Otherwise, the most notable defeat for the government was in 1984 when the Lords rejected proposals to suspend the Greater London Council and the metropolitan authorities in the interim period before their abolition. Yet this only affected the transition and the authorities were still abolished.

Each of these cases shows members of the Commons and Lords asserting themselves, but the overall effect on the balance of power and policy has not been great. Almost all the main items of legislation, such as the many privatization measures, have gone through largely unscathed. More significantly, the government has seldom been on the defensive because of what has happened in the Commons, but because of the impact upon MPs of outside events—the recession, high interest rates, inner city riots, etc.— which have affected the public standing of the government.

The departmentally related select committees have been an important innovation in extending the scope of parliamentary scrutiny. They have broadened the public debate on key issues, enabling ministers and civil servants to be questioned more frequently than they were previously. The committees, whose membership has matched party balance in the House, have specific briefs to monitor the affairs of twelve departments plus the Scottish and Welsh Offices. (However, because of a shortage of Scottish Tory back-bench MPs after the 1987 general election, the Scottish Select Committee was not established, to the fury of the opposition parties, which held sixty-two out of seventy-two seats north of the border.)

These committees replaced, and built on, the work of the former Nationalized Industry, Expenditure, and Technology Committees. They are significant not only in being more comprehensive than the former committees but also in establishing a more permanent place in the parliamentary structure than their predecessors. Meanwhile, a number of existing select committees have remained and thrived, notably the Public Accounts Committee, whose role has been enhanced by the establishment in 1983 of the independent National Audit Office.

The committees have frequently annoyed the government. Indeed, it is arguable that they were only set up because of particularly favourable timing in the aftermath of the 1979 general election. The momentum of reform which was created by procedure committee inquiries in the late 1970s and pre-election commitments of first Francis Pym and then Norman

St John-Stevas forced Mrs Thatcher to agree. Subsequently, a number of ministers made no secret of their irritation with what they saw as upstart committees of disaffected colleagues, let alone opposition MPs, questioning their wisdom. But it has essentially been irritation because the role of the committees is limited to scrutiny rather than to policy creation.

The function of the legislature has been to sustain and examine the executive rather than to replace it. So the committees have had a peripheral role in policy formation. Moreover, the fact that MPs on the committees have been primarily party men and women, subject to the discipline of the whips has limited their independence. In practice also much of the available parliamentary talent has been on the front benches—even a lowly parliamentary private secretaryship proving more alluring to most aspiring MPs than service on a committee. For every Terence Higgins, on economic matters, or Frank Field, on health and social security, there are many more second-rank backbenchers on the committees.

The committees have naturally varied in their impact. Their inquiries have ranged from regular items in the calendar, such as the Budget and the public spending White Paper, to immediate crises, such as over health service funding or eggs, to longer-term inquiries—as, say, into Anglo-Soviet relations or the motor component industry. While the collection of evidence for the latter type of inquiry has attracted attention from interested bodies, academics, and the trade press, the resulting reports have seldom had much influence on policy-making. The bigger impact has come from short-term inquiries into topics of the moment. A critical report may not change policy but it does affect the broader public mood on a question. Overall, the committees have expanded Parliament's role in holding the executive to account, no more.

The change of back-bench behaviour towards greater independence, which started in the early 1970s, has continued since 1979 with regular revolts by Government back-benchers. In many cases the whips have been relaxed about such rebellions since fifteen or twenty MPs abstaining or even voting against the government could easily be absorbed by large Commons majorities, particularly after the 1983 and 1987 elections. Such revolts are soon forgotten. Even the defeat in April 1986 of the second reading of the Bill to liberalize shop trading hours was more interesting as a historical curiosity—the first time this century a government with a clear working majority has lost such a measure—than in establishing a trend. Yet the revolts, often on matters of particular concern to the Conservative rank and file, like the setting of rates and the green belt, have reflected an unease about the pace of Thatcherism. The rebels have included not only a hard core of twenty disaffected MPs who have been found in most revolts but also a varying group of others mobilized on particular issues of interest to them or affecting their constituents. But they have not represented a fundamental challenge to the government.

Even in the period of most acute division within the Conservative Party over economic policy in the early 1980s, the groups of back-bench doubters were relatively ineffective—and never threatened the government as the Tribune Group did in opposing the public spending White Paper in 1976. Moreover, in classic Tory fashion, most of the rebels were soon absorbed into the hierarchy. Of the dozen signatories of the 'Changing Gear' pamphlet of September 1981, which questioned the direction of the then economic policy, all but a couple were in the government in one form or another within three or four years. By the mid- to late 1980s the largest Tory back-bench groups were on the free-market or authoritarian right—as represented by the No Turning Back and 92 groups—and they both worked mainly behind the scenes in advancing their ideas.

Indeed, the Thatcher government has been acutely sensitive to back-bench opinion, contrary to its popular image. On several occasions ministers have offered concessions in response to actual, or threatened, back-bench revolts—in 1984 totally recasting proposals on student finances in response to the anger of the middle classes as expressed at a packed meeting of the back-bench Education Committee, and, as noted earlier, offering sizeable concessions on housing benefit and social security in April 1988. Yet these revolts should not be exaggerated. The concessions have been at the margin. They have represented prudent party management by the whips. The core features of the Thatcher revolution have been carried through Parliament largely unaltered.

Mrs Thatcher, like previous prime ministers, can never ignore Parliament. She and her ministers want a contented band of back-benchers rather than a discontented one. Moreover, Mrs Thatcher has to answer questions twice a week, and her mastery for most of the time has been an important part of her general political strength. When she has faltered in Parliament, as over Westland and at times on health and social security issues, it has been reflected in her popular standing. The mood of MPs not only reflects the feelings of constituents on particular issues but is also quickly communicated back to voters. The Commons remains an acute barometer of the mood both of MPs and of the nation generally.

Yet, the dominance of Mrs Thatcher and of the Tories for most of the 1980s has created frustrations in Parliament, particularly for the opposition parties. Labour leaders have faced the particular difficulty of an eager rank and file urging them on to attack and defeat the hated Tories, but knowing that, however well they perform in debate, they will be defeated at the end of the day. And what is more they will be largely ignored by the media. So Labour leaders faced a continuing problem of motivating their back-benchers, many of whom were also concerned to spend more time in their constituencies in order to head off possible reselection prob-lems and defeat at the coming general election. So for much of the 1980s there were the twin problems of empty opposition benches and occasional explosions of anger with demonstrations. There were particularly difficult periods for the Speaker at the beginning of both the 1983 and 1987 parliaments when a number of mainly hard-left MPs were thrown out of the chamber for disruption and when complaints were heard about rowdyism. In reality behaviour was no worse than in earlier decades but the absence of the prospect of power for the foreseeable future was bound to produce bad temper as well as absenteeism. And voters were more aware of the noise because of the radio broadcasting of the proceedings of the Commons. The positioning of the microphones made exchanges seem rowdier than they were to those present.

For much of the period the Labour front bench was ineffective in attack with a few exceptions like veteran Denis Healey, the Scottish lawyers John Smith and Donald Dewar, and, on occasion, Roy Hattersley and John Cunningham. Michael Foot proved to be an abysmal leader of the Opposition, totally outclassed by Mrs Thatcher, and never shining except when constitutional matters were under discussion. Neil Kinnock also seldom showed the oratorical powers he could display on outside platforms. However, from the mid-1980s onwards there was an improvement in the Labour front bench with a new generation of good debaters such as Robin Cook, Bryan Gould, Jack Straw, Gordon Brown, and Tony Blair. While their performances, and a sharper approach by Neil Kinnock in 1989, helped Labour morale, they did not in themselves undermine Mrs Thatcher's dominance.

Mrs Thatcher's impact on both the Cabinet and Parliament has been considerable. But it has been primarily personal rather than institutional. She has been dominant through her use of the existing levers of power rather than by creating new ones. As such, there is nothing necessarily permanent in the way she has run the Cabinet or treated Parliament, unlike say the greater powers which central government has taken over the conduct of local authorities. Moreover, where there have been changes, such as the creation of select committees or the televising of Parliament, they have been outside of her control, and often against her preferences.

The position was best summed up by Sir Douglas Wass, Permanent Secretary to the Treasury until 1983. He said in the BBC series 'The Thatcher Phenomenon': 'the extent to which prime ministers behave like presidents and the extent to which they behave like chairmen of committees varies almost randomly with the occupant of No. 10. It's gone up and down over the course of history and I think it's quite possible we could revert to a chairman-type prime minister again.'

In short, Mrs Thatcher's approach to the Cabinet and to Parliament may not last any longer than she does—unlike much of the rest of the Thatcher revolution.

8

The Civil Service

PETER HENNESSY

Mrs Margaret Thatcher has had more impact on the Civil Service than any peacetime prime minister since Mr Gladstone. Rarely can such simple claims be made with certitude. This one has the status of a self-evident truth.

It raises, however, one serious problem of assessment and invites a second long-term question: has she had *quite* as much impact as her detractors and admirers claim? And will her changes endure? It is the stuff of politics and history A level exam questions well into the twenty-first century.

The prize for undeniable achievement must be awarded for improved public service management. It is a doubly praiseworthy accomplishment. The peacetime Civil Service (Whitehall in conditions of total war 1914–18 and 1939–45 was a very different place—fast, flexible, and effective) had long appeared virtually unreformable.

The reports and White Papers, the tombstones of failed attempts, littered the public admin. shelves of the libraries. Clever permanent secretaries (the 'permanent politicians' of the system) would always in the end, it seemed, see off and out the transient occupants of the ministers' offices or even No. 10 itself. To compound the difficulties, Whitehall—a sprawling federation of departments, each with its enervating traditions and vested interests—was in size and ungovernability second only to the health service in the management problems it threw up.

Conventional wisdom had it in 1979 that Whitehall would indeed swamp Mrs Thatcher for all her determination and suspicion of the official machine, its work practices, and the advice it served up, as it had overwhelmed so many before including both Harold Wilson and Edward Heath.

Conventional wisdom, as in so many areas, was wrong. It

helps, of course, if you keep winning elections. The electorate in the past has been to the Civil Service what the snow has been to Russia when invaded—the ultimate remover of the intruder. After a decade of occupation, however, the intruders become insiders however abrasive and counter-cultural they remain.

In addition to longevity, a crystalline perception of what changes were needed was required. In 1979 Mrs Thatcher had more a gut-feeling than a game-plan—there were too many civil servants (732,000 of them to be precise), they cost too much (over £3.00 a head per week for every man, woman, and child in the country), a handful of the best from the private sector could do in an afternoon what a committee of permanent secretaries would fail to do in a month, they had too much say in the outcome of policy, and were always pushing in a corporatist direction.

Ten years later pretty well all of that has changed (I never believed, however, in the businessman-as-superman notion and reckoned the alleged corporatism of the 1960s and 1970s was overdone), but not because of a detailed strategy thought out in advance and captured in a single document. The transformation has been gradual and incremental.

Mrs Thatcher's first decision, however, was crucial, for virtually everything else has depended on her choice of Sir Derek (now Lord) Rayner of Marks and Spencer as her first efficiency adviser. He had worked in Whitehall before, and knew its good and bad points. Most of all he understood that the best chance of lasting change would be the unchaining of the would-be reformers already in the Civil Service. He kept his own Efficiency Unit small, therefore, and sought and found allies at all managerial levels across the departments. Permanent secretary power he would (and did) trump by prime ministerial power.

The strategy he developed for Mrs Thatcher and presented to the Cabinet in the spring of 1980 as a seminal document, *The Conventions of Government*, identified the enemy as those twin artefacts of bureaucracy—paper and rules. In the short term he would weaken them by ruthless cutting of costs and manpower and by efficiency probes, known as 'scrutinies', into blocks of routine work which would yield swift economies and set an example across the board.

In the long term he would defeat them through lasting reforms (his phrase) which dug up the old power lines of Whitehall's money and personnel systems. For the first time, ministers would be given proper management information and direct responsibility for the stewardship of their departmental resources; the ethos of the senior Civil Service would be changed from a policy-making to a managerial culture when it became plain that the route to the top would be open to those who got the most out of people and cash. Good management was to be a policy in its own right. Parliament would benefit from a clearer picture of what departments were doing and how. The public would benefit by greater value for their taxpayer pound.

Mrs Thatcher backed Rayner at every turn. She called him 'a remarkable and wonderful person' at Question Time. She bullied ministers, who, Michael Heseltine apart, did not throb with pleasure at the idea of managing, into taking Raynerism seriously. She trumpeted his achievements abroad and allowed him to pursue a policy of openness when appearing before parliamentary select committees or speaking to journalists.

Before he returned to the private sector full-time, Rayner's principles were enshrined in a document, *The Financial Management Initiative*, which made permanent the *ad hoc* changes of the first three years of the efficiency drive and established clear lines of managerial responsibility deep down the departmental hierarchies.

By the end of Mrs Thatcher's second term, all the departmental management systems were up and running. Permanent secretaries acknowledged in public and in private how valuable they were as tools of management and urged their retention if the government changed. The efficiency probes, the famous Rayner scrutinies, had produced a cumulative saving of £1 billion which in mid-1980s terms would buy you 22 new hospitals or the M25 motorway or the Chevaline missile system. Also by the close of the second term the Civil Service had contracted by some 20 per cent to 600,000, the smallest since the war, and its running costs were, at last, both measurable and under control. This was a considerable achievement. The Labour Government had conducted a *Cost of Central Government Review* in the mid-1970s which shed 35,000 jobs and saved £140 million, significant but not on the Thatcher scale. If Mr Callaghan had won the 1979 election he could well have split the Treasury into a finance ministry and a department of management and budget. But, as far as is known, Labour had no plans to change the fundamentals of Whitehall's work practices. After 1979 it was most certainly not business as usual. Here, at least, the Thatcher effect is traceable and undeniable.

Characteristically, the stone-cladding of the new way in *The Financial Management Initiative* was not seen by the Prime Minister as the moment to ease off and savour the achievement. There remained an 'unfinished agenda', as Lord Rayner put it in his farewell lecture. For a start, he said, the performance improvements won by the civil servants themselves had not found their way into better working accommodation and conditions for the staff (the other half of the Marks and Spencer philosophy), which he regretted. Nor had the new management techniques penetrated the big spending programmes of government which accounted for 90 per cent of public expenditure as opposed to the 10 per cent absorbed by running costs, where Raynerism was having its effect. Truly big prizes in savings and efficiency remained to be won.

Rayner's successor, Sir Robin Ibbs of ICI (a former director of the by now abolished think-tank), pressed on in his unobtrusive fashion. Savings from the scrutinies continued to accrue. He pursued a policy of quiet evangelism, moving from department to department exhorting ministers and permanent secretaries to do more. The war on paper continued. By 1987, 27,000 forms had been scrapped, 41,000 redesigned, and £14 million saved. A sense of value-for-money was imbuing much of government activity. But Ibbs was restless. Slow, incremental improvements were not enough. The Financial Management Initiative was running out of steam.

In the summer of 1986 he made a dramatic request to Mrs Thatcher. Would she sanction a scrutiny into the efficiency strategy itself? She would. Its terms of reference were genuinely all-embracing. Unlike the Fulton Committee twenty years earlier, the Ibbs inquiry was not kept out of matters touching on ministerial responsibility. The 'obstacles to better management' he and his team were to tackle included the 'political and attitudinal' as well as the 'institutional and administrative'.

Shortly before the 1987 election, the Ibbs Report, *The Next Steps*, reached Mrs Thatcher. For once a Whitehall document deserved the adjective 'radical'. It proposed that a fresh eye be cast over the Civil Service. The bulk of its activities should be seen for what they were—businesses delivering services to the public, sometimes on a vast scale nation-wide like the tax-raising and benefit-paying systems, on a medium scale such as the driver and vehicle licensing establishment at Swansea, or on a small scale like the Royal Parks or the Queen Elizabeth II Conference Centre in London.

If ministers decided these activities were not suitable for privatization, they should, none the less, be placed on as commercial a footing as possible by being cut loose from departmental hierarchies. They would stay answerable to ministers and Parliament. Their staff would, in the main, continue to be civil servants. But these new executive agencies would be free-standing with substantial powers over their own budgets, pay structures, and management methods.

The imminence of the election put paid to any chance of a swift response (or immediate publication) from No. 10. The election over, a battle royal ensued in the summer and autumn of 1987 with the Treasury playing its starring role as institutional sceptic, ever fearful that the devolution of power would mean financial indiscipline, a free-for-all on Civil Service pay, and the busting of their sacred public expenditure targets.

By February 1988, when *The Next Steps* was published, a concordat of a kind had been agreed between the Cabinet Office, which was to implement the plan, and the Treasury, which was to pay for it. Charters, or 'framework agreements', which would somehow reconcile liberty and order with a review every few years, were to be negotiated agency by agency. The programme was, in its way, to follow the pattern of privatization in the early 1980s—initial, cautious experiments which could lead to a rolling programme progressively changing the configurations of our political economy. The aim was certainly ambitious: to have three-quarters of the Civil Service in executive agencies of one kind or another by the end of the century. If this was to be accomplished, with a real outflow of power irrigating the new bodies and allowing a hundred managerial flowers to bloom, it would represent a change in the Whitehall landscape of a magnitude not encountered in peacetime since Gladstone implemented the Northcote–Trevelyan recommendation that a career Civil Service be created by recruiting on the basis of merit rather than political connection.

Will it be achieved? The signs (in the spring of 1989) are promising. An energetic implementer, Peter Kemp, was transferred from the Treasury to the Cabinet Office to manage the project. Key prime ministerial support was, as always, crucial and, as always, in plentiful supply. By the end of 1988, though only three agencies were in operation, the Vehicle Inspectorate, Companies House, and Her Majesty's Stationery Office, another thirty had been earmarked, including some big operations such as the social security system and the employment service. And of the three agencies already chartered, HMSO had managed to squeeze from the Treasury a high degree of autonomy over its pay arrangements. Furthermore, parliamentary interest remained high and an enthusiastic, if occasionally sceptical, tranche of bipartisan support was forthcoming from the all-party House of Commons Select Committee on the Treasury and the Civil Service.

Significantly, the climate of expectation changed during the course of 1988 from a suspicion that *The Next Steps* could easily find its way to the knackers' yard already crammed with failed Civil Service reforms to the feeling that it would be surprising if something substantial had not materialized by the early 1990s. Even if *The Next Steps* were to prove a relative disappointment, however, the cumulative effect of her managerial reforms between 1979 and 1987 would leave Mrs Thatcher a historic figure in Civil Service terms. If *The Next Steps* are truly trodden she will unquestionably rank as historic in Whitehall's history as long as there are historians left to record it.

There is, however, an ever-present danger of taking Mrs

Thatcher too much and too often at voice value. For since becoming leader of the Conservative Party in 1975 she has claimed on several occasions to have 'changed everything'. In the Civil Service context, her detractors say she has with a vengeance and not just in management terms. They contend she has undone Gladstone's reform and politicized its upper ranks. It is a grave charge and a difficult one to resolve either way.

She has had the opportunity to do so. By the end of her second term, the natural turnover among permanent and deputy secretaries had ensured that virtually all of them had been appointed with her approval. And Mrs Thatcher certainly took a keener interest in the work of the Cabinet Secretary's Senior Appointments Selection Committee than any premier in memory. To the permanent secretaries who sat on it she made known her preference for 'can do' officials and she was keen for them to get to the top earlier. At prime ministerial meetings with potential promotees present, members of the selection committee would watch to see if the chemistry was right between the candidate and the boss. Certainly some people did not reach the top rank who would have done if Lord Callaghan had remained in No. 10. But was the chemistry political or more to do with temperament? In my judgement it was the latter, a view shared, incidentally, by an inquiry committee on top appointments commissioned by the independent and respected Royal Institute of Public Administration.

Gazing across the list of late 1980s permanent secretaries I see no outsiders brought in at the top of Whitehall on the basis of an 'is he one of us?' test. A few outsiders there are like Sir Peter Levene, the Chief of Defence Procurement, but he was appointed (by Mr Heseltine when at Defence) on the poacher-turned-gamekeeper principle of getting the best bargainer in the arms world on the other side of the negotiating table. Some names on the permanent secretaries list got there sooner than expected and, occasionally, in surprising departments. But not one was there because of the attractiveness of his or her political beliefs even if they were discernible.

But, that said, Mrs Thatcher *had* created the impression of politicization not just in certain sections of the press, but where it counted, in Labour's Shadow Cabinet. A future Labour government could very easily retire some permanent secretaries early and pick replacements more to its liking, citing Mrs Thatcher as a precedent. They would be wrong to but, in practical terms, that would be immaterial. Politicization would have arrived and with it a profound constitutional change. Already Dr John Cunningham, Labour's environmental spokesman, has said publicly that he would find it difficult to work with Sir Terence Heister, Permanent Secretary to the Department of the Environment.

Top appointments, then, is a grey area of the Thatcher legacy. What is not in question, however, is the relative decline of Civil Service influence since 1979. The influence of its policy advice to ministers is diminished compared to the 1970s let alone to the relatively unpolarized political days of the 1940s, 1950s, and 1960s. The permanent politicians have been largely, though not wholly, eclipsed by the temporaries. This is not necessarily a matter for concern in a democracy where, in the end, elected people (ministers) must always prevail over appointed people (civil servants).

But there is a danger, as Lord Bancroft, retired early by Mrs Thatcher in 1981 as Head of the Civil Service, has pointed out. It lies in the degree to which Whitehall advice is attuned to ensure it falls with a joyous note upon the ministerial ear. There were signs of this happening throughout the Thatcher years. It was disturbing. Civil servants have tenure in the form of a job-for-life for the purpose of enabling them to speak truth unto power. If they don't, who, on the inside track of government, will?

This, I believe, is a more worrying issue than ethical considerations about the confidentiality of advice and the probity of ministerial actions raised in their different ways by the Ponting and Wright affairs. Both the *Belgrano* and *Spycatcher causes célèbres* were important in themselves and because of the issues they raised. But both had to do with exceptional or unusual circumstances (and both protagonists were somewhat singular people). But the fearlessness with which inconvenient fact and analysis is presented to ministers was an every hour of every day matter.

The civil servant as trade unionist was, too, a much weaker

figure in the late 1980s than he or she had been in the late 1970s.
Like many of their public sector equivalents, they had their own
individual showdown on the battlefield of trade union power. A
record twenty-two-week strike took place over pay in 1981
which, from whatever angle it is examined, was not a victory for
the Civil Service unions. And by the end of Mrs Thatcher's second
term they were claiming, with justification, to have fallen nearly
30 per cent behind in pay terms from their position in 1979. The
public did not sympathize. Crown servants in civvies have never
enjoyed a place in popular affection unlike many crown servants
in uniform.

Mrs Thatcher's decision to remove the trade unions from the
Government Communications Headquarters in 1984, however,
did outrage a wide swathe of political and public opinion. It
seemed an illiberal overreaction particularly as, when threatened
with eviction, the unions had offered a 'no-strike' agreement. A
future government is almost certain to reverse this (no other
government would have done it) and let the unions back into the
Cheltenham intelligence station albeit on a 'no-strike' basis.

In machinery-of-government matters generally, Mrs Thatcher
has been cautious. Some departments have been re-merged
(Trade and Industry in 1983), others broken up (Health and
Social Security in 1988). The Central Policy Review Staff,
popularly known as the think-tank, went in 1983 to allow for the
building-up of the more politically attuned Downing Street Policy
Unit. Wisely, she has never shown any sign of succumbing to
Lord Wilson's habit of creating a splash by rushing furniture
from one end of Whitehall to another while recasting departmental nameplates. The creation of a prime minister's department was briefly considered after the Falklands War but quickly
ruled out.

A price has been paid for Mrs Thatcher's impact not just by
civil servants, whose pay has languished, whose office accommodation gone unimproved, or, worse still, whose jobs have
disappeared altogether. There has been a noticeable haemor-
rhage of promising talent in its thirties and forties to the private
sector. In the early 1980s the Civil Service Commission, the image
of a Whitehall career being so dingy to many graduates, found

difficulty in finding the recruits it was seeking, though the position eased a little from the middle of the decade.

Perhaps most important of all, the public service ethic, a great motivator of many of Britain's best and brightest, drawing them into the nation's service relatively cheaply, took a considerable hammering in the Thatcher years. The Civil Service found the Prime Minister a good boss on an individual basis but never lost the feeling that she had little time for them as a breed which, according to her philosophy, had helped bring Britain low through its devotion to the tenets of Maynard Keynes and William Beveridge. This was not an impression designed to sustain the morale of the direct labour force on whom the Prime Minister and her colleagues depended.

In terms of wider Civil Service reform, Mrs Thatcher showed little interest in calls from her ex-Downing Street advisers Sir John Hoskyns and Norman Strauss that she replenish the White-hall talent pool by transfusing large amounts of new blood at regular intervals. The labour market at the top of the Civil Service remained very largely closed. The Civil Service Commission continued to recruit the bulk of its top people thirty years and four or five premiers ahead of the moment they would reach permanent secretary rank. This was a fault as was the reluctance to embrace more open government which, apart from its other benefits, would have exposed Whitehall's policy analysis to the sunlight of wider criticism and discussion.

Changing everything? In Civil Service terms, a great deal, Prime Minister, but not all. Will your changes stick? As Mr Asquith, whose longevity you surpassed last year, liked to say, 'Wait and see'. The question is still open. The interim answer is 'probably'.

9

Local Government

KEN YOUNG

Of all Mrs Thatcher's confrontations with the institutions, that which she has fought with local government has been the most prolonged and is arguably the most significant of all. Significant, that is, in two senses: first, in the sheer scale of its impact; second, in its ultimate political importance. In the same year that we celebrate the centenary of Lord Salisbury's great reform of local government we also witness a series of changes every bit as profound in their impact.

It is important that the changes in local government since 1979 are seen as a whole. Although there has never been a grand strategic plan (for the Prime Minister is too instinctive a politician for that) she and a number of her senior colleagues have a strong antipathy to local government. This has found expression in a consistent drive towards constraining the existing role of local government, displacing it from the centre ground of policy implementation, and setting its future development within the limits of the public's willingness to pay. In short, the subordination of local government to the political market-place and to a central authority that claims a more valid mandate than is to be found locally.

The right questions to pose are surely these. First, to what extent are these changes *uniquely* attributable to Mrs Thatcher and to what extent might they have come from any Conservative administration or indeed any government of any colour? Second, which of them are truly *irreversible* and, among these, which can be credited to 'the Thatcher effect'? Third, what major issues in the reform of local government have been so far neglected and may yet arise as the unintended consequences of her premiership?

CONTROL OF THE PURSE?

The enduring complaint of local government in this decade (and to a lesser extent in most) has been financial restriction. The measures taken by Mrs Thatcher's Environment Secretaries to control local authority spending followed on from the efforts of the Labour government in the late 1970s to apply the brakes by cutting grant and establishing cash limits. In a general sense, there could be said to be considerable similarity between Mrs Thatcher and Lord Callaghan in this regard. Both saw reduction of the overall level of public expenditure as a prime policy aim, to be achieved in part through a more vigorous assault on the rate of growth of local authority expenditure and manpower. Mrs Thatcher's governments have gone further only in the sense of seeking cuts in current, as well as planned, expenditure.

The counter-factual argument is crucial here. Had there not been a Conservative government since 1979 would we still have seen the introduction of the complex system of multipliers, targets, and penalties which dominated the period from 1980 to 1985? If the 1980–2 recession had been the cause, then, given the persistence of Treasury concerns, the answer is probably 'yes'. Mrs Thatcher's first phase was one in which Michael Heseltine, Tom King, and Patrick Jenkin struggled (as *any* Environment Secretary would have struggled) to find the means of bringing local authority spending into line with national priorities. No sign of a Thatcher effect here.

To push the question further, what might have happened when, as by 1985, it became apparent that many local authorities simply responded to these constraints by shifting the fiscal burden from taxpayers to ratepayers? It will be Lord Jenkin's misfortune to be remembered as the architect of the logical next step, direct control over local authority rate levels. Selective ratecapping— and the powers enabled it to be far more general, ensuring that the shadow was every bit as efficacious as the substance— brought ministers into the closest possible scrutiny of local expenditure plans as some of the ratecapped authorities (all but one Labour-controlled) sought redetermination of their permitted levels. It is not unthinkable that Labour ministers would similarly have allowed themselves to be drawn down the slippery slope to which the original controls had so inexorably led. Draconian as the powers were, and an undoubted violation of any principle of local self-government, it is hard to see them as a unique contribution of Mrs Thatcher or of 'Thatcherism'.

We come now to the watershed, when the government's approach shifted sharply from acceptance of the inexorability of increasing controls (for ratecapping was itself partly evaded by the disposal or mortgaging of assets) to the alternative course of radical reform of the structure of local authority finance. By 1986 the government appeared to have realized that containing local expenditure through increased central control of individual authorities' decisions was a lost cause. The dynamic of local needs and demands required an equally powerful dynamic of central containment. Better by far to change the basic dynamic force from one of local expansionism to one of local containment. Hence the Green Paper on *Paying for Local Government*, the introduction of the community charge, and the nationalization of non-domestic rates.

REVERSING THE TIDE

Here we have the first whiff of radicalism in the Thatcher government's approach to local expenditure. It is unthinkable that a Labour government would have taken this road. It is highly unlikely that a more orthodox Conservative administration would have done so. The production of a system in which local authorities wishing to increase their expenditure by a given percentage will drive up their community charge rates far more than proportionately, thus triggering local electoral backlash, sits well with the basic political dispositions which the Prime Minister shares—for the first time—with her Environment Secretary. It is this goal of changing the balance of forces, not a long-given promise to replace domestic rating (so often made by Conservatives, and so often forgotten), that underlies the transformation of local finance.

Moreover, the potential political costs of the community charge—many more losers than gainers, an intrusive system for verifying liability, the exposed flank of inequity—would have daunted most other Conservative leaders. The gains remain hypothetical, and the political calculation a massive gamble of the very type to which Mrs Thatcher seems drawn, and from which less radical Conservatives will shrink. Here, as in a number of other matters, we see Mrs Thatcher increasing her stride and 'Thatcherism' gaining confidence in itself. The probable long-term impact—the eventual 'Thatcher effect' in the field of local finance—is something to which we shall return.

BEYOND LOCAL PROVISION

If the pursuit of economy is one enduring theme to which all governments will subscribe, the linked value of *efficiency* is less evenly honoured. The initial drive towards efficiency—eradicating waste, making better use of resources—came from Michael Heseltine. The disposal of surplus land, the establishment of the Audit Commission, and the first round of competition policy came during his stewardship of Marsham Street. We might expect any Conservative government to have travelled this same path.

Again, what distinguishes Mrs Thatcher's style from that of her possible rivals is the propensity to increase the stride, to advance further and faster down the path of change rather than 'consolidate'. This is as evident in the field of competition policy as in respect of the community charge. The crucial feature of the most recent phase is not the extension of compulsory competitive tendering beyond the obvious target of direct labour organizations but the sense that in principle *no* local authority service—including those providing social care—can claim immunity from the disciplines of the market.

We come now to a matter of great uncertainty. It is possible to read the shift towards market disciplines as no more than a robust device for securing efficiency—local authorities can remain as service providers if they can so discipline their own operations as to provide at costs comparable with those incurred under market provision. But it is equally possible to see competition policy as an instrument for bringing about a fundamental change in the nature of local government, in which local authorities provide little in the way of services directly, but merely secure their provision through contractual relationships with providers.

The key slogan—*enablers not providers*—is of course Nicholas Ridley's. It encapsulates both a positive and radical vision of the future role of local government and an implicit criticism of the past record of local authorities as direct providers. It suggests that the second interpretation of the government's objectives is more accurate. But the ideological cutting edge clearly comes from Mrs Thatcher and Mr Ridley and is undoubtedly regarded with scepticism elsewhere in the ranks of the government. It is all the greater an irony, therefore, that the vision of an enabling local authority, so congenial to the Prime Minister, should evoke a warm response among the new urban left (where the criticisms of the failings of past bureaucratic provision are echoed) and within what might be called the mainstream of the management revolution now being experienced within local government.

Does this broad (and partly covert) concurrence suggest that we are dealing here not with the 'Thatcher effect' at all but with that convergence of radical left and radical right thinking that *Marxism Today* celebrates under the engaging slogan of 'New Times'? Surely not. The latest of the Thatcher government reforms show that same lengthening of stride, that ability to outpace yesterday's radicalism the very moment it becomes today's orthodoxy. Thus both the Housing Act 1988—which empowers the Secretary of State to establish Housing Action Trusts and more generally enables tenants to opt for a change of landlord—and the Education Reform Act 1988 which permits schools to opt out of local education authority control, can be set alongside the Environment Secretary's power to order the subjection of any activity to compulsory competitive tendering. All three might potentially contribute to a fundamental redrawing of the boundaries between local authorities and other bodies. And that outcome would undoubtedly be highly congenial to the Prime Minister.

INVENTING NEW AGENCIES . . .

Focusing attention on this comprehensive redrawing of the map of local politics places some of the other developments of the Thatcher decade in context. Among these features the continuing displacement of local authorities from areas of activity that reflect major government priorities but which are achievable only at the local level, most notably urban renewal and labour market policy. The initial designation by Michael Heseltine of the first two urban development corporations in the London and Mersey docklands was no Thatcherite idea, but a Fabian one. And the extension of the UDC as an instrument in other, less significant, areas of urban dereliction so that we now have three—or rather three and a half—generations of UDCs represents a more general desire, not confined to the Prime Minister, to bypass local authorities and to discount them as potential agents of change and renewal.

The UDCs are often seen as a short-term expedient, justified by the special magnitude of urban problems in these areas. But the exclusion of local authorities from labour market policy represents a basic disposition to see the problems as too important relative to the capacities—or the willingness—of local authorities to grapple with them. While the tendency is in line with Mrs Thatcher's impulses, it does not stem directly from them. Once again, however, a seemingly self-contained area of policy development intersects politically with the larger, and distinctively 'Thatcherite', agenda: to set the people of the inner city free of the institutions that have hitherto oppressed them. The analysis is familiar enough. Welfare dependency, and a more generalized dependency upon the local authority as an omniscient universal provider, has sapped the initiative of inner city residents. The object of Mrs Thatcher's inner city policy—prefigured in her 1987 victory speech—is to reclaim the cities for Toryism. It is for that reason that her inner city policy, as outlined in *Action for Cities*, has little in common with the urban policies of 1976–86 and is strictly speaking not recognizable as an inner city policy at all.

... AND DISINVENTING OTHERS

Mrs Thatcher's attack on the institutions has not prevented the proliferation of new agencies to address specific concrete problems. But it found most characteristic expression in the abolition of the GLC and metropolitan county councils. It is strange today to remember the general disbelief that such a measure would—or could—be put through which was manifest across the political spectrum when *Streamlining the Cities* was first published.

Once again, most commentators missed the point, interpreting the abolition commitment in the 1983 manifesto as a desperate attempt to conceal the fact that on rates reform the empress had no clothes. The lack of Cabinet enthusiasm for so bruising and apparently pointless a parliamentary struggle was similarly cited as evidence that the commitment derived from nothing more substantial than Mrs Thatcher's personal animus towards Ken Livingstone. The full story of the abolition episode has yet to be told, but it scarcely supports the notion that getting rid of the GLC was a bright (or not so bright) *idée fixe* on the Prime Minister's part. True, most of the Cabinet would not have supported the inclusion of such a manifesto promise, but the reasons for doing so were not thereby rendered insubstantial. In this as in other matters, Mrs Thatcher's own sense of political strategy, shared more with policy intimates than with the Cabinet, converged with her generalized dislike for the mega-institutions of the Heath era. Certainly, without this combination, the GLC and the metropolitan county councils would be with us today, functioning still as the Labour Party's most effective bases for the guerrilla war against the government.

WILL IT LAST?

So throughout the last decade there has been a discernible Thatcher effect in the subordination of local government. Many of the things that have happened would have occurred under any Conservative government, some under any government. But the most important of the Thatcher contributions are perhaps the least publicly visible, and the most potent for the future. The Prime Minister has lit the slow-burning fuse of revolution in local government and there are no obvious ways of extinguishing it.

I strongly suspect that a future government—any future government—will want to ride with this tide of change. The introduction of competition into local authority service provision is too convenient a device for securing economy and efficiency for any Environment Secretary willingly to relinquish, while the Labour Party is itself adjusting to the advantages of running public services under market disciplines. The long-term result is likely to be neither monolithic provision nor universal enabling, but rather a rich pattern of diversity in local practice.

Reinforced by the introduction of competition, a revolution in management thought is beginning to make itself felt in local government. The contract mode of working is spreading and becoming more widely adopted as a means of negotiating the provision of services *within* local authorities. The old-established administrative skills are giving way to the more commercial skills of contract management, and the cultural barriers that have always closed off local government from the wider commercial world may well begin to crumble. A new generation of officers is rising to senior and top management positions, and many of them do not regret the passing of the old order.

Three issues remain. The first is the long-term future of one of Mrs Thatcher's most significant legacies, the community charge. Another Conservative leader would be likely to want to temper the more regressive aspects of the flat-rate charge, so as to give fewer hostages to political fortune. A Labour government would abolish it, but could not face the political costs of a return to domestic rating. Ability to pay will become the first consideration in the search for a new system. Some of the wiser observers of the scene are already predicting that Mrs Thatcher's most enduring achievement in the field of local finance will have been to pave the way for local income tax. That would be the first irony.

The second issue is a transformation of the basic structure of local government. Peter Walker's 1972 reforms have been dogged by political instability. The subjugation of strong city governments outside the metropolitan areas to unsympathetic county councils continues to rankle. The abolition of the GLC and metropolitan county councils offers a prototype of single-tier local government. The district councils have made the running in a campaign to bring local government closer to the public and now an element in county opinion is beginning to accept a single tier as the most likely future solution. The debate is echoed in Scotland, where the more populous regional councils remain as one of the last monuments to the Heathite preoccupation with big government. The crucial factor is likely however to be the dynamic one, the shift away from ideas of monopoly provision towards enabling and contracting. Two tiers of providers makes some sense, two tiers of enablers rather less. So Mrs Thatcher, with her impatient disdain for institutional reconstruction, may nevertheless have inadvertently set it in motion. That would be the second irony.

The third and final issue is fundamental, and concerns the rationale for local government. In all of these transformations of the local government scene, something has been conspicuously absent. We have heard nothing of the value that traditional Conservatism places upon local government as a counterbalance to the centre, as a means of community involvement and citizenship, as a celebration of diversity, as a vehicle for political education. Instead, Mrs Thatcher's stance towards local government has been in a literal sense politically rootless. It is hard to believe in this centenary year that the great ferment of change unleashed since 1987 will not bring back to the surface the basic argument of *why* we have a framework of elected bodies at the level of the local community. Despite her distaste for traditional Conservative thought, this larger question—at root a question about the nature of the polity itself—is likely to be forced upon our attention as politicians struggle to find their bearings again. A renewed sense of the political and constitutional importance of local government may then emerge. That would be the most ironic of all the effects of Mrs Thatcher's decade.

IO

The Constitution

VERNON BOGDANOR

Each period of history has its own characteristic motif. The 1970s were marked by a crisis of authority in British politics as the jurisdiction of the state seemed to be threatened by trade unionists, Ulster loyalists, and Scottish nationalists. The most memorable emblems of that decade were the Saltley pickets, the masked gunmen of Northern Ireland, and the cancer patients turned away from hospitals. For political scientists, the central themes were ungovernability and overload. The state was under threat because it was trying to do too much; and, precisely for this reason, it was unable to fulfil its basic responsibilities effectively. The fundamental task of government, so it seemed, was not only to alter the direction of economic management, but to restore the authority of the state.

The 1980s, by contrast, are best understood through a quite different concept—elective dictatorship—coined by Lord Hailsham to characterize the weak Labour governments of the 1970s, but more applicable to the regime of Mrs Thatcher in which he was himself to serve. The juxtaposition—ungovernability, elective dictatorship—neatly sums up both the strengths and weaknesses of Mrs Thatcher's decade. For, having restored the authority of the state, she has also weakened the democratic underpinning which makes that authority tolerable. It would be a mistake, however, to ascribe this duality solely to the personality of Mrs Thatcher, or to that ill-defined jumble of qualities labelled 'Thatcherism'. It stems, rather, from a deep-seated instinct in conservatism itself. Hayek, often cited as one of Mrs Thatcher's ideological mentors, has noticed 'the characteristic complacency of the conservative toward the action of established authority, and his prime concern that this authority be not weakened rather than that its power be kept within bounds—he believes that if government is in the hands of decent men, it ought not to be too restricted by rigid rules'.[1] In her commitment to a strong state and her aversion to any reform of the constitution which might limit its sway, Mrs Thatcher is doing no more than following a well-worn Conservative tradition.

Restoration of the authority of the state required, first and foremost, a positive answer to the constitutional question: could government govern against the wishes of the trade unions? From 1969, when Harold Wilson capitulated to the union barons over *In Place of Strife*, to 1985, when Mrs Thatcher inflicted a final defeat on Arthur Scargill, this was the dilemma which haunted British politics. In four general elections—1970, October 1974, 1979, and 1983—the problem lay in the background as an implicit constraint on government; in the fifth, that of February 1974, it moved into the foreground, becoming an explicitly constitutional issue and bringing about the fall of Edward Heath. As a result, governments found themselves paralysed over wide areas of policy-making—not only in industrial relations, but also in areas such as education and health, where the trade union veto operated to prevent new policy departures. It is the removal of that veto which has, for better or worse, made possible the reforms of Mrs Thatcher's third term—the Education Reform Act and the proposed changes in the NHS. Whether the NUT or the health service unions favour these reforms or not is now irrelevant, for they have lost the power to destroy legislation with which they disagree. The era which Bernard Donoughue christened as one of producer socialism is now quite dead.

Mrs Thatcher has thus taken one major constitutional issue—the government versus the unions—entirely out of politics, prob-ably for good. The removal of this issue from the political agenda was an essential precondition not only for the promotion of a market economy, favoured by the Conservatives, but even perhaps for the policies favoured by the opposition parties. They too may have cause to be grateful to her for removing the union veto, which was a veto on the policies of Labour governments as well as Tory.

Restoration of the authority of government is in essence a Tory idea. Yet it was sought as a means to ends which are far from Tory. For Mrs Thatcher's aim has been to create not a hierarchical society, one governed through rank and degree, but its opposite, a society marked by freedom and individual responsibility. How was this aim to be achieved—by the method of constitutionalism, as in the German Federal Republic, or by the exercise of sovereign power as in Britain.

In Germany, the social market economy is buttressed by constitutional provisions designed to limit state action. Government is constrained by very general constitutional rules, and especially by a federal division of power which ensures that the implementation of much federal legislation is left to the *Länder*. Fundamental to the German constitution is a conception of the dispersal of public authority as an essential concomitant of economic liberalism. For neo-liberal thinkers such as Hayek and Nozick, the constitutional dispersal of power is vital to the achievement of the free economy. For them, the methods by which the state acts, the forms which it takes, are as important as the content of state action. For this reason, Hayek explicitly rejects the notion of parliamentary sovereignty, which he sees as but the legal counterpart of omnicompetent government; it means in effect 'the abandonment of constitutionalism which consists in a limitation of all power by permanent principles of government'.[2] Yet in Britain, by contrast, Mrs Thatcher, far from seeking to limit the power of government, has made use of it to a far greater extent than her predecessors. The ambit of government may be limited, but its scope has become infinite.

The reason for this should be clear. In a Germany ruined by Hitler, there seemed little alternative to the disciplines of the market. In Britain, on the other hand, attitudes conducive to the maintenance of a free economy could not be assumed, but had to be conjured into existence. Thus, Mrs Thatcher's aim has been not only to reconstruct the state, but also to transform society. The impact of over thirty years of social democracy and the Welfare State has been to weaken the primacy of competitive relationships, making individuals over-reliant on 'society', rather than on their own efforts. Thus, the project to re-establish the free economy must also be one that reshapes social relations. In

Andrew Gamble's words, 'The citizens have to be forced to be free and enterprising, otherwise there is no guarantee they will be so'.[3]

Human nature, in the Conservative view, is not naturally inclined towards freedom and individual responsibility. For this reason, Mrs Thatcher's policy for society, as opposed to her policy for the economy, could not be one of *laissez-faire*. The success of a competitive economy, as Japan shows so clearly, rests not upon a sense of rampant individualism, but upon quite different values. The primary need, therefore, was to restore a sense of discipline and morality without which individuals would be ill equipped to take their places in the competitive market. Thus the transformation which Mrs Thatcher has sought is as much cultural as it is economic. This certainly marks a definite break with the past. Previous Conservative administrations—those of Baldwin, Macmillan, even perhaps of Heath—sought to conserve a society whose values they saw as supportive of Conservatism. Mrs Thatcher, by contrast, saw herself living in a society undermined by the permissive 'adversary culture' of the 1960s and saturated with values which were far from Conservative. If the measures taken to correct this situation happened to invade what liberals of the left chose to think of as civil liberties, that had to be accepted in the interests of the broader goal.

Since 1979, therefore, civil liberties issues—freedom of information, rights to freedom of speech and expression, the rights of unpopular minorities such as suspected terrorists and homosexuals—have played a much more prominent part in constitutional debate than in any other period since the end of the war. Indeed, one proposition on which the opposition parties—whether Labour, SLD or SDP—are broadly agreed is that Mrs Thatcher constitutes a threat to civil liberties. This agreement was the basis of the Charter 1988 movement, a critique of what its authors saw as creeping authoritarianism, but also a possible agenda for party realignment. Yet, here again, while Mrs Thatcher may have gone much further than previous administrations, it is difficult to see her basic concerns as being essentially different in kind from those of, say, Lord Salisbury, Sir William Joynson Hicks, or Henry Brooke, all of whom seem to have believed that human beings needed to be fenced around with stern prohibitions if they were to be made fit for the rigours of competitive life.

But Mrs Thatcher's programme had to involve, in addition, policies designed to topple the bastions of social democracy—not only the trade unions, but also local government, the education system, the National Health Service, and even the professions themselves, carriers of a quite different ethos from that of the competitive market. It is in seeking to transform those institutions whose function is to offer collective provision that Mrs Thatcher has, unwittingly, brought the constitution back into the centre of British politics.

As head of a government dedicated to turning back the tide of collectivism, Mrs Thatcher found herself confronted by institutions whose very purpose was that of providing for collective needs. The most important of these institutions is local government, and it is no coincidence that Mrs Thatcher's administrations have raised, in a very acute form, the constitutional question of the proper relationship between central government and local authorities. It is, in particular, in Scotland and the great conurbations of the North of England that this relationship has been put under strain to such an extent that there is now, in some parts of Britain, a real question mark over the moral legitimacy of the actions of central government.

To criticisms that the government's actions strain the limits of the constitution, ministers reply that Britain is a unitary state in which Parliament enjoys the power to alter political relationships as and when it pleases. This conception of the constitution, however, allows too much weight to be placed upon one of Dicey's principles—the sovereignty of Parliament—while ignoring another—the conventions of the constitution. For the territorial constitution of the United Kingdom is governed less by statute than by convention; it depends upon a spirit of mutual accommodation, and it rests upon a sense of identification by the governed with those who have authority over them. An assertion of the unbridled right of an omnicompetent government is apt to conflict with the practicalities of political management in a country already sharply polarized by an electoral system which effectively excludes much of the North of England and Scotland from a share in the exercise of political power. The traditional defence of territories so excluded has been the power of constitutional convention. But the years of Mrs Thatcher's rule have seen the death of convention.

It is a paradox that a programme designed to widen individual choice has as one of its consequences a massive increase in the power of central government, and a decline in the influence of local communities and intermediate institutions. The explanation for this paradox was foreseen as long ago as 1946 in a brilliant if little-noticed reply to Hayek by Herman Finer, entitled *The Road to Reaction*. Finer argued perceptively that the free-market programme, like its seeming opposite, socialism, was a global philosophy of politics, and that it could not coexist with other centres of power. As *The Economist* noticed in December 1979, 'The trouble with being a non-interventionist government is that in order to go from intervention to non-intervention you have to intervene to challenge the way things are done'.

In a democracy, any government, whatever its political colour, will find itself faced with a society in which competing conceptions of the good life jostle for attention. Faced with the reality of social pluralism, two responses are possible: to share power or to curb its competitors. An ideological government, whether free market or socialist, finds itself compelled to adopt the latter alternative. For it is of the essence of its philosophy that any competing viewpoint is somehow illegitimate and its continued expression a threat to good government. It was Thomas Hobbes who called institutions which lie between government and the individual, worms in the entrails of the body politic; for they serve to eat away at the sovereignty of Leviathan. It is this conception of sovereignty which Mrs Thatcher has carried to its limits.

At first sight, this view of the role of the state seems peculiarly associated with the brand of Conservatism espoused by Mrs Thatcher. Previous Conservative governments, whether led by Churchill, Macmillan, or Heath, felt little impulse to reconstruct society, seeking instead to coexist with other centres of power, rather than to transform them. And yet Mrs Thatcher's approach was perhaps an inevitable response to the perceived unworkability of a Conservatism which sought to remain within the constraints of the post-war consensus. The Heath government sought desperately, in its final eighteen months, to accommodate itself to a society whose values were deeply un-Conservative. The only way to escape from such appeasement was to break the constraints of social democracy, and seek to confront society with a radically different philosophy of government. The probability is, therefore, that any Tory leader, having lived through the crisis of Conservatism between 1972 and 1974, would react as Mrs Thatcher has done, and abandon the philosophy which led her predecessor to grief. All the same, the very determination with which Mrs Thatcher has pursued her goals has brought into sharp focus the limitations of traditional conceptions of the British constitution. For, when confronted with a determined government, insistent upon its will, the constitution seems to have no devices which can serve to restrain or limit the powers of government. 'The hollowness of the Diceyan liberal constitution, now exposed, is that when confronted with this drive for centralised, uncheckable power, it has no answer.'[4]

'In England,' Tocqueville declared, 'Parliament has the right to modify the Constitution. In England, therefore, the Constitution can change constantly, or rather it does not exist at all.'[5] It is a paradox that a government so determined to resist constitutional change has made the constitution itself a political issue. The existence of a constitution implies a set of rules determining political behaviour; but the peculiarity of the British constitution is that it lacks an umpire. It is the players themselves, the government of the day, who interpret the way in which the rules are to be applied. There is no reference point, no *pouvoir neutre*, over and above government which can offer a criterion for what is allowable and what is not. It is this deficiency which proponents of constitutional reform seek to remedy, either by establishing such a reference point in the form of a Bill of Rights or, alternatively, by ensuring, through electoral reform or reform of the House of Lords, that a single party cannot enjoy unlimited power on a minority of the popular vote. It is a striking consequence of Mrs Thatcher's decade that all of the opposition parties, without exception, now favour constitutional change of one sort or another, so that the constitution, as it now exists, depends for its survival upon the continuation of Conservative government.

But conceptions of the constitution themselves rely on alternative conceptions of human nature and of political liberty. For Mrs Thatcher, as for most modern Conservatives, freedom is in essence the freedom to compete in the market-place. By reducing the role of the state in the economy, through abolishing controls over prices, incomes, and foreign exchange, she has increased the sum total of freedom in society. By policies which encourage the ownership of property, shares and other forms of wealth, she has contributed towards a genuine decentralization of power. Freedom is devolution of power to the individual citizen; it is not something which can be guaranteed by institutions. To regard participation in government as the essence of freedom is to misunderstand the basic needs of human nature. For, as Oscar Wilde once wrote, what was wrong with socialism was that it took up too many evenings. Mrs Thatcher, by reducing the influence of intermediate institutions such as local authorities, has succeeded in diminishing the scope of the political over people's lives. For the only real participation that is worth the name is participation in the market-place; and political freedom is nothing but the withdrawal of the state from all but its most essential tasks.

The trouble with this view of freedom, however, is that it assumes away any notion of the public good. It transforms questions about, for example, the best system of education and health care for society as a whole into questions about the best system of education and health care for myself and my family. In assuming that the community is nothing more than the mere sum of individual wants, it commits the fallacy of composition. It offends against Burke's notion of a society as being a contract between generations as well as between individuals. There is, however, an alternative conception of freedom capable of taking full account of those communitarian instincts which are, in some sense, natural to mankind; and it is this alternative conception which lies at the root of the constitutionalist critique of Mrs Thatcher.

Liberty, it has been said, is power cut into pieces; and the purpose of dividing power is to make it properly accountable. Thus intermediate institutions, far from being barriers to freedom, are actually essential to it since they provide opportunities by which citizens are enabled to make decisions as to the relative priorities for society. For, whether services are to be provided publicly or privately, the determination of priorities must, in the last resort, be made politically. The market itself cannot decide how much should be spent on schools, and how much on housing. The decision must be made by a political body, either by central government or by decentralized institutions. The great advantage of the sharing of power is the much greater opportunity for popular participation which it provides. For, whereas there are only 650 MPs, and being an MP is today a full-time professional career, there are around 25,000 local government councillors, as well as a large number of people involved in local pressure groups and similar bodies. Thus the existence of a wide range of intermediate bodies allows for the diffusion of political understanding, and is part of the very essence of democracy. For it is these institutions which help to produce the 'active citizen' which ministers such as Douglas Hurd have sought to call into existence to supplement gaps in welfare provision. The active citizen, however, is unlikely to be the product of a system based upon the authority of parliamentary sovereignty; he or she is far more likely to arise out of a society which diffuses and shares power. For it is, as John Stuart Mill understood, 'the discussion and management of collective interests' which 'is the great school of—public spirit'.[6]

It is, in the last resort, impossible to bifurcate human beings, impossible for someone who is expected to be independent and self-reliant in his or her economic dealings not also to demand wider social and political rights. Moreover, one fundamental consequence of the information society is the dispersal of decision-making which it makes possible. Individuals, freed from the tyranny of mass production and large public sector unions, will no longer be content to see themselves as subjects, but will, increasingly, seek to be citizens.

Mrs Thatcher's constitution is at bottom a heroic attempt to restore the authority of the state in a period when the social preconditions for the restoration of authority are absent. What is distinctive about the changes she has wrought is less their originality than the colossal effort of individual will needed to bring them about. Indeed, she has so strained the conventional limits of the British constitution that the constitution itself has become a part of party politics, rather than a set of rules lying above politics. Whether Mrs Thatcher will be able to preserve the constitution, unsullied, to hand on to her successor, or whether she has helped build up irresistible pressure for constitutional reform, must remain an open question. For constitutions depend not only upon political leaders, but also upon the social and economic patterns which underpin their operation, upon a country's political culture. Who is there yet able to tell whether this culture has been permanently transformed by our remarkable Prime Minister?

Notes

1. F. A. Hayek, *The Constitution of Liberty* (Routledge & Kegan Paul, 1960), p. 401.
2. F. A. Hayek, *The Political Order of a Free People* (Routledge & Kegan Paul, 1979), p. 3.
3. Andrew Gamble, *The Free Economy and the Strong State: The Politics of Thatcherism* (Macmillan, 1988), p. 35.
4. Patrick McAuslan and John F. McEldowney, 'Legitimacy and the Constitution: The Dissonance between Theory and Practice', in McAuslan and McEldowney (eds.), *Law, Legitimacy and the Constitution* (Sweet and Maxwell, 1985), p. 38.
5. A. de Tocqueville, *De la démocratie en Amérique*, pt. 1, ch. 6.
6. Cited in David Marquand, 'Preceptoral Politics, Yeoman Democracy and the Enabling State', *Government and Opposition*, 23/3 (Summer 1988), p. 273. This essay is a splendid example of an approach to constitutional thinking which lies at the opposite pole to that favoured by Mrs Thatcher.

II

Thatcherism and Defence

LAWRENCE FREEDMAN

Defence has been one of those issues closely associated with Mrs Thatcher and which she pushed to the fore in two election campaigns. The stress on the importance of maintaining robust military capabilities meant that she was often twinned with Ronald Reagan as the architect of the more hard-line policies adopted by the West during the early 1980s. However, while there might have been similarities between the two leaders in their intuitive hawkishness and evident readiness to use armed force in pursuit of national objectives, Thatcherism turned out to be quite distinct from Reaganism.

Mrs Thatcher's ostentatious enthusiasm for Reagan, reciprocated to the point where their joint appearances became embarrassing to spectators, reflected a traditional calculation of security interests. Her scepticism over the European project meant that, unlike Edward Heath, she rarely showed any interest in European defence co-operation beyond ensuring the degree of common effort necessary to persuade the Americans that Europe was still worth defending. Mr Heseltine got no support when as Defence Minister he took a strongly European line during the Westland Affair at the end of 1985. The Prime Minister's conviction that the American guarantee was central to European security was why she welcomed Reagan's commitment to raising American self-esteem and his readiness to accept international responsibilities, and also why she tolerated the President himself, despite his tendency towards heresy and a 'management style' (to use the euphemism of the Tower Commission) almost the opposite of her own.

This emphasis on reinforcing established security arrangements reflects the hallmark of Thatcherism in the defence sphere. She has supported the orthodoxy in the face of a series of challenges, of which in practice one of the most significant came from Reagan. This has been most evident with nuclear deterrence, but the judgement also applies to the generality of British defence policy. When this was considered early in Mrs Thatcher's tenure, in the course of John Nott's 1981 defence review, the conclusion was wholly orthodox—the priority commitment was to NATO's central front in Germany and nuclear deterrence. Although she toyed in her first eighteen months with some of the ideas promoted by the maritime lobby for meeting an alleged communist threat in the Third World, when it came to the crunch the Navy suffered the most. In this particular sense her defence build-up in no way followed that of the Reagan administration, which was largely devoted to the US Navy.

The conduct of Thatcher's defence build-up was also different from that of Reagan's. Both inherited from their predecessors a NATO commitment to a steady 3 per cent rise in defence budgets. Reagan accelerated spending even faster and with his Secretary of Defense Caspar Weinberger gave the impression that the military was exempt from the constraints that were applying to all other areas of public spending. By the end of his term he was becoming embarrassed by reports of waste and mismanagement. Thatcher moved her first Defence Minister, Francis Pym, in part because he was not exercising enough control over the defence budget, and reverted back to level spending as soon as the NATO commitment for 3 per cent rises up to 1986 lapsed, apart from the extra costs consequent on the Falklands War. There were examples of waste and mismanagement in British defence procurement, most notably with the development of the Nimrod Early Warning aircraft which had to be scrapped in favour of the US AWACS. Mrs Thatcher took such examples to justify holding down defence spending (senior Ministry of Defence officials are convinced she carries a list in her handbag). Necessary improvements in the defence effort had to be financed by greater efficiency in the management of the budget. Typically this argument was never pushed too far. It can now be said that the defence budget is set at that level necessary to avoid another major—and so politically controversial—defence review, so recently there has been limited growth.

The embrace of orthodoxy was not confined to the hard-line aspects of defence policy. While Mrs Thatcher complained early in 1988 to NATO ambassadors that the Soviet bear was no longer ferocious enough when it came to gaining popular support for a constant defence effort, it was she who had first signalled the start of the 'Gorbachev era' by declaring the then heir apparent to the Soviet leadership, on his visit to London in December 1984, a man she 'could do business with'. Indeed the Thatcher–Gorbachev relationship may have worked more to their mutual benefit than the Thatcher–Reagan relationship, for they helped to give each other credibility on the international stage.

Even before Gorbachev came along policy towards the Soviet Union followed a well-trodden path. A Labour government might not have reacted so severely to the Soviet invasion of Afghanistan (although given the strength of American feeling it would have been hard to do much less). However on questions such as sanctions over Poland she resisted American pressure. Moreover as it became necessary to calm the anxieties that were building up during the early 1980s over the deterioration in East–West relations, the apparent bellicose nature of the Reagan administration, and the coincident prominence of a series of nuclear weapons issues, the government mouthed familiar platitudes on the importance of arms control negotiations. Yet arms control was an obvious candidate for some Thatcherite revisionism, which might have challenged the interventionist, regulatory ethos and pointed to the contrived conclusions reached by the negotiations. No such critique was ever launched.

There was a clear determination to protect the British nuclear force from arms control but it was not an outright rejection ('we never say never'—Geoffrey Howe) but rather a list of conditions that had to be met before this exercise could possibly be suitable for Polaris/ Trident.

In all its aspects the nuclear issue required a hawkish military orthodoxy to be balanced by a doveish diplomatic orthodoxy. The first few years of government were marked by a dramatic rise in Campaign for Nuclear Disarmament (CND) membership and regular large-scale demonstrations, with the first US cruise missile base at Greenham Common a popular target.

Cruise missiles raised no financial issues, but they did play on fears generated by the tense international climate, which had been given a push by the December 1979 Soviet invasion of Afghanistan (just two weeks after the NATO decision on cruise missiles). This decision was to a significant extent inherited from the Labour government. Although Callaghan had been spared the need to agree to accept US cruise missiles into Britain, his role at the four-nation Guadeloupe summit at the start of 1979 was central to the development of NATO policy.

Initially the government did not engage the anti-nuclear movement effectively. Its sophistication and popular appeal was underestimated and the debate often left to junior ministers. The departure of John Nott to the City at the end of 1982 gave Thatcher the opportunity to put in a Defence Minister, Michael Heseltine, who relished taking on CND. In early 1983 the counter-attack began, with vigorous speeches by both Heseltine and Thatcher, and this was carried through into the 1983 election. After this point the Conservatives stayed on the offensive on the nuclear issue.

The Labour Party had found the embrace of the anti-nuclear movement irresistible, and was tempted to exploit the evident popular hostility towards hosting American nuclear bases. However this hostility did not extend to unilateral *British* nuclear disarmament and this became the Opposition's Achilles' heel, to the point where for most of the 1980s the 'defence' issue in British politics was the future of the country's nuclear deterrent.

In fact the preparatory work on the future of British nuclear forces, which revolved around the question of whether and how to replace the ageing Polaris nuclear force, had also been undertaken by the Callaghan government. There was never any doubt that the Conservatives would stick with the nuclear deterrent; the commitment was made clear in the 1979 manifesto. Labour's preparatory work confirmed that the Ministry of Defence wanted to take the course of least resistance, to follow the same formula as before—British submarines carrying American ballistic missiles carrying, in turn, British warheads. This means adopting the most modern American missile available, Trident.

This approach had the advantage of exploiting American economies of the scale and the infrastructure originally created for Polaris, as well as a sound strategic rationale, in that sea-based systems are relatively invulnerable to surprise attack while missile warheads should face little difficulty from Soviet defences in reaching their targets.

The decision, when announced in July 1980, was inevitably controversial. The Opposition was placed in an awkward position. James Callaghan had clearly been content to maintain the deterrent. On the other hand, there was now no Labour Party support for any replacement for Polaris so it could not follow the line taken, most notably by Dr David Owen, to the effect that cruise missiles should have been chosen instead of Trident. Labour therefore criticized Trident for being excessively sophisticated, with its long-range and accurate multiple warheads, and far too expensive. In the harsh economic conditions of the early 1980s Trident's price-tag, which was initially put at £5 billion and soon went up to £7.5 billion, could be presented as a gross extravagance, even inimical to the wider defence effort, for it would use up a large chunk of the available funds for new conventional military equipment. At a time when NATO was increasingly talking of relying more on conventional and less on nuclear forces, Britain would be moving its defence priorities in exactly the opposite direction.

Labour was unable to make the most of this critique because it was arguing that the shift away from nuclear deterrence should be total. This may have found favour with an active portion of the British electorate but left a more passive majority unimpressed. It must be doubted whether even a more moderate critique based on the nuances of NATO strategy would have swayed public opinion, in the face of the more gut appeal of a nuclear status for Britain.

The other difficulty with the economic argument for Labour was that it was going to be most powerful during the early stages of the programme. As the money was spent and committed the potential for savings gradually declined. The point has now been reached where it would cost almost as much to get out of the nuclear business as to stay in it. Here the government has been helped, in contrast to other major military procurement programmes, by the fact that Trident has, thus far, remained on schedule and within budget. Indeed, almost uniquely, the cost estimates have been reduced by some 20 per cent.

In practice more problems have been created for the Trident programme—and indeed the government's overall nuclear policies—by the United States than by Labour. The only serious rise in the Trident estimate resulted from the early Reagan decision to modernize its strategic nuclear arsenal, which involved bringing along the even more capable and larger Trident D-5 missile as against the perfectly adequate C-4 version. In order to be able to take advantage of what was dubbed 'commonality' with the United States, Britain was obliged to follow suit and shift to more sophisticated missiles and much bigger submarines than required.

The second and more fundamental Reagan challenge came as the President entered his 'anti-nuclear phase'. This began with the Strategic Defence Initiative (SDI or 'star wars') of 1983, and reached its peak with the Reykjavik summit with Gorbachev in October 1986. Reagan's tendency towards an absolutist critique of nuclear deterrence during this period caused a series of problems for Thatcher.

With SDI Reagan was arguing that the world would be safer if both sides were able to defend themselves against ballistic missile attack. There was a natural question to ask as to whether Britain could expect to be protected by the US defensive shield, given its proximity to the Soviet Union, while its own missiles might not be able to penetrate the Soviet defensive shield, and so fail to function as a deterrent. The government's analysts convinced themselves that the Trident system would be able to cope with any shield that the Soviet Union would be able to put up during its lifetime, but if a 'strategic-defence race' had developed then the government would have been hard put to convince Parliament and the electorate that it was worth bothering with Trident without casting doubt on Reagan's whole enterprise.

With arms control there was always a risk that the United States would agree to measures that would limit its ability to provide Trident. In the early 1980s this seemed unlikely in that submarine-based systems have not been controversial in the United States and so there was only a slight risk of an outright cancellation. However, as Reagan began to pick on ballistic missiles as the target for SDI this came to be reflected in his proposals for strategic arms control. In the summer of 1986 he proposed a ban on all ballistic missiles. The disastrous consequences of this for the British programme resulted in an anxious letter from Mrs Thatcher. This, British officials believed, led to the rejection of the heresy and so they were horrified to see it return so publicly to the US position during the Reykjavik summit. Fortunately for the government this idea did not seem over-attractive to Gorbachev and it has not been put into the draft Strategic Arms Reduction Treaty.

In both December 1984 and December 1986 Mrs Thatcher was obliged to scuttle across the Atlantic to encourage the President to correct the impression he had created as a result of SDI and Reykjavik respectively. As Mrs Thatcher had argued that nuclear deterrence based on the threat of devastating retaliation was moral, durable, and essential for security it was alarming to hear President Reagan suggest that it was none of those things. Although in both visits Mrs Thatcher was speaking for European conservative orthodoxy, perhaps even more disturbing to her in more recent years has been the growth in doubts over nuclear deterrence amongst her natural allies, such as the CDU in West Germany. The combination of the unease created during the great nuclear debate and Gorbachev's 'charm offensive' has taken its toll.

One consequence of the controversy over nuclear matters is that it has not been matched with comparable controversy over conventional forces. For the Labour Party any credibility on the defence issue required promises to keep the armed services moderately well paid and well equipped. The charge over Trident was that it was taking resources away from tanks and frigates, not from schools and hospitals. Surprisingly the growth in the defence budget during the first half of the 1980s while other areas of public expenditure were being visibly cut did not result in a 'guns versus butter' debate, and by the time health and education were becoming major issues the defence budget was being held down. With the growth in the economy, the proportion of GDP spent on defence this year will be less than was spent in the final years of the Labour government.

The problem for the government was the traditional British defence problem of matching resources to commitments. The June 1981 White Paper, *The Way Forward*, arose from a recognition that, even with the increased spending planned, available funds were unlikely to be able to pay for the existing programme. It is true that there probably would have been a review sooner or later without Trident, and that the pressure on funds was going to make itself felt well before Trident costs were going to bite. Nevertheless, the fact that the amount of money to be saved was not dissimilar to the cost of Trident, and that the service which took the brunt of the cuts was the Navy, which had been grumbling since it had been told that Trident was to be counted within its budget, encouraged the idea that this was a Trident-induced review.

Although there were many parts to the 1981 review, the most dramatic were cuts to the Royal Navy—a reduction from 59 front-line frigates and destroyers to 42. Many government critics believe that it was these cuts, along with the very special message conveyed by the decision to scrap HMS *Endurance*, which had been patrolling around the Falklands, that convinced the Argentine junta to risk the reoccupation of the Falkland Islands on 2 April 1982.

The Falklands campaign of April to June 1982 was a watershed in the development of government defence policy, although John Nott insisted that the Falklands experience in no way affected the broad strategic judgements behind the 1981 review, and he rather boldly, if belatedly, published the 1982 White Paper as the campaign drew to a close, despite the fact that it had been written prior to the campaign and so the situation which it described no longer obtained.

However, the Falklands qualified the defence review in a number of important respects. The conduct of the campaign raised the profile of the armed forces and showed them in a positive light. The new commitment established by the need, having repossessed the islands, to hold on to them in the future created demanding new tasks for the services, which were especially heavy before the completion of the new runway at Stanley. For both these reasons it now became difficult to scrap HMS *Endurance* or sell off carrier HMS *Invincible* to Australia.

Nott's successor at the Defence Ministry, Michael Heseltine, in 1983 and 1984 presided over a steady retreat from some of the harsher judgements of 1981. In 1984 the retreat from the 1981 review continued with the decision to move eight ships from the stand-by squadron to the front-line Navy, in practice halving the 1981 cuts. Meanwhile the Air Force was not only increasing its front-line forces but insinuated the Advanced Combat Aircraft as a much more substantial prospect than previously described. Soon this became the European Fighter Aircraft as Michael Heseltine engaged in an effective if expensive piece of European enterprise, of a sort that was soon to be his undoing when he applied it to helicopters and sought to persuade a reluctant Westland to enter into collaboration with European partners in whom it had little confidence.

When Heseltine stormed out of government over this issue at the start of 1986 he was replaced by the calmer figure of George Younger, who was welcomed in the Ministry as a man who took decisions rather than talking all the time about how they could be made better. Under Younger the Army got its major modernization programme—a new main battle tank—agreed at the start of 1989.

All this modernization might please the Chiefs but it was not evident how it was to be paid for. The promise has been that what cannot be achieved by extra funds can be achieved by the more efficient use of available resources. In 1984 Heseltine outlined proposals for reorganizing MOD with the objective of drawing 'a clearer distinction between the formulation of advice on operation, defence policy and resource allocations, on the one hand, and the management of defence resources on the other'. The approach was to centralize further and form 'a fully unified and integrated military/civilian Defence Policy and Operational Staff', and reduce the individual service staffs, a prospect that led retired senior officers to write to the press with expressions of great alarm, but in practice turned out to be moderately successful.

The effort to sustain improvements in front-line forces without much by way of extra resources risks coming at the expense of the quality of logistical support and training which had made such a vital contribution in the Falklands. The other theme in the managerial revolution has been the introduction of greater competition in procurement in an effort to undermine the cosy relationship that can develop between the Ministry and its major suppliers. This has helped MOD to secure its industrial base, develop realistic specifications, and achieve economies of scale, but at the expense of a certain loss of financial discipline. Now the contractors must take nothing for granted: at every stage there is notionally competition: after research; after development; after first-batch production; and so on. Where competition is impossible because there is only one obvious source, then the prime contractor will be expected to twist the arm of the subcontractors. Again modest successes can be noted: the question is whether in the high-cost high-technology area that puts the real pressure on the procurement budget there can be a genuine change. The problem is that much of the competition will be artificial, without a rapid increase in overseas purchases. This policy can offer little more than an easing of the persistent upward thrust of equipment costs.

All this has been revolutionary enough in terms of the standards of the Ministry of Defence, and at the end of Mrs Thatcher's decade in office the Ministry is certainly leaner. Given the desire to avoid the political hurdles of yet another defence review, the prospect if the budget stays around its current level is of new equipment being delayed, abandoned, or diminished in quantity and/or quality—incremental and opportunistic decline rather than deliberate and discriminating reduction.

Up to now there have been declines here and improvements there but broadly speaking the composition of the armed forces and the underlying strategic rationale are remarkably similar to those inherited. The great change has been in the international environment, with political changes underway which have yet to be reflected in British defence policy but which show signs of posing quite novel challenges to the assumptions on which this policy rests during Mrs Thatcher's remaining years in office.

12

Britain and the World

SIR ANTHONY PARSONS

Governments of states which, for reasons of real power (the United States and the Soviet Union) or for historical reasons (Britain and France), conduct global foreign policies slip easily into a habit of exaggerated public self-congratulation regarding their importance in world affairs. This practice is harmless enough and can be good for national morale, provided that those responsible do not fall into the trap of believing their own propaganda and that the audience keep their salt-cellars handy. In the past few years we have heard a lot about the unparalleled, since Winston Churchill, excellence of Britain's 'special relationship' with the United States, about trenchant prime ministerial campaigns to prevent grasping Europeans from making off with excessive amounts of the British taxpayers' money, about the forging of a fresh 'special relationship' between Mrs Thatcher and President Gorbachev, about the routing of clamorous Commonwealth governments which have urged Britain to impose economic sanctions against South Africa, and so on and so on. What is the truth? Is Britain a more potent force in today's world than she was in the 1970s or has nothing changed except for the effectiveness of the government's public relations apparatus?

In most important respects, the present government has had an easier foreign policy ride than its predecessors of the 1970s, indeed than any government since 1945. By 1974, with a few difficult exceptions (see below), the process of decolonization was completed and, with the 'East of Suez' withdrawal in 1971, Britain was no longer burdened with maintaining and protecting a chain of overseas military bases and other quasi-imperial fixed assets. Entry into the European Community in 1972 had brought Britain into line with her old imperial rival France, establishing us, as we should have been years before, as an upper-middle-rank European power with distinctive residual features from the past, namely nuclear status, Permanent Membership of the UN Security Council, plus a network of intimate relationships with a majority of the membership of the Non-Aligned Movement arising out of the transformation of Empire into Commonwealth. Moreover, the Labour government of the 1970s has maintained the Anglo-American relationship in good shape. Finally, with the exploitation of North Sea oil, Britain was no longer dependent in times of crisis on the vagaries of Middle Eastern oil supplies and our last strategic commitment 'East of Suez', the Central Treaty Organisation, had disappeared with the Iranian Revolution only months before the present government took office.

During that period, the performance of our domestic economy had been as always the most reliable barometer of our overseas influence. The 1970s had been a dark period in this regard. Internal factors, which are not my concern in this essay, had combined with external forces, notably the quadrupling of the price of crude oil in the early 1970s, to produce stagnation, inflation, and incipient recession. By the end of the decade I was becoming increasingly conscious of the fact that, in the overseas countries with which I was involved, our influence was based on the wasting asset of past glory rather than on present performance, in which we were being outstripped by the majority of our European partners, not to mention Japan. Furthermore, the unsolved problem of Southern Rhodesia had assumed international dimensions and was permeating the whole spectrum of British foreign policy, in the United Nations, in the Commonwealth, and with our closest allies and partners. In a nutshell Britain's standing world-wide had drifted downwards from the high point of 1972, when Mr Edward Heath had brought the country into the European Community, thus, as it seemed, at last solving the problem of Britain's role in the world.

In the first year in office, the government's outstanding success was the negotiation of a peaceful settlement of the Southern Rhodesian problem, bringing into being the Republic of Zimbabwe. The time was ripe. The confidence of the white regime had been eroded by the guerrilla campaign of the Patriotic Front and by the pressure of the Anglo-American proposals devised by the Labour Foreign Secretary Dr David Owen and Secretary Cyrus Vance. The 'internal solution', under which Bishop Muzorewa assumed nominal power in 'Zimbabwe-Rhodesia', had failed to stop the war and had left the international community unmoved. But the Patriotic Front and its sponsors, the Front Line States, knew that victory on the battlefield was still remote, and the latter were suffering acutely from the incursions of the Rhodesian armed forces. Although it was not apparent at the time, all the parties, including the South African government (which must have feared having to make a decision in the not too distant future whether to incorporate an increasingly crippled Rhodesia into the Union), needed a settlement simultaneously; the first time that this necessary conjuncture had emerged.

However, even in these favourable circumstances, a settlement would not have come about without skilful and energetic diplomacy. When they came to power in May 1979 Conservative ministers were disposed to recognize the Muzorewa regime, lift sanctions, and hope that the rest of the world would follow suit. When it was appreciated that this course of action would leave Bishop Muzorewa and Britain isolated in a world which, including the United States, would continue to withhold recognition of and apply sanctions to Rhodesia, it was decided to avoid plunging into another labyrinth of complex negotiations on the lines of the Anglo-American proposals, but to simplify the problem by treating Rhodesia as if it were a normal colony approaching independence. This meant summoning all parties to a conference at Lancaster House at which a constitution would be drafted and agreed. The independence elections would be held in accordance with this constitution.

Before embarking on this course it was necessary to secure an international imprimatur: otherwise, the proceedings would be derailed by hostile states suspicious of Britain's motives. The United Nations was too divided, too adversarial and too cumbersome to be mobilized in this sense. The Commonwealth, comprising as it does nearly 50 per cent of the membership of the Non-Aligned Movement, provided the answer. At the Lusaka Commonwealth summit in July the Prime Minister persuaded

Commonwealth leaders to co-operate with the proposed British initiative.

In the autumn, the Lancaster House Conference was convened and, by December, agreement had been reached after a series of extremely delicate negotiations. Britain resumed control in Salisbury, sanctions were lifted, and the transitional period safely weathered in spite of many storms along the way. In April Zimbabwe emerged into independence. For the success of this enterprise great credit must go, on the British side, to the Prime Minister, to Lord Carrington, Sir Ian Gilmour, and the late Lord Soames, the principal political players. There is no doubt that the successful consummation did much to restore foreign confidence in Britain.

Had it not been for the improved international atmosphere generated by the settlement of this apparently intractable dispute, it is doubtful whether Britain would have been able to mobilize such effective Commonwealth support in neutralizing Latin American backing for the Guatemalan claim to Belize, which had obstructed Belizian independence for many years. In the event, Belize was welcomed into the United Nations almost unanimously in 1981, another obstinate problem of decolonization out of the way.

There is equally no doubt that, had the Rhodesian problem remained unsettled, Britain would not have secured the measure of support which she did in the United Nations when Argentina invaded the Falkland Islands at the beginning of April 1982. Paradoxically, this failure of diplomacy to prevent war resulted in a major boost for British international prestige. The Argentine military junta must have calculated that, with its popularity in the new administration in Washington and with the endorsement by the Non-Aligned Movement of the Argentine claim to sovereignty, Britain would find herself too isolated to risk unilateral military action and, after some routine huffing and puffing, would accept the new status quo. They were wrong. I can testify from my experience in New York that all elements in the international community, with the exception of some Latin American diehards, appreciated that the British government did its best to bring about a peaceful Argentine withdrawal from the islands, first through the bilateral negotiations conducted by Secretary Haig and thereafter through the UN Secretary-General Sr. Perez de Cuellar, and that it was only as a last resort that force was used. The efficiency with which the military operation was conducted won widespread respect and British prestige rose to a higher level in the summer of 1982 than it had reached for years— even the ranks of Tuscany (Eastern Europe and the Non-Aligned Movement) could scarce forbear to cheer.

Meanwhile the wider international scene had darkened. The age of *détente* ended abruptly with the Soviet invasion of Afghanistan in 1979. In the same year the agony of the American hostages in Tehran began, to be followed in 1980 by the Iran–Iraq war and, in 1982, by the Israeli invasion of Lebanon. By 1983, public opinion in Western Europe was divided over the impending deployment of cruise and Pershing missiles in response to the deployment by the Soviet Union of SS 20s. In these areas British foreign policy focused on firm adherence to the transatlantic alliance combined with intensified political co-ordination within Europe, separating the political ingredient from the bad-tempered wrangling over the Community budget.

By the beginning of the government's second term in office, that is, by 1984, Britain's standing in the world was fast improving from the low point of the late 1970s. This was due principally to the determination shown, for which the Prime Minister was given much personal credit internationally, in tackling the problems for which Britain was directly responsible. In this context I have already mentioned Rhodesia, Belize, and the Falklands War. Another important issue was the future of Hong Kong. Discussion of this could not be postponed: British leases of over 90 per cent of the territories involved are due to expire in 1997. This fact was already creating uncertainty in financial and business circles. After a protracted negotiation a more detailed agreement on Hong Kong's future, in terms of safeguarding its autonomy and economic freedom, was reached in 1984 with the government of the People's Republic of China than the negotiators could have hoped for at the outset.

In spite of these successes, the performance of the British economy still inhibited Britain from exercising full influence in the international arena. The country was seen by outsiders as still being plagued by recession, rising unemployment, and industrial unrest.

During the last four or five years, the government in its second and third terms has had its hands relatively free of difficult bilateral problems, with all that they involve in expenditure of diplomatic and military effort; more so than any of its predecessors in the post-1945 period. Although the recovery of the Falkland Islands did nothing to facilitate a settlement with Argentina, the latter has been so preoccupied with the re-establishment of democratic politics and with apparently insoluble economic difficulties that the quarrel with Britain has been given low priority. Anglo-Chinese relations cleared with the Hong Kong agreement. Even the dispute with Spain over Gibraltar changed to a more manageable and less jagged shape with the accession of Spain to NATO and her entry into the European Community.

Hence the second half of my analysis is concerned more with trends and the development of lines of policy than with dramatic episodes. First and foremost, perceptions both at home and abroad have crystallized into the belief that the formulation and conduct of British foreign policy has increasingly passed from the Foreign and Commonwealth Office to No 10 Downing Street. If true, this is far from being historically unprecedented. Not a few prime ministers, especially as their terms of office have lengthened, have found foreign policy excursions more intriguing and enjoyable than the often frustrating and controversial grind of domestic affairs.

In regard to the formulation of foreign policy, I do not believe, although many would argue to the contrary, that there has been qualitative change under Mrs Thatcher's premiership. When she came to power, she probably had less direct experience of the conduct of foreign policy than any of her predecessors for many years; and I doubt whether her perception of the Foreign and Commonwealth Office as being prone to favour woolly compromises and consensus over clear-cut policy differed from her perception of the existence of such characteristics in other departments of state. Until April 1982 she had a strong, experienced, and internationally well-known Foreign Secretary in Lord Carrington.

Any change that there has been post-dates Lord Carrington's resignation and the circumstances which surrounded it. The surprise of the Argentine invasion of the Falklands sent a violent shock wave through the system and may well have convinced the Prime Minister that she must take a closer interest in foreign policy questions, particularly those which contained the seeds of sudden crisis, in order to avoid the government being taken by surprise in future. Accordingly, she strengthened her personal staff in No 10 in 1982, but not to the extent of creating an alternative source of foreign policy formulation on the lines of the National Security Council in Washington. Basically the system has continued to function as before, with the Prime Minister playing a greater supervisory role over important areas of policy. But I doubt whether this change of emphasis is much greater than was the case under previous prime ministers who have developed, or come into office with, predilections for foreign affairs: Sir Anthony Eden, Mr Edward Heath, and Mr Harold Wilson come to mind. It should also not be forgotten that Sir Geoffrey Howe must now be one of the longest continuously serving Foreign Secretaries in the twentieth century.

However, in this particular case, there are important differences. The fact that the Prime Minister is a woman has in itself generated special interest amongst foreign leaders. She is in fact the first ever elected female head of government in a Western democracy, if Israel will forgive me for classifying Mrs Golda Meir with her Asian counterparts Mrs Indira Gandhi and Mrs Bandaranaika. (Is it not strange that, as the twentieth century draws to a close, the sum total of elected female heads of government in the whole of history is, according to my calculations, only eight?) In the overwhelmingly male congeries of foreign governments, Mrs Thatcher has been a phenomenon, originally because of her sex, progressively because she has now long outlasted all her Western colleagues, and last but not least, because of her forceful and straight-talking personality. All these factors have combined to heighten interest in Britain throughout the world.

Moreover, the Prime Minister's political and economic ideology, namely free-market capitalism, has caught a tide which has been flowing in the second half of the 1980s from China, through the Soviet Union and Eastern Europe, to the Third World itself, where the trappings of state socialism are in many cases a mere cloak for a growing measure of free enterprise. Britain was an early starter in this revolution and 'Thatcherism' is a word which has entered the international vocabulary. Most important, in the light of my earlier comments, the British economy has forged ahead in the past three or four years and is seen by the outside world as one of the success stories of the decade. This factor has in itself, and for the first time for many years, removed an important obstacle to the growth of British influence.

In what ways and to what extent has Britain succeeded in exploiting these assets? The Anglo-American relationship springs first to mind. It is many years since there was such ideological compatibility between an American president and a British prime minister as there was between Mrs Thatcher and President Reagan; both leaders made the most of this nexus. (It would not have been quite the same had President Carter won a second term in 1980.) This political love affair, not too strong a term when one considers the embarrassingly hyperbolic eulogies which each has delivered to the other on public occasions, has given the impression that America is a higher priority than Europe in the eyes of the British leadership and that Britain has on the whole been over-anxious to parade loyalty to the United States. The government would claim that overt demonstration of unity leads to greater private influence. There has certainly been straight talking, some of which has seeped through into the public domain, examples being in the reaction to the invasion of Grenada and the Reykjavik summit. And Mrs Thatcher has not been slow to proffer advice on a multitude of subjects: for example the Middle East crisis and the Gulf War. I am equally sure that her views have carried weight: her long experience has been a cumulative advantage. Taking all in all, it must be true that British influence in Washington today is greater than it was ten years ago and that Mrs Thatcher is well placed to carry on the good work with the new president, in a world which, in the past year or so, has been entering a period of change more profound than at any time in the past forty years.

The advent of President Gorbachev has altered the nature of the ball game. Where there had been a long freeze on the Central Front and in Eastern Europe, the glacier is melting and a new landscape is emerging. Nuclear, even conventional, disarmament is no longer a chimera. Nationalism is stirring within the Soviet Union and aspirations towards greater independence of Moscow are growing in the Warsaw Pact countries. By contrast the super-powers are beginning to co-operate within the United Nations and apparently intractable regional conflicts are starting to move towards solutions—examples are Vietnam–Cambodia, Afghanistan, Iran–Iraq and Angola–Namibia: even the Palestine problem is changing shape.

In this more fluid environment, it is of the utmost importance that there should be solidarity within NATO and close co-ordination of foreign policies within the expanded European Community. The British government, with a longer experience in office than all its allies and partners, should be able to play an important part in both these areas. For the first time in recent memory Britain has simultaneously warm relations with both super-powers and with China. As an outsider, I get the impression that we have been pulling our full weight in NATO and in regard to the new look developing in Eastern Europe.

The Prime Minister is seen by other foreign leaders as having been amongst the first to recognize, even before he came to power, that Mr Gorbachev would be a new type of leader for the Soviet Union, especially in contrast to the Brezhnev years. Her visits to Eastern Europe, particularly to the Soviet Union and Poland, received wide publicity, emphasizing not only her good personal relationship with Mr Gorbachev but her recognition that a new wind is blowing throughout the communist world. All this is very much on the credit side.

Can the same be said about developments in the European Community? It is difficult not to feel that the promising move towards a co-ordinated foreign policy in the early 1980s has slackened in recent years, perhaps because of the expansion of the Community to include more Southern European members, because of concentration on 1992, distractions in the form of bilateral rows over, for example, Northern Ireland, wholly justifiable preoccupation with international terrorism, and the disagreement over the future of 'Europe' itself so fiercely highlighted by the Prime Minister's recent speech at Bruges (although it has to be said that the speech in question could equally well have been publicized as 'pro' rather than 'anti' European). I may be in a minority, but I have long regarded political co-operation as being in the long term one of the most important Community activities and I would like to see firmer publicly stated positions on the main issues—East–West relations, the whole range of 'regional conflicts', and so on. Renascent Britain should be in the forefront here even if some of the end results might not (like the Venice Declaration of 1980 on the Middle East) be entirely to Washington's liking.

It may be that history will judge the foreign policy of the Thatcher epoch in terms more of the balance between Britain's relationship with the United States and Britain's role within the European Community than of any other factor. In addressing the questions, historians will have to concede that, up to the present day, Britain has had only one post-war government which was 'European' in the fullest sense of the word, namely that of Mr Edward Heath from 1970 to 1974. They will also have to admit that a prime minister who was either lukewarm (as with the Labour governments of the 1970s) or abrasive towards the Community and, by contrast, enthusiastic about the 'special relationship' with the United States could count on a fair degree of public support amongst a wide cross-section of British society. Against this background those of us who have long believed that Britain's post-imperial future lies primarily with Europe, while maintaining strong transatlantic and Commonwealth ties, have looked in vain for vigorous leadership in this direction since 1979. Instead the public perception is, I believe, one of British exasperation with the economic and budgetary shortcomings of the Community; coupled with a nationalistic determination not to be drawn towards wider horizons of a Western European conglomerate of democratic states so closely bound to each other in all aspects of life as to neutralize any possibility of a return to the bad old days of shifting balances of power; plus an inclination to turn with relief from the high-flown notions of Euro-idealists to the cosy pragmatism and cultural familiarity of Anglo-American relations.

In the Commonwealth and elsewhere in the non-aligned world, for example in the Middle East, where Britain still has important interests to protect, the same heightened profile can be found, but it is not easy to prove greater British influence. Relations with the Arab world are generally good, in some cases exceptionally warm, and the government conducted a skilful policy of neutrality throughout the Iran–Iraq war. But British power and leverage are things of the past. The regional governments look to Britain as part of Europe to concert influence on United States policy, especially in the Arab–Israeli context. Individual initiatives, such as Mrs Thatcher's apparent efforts to foster a 'Jordanian option' between Mr Shimon Peres and King Hussein, have not come to fruition, and there is no evidence that, in this sensitive area, British or European influence on Washington (or Tel Aviv for that matter) has been greater than in the days of Messrs Wilson and Callaghan).

In the Commonwealth, it is even harder to draw positive conclusions. Although the importance of the Commonwealth as a political forum with a greater degree of like-mindedness than could be found in the United Nations was demonstrated in cases such as Southern Rhodesia, Belize, and the Falklands War, the resultant favourable atmosphere was partially dissipated in the obsessive row over sanctions against South Africa which left Britain virtually isolated. Comprising as it does nearly 50 per cent of the membership of the Non-Aligned Movement, it is not surprising that the Commonwealth is fixated on the question of the elimination of apartheid and, regardless of the merits of the sanctions argument, it is surely a pity that unnecessarily crude public positions on all sides should have been allowed to carry the organization in its political dimension back to the bad old days when it was equally obsessed with Southern Rhodesia, to the discomfiture and irritation of British governments of the time.

Power, be it global or regional, is an easier commodity to measure than influence, and Britain is no super-power. I do not believe that the present government cherishes the illusions of grandeur which bedevilled Britain's search for a post-imperial role until as recently as the mid-1960s. British influence has not invariably followed an exact correlation between economic performance and foreign policy successes. Did we not for example play a leading part in the difficult negotiations leading up to the adoption of Security Council Resolution 242 of 1967 on the Middle East when the country was in the throes of a serious financial crisis and only two years after we had failed either to prevent or to reverse the unilateral declaration of independence in Rhodesia? However, none would doubt that, over the past decade, the curve of the graph has been upward. For the reasons I have suggested—determination in settling bilateral problems, the improvement in the economy, the personality and political longevity of the Prime Minister, the excellence of the Anglo-American relationship—Britain today cuts a more impressive figure on the world stage. But we still need to resolve the fundamental question of priority between the Atlantic and the continent of Europe—Mr Heath did not last long enough to consolidate his initial achievement—and we must still envy the relationship which France has forged with her former territories compared to the squabbling which persists within the Commonwealth.

In this world of bewildering change, Britain will need to deploy her skills and advantages to the full. To paraphrase Prufrock, we may not be one of the princes but we have certainly risen in the pecking order of attendant lords. They have their part to play in the unfolding of the drama.

13

The Health Service

CHARLES WEBSTER

Whatever the forms of health care adopted, all Western nations are faced with problems of escalating costs and they are beset by doubts concerning the adequacy of their systems to meet the challenges of the future. Their problems are not new, but as in some countries the cost of health care has risen to above 10 per cent of GNP during the last decade, health provision has emerged as a major social and political issue. The increasing preponderance of the elderly in the population, together with the mounting cost of high-technology medicine, are steadily increasing strains on the health services, and it is clear these pressures will become ever more acute.

In Britain, the above problems have been compounded by a record of persistent underfunding made worse by a hostile economic environment taking root in the mid-1970s, and also by in-built inefficiencies of the system exacerbated by the Joseph health service reorganization of 1974. Even before the Thatcher administration Britain was straining to maintain a Western-style health service on the basis of 6 per cent of GNP. Despite its many virtues the NHS was not capable of competing on a half-price basis. This difficulty drove the Labour government in 1976 to establish a Royal Commission to look into the NHS. This was the first and only thorough review of the British health service in its forty-year history.

Because Britain is the only major Western nation to possess a centralized, tax-funded system of health care, the health service has always maintained a higher public profile, and it easily becomes an issue of major political importance. The NHS was brought into existence by Bevan in a highly charged political atmosphere. Thereafter there emerged a consensus, which proved less durable than it seemed at the time.

Consensus rapidly dissolved after 1979. When Mrs Thatcher assumed office the National Health Service entered the headlines and it has resolutely stayed there. During the 1980s health has also emerged as a high-profile political problem. For the first time, the National Health Service, for long regarded as the pillar of the Welfare State, no longer enjoyed the prospect of a certain future. The government has been attacked for lack of radicalism by the Tory right, and for departing from the basic principles of the NHS by Labour. Despite the effort devoted by Mrs Thatcher's team to proving that the NHS is 'safe with us' the public remains stoically unconvinced. Even the much heralded and massively publicized White Paper *Working for Patients: The Health Service: Caring for the 1990s* (January 1989) damaged the Conservative Party's performance in the opinion polls. According to the verdict of the *Daily Telegraph* headline: 'Gallup puts Labour 1.5 pc behind. Tory poll lead hit by doubts over NHS plan' (16 February 1989). Before the end of the month, uncertainty over the NHS, together with a mounting public health scare, contributed to the fiasco of the Richmond by-election and a further slump in Conservative standing in the opinion polls. Finally, in May the NHS helped Labour to its by-election triumph in the Vale of Glamorgan. In the spring of 1989 it seemed as if health, always an Achilles' heel for Mrs Thatcher, might prove the undoing of the revolution of the right.

COLLAPSE OF CONFIDENCE

By 1979 earlier optimism concerning the ability of modern medicine to transform health care into a cheap and painless process was becoming dissipated. It was clear that high-technology medicine would create as many problems as it solved, and those problems duly crowded in on Mrs Thatcher's government. New openings in transplant surgery, *in vitro* fertilization, or cancer screening revealed ethical dilemmas and shortcomings of the system. In many cases problems that had been swept under the carpet for years could no longer be evaded. Yet the habit to evade persisted with the result that crucial instances were provided to provoke anxieties about the safety and effectiveness of

the health service. Even single incidents were sufficient to provoke panic, and too often further inquiry showed that there was
ample room for concern. For instance, the death in 1985 of an
Oxfordshire mother who had not been informed about a positive
smear test for cervical cancer revealed the deficiencies of cervical
cancer screening procedures. The scandal looked worse when it
became known that recommendations of the government's own
Committee on Gynaecological Cytology for radical restructuring
of the screening programme, dating back to 1981, had not been
implemented. The public was alarmed by the prospect of 2,000
unnecessary deaths each year due to deficiencies in the screening
programme. Concern over cervical cancer extended to breast
cancer, and then other cancers. It soon became apparent that
substantial loss of life was occasioned by failure of the NHS to
adopt a modern mechanized and computerized screening
programme.

A further incident with wide repercussions was the outbreak of
Salmonella poisoning at Stanley Royd Hospital, Wakefield, in
1984, which was responsible for nineteen deaths. The report into
this affair in January 1986 criticized the health authority for
'appalling mismanagement'. Providentially reinforcing this message, another outbreak of *Salmonella* poisoning was traced back
to the Farley's baby food factory at Kendal, sending Farley's into
liquidation, with considerable loss to the parent company Glaxo.

The Stanley Royd affair had a major impact. It prompted the
Acheson inquiry into public health and community medicine.
Public health as medical specialism had long been in decline, but
especially after the 1974 reorganization it had dwindled into
insignificance within health authorities. This was to some extent
compensated for by the rise of environmental health in local
authorities, but under the present administration environmental
health departments suffered from local government economies
and they became seriously understaffed.

Stanley Royd also drew attention to the use of crown immunity
to evade environmental health sanctions. A survey by the Institution of Environmental Health Officers suggested that a majority
of hospital kitchens failed to meet food hygiene standards.
Responding to all-party protests in Parliament in 1986 the

government ended crown immunity of hospitals, exposing the need for massive investment in hospital kitchen modernization.

During the 1980s environmental health, communicable diseases, nutrition, and food safety have reappeared as major questions of health policy. The capacity of such issues to provoke alarm is evident from the newspaper headlines between December 1988 and March 1989. *Legionella*, *Listeria*, and *Salmonella* have emerged as matters of public concern and ministerial discomfort. The inadequacy of the mechanisms for dealing with such problems has been evident for some time. The Acheson inquiry was designed to reinvigorate public health. The government reversed its decision to abolish the Public Health Laboratory Service. The government's record over changes in the machinery for health education and nutritional advice is more doubtful. It is far from evident that expert advisory bodies are sufficiently protected from vested interests or bureaucratic pressures. The government's reputation has been damaged by accounts of suppression or unnecessary delays in publication of reports on vital questions of health. Collectively these experiences have undermined public confidence in the handling of preventive medicine, and these doubts have contributed to the mood of general dissatisfaction about the health service.

CRISIS OF EXPENDITURE

Most of the shortcomings mentioned above relate in some way to the increasing financial stringency affecting the health services in the 1980s. The drive to curtail expenditure has been the most conspicuous feature of the Thatcher administration's intervention in the field of health, forming an important element in the government's general assault on public expenditure.

Granted, the Thatcher government, like all of its predecessors, has steadily increased its spending on the health service. In cash terms UK health service spending increased from £8bn. in 1978/9 to £23bn. in 1988/9. Most of this increase was accounted for by inflation. One representative computation indicating the contrast between current spending and the change in purchasing power for the NHS in England is given in Table 13.1.

TABLE 13.1. *Resources available for services 1980/1–1986/7*

	1980/1	1981/2	1982/3	1983/4	1984/5	1985/6	1986
HCHS current							
Total spending (£m.)	6,963	7,688	8,251	8,674	9,168	9,660	10,35
Increase (%)	—	10·3	7·3	5·1	5·7	5·4	7·2
Inflation etc. in service (%)	—	8·2	6·5	5·1	5·8	5·2	6·9
Change in purchasing power (%)	—	2·0	0·8	0·0	−0·1	0·2	0·3
FPS current							
Total spending (£m.)	2,173	2,504	2,894	3,110	3,419	3,600	3,908
Increase (%)	—	15·2	15·6	7·5	9·9	5·3	8·5
Inflation etc. in service (%)	—	12·9	11·6	5·4	6·9	6·1	6·0
Change in purchasing power (%)	—	2·0	3·6	2·0	2·8	−0·7	2·4
NHS total							
Total spending (£m.)	9,971	11,182	12,195	12,919	13,870	14,675	15,81
Increase (%)	—	12·1	9·1	5·9	7·4	5·8	7·7
Inflation etc. in service (%)	—	9·0	7·4	5·0	5·9	5·4	6·5
Change in purchasing power (%)	—	2·9	1·5	0·9	1·3	0·3	1·1

Note: The figures for NHS total spending include both capital expenditure and Central Health and Miscellaneous Service, therefore these figures will not equal the sum of HCHS and FPS expenditure.

Source: Social Services Committee, Session 1985–86 Public Expenditure on the Social Services HC 387 and DHSS memorandum to Social Services Committee, Session 1986–87 Public Expenditure on the Social Services HC 413. (From Soci: Services Committee, *Resourcing the National Health Service*, HC 264–II, p. 15.)

In presenting these conclusions the National Association of Health Authorities (NAHA) points out that the Family Practitioner Services (FPS) had fared better than the Hospital and Community Health Services (HCHS). Over the period 1980/1 to 1986/7 the cash available to the NHS in England increased by 58.6 per cent from £9,971m. to £15,811m. For the FPS it increased by 79.8 per cent from £2,173m. to £3,908m. For the

HCHS, the increase was 48.7 per cent from £6,963m. to £10,355m. over the same period. The most significant feature of the government's policy was the virtual standstill in purchasing power in the HCHS sector since 1982/3. The steady growth experienced by the HCHS up to 1982/3 came to a sudden halt in 1983/4. Consequently since that date the hospital services have been forced to accommodate development and mounting demands from the elderly without an increase in their resources. On the other hand the non-cash-limited FPS services continued to expand to meet the increasing demands imposed by demographic change. If the HCHS had received cash increases equivalent to those of the FPS, its cash limits would have been £12,522m. in 1986/7, almost 21 per cent higher than was the case. The government would argue that its regime of 'efficiency savings' had offset this shortfall, but these savings had reached only about £160m. in 1986/7, while in many cases they represented cuts in vital services rather than genuine gains in efficiency.

Thus after being carried along for a brief time on a tide of obligation inherited from the Labour government, the Thatcher administration succeeded in checking the increase of resources flowing into the HCHS sector. In achieving this objective the partnership of Lawson and Fowler was interrupting a trend dating back to the beginning of the health service.

Taking Mrs Thatcher's term of office as a whole the average annual real rise in NHS expenditure on current goods and services is smaller than that of any previous administration. In fact it is only half the level of any administration since 1960. The present government's effort has only marginally reduced the share of national resources devoted to health care, but Britain is now resolutely located at the foot of the league table of health expenditure of comparable Western nations. The average OECD nation now spends 2 per cent more of its GNP on health than Britain. Britain's 6 per cent compares particularly unfavourably with the 11 per cent in the USA.

THE OUTPUT ENIGMA

Resource restrictions have not of course totally inhibited development within the NHS. The Prime Minister frequently points out that front-line medical and nursing staff have increased in numbers, and that output of the NHS has expanded. Table 13.2 indicates growth criteria cited by the DHSS in its evidence to the Social Services Committee in 1988.

TABLE 13.2. *Increase in NHS staff and output 1980–1986*
(Index 1980=100)

HCHS	101·0
HCHS doctors	107·6
Nurses (not adjusted for reduction in contractual hours in 1981)	108·8
Professions allied to medicine	121·3
FPS practitioners	113·0
In-patients	111·9
Day cases	157·0
Out-patients	109·1
Cases treated in acute sector (1980–5)	110·4
Acute conditions seen by consultants (1980–5)	111·2
All operations (1980–5)	109·7

Source: Recalculated from DHSS evidence to Social Services Committee, Feb. 1988, *Resourcing the NHS*, HC 264-II, pp. 96–9, Tables 1–8.

Although these changes have occurred under the present government, Mrs Thatcher's administration can only claim the credit in an indirect sense. Britain has shared in the general progress of medical innovation which has been gathering momentum since World War II. On the whole innovation has increased the cost of medical treatment. The cases where new drugs or vaccines have reduced costs and liberated hospital beds are outweighed by examples in which full exploitation of medical advances has raised costs. Modernization has increased demands for personnel and plant. The present government has faced successive waves of demand for additional resources to support community care, transplant or cardiovascular surgery, cancer screening, or treatment for AIDS. Given no more than limited concession to these pressures, innovation has only been possible at the cost of diversion of resources within the service, involving closure of wards, more efficient use of beds, exploitation of day-surgery, and increasing dependency on resources derived from private and charitable agencies.

Paradoxically, government resistance to funding development has on occasions produced marginal benefits by hastening the drift towards more active clinical regimes and economical application of new techniques. But it has also carried the danger of premature discharge and undesirable short cuts in care. Shortage of resources has also prevented optimization of medical innovation, with the result that Britain's standing in the international medical league table has been prejudiced. Hence, compared with its Western neighbours, the NHS has been increasingly censured for its low expectations and declining standards. This is a recurrent theme of right-wing critics of the NHS.

Shortcomings in meeting the obligation incurred by modern methods have periodically discomforted the present government. The anxieties provoked over deficiencies in the cancer screening programme have already been noted. Superficially the cervical screening programme seemed to show preventive medicine at its best. Between 1973 and 1986 the number of cervical smears examined rose by 35 per cent. But a National Audit Office report in 1986 showed that women most at risk tended to be least screened, while the majority of authorities had failed to develop comprehensive arrangements for calling and recalling women in the relevant age groups. Consequently, despite its screening programme Britain had a poor record over deaths from cervical cancer.

It was not until 1988 that concerted effort was made to tighten up screening for cervical cancer. Even now Britain is some way off the target of triennial screening, computerization, and linking of health authority and Family Practitioner Committee (FPC) records. Once the cancer screening problems are overcome it will be necessary to face defects in the acute services for cancer. In 1984 the working group on these services concluded that 'the NHS generally cannot be insulated from economic realities, but current resource constraints do have particularly significant implications for services to cancer patients. The gap between the level of services generally available and the level that it is now possible to achieve has increased considerably.' It is arguable that this gap has further increased since 1984, and this conclusion could be applied to other acute services.

Improvements in treatment of end state renal failure is one of the major success stories of high-technology medicine. Between 1968 and 1986 the acceptance rate of new patients for renal replacement therapy increased from 7 to 47 per million population. Transplants performed per million population increased from 11 in 1976 to 29 in 1986. Whereas in 1968 no patients were accepted for transplants above the age of 55, in 1986 17 per cent fell into this category. The target set by the DHSS in 1985 has been met. Nevertheless it has not been met in all regions and by comparison with European neighbours Britain's performance is not outstanding, particularly in the field of dialysis. In 1986 the German Federal Republic recorded 66 new patients per million population for renal replacement therapy and Britain was six-teenth in the European league table. Even in the transplant area, where Britain recorded five times as many grafts in 1976, the German Federal Republic has now caught up; and the Germans have six times as many transplant centres per million population. Also Britain's position has not been comfortably maintained. The renal service has been successful in the competition for NHS resources, but modernization has been conducted at the cost of less favoured specialisms, while in general the maintenance of standards in high-technology medicine has been at the cost of the development of community care. Reduction in reliance on institutional services has been policy since the beginning of the NHS. In the 1960s community care policies received the backing of Enoch Powell as Minister of Health. There was renewed emphasis on community care in the context of NHS reorganization in the 1970s. Finally, under Patrick Jenkin, the present government designated community care as a major health service priority and the rundown of mental and mental handicap hospitals has proceeded more quickly than ever before. Realization of the community care initiative has exposed weaknesses in the capacity of present health service administration to deal with problems at the interface between the health authorities and local authorities. In practice, community care has not attained the high priority promised in official policy pronouncements. Taking account of reduction in working hours, the community nursing work-force has remained static. When allowing for the increased burden of handicapped and elderly dependency imposed by demographic change and policy initiatives it is clear that community care provision is sliding into a state of serious crisis. This example indicates that government claims about increase in health service manpower cannot be taken at face value. The nursing work-force as a whole has remained static since 1982, and the increase before that date brought limited benefit in output because of the reduction of the working week in 1981 from 40 to 37.5 hours. The increase in numbers of doctors or nurses employed in the NHS has not been sufficient to keep up with the demands imposed by demographic change or the increased workload of hospital care. For this reason the long-running scandal of excessive hours worked by junior hospital doctors has been allowed to drag on.

BREAKING POINT

Curtailment of health expenditure exactly coincides with Mr Fowler's long tenure as Secretary of State for Social Services, following the brief and inconsequential performance of Patrick Jenkin. As the *Guardian* pronounced on 16 July 1982, 'the expansion of the NHS was brought to a halt by Mr. Norman Fowler, the Social Services Secretary, last night'. This objective was not achieved without pain and resistance. At the first hurdle Mr Fowler ran into an eight-month industrial dispute with nurses and ancillary workers. Apart from the miners' strike this was the government's most prolonged contest with organized labour. Mr Fowler made only minor concessions. The unions were humiliated, while nurses were bought off by the grant of a pay review body.

After an initial perturbation the Fowler economies were pursued without effective resistance. The headlines were regularly occupied with accounts of local closures and cuts in service. Some

District Health Authorities temporarily refused to implement staff cuts, but local health authorities were whipped into line by the regions. Nevertheless the DHSS was warned of the cost to services, and it became increasingly clear that the annual regime of cuts followed in some cases by last minute minor concessions was stretching the tolerance of the system to its limit.

The breaking point was reached at the end of November 1987, conveniently just after the departure of Norman Fowler and his replacement by John Moore. Once again a tragic individual case provoked a chain reaction. The death of David Barber, the Birmingham baby, whose hole-in-the-heart operation was carried out only after five postponements, court cases, and much publicity, set off a wave of public outrage. Dame Jill Knight used the moment to mobilize a substantial back-bench revolt against the government's plans to impose charges for dental and eyesight checks. Since 1951 dental and spectacle charges had become an established feature of the NHS, and they were periodically increased, but charges on checks were always resisted because they were seen as a disincentive to prevention and early treatment. Mrs Thatcher broke this taboo. The charges were introduced in 1988, but only after a prolonged and damaging political battle with Conservative dissidents in both Houses. The second reading of the Bill to impose these charges was seized by the Presidents of the three premier Royal Colleges to unleash a blistering attack on the government's record in health care and medical research. The government reacted with its habitual nostrum, a small increment in health authority expenditure to relieve the deficit for 1987/8.

More than any previous government since the emergence of consensus the government had sacrificed the goodwill of the NHS work-force. The breaking of union influence was consistent with general government policy. But the government risked making more powerful enemies by riding roughshod over the British Medical Association, the Royal Colleges, and other organizations representing the professions and scientific expertise. This policy too was in line with the government's assault on the vested interest of the professions, but in this case the action risked breaking up the corporate consensus that had been important for sustaining the NHS. Furthermore, in general, the public retained its high estimate of the work of the professions involved in medicine. Particularly damaging to the government was its treatment of nursing. Even the pay restructuring was mishandled, with the result that nurses again resorted to industrial action in January 1988 and their grievances remained unsettled.

With a view to a longer-term solution, the Social Services Committee began a thorough review of NHS funding. Following rumours in April, in July 1988 Mrs Thatcher also intervened to set up her own confidential ministerial review, with the idea of providing for the first time in the history of her administration a positive policy for health funding. The elevated expectations concerning this high-level review defused the crisis and granted Mr Moore much needed breathing space so that he could extricate himself from the controversies surrounding social security before solving the problems of health care. It also gave him time to recover from a spell of ill-health. In the event Mr Moore was relieved of the responsibility. Mrs Thatcher broke up the DHSS and placed the new Department of Health in the hands of Kenneth Clarke, who had from 1982 to 1985 headed Mr Fowler's health team. She was returning health administration to the situation existing between 1951 and 1968, with the difference that the Ministers of Health for almost all of that period were excluded from the Cabinet. There were obvious advantages in recreating a department entirely committed to health, but in taking this step Mrs Thatcher generated other problems. First she was faced by two spending ministers in the Cabinet whereas formerly there had been one. Secondly, the rationalization was still incomplete because various spheres of health responsibility were left with such departments as Agriculture, Education, and Environment. The awkwardness of this division of responsibility was soon to be exposed. Finally, the small Health Department, especially if its functions are further devolved in line with rightist ideology, is destined to become an unattractive backwater of the Civil Service.

INCESSANT REORGANIZATION

The discipline of retrenchment does not entirely exhaust the contribution to health care of Mrs Thatcher's administration. Election manifestos have given relatively little guidance on Conservative commitments. In the main they have reiterated commonplace objectives concerning the improvement of efficiency. Hints about the encouragement of private medicine or consideration of alternative funding for health care have not in practice led to dramatic initiatives.

During Jenkin's brief tenure as Secretary of State the main initiatives were completion of business left over by the previous Labour administration, especially simplification of health administration by removal of the superfluous area tier. Retention of the district rather than the area in the 1982 reorganization raised the question of the relationship between FPCs and health authorities. Against the recommendations of the 1979 Royal Commission the FPCs were given statutory independence. This move protected general practitioners from cash limits, at the cost of sacrificing a final opportunity for unified health administration at the local level. The radical step of abolishing the regional tier was considered, but in the end the region was reprieved. Unexpectedly a stir was created over the government's wish to abolish Community Health Councils, as a result of which these too were reprieved.

As noted above Mr Fowler's tenure was characterized by a standstill in real spending. This was only rendered possible by a frantic search for economies in spending, including the first manpower cuts and controls to be introduced since 1951. Mr Fowler was not always more successful than his predecessors in dealing with intractable problems, for instance in reversing the steady growth in the NHS drugs bill and controlling the profits of the drug industry. He was driven by the Treasury and Public Accounts Committee to take more concerted action than his predecessors. Even then his progress was halting and irresolute. In 1983 the Greenfield Report proposed the adoption of generic prescribing. Instead in 1984 Fowler opted for the more modest savings offered by limiting the drugs available for minor ailments.

Even this scheme was liberalized in the light of criticism from doctors and the industry. Mr Fowler's other main hope for containment of the drugs bill lay in renegotiation of the Pharmaceutical Price Regulation Scheme. As in previous negotiations the outcome proved more generous to the drug industry than was intended, exposing the Health Department to further criticism from the Public Accounts Committee for permitting excessive profits on a drug bill which has now reached £2bn.

Many of the actions of Mr Fowler reflect Mrs Thatcher's drive to incorporate business and market principles into the public services. Thus Rayner scrutinies were undertaken into ten areas of NHS activity. One of the major proposals of these reviews involved the disposal of huge amounts of NHS property, including nurses' homes. Rich opportunities were detected for the privatization of NHS services, but in the event cleaning, laundry, and catering services were the only functions in which private contractors were employed on any scale.

The boldest and most important initiative undertaken by Mr Fowler involved the scrapping of the consensus form of management adopted in 1974 and maintained in the 1982 reorganization. Advice on this action emanated from Mr (later Sir) Roy Griffiths, the deputy chairman and managing director of Sainsbury's, whose report was commissioned in 1983. The Griffiths proposals received a mixed reception but they were immediately implemented. General Managers replaced consensus teams at unit, district, and regional levels, while within the DHSS responsibility for NHS affairs was transferred to a Management Board answerable to the Secretary of State's Health Services Supervisory Board. The businessman appointed to head the Management Board lasted only for a short time, after which the Board came under the chairmanship of the Health Minister. But even the revised arrangement was unsatisfactory, with the result that further changes are proposed in the 1989 White Paper. The management structure and divisions of the Department of Health coexist in uneasy partnership.

Although presented as an innovation the Griffiths reforms are little different from the changes advocated in the mid-1960s when NHS reorganization was first discussed. In general, neither

Mr Fowler's economies nor his reforms have fundamentally altered the NHS, and his few general policy statements confirmed his support for the basic principles upon which the NHS was founded. Periodically Mrs Thatcher has subscribed to the same theme. Their emollient speeches have not reassured the public because much publicity has been attracted by an undercurrent of rival policy proposals, most of them stemming from sources near to Mrs Thatcher, calling for a radical shake-up of the NHS. Typical packages envisage abandonment of the present tax-funded health service in favour of social or private insurance. It is also proposed that privatization of health service facilities should be drastically extended.

The report of the Social Services Committee, *The Future of the National Health Service* (July 1988), considered 'new ideas for the organisation and provision of services' sympathetically, but rejected most of them. The government's White Paper of January 1989 is little more sympathetic to the radicals on the question of funding the NHS. Once again Mrs Thatcher confirms that 'the National Health Service will continue to be available to all, regardless of income, and to be financed mainly out of general taxation'. Only token encouragement to the extension of private insurance is given in the provision for tax relief on health insurance premiums for the elderly. No general incentive is provided for opting out of the state system. The radicals will be more satisfied with the White Paper's scheme for the opting out of hospitals and introduction of market principles into primary care and acute hospital services. It seems that regional and district health authorities will fade into the background and no longer exercise the strong planning and supervisory role which has been developing since 1948. The age of planning bodies is giving way to the age of the manager and the market. However, by contrast with previous major planning documents the White Paper and its associated working papers contain serious omissions and they are deficient in detail. The proposed reforms concentrate on general medical practice and acute hospital care to the exclusion of virtually everything else. The growing numbers of the handicapped, the old, and those requiring care within the community will no doubt be wondering about their place in the future medical market. Their fears will be compounded by the embarrassing delay in the government's response to the Griffiths Report on community care services published in March 1988. Community care, the pillar of earlier government pronouncements concerning the future health services, now seems to have disappeared from the horizon. In a further serious miscalculation, public health has been omitted from the blueprint for the future. Although the impression is given that the changes proposed represent an extension of the government's good housekeeping campaign, it is evident that the reforms, if carried to their logical conclusion, will fundamentally alter the character of the NHS.

The White Paper proposals arguably represent reversion to the pre-NHS state of affairs. No authority will exercise planning and executive responsibility for health services in a particular area. As before World War II health authorities are likely to retain direct responsibility for the chronic hospital sector. The former voluntary hospitals will regain their independence and compete with one another. The way will be clear for a repetition of the inefficiencies and defects of the competitive system that the NHS was designed to correct.

A DANGEROUS EXPERIMENT

No institution in Britain has commanded wider respect than the National Health Service. But successive administrations have neglected their responsibilities towards this service. For a long period the NHS was a low priority issue. Consensus proved to be the passport to inertia and underfunding. By the arrival of Mrs Thatcher's administration, Britain has achieved a worst-of-both-worlds situation, a health service that was underfunded and in serious respects inefficient. The intrinsic strengths of the NHS and the dedication of its work-force were still sufficient to preserve a remarkable level of service and public satisfaction. However, the cracks were beginning to appear and under the tight regime of retrenchment introduced by Mrs Thatcher these difficulties intensified to crisis point. The pressure under which the NHS operated forced the Secretary of State to look more seriously into questions of efficiency than any of his predecessors.

The Thatcher administration will therefore be remembered for its efficiency campaigns, and especially for its decision to apply management practices taken from the private sector. However, economy was pursued without any clear guiding strategy. Crisis management has dictated most of the government's interventions.

For an administration renowned for its resolve and clarity of purpose the NHS has proved an embarrassment. The government has committed itself neither to optimize the working of the socialized system nor to opt for a new model consistent with market principles. Throughout Mrs Thatcher's term of office formal support for the existing system has been maintained against pressure from the right for imitation of American models of health care. To the degree that the intentions of the 1989 White Paper can be deciphered, the government now seems to have reached a compromise. Funding of the NHS by general taxation will be maintained, but the services will be organized according to market principles. But it is by no means clear that the government's formula will produce a stable equilibrium. Much greater consumer satisfaction is promised from the new system, but neither the public nor providers of services are convinced. It is argued that the essential objectives of the reforms could be achieved within the existing framework. Improvements in service promised from the reforms are by no means certain to materialize. The prospect of a regime of extended and unrealistic cash limits, lack of local accountability, collapse of integrated planning, escalating bureaucratic complexity and administrative costs, and destabilization of essential services suggests that the NHS is on the verge of an experiment more dangerous than anything experienced in its forty-year history. Mrs Thatcher's administration is therefore marking its tenth anniversary by taking its first major initiative on health service reform. Unless wise counsels prevail Mrs Thatcher will be remembered for delivering a blow from which the NHS might never recover.

14

The Schools

J. R. G. TOMLINSON

The agenda for educational change which arose from the breakdown of the post-war consensus, and which was publicly announced by James Callaghan in his Ruskin speech of 1976, occupied the following decade. It was not essentially altered by the advent of the Conservative Administration in 1979, although some of the methods employed were novel. However, from 1986, a new hard-right ideology supervened, dominated the 1988 Reform Act, and may shape the 1990s.

Callaghan said that schools should pay more attention to preparing pupils for working life, reconsider the curriculum and teaching methods, and be more willing to share curriculum concerns with parents and the public. He also called for a core curriculum, a more interventionist role for the DES and Inspectorate, and more lay influence on and through governing bodies (*TES*, 22 October 1976).

The background to this intervention by a Prime Minister into the purposes and methods of education included the Black Papers (starting in 1969),[1] the economic crisis from 1973, and the desire of the DES, especially its officials, to strengthen its role, particularly since it had been criticized in a report by OECD for not being sufficiently active in planning the education system. The DES's position was summed up in the 'Yellow Book' of July 1976, their response to Downing Street's request for a view of the educational scene.[2] It was faithfully followed in the Ruskin speech.

The Great Debate which Callaghan called for about the purposes and means of education led to the ten most hectic years ever experienced by the public education system. A stream of policy papers from both DES and the Inspectorate touching virtually every aspect of the service was paralleled by a series of education Acts culminating in the Education Reform Act of 1988, unquestionably the most significant piece of educational legislation since 1944.

By 1988 the maintained schools of England and Wales faced radically different demands from government, demands which were expected to be met by radically different means. Each school had to produce an individual curriculum statement to meet the requirements of the national curriculum and take account of additions and comments from the LEA. Their pupils would be assessed at ages 7, 11, 14, and 16 through a national assessment system and the results at 11, 14, and 16 made public. Schools must provide information about their objectives, work, and results, including any public examination results. Admission procedures allowed parents to choose a school, even in another LEA, if there was room (which would be decided by the DES). Thus schools would be in competition for pupils especially if school rolls were falling. The teachers had lost rights to negotiate pay and were subject to national conditions of service. The governing body had the power to hire and fire teachers, including the Head. The annual appraisal of teachers was imminent. Every school of more than 200 pupils would be provided by the LEA with a budget fixed by formula and expected to manage its own finances. The examination system at 16+ had been reformed and the GCSE set in place; the requirement for every pupil to have a record of personal achievement following national guidelines was imminent (1990). Primary schools faced the first impact of the national curriculum and testing programme for 5–7 year olds, to be introduced in 1989.

A good deal of the work of schools was subject to earmarked grant from central government (often a department other than the DES) usually connected with a management contract for its delivery against predetermined criteria. Examples included the Technical and Vocational Education Initiative, which required work experience for all pupils of 14+ (an initiative of the MSC), the promotion of an enterprise culture (a DTI initiative), a range of curriculum developments funded by DES Education Support Grants, and programmes of in-service training for teachers largely paid for by DES grant and subject to prior DES approval.

In short, a system deriving from broad legislative objectives, convention, and consensus had been replaced by one based on contract and management.

Between 1979 and 1986 it was the methods not the objectives that were new. They produced an acceleration effect which it is most unlikely would have been achieved by any government continuing to use the traditional tools of consultation and consensus. Consultative bodies were disbanded and procedures compressed. Where new consultative or executive machinery was created its members were not appointed as representing a balance of interests but were nominated by government. Schools and LEAs were loaded with a quantity of innovation which would formerly have been regarded as counter-productive. Underlying these processes were deeper objectives of the neo-liberal political programme of removing or neutralizing institutions and power groupings which intervene between the state and the individual, notably the breaking of the power of the teacher trade unions (over pay, conditions of service, and curriculum), a considerable reduction in the powers of local government and its realignment towards being an agency of central government, and an orchestrated denigration of the profession. It was possible, because of the teachers' associations' claim to be both professional association and trade union, to attack the professionalism of teachers at the same time as their unions. In this latter respect above all Sir Keith Joseph's prescription broke with the Callaghan consensus: Callaghan had said, 'We must carry the teaching profession with us.' These factors and the prolonged and bitter teachers' pay dispute of 1984–7 softened up both public opinion and the 'educational establishment' for a complete break with tradition. There was no longer any expectation that a consensus would be sought and therefore no need to seek one.

Thus by 1986 the stage had been set for the radical phase of Thatcherite educational policy. Although there were some intended leaks, the manifesto of 1987, which provided the 'mandate' for the 1988 Reform Act, was prepared in secret during the previous nine months under the general direction of the Prime Minister's Policy Unit. The aim was to make an irreversible change in the public education system, similar to that already achieved in other aspects of social and economic policy such as trade union legislation, the sale of council houses, and the privatization of industry.

There was also an international context for a new radicalism towards public education. Thinking and action in the USA has perhaps been the most influential upon government during the 1980s. The report of the US National Commission for Excellence in Education, *A Nation at Risk: The Imperative for Educational Reform* (1983), typified the many reports and concerns of that period in the USA that 'the educational foundations of our society are presently being eroded by a rising tide of mediocrity that threatens our very future as a nation and a people'. Interestingly, as in Great Britain, the main focus for criticism was the secondary school and the criticism came not only from the right wing, over the need for greater economic effectiveness, but also from the radical left, which considered that the public schools had failed the poor and deprived.[3] The feeling that the time had come to reconsider both the instrumental and the altruistic purposes and achievements of the publicly provided school systems in countries with broadly similar political aspirations was an important influence on both politicians and professionals during the first half of the 'Thatcher decade'.

The years 1979–89 may therefore be seen as having two distinct phases. Until 1986 the broadly bipartisan agenda already set in the 1970s was worked through, though in a new spirit. But the novel methods employed had eroded the vitality and self-confidence of the system in many essential aspects—the morale of the teachers, the place of the teachers' unions, and the authority of the LEAs. The third term of office provided the opportunity for a radical programme. Yet the 1988 Education Reform Act contained elements of both old and new thinking, reflecting the differences of ideology within the Conservative Party between the hard-right 'free marketeers' and the more traditional 'centralizers'. The contradictions inherent in the legislation will be worked out during the 1990s and it is impossible to tell which element will gain the upper hand, that is to say whether as we approach the twenty-first century the English and Welsh public education system will be highly centralized or largely privatized.

Or, as some fear as the worst option, there will be a privatized and successful middle-class sector supported by both public and private funds, alongside a remnant public sector 'educating' an under-class.

One of the most interesting aspects of the Ruskin speech was the way that it released not only a political agenda for change, but also the professional agenda which had been suppressed by the inertia of the formal, academic traditions and the vested interests they had accreted. Once it had been agreed to discuss curriculum more openly and admit new 'stakeholders', once the Taylor Committee,[4] appointed by the Labour government, had suggested broadening membership of school governing bodies, once the connection between education and the world of work had been accepted, and once it had been admitted that new forms of education required new forms of teaching and assessment, then a good deal of the professional–administrative debate of the previous decade or so surfaced and found a favourable tide. It seems unlikely that the changes wrought in the 1980s could have been so profound had not this coincidence occurred.

By the mid-1950s it had been accepted in professional circles that the 'explosion of knowledge', which forced greater selectivity and yet more attention to principles rather than 'facts' into the school curriculum, and the changing social structure and mores of the UK, had made the curriculum problematic. Once 'secondary education for all' (after 1972 until age 16) was actually attempted, whether in divided or comprehensive systems, it became even more urgent to find new ways of teaching old knowledge as well as new knowledge and skills appropriate for the changed social and economic structure. A month before the Ruskin speech, the foundations were laid for the joint HMI–LEA secondary curriculum 11–16 project, which produced a series of influential reports from 1977 to 1983.[5] The notion of a broad and balanced curriculum, diversified according to individual pupil need, coherent as received by the pupil, and progressing in a planned way through time is reflected in much professional writing, including the HMI documents of the 1980s, in *Better Schools*,[6] and in the opening section of the 1988 Reform Act. This stream of thinking had wide support beyond the profession. For example, in 1978 a number of figures from public life had signed the manifesto 'Education for Capability'. This argued that,

There is a serious imbalance in Britain today in the full process which is described by the two words 'education' and 'training' ... [which] is harmful to individuals, to industry and to society. A well-balanced education should, of course, embrace analysis and the acquisition of knowledge. But it must also include the exercise of creative skills, the competence to undertake and complete tasks and the ability to cope with everyday life; and also doing all these things in cooperation with others.[7]

Such 'practical' opinions had support from research into the psychology of learning, where the notion, prevalent in the inter-war period, that there were two kinds of intelligence and there-fore of people, the academic and the practical, had been super-seded. Thus the intellectual and economic basis had been laid for a common form of schooling and one that required a more open, practical, and co-operative approach from educators. The move-ment towards a redrawn secondary school curriculum (closer in ethos to the primary school) and towards closer links between education and the world of work received a boost from an unexpected quarter in 1982. At the initiative of David (later Lord) Young, then chairman of the Manpower Services Commis-sion, and the Prime Minister, but without the prior involvement of officials in the DES, the Technical and Vocational Education Initiative was announced. This was to apply to the age group 14–18, whether in schools or further education. It provided addi-tional money specifically to achieve such objectives as work experience, the teaching of technology, and new forms of active learning. At first much of the education establishment was uneasy. It seemed a narrowly conceived vocational intrusion by a non-educational department of state. Moreover it was to be managed in a new way through LEAs contracting with the MSC to deliver against predetermined criteria. But the early experience of teachers, at a time when schools were suffering reductions in budgets over and above the losses due to falling rolls, was that the new money could fund equipment and extra teachers which could be used to realize many of the objectives of the suppressed agenda of broader and more active learning. For most schools there was no novelty in forming links with industry or encouraging the use of computers, but it was unusual to be funded to do so. Without waiting for the formal evaluation reports from the pilot schemes the government decided to extend TVEI to all students 14–18 at a cost between 1985 and 1995 of £900 million. This process was well under way when plans for the national curriculum were announced by the DES. The subject-defined national curriculum could be at odds with an approach which relies on the promotion of economic awareness, active and cooperative learning, and technology across the curriculum as well as for its own sake. In particular TVEI requires schools in an area to work co-operatively, not competitively, and that LEAs should manage the contract. The two departments of state have patched together a joint approach, and the National Curriculum Council is working on 'cross-curricular themes', but it remains notable that an initiative taken as recently as 1982, which seemed so Thatcherite at the time, should have been fighting for its corner only five years later. It illustrates the new political–educational philosophy that has appeared in the third term.

New forms of knowledge and achievement necessitated teaching methods that involved active learning and provided new kinds of motivation (especially as widespread youth unemployment destroyed the traditional reasons for wanting to succeed at school) and the involvement of pupils and teachers together in much of the assessment and recording of what had been learned.[8] Mark Carlisle as Secretary of State in 1980 accepted the need for GCSE; at first Sir Keith Joseph was not convinced, but on learning the arguments he rapidly set the new examination in place. It involves, as well as written examinations, the assessment of pupils' work over time and the opportunity for the examinee to demonstrate his or her level of achievement rather than have it predetermined by curriculum or the examination entered. It contains more elements of criterion-referencing than did GCE.

The new objectives for schooling also required new forms of organization within and between schools. It had become clear that successful curriculum and staff development required a 'whole-school', collegiate, approach. Teachers needed to be able to work as a team as well as being individual practitioners. This has considerable implications for the management of schools and in particular for the role and style of management of the Head. The trend was established from narrow hierarchies to open management among interlocking, often task-centred, groups. This emphasis on the school as the instrument of change was reinforced in the political decisions of the period. The 1980 Education Act required schools to publish a prospectus, the LEA to publish school admission policies, and the election of parent governers. The school was the focus both for the promotion of parents' rights and for greater public accountability. By 1985, Sir Keith Joseph's White Paper summarizing his review of policy for school education was called *Better Schools*. Schools were the focus for improvements in teaching, curriculum, and assessment as well as the unit for parental choice and for maximizing value for money. This approach was strongly projected forward into the 1988 Education Act where there is emphasis on the school as the unit of parental choice in the market-place, as the vehicle for change, and as the unit for financial management and accountability. 'Head teachers and their deputies are the cutting edge of our reforms' (Kenneth Baker, *Daily Mail*, 30 November 1988).

The question of how far resources for education increased or declined in the 1980s is obfuscated by frequent changes in the Rate Support Grant formula,[9] enforced 'efficiency savings', the ratio of resources to declining school rolls, and the introduction of an array of specific government grants for educational purposes. The broad picture which most of those working in the service might accept would be that though resources increased in real terms it was not sufficient to maintain the former level of service. The government's public spending plans for 1988–92 (White Paper, January 1989) state that the rise in real terms since 1979 has been 10 per cent. Alongside this must be set the labour-intensive nature of the service, so that costs rise by a greater index than RPI because wages generally tend so to do. Moreover, as first the primary schools and then the secondary schools experienced falling rolls, so there was unavoidable 'disefficiency' as teachers and buildings could not be shed as quickly as pupils disappeared. Government plans for school closures expected only about 50 per cent of the surplus places to be taken out of use, and this was rarely achieved, since school closures arouse political opposition and often even ministers could not approve LEAs' proposals for closure.

The overall pupil–teacher ratio in schools in England and Wales 'has fallen from 20 : 1 in 1975–76 to 17 : 1 now ... predominantly it is the result of reductions in teacher numbers not having kept pace with the rapid decline in the number of pupils'.[10] This confirms the view, taken in the profession, that the 'improvement' in the PTR, claimed by ministers at various times as a planned betterment in the service, is in fact an accidental effect. Moreover, in conseqence, the additional teachers are not in the places where their services could best be utilized, nor are their skills and experience necessarily those required in the schools where there are vacancies. Hence the paradox of teacher shortage and mismatch in a period of apparently improved pupil–teacher ratios.

The Thatcher decade may therefore be interpreted as one in which fundamental change in educational policy for schools came about through the confluence of many streams: a generalized political and public concern about whether schools were doing their job adequately, a professional concern to further the effectiveness of schooling for all, and a sharp party political determination to raise educational standards but at the same time break 'producer domination' and substitute 'consumer' control and choice. Central government departments took new policy initiatives driven by earmarked funding and the DES ended the period with virtual control over the objectives of a national curriculum and its associated system of attainment targets and testing, the curriculum of initial teacher-training (it had always accredited and struck off teachers), the pay and conditions of service of teachers, and their in-service training. The DES also strengthened its general power over LEAs to determine parental choice of school and whether schools should opt out of LEA control. With the advent of the community charge only 20–25 per cent of local government funding will be raised locally, and the process of the LEAs' conversion from an alternative basis for political initiative (an 'Authority') to virtually an agency of central government will be complete. After the 1988 Education

Act it was no longer possible to regard the schools of an LEA as constituting a 'system', with the LEA having responsibility to manage and plan for them as a system. The atomization of the service into semi-autonomous schools moved the schools towards a free market rather than a planned system. Significantly the same processes, designed to reduce LEA influence, impinge on the Churches—the third partner in the 1944 settlement. It will be equally difficult for the diocesan authorities for voluntary-aided C. of E. and RC schools to plan systematically; and they are equally vulnerable to the possibility of 'their' schools choosing to opt out. None the less, schools will have important relationships with the LEA, over monitoring of standards, financial delegation, appraisal of teachers, publication of information, and so on. Most LEAs appear to be planning robustly to take on their new role of regulators rather than providers.

The introduction of a national curriculum, especially as an 'entitlement' for all, is not a party political issue; it was advocated by the House of Commons Select Committee (1986), and by professionals, as for example in the documents from HMI, *Curriculum 11–16* and *Curriculum 5–16*,[11] as well as by educationalists committed to a common curriculum.[12] Its appeal lies in the promise of further movement towards equality of opportunity. A major concern about the former system was the differential opportunities it offered, whether analysed in terms of race, gender, or class. Differences between LEAs and between schools within them had stubbornly remained. However, a centrally controlled curriculum is at odds with the ideology of the free market, where the stress is upon opportunity, not equality. In a truly free market of schools there could not be any predetermined curriculum, only the various curricula produced as a result of negotiation between parental choices and schools' offerings. If the elements in the 1988 Act which promote the free market prove to be its predominant effect, then a national curriculum will seem increasingly paradoxical and inappropriate. It will become a façade behind which differences multiply.[13] Whereas greater community control, even opting out, might offer greater opportunity to minorities, especially in the inner cities, to have schools more capable of meeting the aspirations of their children, the same process could also create 'ghettoization' as choice comes to be exercised on grounds of social and racial prejudice. It has also been pointed out that once school budgets based on the aggregation of per capita payments are established, it would be a short step to giving the equivalence in monetary value to the parents instead of the schools. In this sense local financial management may become a staging post towards vouchers, the cynosure of the New Right and a policy which Sir Keith Joseph found it impossible to introduce at one step.[14] The question must therefore be whether we shall move not towards a general improvement of schools, but towards a three-tier system made up of independent schools (the existing public and private schools and the City Technology Colleges), public sector schools (both grant maintained and LEA) well enough reinforced by parental choice and voluntary funding, and a third tier, an under-class of schools located in areas of poverty, forced to exist on basic funding and less cushioned than previously by discretionary funding from the LEA. It is questionable whether such an outcome would achieve the government's general objectives of creating a highly educated and trained work-force for the technological society of the future. However, the new assertion of 'standards', testing, and selection might help to re-establish hierarchy and ensure that those enjoying access to power and prosperity as a result of the former selective education system do not have their position or the prospects for their children eroded too quickly. What is interesting for the analyst is how so many of the events of the decade in respect of school education can appear to fit such interpretations, which would be favoured by, say, functionalists or Marxists, while at the same time the triumph of neo-liberalism or at least of determined conservatism is also being proclaimed. The question must be whether the new, authoritarian powers taken by a government dedicated to 'rolling back the frontiers of the state' have been and will be used only in order to regulate a free market in the interests of the consumer; or whether they are a new example of social engineering.

As to the schools and teachers themselves, the new competitiveness between schools is an alien and uncomfortable notion to most. For many years LEAs and teachers have been encouraging the interchange of ideas, equipment, and teachers. If the market and the arrival of new types of school should indeed lead to overt stratification, then one vital and hard-won aspect of the professionalism of teachers in the public domain will have been discarded—apparently without thought for the values thus lost. At the same time, the prospects for an adequate supply of teachers in the 1990s look dim, and plans are being laid for the use of unqualified licensed teachers. The first government to set down national criteria for the training of teachers may also be the first to abandon them. Another, more ironic, consequence of the atomization of the system into competing units is that if they thus become more like public schools, there will be a reprofession-alization of the schools. Those who send their sons and daughters to the independent schools do not generally expect to play a great part in setting the curriculum or helping manage the school; they prefer to let the professionals get on with it and hold the school accountable by its results and reputation.

Such speculation raises the final and most important question, which for the moment must also be the most impenetrable. That is, what fundamental purposes is society expecting its maintained schools to pursue in this new future? The 'consensus' value basis was pluralism. The language of discourse in education has changed profoundly over the decade in question. Education seems to have become more a tool of economic than of social policy. But the question presses in, what ends would be served? 'Maintaining a competitive edge' may seem categorically inferior to earlier aspirations towards a liberal education or greater social justice, or fraternity or even equality. This is a phenomenon known to policy analysts as the reversal of means and ends.[15]

The neo-liberal has a comprehensive answer. The individual choices of those in the market will produce a more satisfactory result than the rational plans of either politicians or bureaucrats. They may lead to greater differences within society, but *all* will be better off, because more wealth will have been created. Individual liberty is the dominant value; what the individual does with wealth and freedom is his or her own affair.

However, that raises a problem that is well known: how do you ensure there is enough 'moral and social glue' to hold together an individualistic society? Are we aiming for a minimalist morality in which you do good (or avoid doing harm) to others only if it is in your own interests (the philosophical problem of deriving moral imperatives from contractarian ethics)? Or are we saying there are other (higher) moral principles that should govern human life? How can the schools avoid, in promoting an enterprise culture, mere social Darwinism? How are we to know, for ourselves as individuals, when enterprise becomes aggression, acquisitiveness greed, individualism selfishness? The Prime Minister gave the General Assembly of the Church of Scotland one answer—the Hobbesian: the unseen country of the spirit grows 'soul by soul', not through social interaction. Douglas Hurd has given another, from the other tradition of Burke and Mill, that 'men and women are social beings'.[16] The problem is an intensely practical one for the schools; teaching cannot avoid being a moral activity. To legislate that school assemblies should be 'broadly Christian' in character is no solution, even for Christians. The philosophy of individualism has contained two different moral teachings and the difference is starkly unresolved in current educational policy. The one, a 'republican individualism' that puts duties along with or before rights, and which, as Kant's moral philosophy demonstrated, is the kind of individualism which is no threat to morality and civic duty; the other, which, though denounced in the nineteenth century, still flourishes and puts rights before duties. 'It treats society as a mere association of individuals who owe nothing to others'.[17] For schools, the question whether they are still to attempt to be moral communities, in which all are treated with equal respect, given equal opportunities for service, but are not all expected to be alike, or whether it is, indeed, to be social Darwinism, may prove the most troublesome problem in the 1990s and Thatcherism's most ambivalent bequest.

Notes

1. Black Papers (1969–77) ed. C. B. Cox, A. E. Dyson (Cox and Rhodes Boyson 1977), Maurice Temple.
2. DES, 'School Education in England—Problems and Initiatives' ('The Yellow Book'), July 1976, 'for official use only'. Quoted TES, 15 Oct. 1976.
3. John H. Bunzel (ed.), Challenge to American Schools: The Case for

Standards and Values (OUP, 1985); I. Shor, *Culture Wars: School & Society in the Conservaive Restoration 1969–84* (Routledge & Kegan Paul, 1986).

4. Taylor Committee, *A New Partnership for Our Schools* (HMSO, 1977) (The Taylor Report).

5. DES, *Curriculum 11–16*, Working Papers by HMI (1977); DES, *Curriculum 11–16* (Supplementary Papers, 1979); DES, *Curriculum 11–16: A Review of Progress* (1981); DES, *Curriculum 11–16: Towards a Statement of Entitlement* (1983).

6. DES, *Better Schools*, Cmnd. 9469 (1985).

7. T. Burgess (ed.), *Education for Capability* (NFER-Nelson, 1986), p. ix.

8. J. R. G. Tomlinson, *Changes in Education* (CRAC Occasional Paper, 1986).

9. T. Travers, 'Finance of Education', in S. Ranson and J. R. G. Tomlinson (eds.), *The Changing Government of Education* (Allen & Unwin, 1986).

10. DES, 'The Supply of Teachers for the 1990s', Note for the Education, Science and Arts Committee of the House of Commons (1988).

11. DES, *Curriculum 11–16*, Working Papers by HMI; DES, *Curriculum 11–16: A Review of Progress*; DES, *Curriculum 11–16: Towards a Statement of Entitlement*; DES, 'The Curriculum from 5–16', HMI series, *Curriculum Matters*, 2 (1985).

12. e.g. M. Arnot (ed.), *Race and Gender: Equal Opportunities Policies in Education* (Pergamon, 1985); A. Kelly, *The Missing Half: Girls and Science Education* (Manchester University Press, 1981); D. Lawton, *Class, Culture and the Curriculum* (Routledge & Kegan Paul, 1975); M. Stone, *The Education of the Black Child in Britain* (Fontana, 1981); J. White, *Towards a Compulsory Curriculum* (Routledge & Kegan Paul, 1973).

13. R. J. Campbell, V. Little, and J. R. G. Tomlinson, *Public Education Policy: The Case Explored*, special issue, *Journal of Education Policy*, 2/4 (Taylor & Francis, 1987); J. R. G. Tomlinson, 'Curriculum and Market: Are they Compatible?', in J. Haviland (ed.), *Take Care Mr. Baker* (Fourth Estate, 1988).

14. Stuart Maclure, *Education Re-formed* (Hodder & Stoughton, 1988).

15. G. Neave, 'Education & Social Policy: Demise of an Ethic or Change of Values?', *Oxford Review of Education*, 14/3 (1988).

16. D. Hurd, in *New Statesman*, 27 Apr. 1988; Martin Hollis, 'Atomic Energy and Moral Glue', paper given 15 Oct. 1988 to the conference 'The Philosopher's Eye', organized by Cheshire LEA, Warwick University Institute of Education, and the Royal Institute of Philosophy.

17. Hollis, op, cit.

Further references

Hirschman, A. O., *Exit, Voice and Loyalty: Responses to Decline in Organisations and States* (OUP, 1970).

Ranson, S., and Tomlinson, J. R. G. (eds.), *The Changing Government of Education* (Allen & Unwin, 1986).

Schools Council, *Schools Council Report 1970/71* (Evans/Methuen Educational, 1971).

SKIDELSKI, R., *Thatcherism* (Chatto & Windus, 1988).

TOMLINSON, J. R. G., *The Schools Council: A Chairman's Salute & Envoi* (Schools Council, 1981).

——— 'Public Education, Public Good', *Oxford Review of Education*, 12/3 (1986).

WARNOCK, M., *A Common Policy for Education* (OUP, 1988).

15

Higher Education

PETER SCOTT

Three different, and apparently contradictory, accounts are available of the impact of Mrs Thatcher's ten years in government on higher education. The first is a story of the radical modernization of an inward and anachronistic academic system—in a word, reform. The second is a story of the evolution, although in a more abrasive form, of trends in higher education policy that go back to the 1960s or even the 1940s—in a word, continuity. The third is a story of the retreat from the populist ambitions of post-war Britain, the abandonment of the liberal agenda prepared by the Robbins Committee and revised by Mr Anthony Crosland in the binary policy a generation ago—in a word, reaction. The difficulty with measuring the 'Thatcher effect' on higher education is that all three accounts contain important elements of truth.

The government's policies towards higher education in the Thatcher decade are best divided into four phases: first, immobility; second, crisis; third, consolidation; and fourth, reform or, depending on political taste, reaction. When the Conservatives came to power in 1979 they had no settled policy on universities and polytechnics, but they were determined to curb public expenditure. Talk of introducing 'vouchers', which students would be free to 'spend' at the institutions of their choice, so creating an internal market in higher education, was still confined to the right-wing fringe of the party. Their main proponent, Dr Rhodes Boyson, who was appointed junior minister responsible for higher education, failed to persuade either of the first two Secretaries of State, Mr Mark Carlisle and Sir Keith (now Lord) Joseph, to adopt this radical course. Instead they were largely content with the binary framework established in the Harold Wilson years. Their broad aims were the same as those of

Mrs Shirley Williams, their Labour predecessor—to modernize the University Grants Committee system, which had been severely tested by the collapse of arm's-length quinquennial planning during the inflation and retrenchment of the 1970s; and to develop the means for the effective national co-ordination of the work of the polytechnics and colleges, but without altering their status as part of local authority education. Indeed in the first eighteen months of Conservative rule, although there was little change of direction, there seemed to be a loss of momentum on both fronts. Mr Carlisle promised the universities 'level funding', which took off some of the pressure to reform. And he abandoned the tentative initiative to co-ordinate the work of the polytechnics and colleges which had been begun by the Labour junior minister Mr Gordon Oakes.

It was the desire and, after the inexorable growth of mass unemployment with its insatiable demands on social security, the need to curb public expenditure that forced the government to review its higher education policies. An early indication of this mounting pressure was the decision to charge overseas students 'full cost' fees, in the hope that the burden on the Treasury could be reduced. In the short term this decision led to serious financial instability in many universities (polytechnics and colleges were better protected from this turbulence because they were sheltered by local government). In the medium term the government was obliged, largely by diplomatic and commercial pressures, to reintroduce subsidies for overseas students, although these were no longer indiscriminate but targeted on selected groups of students. In the long term the policy worked, in the sense that most institutions were able by the aggressive recruitment of fee-paying students from overseas to recover the income they lost in 1979–80. But doubts persist about whether, in the even longer term, this policy may not have undermined once high academic standards.

The second phase, that of crisis, quickly followed. The financial squeeze on higher education became acute in the autumn of 1980 when Mrs Thatcher appeared successfully to overcome the objections of her more liberally minded Cabinet colleagues to deep cuts in public expenditure. As a result Mr

Carlisle's promise of 'level funding' was abandoned and a 15 per cent cut over three years agreed. In a confidential memorandum the UGC warned that cuts on that scale and at that speed would lead to serious diseconomy. But the warning was ignored. In July 1981 the UGC accordingly made public its distribution of the much reduced grant. The explosion of dismay that followed was intensified by two further UGC decisions. First, the committee's distribution was highly selective; some universities, like Bath and York, suffered no cut in their grant; others, like Aston and Salford, had their allocations cut by up to 40 per cent. Second, the UGC also reduced the recommended intake of students—partly to protect the already battered unit of resource and to safeguard the universities' shrinking research base; partly because the Treasury, which was not prepared to allow higher enrolments that would lead to increased public expenditure on fees and grants, left the committee with no choice. When it became clear subsequently that the government was unable to limit enrolment, because the displaced students simply flowed into the polytechnics and colleges, where numbers could not be controlled, the UGC was heavily criticized for limiting access. But only with hindsight.

The dramatic events of the summer of 1981 were the start of a lengthy period of financial instability, which for some universities has been prolonged throughout the Thatcher decade. The collapse of universities was only avoided when the government agreed to put back some of the money it had taken out of the system, under the guises of a 'restructuring fund' (to compensate lecturers who could no longer be paid) and a 'new blood' scheme, a limited initiative to recruit younger lecturers to avoid the complete sclerosis of the academic profession. This initiative was repeated in the late 1980s. In 1981 the government's policy towards polytechnics and colleges also went into spasm; it lurched from apparent immobility to premature radicalism and then settled back to modest reform. After abandoning the Oakes initiative the Department of Education and Science dawdled for more than a year. Then it conceived a plan to separate the polytechnics and colleges from local authority education entirely. When it was prematurely revealed, leading Conservatives in local

government persuaded Mrs Thatcher to overrule the DES.
Instead a compromise was reached. The polytechnics and colleges continued to be maintained by local authorities but a
National Advisory Body was established to undertake national
planning of this locally managed system. Unlike the UGC the
NAB was a representative body with an unwieldy two-tier
structure. But it seemed to work. The local authorities—not yet
pariahs in the eyes of the Prime Minister—felt their honour had
been satisfied and were content with the new NAB arrangements;
the polytechnics and colleges felt their institutional maturity had
at last begun to be recognized and looked on the NAB constitution as the first step towards a more complete independence. In
both sectors, therefore, the crisis of the early 1980s was, if not
resolved, at any rate domesticated.

The third phase, that of consolidation, occupied the middle
years of the decade. The direst threats to the viability of the
weaker universities had been lifted. The implicit agreement that
no university would be allowed to close was translated in 1986
into an explicit promise by Mr Kenneth Baker, the new Secretary
of State. The promise was honoured when next year University
College Cardiff was rescued from bankruptcy, although the
delinquent institution effectively forfeited its former independence by being forced into an unwelcome merger. In order to
help universities cope with financial austerity and to reassure the
government that they were tightly managed, the vice-chancellors
established the Jarratt inquiry into university efficiency.[1] A
similar inquiry into good management practice in polytechnics
and colleges was commissioned by the NAB.[2]

A chastened UGC now worked more closely with the DES,
prompting fears that it no longer acted as buffer between universities and government. Its new chairman, Sir Peter Swinnerton-
Dyer, welcomed frequent contact with ministers and civil
servants, which his predecessor Sir Edward Parkes and earlier
chairmen had shunned. The reform of the UGC system, tentatively begun in the mid-1970s but interrupted first by the
immobility of the incoming Conservative government and then
by the crisis of 1981–2, was resumed with renewed purpose. The
old pattern of funding was modernized; grants for teaching and

research were separated, with the former linked explicitly to planned student numbers and the latter to the UGC's own controversial assessments of the standing of departments. A series of subject reviews was commissioned to rationalize and strengthen courses, teams, and departments, most conspicuously in earth sciences, physics, chemistry, and veterinary science but perhaps more successfully in some arts subjects.[3]

For the polytechnics, without question, and the colleges, more debatably, the mid-1980s were a period of forward-looking development. The number of their students grew rapidly until in 1987 it surpassed the universities' total in terms of full-time equivalents. Although unit costs fell by 20 per cent during the decade, these institutions suffered no serious budget cuts (partly because some continued to be subsidized, or 'topped-up', by their local authorities). The NAB began to unravel the tangled web of polytechnic and college funding. After several attempts it produced an allocation formula that was, approximately, rational. The NAB also developed policies to encourage more students to study, or switch to, science and engineering (in particular information technology). Like the UGC, and sometimes in partnership with it, the NAB also become embroiled in the rationalization of courses and departments, although perhaps with less success because academic intelligence was not so well developed in the polytechnic and college sector. In the case of town and country planning and architecture there were nasty political rows, while the DES refused to relax its grip on teacher education. But when it celebrated its fifth birthday at the beginning of 1987 the NAB was justly proud of how much it had achieved in its short life.[4]

However, although in the mid-1980s both the UGC and the NAB pursued active, and generally positive, policies and although the universities got on top of the worst of their financial troubles and the polytechnics flourished, a coherent national policy failed to develop. The privately funded Leverhulme inquiry between 1981 and 1983 helped to stimulate debate about the possible shape of a post-Robbins (and post-Crosland) higher education, a system designed to meet the needs of the 1990s.[5] This debate was carried forward by both the UGC and the NAB, which in 1984 presented the DES with their considered views of the future of higher education based on widespread consultation with their respective sectors.[6] But the DES's Green Paper next year was greeted with disappointment.[7] Instead of carrying the debate on further, its effect was to stifle it in recriminations about short-sighted philistinism. The DES, and Sir Keith himself, were upset by the critical reception of the Green Paper. It seemed to them that higher education was repudiating the *rapprochement* that had followed the 1981–2 crisis. Oxford University's refusal to award Mrs Thatcher an honorary degree seemed to confirm the breakdown of trust between the politicians and the dons, although the more lurid accounts of the Prime Minister's later revenge on the universities can probably be discounted. The snub no doubt was felt more keenly by her supporters than by Mrs Thatcher herself. On the other side the government's academic critics felt the period of consolidation in the mid-1980s had not been accompanied by a recovery of a wider vision of the reworked purposes of higher education. The binary structure, in all its rigidity and inequity, had been maintained. Questions about the impact of demographic decline on student enrolment in the 1990s had been left unanswered. And, despite the series of urgent reports on the state of science, the decaying dual-support system for university research had been neither repaired nor reformed.

The beginning of the fourth phase, that of radical reform, coincided with the arrival of Mr Baker as Secretary of State. A puzzled and intense thinker was replaced by a confident and articulate politician. The new Secretary of State was never likely to tolerate the weakening of the thrust to reform, which was how critics of higher education saw the period of consolidation. In any case the reform of schools was an important issue in the general election campaign that led to Mrs Thatcher's third victory. A major education Bill, to recast the 1944 Act in Thatcherite terms, was promised. Higher education could not hope to be ignored in any comprehensive package of reforms. Within a year of taking office Mr Baker published a White Paper that proposed the radical reconstruction of the higher education system.[8] In the subsequent Education Reform Act both the UGC and the NAB were abolished, to be replaced by the Universities Funding

Council and the Polytechnics and Colleges Funding Council. The new councils took over in April 1989 with part-time chairmen and full-time chief executives. At least half their members were drawn from outside higher education, unlike the UGC which had a largely academic membership and the NAB which was a representative body. The polytechnics and colleges were removed from local authority control and established as separate corporations. Both they and the universities were no longer to be funded by 'grants', which suggested to ministers an unhealthy entitlement to public funds, but by 'contracts', which implied a welcome reciprocity. Finally academic tenure was abolished in universities. Commissioners were dispatched to amend their statutes accordingly.

But the Act was not the only expression of the government's new enthusiasm for reform. Four other developments were important in this fourth phase. First, movement towards a more open system with wider access was resumed after the stagnation and even regression that had marked Mrs Thatcher's first two terms as Prime Minister. The White Paper envisaged a rise in the age participation index (the proportion of young people going on to higher education) from 14 to 18 per cent. In a speech at Lancaster University in January 1989 Mr Baker even talked of a mass system enrolling up to a third of the relevant population in the next century. Second, Conservative ministers encouraged a right-leaning debate about alternative methods of funding the present system and paying for future expansion. One option was vouchers, no longer an exclusive device of the free-market right. Traditional Tories and even liberals also dabbled with the idea, in the belief that enhanced student choice might curb the growing power of the government over higher education.[9] The other was to encourage, or order, institutions to charge more for tuition. As higher tuition need not necessarily be fully covered by local authority fees students would be forced to contribute their own resources. The principle of free higher education would be abandoned. Lord Chilver, the UFC chairman, supported such a change. He suggested that a student's willingness to contribute should supersede, or at any rate supplement, the Robbins principle which stated that entry to higher education should be determined solely by ability and attainment.[10] Although the government did not offer Lord Chilver explicit support, ministers also hoped that the notion of higher education as a private investment rather than a public right would take hold. Closely linked to this debate about funding institutions was the DES's plan to reform student support. A second White Paper proposed that the universal system of student grants introduced following the Anderson Report in 1962 should be phased out and replaced by loans.[11]

Third, respect among Conservative politicians for higher education's liberal pieties rapidly dwindled. The government's ideological project became more coherent. What had begun as a series of scattered raids against isolated institutions—the former Social Science Research Council, the Open University, the Polytechnic of North London—became a concerted campaign against what ministers took to be the anti-entrepreneurial mentality in which higher education, and in particular the universities, were steeped. An 'Enterprise in Higher Education' initiative was launched and Lord Chilver emphasized the need to make even history 'relevant'. The final development in this reform phase was different. For once the government failed to act. As in the preceding consolidation phase, it shrank from a bold remodelling of the system. In 1987 the Advisory Board for the Research Councils recommended a rearrangement of higher education. Institutions would be divided into three categories—'R' for those with a comprehensive research mission; 'X' for those with a research capability only in selected fields; and 'T' for those dedicated predominantly to teaching.[12] But the government shied away from the plan. A stratification of higher education along Californian lines, although it would have modernized the creaking binary structure, smelt too strongly of central planning. A three-tier system would have been difficult to reconcile with the competitive regime envisaged by ministers; it would have provoked determined opposition from down-graded institutions; and its implementation would have presented intractable technical difficulties. Nevertheless, the episode clearly marked out the limits of the government's radicalism and its lack of a strategic vision.

In this tangled history of higher education under Mrs Thatcher four trends can be picked out, although not all are directly attributable to the 'Thatcher effect'. The first was the reduction in public expenditure, the cuts that seem to sum up higher education's common experience over the past decade. In the universities the cuts were severe; in the polytechnics and colleges less so. But because of the rapid growth in student numbers outside the universities the funding gap between the two sectors actually widened. It was the cuts that, perhaps unintentionally, provoked the crisis of 1981–2 which undermined the Robbins–Crosland settlement reached in the 1960s. It was the cuts that forced institutions to operate as business rather than as academic enterprises. It was the cuts that led to the closure of departments and the rationalization of subjects. It was the cuts that allowed the government, under the guise of value-for-money accountability, to extend its political control over the system.

On their side Conservative ministers deployed three arguments. The first, more popular in the early 1980s under Keith Joseph, was that universities and, to a lesser extent, polytechnics and colleges were flabby institutions which could be made much more effective by a good dose of 'efficiency'-enhancing austerity. The second, more popular later when Mr Baker took over, was that the cuts, if any, had been slight in terms of the system's total income. This improbable conclusion was supported by the statistical sleight-of-hand at which late-Thatcher Whitehall had become adept, although this was difficult to reconcile with the admission by Robert Jackson, the responsible junior minister, in a private paper to ministerial colleagues in the summer of 1988 that the best universities faced the prospect of 'progressive degradation'. Ministers even brandished international comparisons which claimed to prove that Britain already spent a much higher proportion of its gross national product on higher education than most other European countries. By such devices the cuts were made, almost, to disappear—except, of course from the remembered experience of higher education teachers.[13] The third argument was that any government, even a left-leaning one, would have been forced to make similar cuts. In one sense this was fair. Higher education's troubles began not in 1979 but in 1976 when the Labour government changed course. In another sense it was beside the point. Perhaps things might not have been better under another government, but could they have been worse? The impact of the 'Thatcher effect' on the level of public support for higher education is difficult to argue away.

The second trend was that, against the odds, the system continued to expand. In Mrs Thatcher's third term Britain had more students than ever before. But whether this outcome was engineered, or even desired, by the government was doubtful. When the Conservatives came to power in 1979, many still suspected that the recent expansion of higher education had led to an erosion of academic quality. As the party of high standards they were in no mood to encourage further growth. They were the heirs of the 'more means worse' brigade that had opposed Robbins a generation before. This preoccupation with quality persisted, although from the mid-1980s it was diverted away from general opposition to expansion into particular concern about bad teaching (where, of course, it merged with the Conservative attack on 'left-wing' social science). Nor was the DES in an expansionary mood at the end of the 1970s. Civil servants were mesmerized by gloomy projections of future student demand. So when the UGC in 1981 decided to cut student intakes, neither the department nor its ministers objected. Indeed there was concern about their inability to discourage an inflow of displaced students into the polytechnics.

This restrictive attitude did not change until the mid-1980s, when actual student enrolments began regularly to outstrip earlier projections. The growth of higher education clearly was the product of sweeping secular changes which governments of whatever political persuasion had little power to influence. The higher education surge of the 1980s probably owed much to the comprehensive reorganization of secondary schools in the 1960s which many Conservatives had opposed. The government was carried along by this tide of deeper social and educational change. But their driving down of unit costs, particularly in the polytechnics which became the engines of the new expansion, did help. These productivity gains undermined the Treasury's opposition to growth. In retrospect Mrs Thatcher's ten years in office may come to be regarded as the time when higher education, at long last, abandoned the gold standard. When she became Prime Minister Britain still had an élite system. A decade later this was no longer the case. How this historic change will be interpreted, of course, is not yet clear—the destruction of high academic excellence, as Keith Joseph may have secretly feared and the government's critics, expecially in the science community, openly charged, or the growing pains of a more popular system, as Kenneth Baker believed (and his liberal enemies secretly hoped?). To some extent this primary question was obscured by a secondary issue misleadingly presented by ministers. This was whether Britain should follow the European or the American path to mass higher education. The suggested contrast, of course, was between a state-directed and a market-driven system and the implied conclusion that, by choosing the latter, wider access could be achieved without substantially increasing public expenditure. But higher education in the United States, although more heterodox than in Europe, is largely (and massively) tax-supported.

The third trend was the subordination of the universities to the commands of the state. The abolition of the UGC, that celebrated buffer so much admired by foreign observers, was a dramatic episode. It seemed to break the old concordat between academic and polity, to shatter university autonomy, and to deny the universities' claim, as an estate of the nation, to enjoy a special relationship with government. But to attribute these changes solely to the 'Thatcher effect' is wrong. The UGC had already ceased to be a discreetly donnish body charged with passing on to the universities as inconspicuously as possible grants made available by the state. Already in the 1950s and 1960s it had begun to plan the university system in outline. In the 1970s it dug into detail. And in the 1980s, of course, it came to determine most important aspects of university policy. Over a similar period the UGC lost its arm's-length privileges within Whitehall. Long before Mrs Thatcher came to power the university sector had ceased to be a loose-knit club of autonomous institutions and had become a coherent system supervised by the state.

Only in three subsidiary ways did the Conservative government influence the course that had already been set. First, ministers were irritated by the universities' apparent unwilling-ness, or inability, to adapt quickly enough to the new 1980s demands for efficiency and relevance. This they attributed, perhaps unfairly, to the universities' links with a stuffy 'social democratic' Establishment determined to thwart the radical intentions of the Prime Minister. Second, the government having decided to undertake the wholesale reform of education, the universities inevitably became embroiled. They could not be left out. But if there had been no Education Reform Act the pace of change might have been slower and its aim more oblique. Third, the Act made explicit what previously had been implicit in the evolving relations between universities and the state. When these came to be described in statutory terms they inevitably acquired a specific rigour that was new. In these minor ways the 'Thatcher effect' accelerated the subordination of the universities to the state. But this had been foreshadowed long before the Conservatives came to power.

The fourth trend was the nationalization of the polytechnics and major colleges, a process that was completed in the Thatcher period. But, as with the subordination of universities to state power, it had deeper roots. The post-war Percy Report on technical education first recognized that a significant number of advanced courses would have to be provided outside the universities. The 1956 White Paper created the colleges of advanced technology, so affirming that these courses were too important to be left solely to the discretion of local authorities. The 1966 White Paper, although it left the newly created polytechnics under local authority management, confirmed that non-university higher education could not be treated as simply a local affair. Efforts were made in the 1970s to strengthen the national framework for the polytechnics and colleges, most notably the Oakes initiative. So, before the Conservatives came to power, the slow but sure differentiation of the polytechnics and major colleges from the mass of local authority further education, the concentration of this advanced sector in large comprehensive institutions of university size (and character?), and the dissolution of their ties with local government had been under way for many years. The creation of the NAB in 1982 was just another stage on this long march. The ambiguous character of this new agency was announced in its original title—the *National*

Advisory Body for *local* authority higher education.

The replacement of the NAB by the PCFC seven years later was not, therefore, a sharp turn of policy. Rather it was the culmination of forty years of creeping nationalization. Nor was the incorporation of the polytechnics and major colleges a sudden rupture with the local authority past. The NAB itself had recommended a similar enfranchisement in its 1979 good management practice report. But there were two new factors that encouraged the government to go faster and further. The first was its increasing hostility to local government where welfarist values and corporatist practices seemed to be entrenched. At a time when local authorities were being stripped of one function after another it would have been surprising if they had clung on to advanced further education, already one of their most peripheral responsibilities. The second was the rapid expansion of the polytechnics and colleges during the 1980s which made their old dependent status seem increasingly anomalous. During the decade they became the government's favourite higher education institutions, a strange fate for Labour's populist alternative to the liberal university. But in Conservative eyes the polytechnics were more efficient, because they had lower unit costs, and more relevant, because they seemed to have fewer inhibitions about enterprise than the universities.

The 'Thatcher effect' on higher education is difficult to weigh up, even when the detailed impact of the government's various policies on the system has been discussed. One reason, no doubt, is the nature of 'Thatcherism' itself. Although clearly an ideological project in the sense that its aim is to overturn the post-war social settlement, it is more a set of attitudes than a collection of coherent policies. It is a way of doing things, brisk, unreflective, even abrasive, as much as a clearly articulated programme. In some policy fields this absence of a sustained strategy is not so serious. The government's purpose is limited to creating the conditions in which free competition can thrive. Events and outcomes will be shaped by the market, not by the government. Something of this rhetoric has seeped into higher education policy. The universities and polytechnics, we are told, have not been subordinated to the new funding councils but have been freed to pursue their own enterprising destinies. But it is not an especially convincing claim. The practice of higher education is far too close to notions of our nation's culture and grandeur to be left to an agnostic and amoral market. The interests of nation and state are too closely tied up in the academic system for it to be likely that any government will, or should, leave it alone.

So the choice between the three accounts of the 'Thatcher effect' on higher education remains—reform, continuity, or reaction? According to the first account the antique constitution that governed higher education has been rewritten; the inner practices of the system modernized; and the ice of the old academic tradition has begun to break up. A blow against intellectual aristocracy has been struck. According to the second the policies of the Thatcher government, as of the Callaghan, Heath, Wilson, and all post-war governments, have flowed with higher education's *longue durée*. The two essential elements in this have been the subordination of the universities to the commands of the democratic state, and the nationalization of the polytechnics and colleges despite the claims of local particularism. According to the third account the Conservatives have tried to turn back the liberal tide that has flowed so powerfully through British society, and especially education, since the nineteenth century. More particularly Mrs Thatcher's government has attempted to curb the radical potential of a university system that had grown too big to be controlled by a donnish great and good, and of a polytechnic and college system with open frontiers to further and adult education. Otherwise there could be no guarantee that the universities would serve the interests of the national élite, whether 'Thatcherite' or 'social democratic', and that the whole idea of higher education would not be swallowed up in populist post-secondary education. In other words the government acted to preserve crucial intellectual and social hegemonies. In the end none of these accounts is convincing by itself. Perhaps the safest assessment of the 'Thatcher effect' on higher education is that her government pursued conventional policies by radical means and with reactionary intentions.

Notes

1. Committee of Vice-Chancellors and Principals, *Report of the Steering Group on University Efficiency* (1985).
2. National Advisory Body, *Report of the Working Group on Good Management Practice* (1987).
3. University Grants Committee, *The Future of University Physics* and *University Chemistry: The Way Forward* (HMSO, 1988).
4. National Advisory Body, *Policies and Achievements* (1988).
5. Society for Research into Higher Education, *Excellence and Diversity* (1983).
6. University Grants Committee, *A Strategy for Higher Education into the 1990s* (HMSO, 1984); National Advisory Body, *A Strategy for Higher Education in the Late 1980s and Beyond* (1984).
7. Department of Education and Science, *The Development of Higher Education into the 1990s* (HMSO, 1985).
8. Department of Education and Science, *Higher Education: Meeting the Challenge* (HMSO, 1987).
9. John Barnes and Nicholas Barr, *Strategies for Higher Education: The Alternative White Paper* (Aberdeen University Press, 1988).
10. 'The Chilver Principle', interview in *The Times Higher Education Supplement*, 10 Oct. 1988.
11. Department of Education and Science, *Top-up Loans for Students* (HMSO, 1988).
12. Advisory Board for the Research Councils, *A Strategy for the Science Base* (HMSO, 1987).
13. In a Market and Opinion Research International (MORI) poll conducted on behalf of *The Times Higher Education Supplement* in June 1987, 84% of university and polytechnic teachers agreed with the statement 'Cuts in higher education have reduced opportunities to enter universities and polytechnics, undermined the quality of teaching and research and produced chaos in many institutions.'

16

Housing and the Environment

ALAN MURIE

The years since 1979 have been ones of significant change in housing and the environment. There has been more legislation concerned with housing than in any equivalent period—and more is in the pipeline. New legislation and controls on housing finance have involved a greater role for central government and conflicts with local government. And in 1989 the housing debate and the housing situation are different from 10 years before. Home ownership is significantly higher, and the rented sectors have been in decline for some years. High house prices and the gains made through home ownership are more prominent features of debate, but so are affordability problems and homelessness. The problems associated with inner cities and high-rise housing estates are no less apparent. The level of new investment in housing is considerably lower while the housing finance system remains little different from what Anthony Crosland, when Secretary of State for the Environment between 1974 and 1976, referred to as a 'dog's breakfast'.

When the Conservative government was elected in 1979 housing public expenditure had already been trimmed back (from 1976) and new local authority building was in decline. The support and encouragement of home ownership was already well established in financial and legislative arrangements developed by Labour governments as well as Conservative. The preoccupation of post-war policy-makers with housing shortage and slum clearance had already given way to an emphasis on the need to develop locally sensitive housing strategies. New (1977) legislation on homelessness involved new responsibilities, and a clearer focus on those in greatest need, for local authorities whose role in housing was already changing. With the long-established decline of private renting local authorities were housing an increasing proportion of the poorest sections of the population and a social polarization between home ownership and council housing was already significant.

POLICY INTENTIONS

The Conservative manifesto of 1979 had placed considerable emphasis on housing. Under the heading 'Helping the Family' housing received one and a half pages—more than social security or health and welfare or education. The emphasis in the manifesto was on home ownership and on tax cuts, lower mortgage rates, and special schemes to make purchase easier. More prominent than anything else in this approach was the sale of council houses and the commitment to provide a legal right to buy, backed by larger discounts to reduce purchase price and mortgages to enable such purchase to go ahead. New short-hold and assured tenancies were also to be introduced to allow short, fixed-term lettings to make better use of the existing stock of houses and of empty houses in the private sector.

On taking office the government quickly set about implementing these manifesto commitments. New housing legislation (the Housing Act 1980) was introduced and new general consents enabled local authorities to sell council houses on the same terms ahead of this being enacted. The 1980 Housing Act was the first of a series. It introduced the right to buy and changed the rights of council tenants in other ways. It revised the subsidy system for council housing but did not attempt any more general rationalization of housing finance. Subsequent legislation in 1984, 1986, and 1988 has amended the arrangements for the Right to Buy—increasing discounts and reducing the scope for local variation in implementation. The 1989 Local Government and Housing Bill involves another revision of the subsidy system for council housing—but not more generally. Neither system has represented an attempt to resolve the widely acknowledged anomalies in housing finance.

This continuous interventionist legislative programme has had a direct impact on the housing situation. But new legislation does not operate in a vacuum. The impact of the legislation has been affected by parallel changes especially relating to public expenditure. Just as importantly it has been affected by changes in house prices, interest rates, inflation, unemployment, and the general economic environment.

TABLE 16.1. *Principal housing and related legislation of the Conservative governments 1979–1989*

Year	Title
1980	Housing Act
1980	Local Government Planning and Land Act
1982	Social Security and Housing Benefit Act
1984	Housing and Building Control Act
1984	Housing Defects Act
1985	Housing Act
1985	Housing Associations Act
1986	Building Societies Act
1986	Housing and Planning Act
1986	Social Security Act
1988	Housing Act
1989	Local Government and Housing Bill

PUBLIC EXPENDITURE AND CAPITAL RECEIPTS

The most striking changes in policy outputs relate to overall public expenditure on housing and to council house sales. Throughout the period housing has been the spending area achieving the largest cuts in expenditure. In real terms the public expenditure planning total for housing has fallen from £7.3 billion to £1.9 billion.[1] Housing has consistently spent less than anticipated especially because estimates of the capital receipts generated by council house sales have been consistently low. The position has been best illustrated over the last year. Public expenditure calculations build in estimates of capital receipts. In 1988/9 the number of council house sales increased but, more importantly, house price increases raised the value of the properties being sold. Consequently the estimates of housing capital

receipts in the Chancellor's autumn statement in 1988 were
£3,801 million compared with the previous estimate for the same
year of £2,077 million.

Since 1980 council house sales have consistently exceeded new
council house building (Fig. 16.1). The share of private financing
of mortages has also risen (from 43 per cent in 1981–2 to 93 per
cent in 1987–8) and added to initial capital receipts. The pressure
to maintain capital receipts from the housing programme has
become a real factor in policy and an influence on the development of new approaches to privatization and demunicipalization
which have less evident consumer support than sales to sitting
tenants have. Thus the more recent measures to encourage sales
of estates, the development of Housing Action Trusts, and the
early ballots of tenants relating to change of landlord have all
showed strong tenant resistance.

HOUSING CHANGES

The picture of reduced housing public expenditure has not been
the whole story. Some items not included in the housing public
expenditure total have increased. Most notable in these are tax
reliefs related to housing. Mortage interest tax relief has risen
from £1,639 million in 1979/80 to £5,500 million in 1988/9 and
exemption from capital gains tax had an estimated value of
£2,800 million in 1981/2 and £10,000 million in 1988/9. In
addition the social security costs associated with housing benefits
have increased as rents have risen and reflecting the economic
circumstances of tenants. One effect of policy has been to switch
the cost of housing subsidy to the social security and taxation
system.

What has occurred since 1979 has been a major increase in the
level of support for home owners through the increasing value of
mortgage tax relief, council house sales discounts, and capital
gains tax relief. The extent of these increases has been particularly
affected by house price inflation and the growth of home ownership. Mortgage interest tax relief has grown in volume but for
individual owners and especially those with larger mortgages it
represents a smaller proportion of their costs. It is probably not

TABLE 16.2. *Elements of housing activity in England 1979 and 1989*

	1979–80	1988–9
Growth of home ownership	54%	67%
Sale of council houses (no.)	42,000	150,000
Local authority new building (completions)	67,000	15,000
Renovation of local authority and new town dwellings (no.)	76,000	160,000
House association loan approved (no. of dwellings)	34,500	19,000
Total Exchequer subsidy to local authority housing	£1,258 m.	£520 m.
Mortgage interest tax relief	£1,639 m.	£5,500 m.

Sources: The Government's Expenditure Plans 1989–90 to 1991–92, Cm. 609 (1989); The Government's Expenditure Plans 1985–86 to 1987–88, Cmnd. 9428-II (1985); P. Malpass and A. Murie, Housing Policy and Practice (Macmillan, 1987).

crucial to house purchase decisions and is not well targeted. Nevertheless the contrast between what has happened to home owners and the position of tenants affected by reduced public housing subsidies and downward revision of housing benefits is striking. The issues of equity between tenures are clear.

Other switches in expenditure have occurred. The new-town rented housing programme has effectively been terminated and is a net contributor through capital receipts. Local authorities have switched their energies away from new building and towards rehabilitation of the council stock. Ministers have been enthusiastic about other switches in activity with less justification. Low-cost home ownership initiatives (other than council house sales) have not made a major numerical contribution. The recent enthusiasm for housing association investment must be seen against a backdrop of a decline in new housing association completions from earlier figures. The climate which would encourage private sector development proved insufficient to

FIG. 16.1. Public sector housing: sales and new building
(1977–1988)

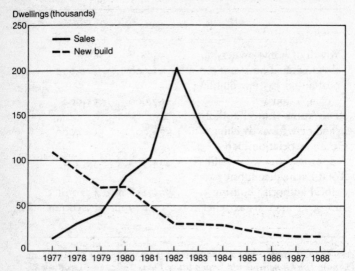

Dwellings (thousands)

Note: Figures refer to local authorities in England and Wales; figures
for 1988 are estimates.

Source: Housing and Construction Statistics.

persuade the private sector to fill the gap in new building left by
reduced public sector building and it has been the high demand
and house prices of the last two years rather than deregulation
which have led to the highest levels of private sector building.
Home improvement grants fluctuated wildly with their temporary release from expenditure control in 1983. While a higher
proportion of local authority new building has been targeted on
dwellings for the elderly and chronically sick and disabled the
actual number of such completions has declined.

COUNCIL HOUSE SALES

Council house sales had matured over a long period and grown
out of local government experience. In 1979 it was seen as an
electorally popular policy which would help to make a reality of
Anthony Eden's dream of a property owning democracy. With

TABLE 16.3. *Proceeds from housing and other privatization 1979–1989 (£m.)*

	Housing[a]	Other[b]
1979–80	472	377
1980–1	603	405
1981–2	1,045	493
1982–3	1,877	488
1983–4	1,958	1,139
1984–5	1,804	2,171
1985–6	1,787	2,707
1986–7	2,132	4,460
1987–8	2,462	5,139
1988–9 (estimated)	3,440	6,100
TOTAL 1979–89	17,580	23,479

[a] Total capital receipts from the housing programme (housing corporation, local authorities, new towns, and central government).
[b] Excludes proceeds from sales of subsidiaries.

Source: The Government's Expenditure Plans 1989–90 to 1991–92, Cm. 621 (1989), p. 33; The Government's Expenditure Plans 1989–90 to 1991–92, Cm. 609 (1989).

over a million sales achieved the policy has been regarded as a success by ministers. Council house sales have also represented the most significant act of privatization carried out in the period. The sales of British Gas, British Telecommunications, and British Petroleum have in later years led other privatization to exceed housing privatization proceeds in any one year. Taking the period 1979–89 as a whole housing has accounted for 43 per cent of the total of these privatization proceeds (Table 16.3).

The actual level of capital receipts generated through housing have been affected by changes in house prices. Initially however they relate to the rate of council house sales. Sales have fluctuated over time and have varied considerably from place to place. Central government's interventions through legislation and finance are not sufficiently sensitive to local or other circumstances to orchestrate the outcomes. While central government has taken steps which have expanded home ownership generally it has not been able to control or achieve a uniform pattern of change. Other factors have meant that sales have been much higher in the South and East and lowest in the North and Inner London. In England, by June 1988, 15 local authorities had sold 30 per cent of their stock or more (since 1979) (Table 16.4). None of these were in the Northern region, Yorkshire and Humberside, the West Midlands, the North West, or Inner London. Sales were highest in shire districts where the housing stock included fewest flats and where home ownership rates were already high. In contrast there were 21 local authorities recording below 10 per cent of their stock sold. Ten of these were London boroughs and the others were mainly but not only metropolitan districts. Analysis of the pattern of sales suggests that rather than political control it is property valuation, dwelling type (flats rather than houses), and local economic circumstances which explain variation.[2]

TABLE 16.4. *Council house sales: local authorities in England reporting sales of 30% and over between 1979 and June 1988*

	%
Havant	34·1
Corby	33·9
Bracknell	33·3
Fenland	32·4
Crawley	32·2
Bromley	31·6
Gedling	31·5
Fareham	31·4
Rochester upon Medway	30·8
Weymouth and Portland	30·5
Wycombe	30·4
Castle Point	30·2
Wealden	30·2
Huntingdonshire	30·1
South Northamptonshire	30·0

Source: DOE statistics.

Throughout the housing programme it is clear that some favourite government schemes have failed to deliver. Others, and council house sales is the clearest example, have produced results which the government regards as a success. Use of subsidy mechanisms to lever rents upwards, increased levels of discount, and, latterly, uncertainties about who the landlord will be have maintained sales. But even in this case government has not been able to orchestrate change in detail. One last housing example makes this position clear. The election manifesto of 1979 and the Housing Act 1980 emphasized reviving the private rented sector. New assured and short-hold tenancies introduced in 1980 were to be the mechanism to do this but they have failed to do so. Further deregulation of private renting in the Housing Act 1988 represents another attempt to revive a declining sector. But few experts think that this is likely and the combination of favourable financial treatment of owner occupation and opportunities for profit taking through sales of properties (especially when house prices are high) is likely to frustrate government's intentions.

NEW AGENCIES, PLANNING, AND INNER CITIES

In both housing and environment central government has looked unfavourably on local authorities. There has been a development of new centrally run agencies or of agencies which are not accountable to local authorities. Estate Action, Housing Action Trusts, Urban Development Corporations, have become important elements in the organization of policy. In each case either expenditure has grown rapidly or, with newer schemes, is planned to do so. The sums involved fall well short of the level of capital receipts from the housing programme. The 1987 conversion of the government to inner city policies has seen expenditure on Urban Development Corporations more than double. The two UDCs set up in 1981 have been followed by four in 1987 and a further four in 1988–9. The longer established Urban Programme has not been so favoured. The experience of the inner cities has arguably been less affected by these high profile interventions than by the effects of economic restructuring and unemployment and by main expenditure programmes—including housing—which have involved changed levels of investment in inner city areas.

Government's preference for bypassing local authorities is also apparent in changes in arrangements for various grant payments relating to inner cities. In these and other ways central government has become more directly involved in scrutiny and supervision of local projects than in the past. Changes in legislation on land and planning were designed to remove constraints on the private sector. Registers of unused and underused land in public ownership, powers for the Secretary of State to direct release of registered land, detailed measures to streamline development control and appeals procedures, and the creation of enterprise zones were all designed to create the climate for private development. One view is that they have created the climate for planning by appeal and have given the Secretary of State more control over local decisions. Anxieties over green belt development, development associated with the Channel tunnel, and the plans of developers to create private new towns in the rural South East have become more prominent. While the government in relation to housing benefits and council housing has attempted to adopt an approach which distances itself from problems and associates itself with successes it has been less successful in achieving this in relation to planning issues.

DISCOVERING ENVIRONMENT

The increased emphasis placed on inner cities since 1987 has been followed by a greater emphasis on environmental protection issues. Ministers assert the continuity of effort in this area. The views of other organizations and earlier responses to the Environment Select Committee do not support this interpretation. A series of speeches and the sponsorship of major international conferences are represented in the media as the greening of Mrs Thatcher and the Conservative Party. Some of the enthusiasm for environmental issues has no doubt arisen in order to make a merit of responses required under European Community legislation. Party competition to capture the green issue has also been a factor. Wider discussion of environmental issues was already apparent not just in relation to nuclear accidents (and Chernobyl) or the damage to the ozone layer but in relation to acid rain, the disposal of radioactive and toxic waste, and the quality of drinking water. The implications both of a wider agenda and of a more active concern for the environment are of increased regulation and control.

The early years of the Thatcher administration saw some continued reductions in air pollution with the decline in industrial output and reduced use of domestic coal. Increased control over the lead content of petrol meant that emissions of lead by petrol-driven vehicles had declined in spite of increased consumption of petrol. But these favourable (mainly unplanned) developments were offset by others. The proportion of sulphur-dioxide emissions accounted for by power stations focused attention upon them. Increased carbon monoxide emissions associated with road transport focused attention on the growth in use of private road vehicles. Anxiety about the impact of acid rain on woodlands and historic buildings related to various sources including the burning of coal, oil, and natural gas, and car exhausts. While water quality had appeared to be improving steadily before 1980 a small increase in the length of poor and bad quality rivers was apparent between 1980 and 1985. Evidence about the cumulative damage to the environment makes the neglect of specific policy initiatives in the early years of the Thatcher administration striking. European community legislation required more rapid improvements than were planned and challenged complacent assumptions over matters such as the quality of drinking water in Britain. The protracted dispute with the EC and other member states over control of substances discharged into water and sewers is generally regarded as evidence of a reluctance to adopt policies which incurred new costs for industry or government.

Steps have latterly been taken to increase expenditure on environmental issues and to adopt a more integrated approach. In April 1987 the establishment of Her Majesty's Inspectorate of Pollution within the Department of the Environment meant a switch from the fragmented system of pollution control and towards the more integrated approach. It meant adopting an

approach urged by the Royal Commission on Environmental
Pollution as long ago as 1976. The new Inspectorate of Pollution
was set up following an efficiency scrutiny by the Cabinet Office
and the persuasive formula of rationalization without increasing
staffing leaves doubts about the adequacy of resources for the
task. Other doubts relate to the focus on industrial pollution and
lack of control over other important sources such as pesticides
and radioactive wastes.

As well as highlighting the need for inspection and regulation
environmental issues raise more direct questions about
established policy approaches in relation to energy, agriculture,
and transport. The growth in the use of private road-vehicles
presents environmental problems as well as leading to congestion
on motorways and other roads. Plans for water and electricity
privatization have both posed problems in relation to pollution.
The electricity industry is resistant to proposals which would
force it to cut down pollution, and privatization will be less
attractive if the industry is faced with an anti-pollution agenda.
Similarly water privatization offers a less attractive proposition if
the control of water standards and other activities is tightened.
How issues about public access for leisure activities, wildlife
protection, water purity, working conditions, customer care,
customer charges, planning and development-related decisions,
and accountability in the water industry are resolved has implications for both the process and proceeds of privatization. The
preoccupations with privatization, contracting out, and adopting
the lowest-cost approaches are not always in harmony with a
concern with the environment which recognizes substantial
indirect and social costs. A reduction of emphasis on energy
conservation and a continuing debate about waste disposal have
raised the same broad concerns about how far the overall policy
approach does represent a coherent package for the environment
as a whole.

After ten years of government the long-term build-up of
environmental damage is more apparent. The failure to invest in
the infrastructure of roads, sewers, and water supply is more
evident and presents a picture of public squalor and declining
standards alongside private affluence. No major programmes for

replacing and rebuilding a declining infrastructure have emerged, and the major new programmes are linked to new development such as the Channel tunnel rather than to renewal. The opportunities created by capital receipts from the sale of land and housing have been used to reduce the Public Sector Borrowing Requirement and to contribute to Public Sector Debt Repayment rather than to invest in housing and the environment. In both housing and the environment changes in the last ten years as well as those now being discussed have the capacity to make a real impact and there will be gainers and losers as a result. Aspects of this are readily apparent in housing. The other side of rapid privatization and the growth of home ownership is homelessness and increasing social divisions. Polarization of housing conditions, of housing subsidies, and of housing opportunities is apparent. The conditions which have enabled privatization to benefit the present generation of tenants—public investment to create a desirable housing stock—are not being maintained or recreated to make the same process possible for the benefit of the next generation. The volatility of the private housing market is no longer cushioned by a relatively stable level of public sector activity and generates real problems for newly forming households, first-time buyers, and lower income households generally—especially in high house price areas. While the expansion of home ownership has been a popular form of privatization it is not clear that demunicipalization or privatization generally is so popular. Indeed the arguments for more public investment for example in rented housing come from Conservative-controlled local authorities, employers affected by housing shortages and costs, and households unable to obtain a home.

Notes

1. *The Government's Expenditure Plans 1989–90 to 1991–92*, Cm. 621 (1989), p. 75.
2. R. Forrest and A. Murie, *Selling the Welfare State* (Routledge & Kegan Paul, 1988).

17

The Irish Connection

D. GEORGE BOYCE

Whatever the electorate expected from the Conservative government in May 1979, they did not expect it to solve the Ulster crisis; nor did the party promise a radical or innovative policy. Indeed, the only policy statement it made in its election manifesto was to 'maintain the Union', and to reform local government, adding a strengthened system of elected regional councils which would fill the gap left in 1972 when the Stormont Parliament was suspended. This was hardly surprising. The whole purpose of British policy after the Ulster crisis assumed serious proportions in the summer of 1969 was to maintain what was characterized as a 'bipartisan policy', one that successive governments, whatever their political complexion, could defend and, possibly, build upon. When in 1973 Edward Heath's government constructed its power-sharing executive and negotiated the Sunningdale Agreement (which created a Council of Ireland to discuss matters of common concern between North and South) it was Wilson's Labour government that had to take up the task of defending that settlement after February 1974. And however much Labour may be criticized for its lack of vigour in so doing, there was never a possibility that the incoming government would *willingly* jettison the policy of its predecessor.

Between 1974 and 1979, however, the Labour government recoiled from anything as bold as power-sharing and the Sunningdale option. Its most ambitious endeavour was the short-lived truce which it managed to make with the Provisional IRA in 1975, in an effort to divide them and their political wing, Sinn Fein, and to encourage more politically minded members of those organizations to abandon their armed struggle. This truce was arranged while a convention of Northern Ireland parties was sitting; when the convention failed to come up with any new or workable proposals, there followed a period of quiescence in British policy, which reflected both the intractability of the problem, and the understandable desire of Labour to leave well enough alone. But, generally, the overall commitment of British political parties to the creation of a government in Northern Ireland which would command the support of both communities remained on the table; or perhaps now under it; it was never formally set aside, at least.

The Conservative government of 1979 had no desire to abandon the policy of seeking government by consent in the North; but neither did it have any clear-cut idea of how it might secure that general objective. It was certainly made all too well aware of the violent and dangerous way in which the simmering crisis could erupt, with the murder of Mr Airey Neave outside the House of Commons in March, followed in August 1979 by the slaughter of Earl Mountbatten and eighteen British soldiers in Ireland. The government abandoned its manifesto commitment to the reconstruction of local government and set out in pursuit of the by now familiar goal of Secretaries of State for Northern Ireland: to explore the possibility of partnership in a devolved government for the province. Humphrey Atkins, Northern Ireland Secretary 1979–81, first suggested an assembly with wide powers but with firm and definite arrangements which would ensure partnership within such a body and within any executive responsible to it;[1] James Prior in 1982 came up with the notion of an assembly whose powers might be extended by the method of 'rolling devolution', whereby if 70 per cent of assembly members agreed on the assembly taking responsibility for a subject (e.g. education) then Prior could if he wished devolve it.[2] These initiatives were unsuccessful; but they were accompanied by statements which, in retrospect at least, bore implications of a more radical look at the Ulster predicament. On 12 November 1979 the *New York Times* quoted Mrs Thatcher as declaring that if political parties in Northern Ireland said that ' "you can't do anything unless we all agree", she would impose a decision. Otherwise "you'll never get anywhere and we must".'[3] There was a hint of impatience, too, in July 1982 when Lord Gowrie,

Deputy to the Secretary of State for Northern Ireland 1981–3, warned that the British taxpayer, 'who puts British Governments in office', had the right to ask Northern Ireland to play a part in 'the alleviation of its own suffering'.[4]

But these were merely hints; and the fact that James Prior was dispatched to Northern Ireland was widely, and no doubt accurately, taken as a kind of political demotion, if not banishment: an example of the way in which Northern Ireland followed the trend under the Conservatives that it had under Labour, that of slipping down everyone's agenda. Yet there were signs that the government had a second string to its bow: in December 1980 the London and Dublin governments initiated a series of Anglo-Irish discussions and began to talk in terms of the special consideration of the totality of relationships within 'these islands', leading to the reconciliation of the two political traditions of Ireland.[5] The IRA hunger strike of 1981, which caused sharp disagreement between the British and Irish governments on how best such a harrowing and politically explosive crisis should be handled, indicated how difficult reconciliation might prove to be.[6] But a year later it became evident that the problem of Anglo-Irish relations was not confined to Ulster: and that Dublin and London were perfectly capable of dredging up differences among themselves.

At the summit meeting of 6 November 1981 an Anglo-Irish Inter-Governmental Council was established to express in institutional form the 'unique character of the relationship between the two governments';[7] but within a short time the uniqueness of that relationship seemed to be its liability to collapse into inter-governmental bickering. When Britain became involved in her dispute with the Argentine over the Falklands, and felt it imperative to send a fleet to the South Atlantic, she naturally looked to her European partners for moral and economic support. This was generally forthcoming; but Dublin called for United Nations action *against* the British, who were denounced as colonial aggressors; and the Republic's criticism of British policy had an element of self-indulgence about it, giving some evidence that twisting the lion's tail was still a political pastime in the South. For Ulster Unionists, the spectacle of an unprecedented display of British patriotism was gratifying and hopeful; for here was Britain expending blood and treasure to assert her sovereignty over a far away place of which most Britons knew nothing. What Unionists did not appreciate was that this far away place could arouse emotions which their own all too near place could not. And so the Anglo-Irish process, blown off course, was soon resumed.

It was taken up partly because the death of several hunger strikers in 1981 gave Provisional Sinn Fein the opportunity of a major breakthrough in the elections for James Prior's 'rolling devolution' assembly in October 1982;[8] for it was clear that the British government had to work harder at establishing a framework for Anglo-Irish relations which would reassure the Roman Catholic minority that it need not set its face against constitutional progress. But as early as July 1982 Lord Gowrie declared that an accommodation to the tradition of Irish unity was as important to good political progress in Northern Ireland as it was to relations between the United Kingdom and Dublin. 'It is surely also a fantasy', he remarked, 'to suppose that the Republic has no proper concern with Northern Ireland affairs. That is why the Government have tried to recognise and honour the minority identity as being in the main Irish, just as they recognise and honour the majority for being British. The one recognition in no way threatens the other.' The recognition of the minority was 'the other side of the coin to the constitutional guarantee to Unionists of their position as part of the United Kingdom . . . Thus we have to establish a framework for Anglo-Irish relations in which representatives of the minority, as well as of the majority if they wished, could in time take part.'[9]

This harked back to the summit meeting of November 1981, when the joint communiqué spoke of the possibility of the British and Irish parliaments considering 'at an appropriate time whether there should be an Anglo-Irish body at parliamentary level comprising members to be drawn from the British and Irish Parliaments, the European Parliament and any elected assembly that may be established for Northern Ireland';[10] but within a week of Gowrie's statement the tender nature of the new plant of Anglo-Irish co-operation was exposed again, as Dublin found fault with Britain on two counts: that Prior's rolling devolution scheme contained no 'Irish dimension'; and that Mrs Thatcher was guilty of insensitivity when she referred to the Republic as the 'Irish Free State'.[11]

These differences revealed yet again the way in which not even carefully chosen words and carefully managed diplomacy could prevent the British and the Irish, with their less than satisfactory history, from lapsing into mutual incomprehension. The tendency of nationalists to hold Britain responsible for all the ills of Northern Ireland, and of Ireland as a whole, was expressed in the New Ireland Forum, a gathering of constitutional nationalists and other representatives of Irish opinion which met in May 1983 and produced a report in 1984 accusing Britain of a 'crisis management' response to the Northern Ireland problem. The Forum outlined three possibilities: a unitary Irish state; a federal Ireland; and joint British–Irish authority over Northern Ireland.[12] This was much too fast for the British; but the Forum Report met with a guarded, but by no means unfavourable, reaction in the House of Commons, where Nicholas Scott, Under-Secretary of State for Northern Ireland, agreed that 'within these islands we must build the closest possible working relationship between the sovereign Governments in London and Dublin'.[13]

This seemed at odds with the celebrated occasion when, following the November 1984 session of the Anglo-Irish Inter-Governmental Council (with Dr Garret Fitzgerald representing the Republic), Mrs Thatcher declared that all the Forum options were 'out'. These remarks caused great offence in Dublin;[14] but they did not mark any permanent rupture in the tendencies towards Anglo-Irish co-operation, tendencies which were now on the verge of becoming a process. For after all the British government wanted an Irish dimension; it wanted more positive moves towards the defeat of the IRA; and it was gathering the nerve to do to the Ulster Unionists what it had already done to other groups in the United Kingdom: override them in the broad interests of the nation, otherwise the North of Ireland would inflict on Thatcherism what it had inflicted on the less than vigorous politics of the Wilson years: frustration.

But what was the 'nation' whose interests must not be sacri-

ficed for Ulster Unionist intransigence? After all Mrs Thatcher led
the Conservative and Unionist Party, even if the 'Unionist' part of
that appellation had been overshadowed for some years, or even
decades. She had decisively rejected devolution for Wales and
Scotland in 1979. Certainly there was always a section of Conservative back-benchers, led by such figures as Sir John Biggs-
Davison and Ivor Stanbrook, who could be relied upon to adopt a
more identifiably 'Ulster Unionist' line; Ian Gow, the Prime
Minister's parliamentary private secretary 1979–83, and Minister of State at the Treasury, was a man of some political stature
who showed unfashionable sympathy with an increasingly
unfashionable people. But this did not colour the government's
thinking, which was increasingly attracted by benefits of firm co-
operation with Dublin, and the rescuing of Northern Ireland
nationalist politics from the thrall of Sinn Fein. Paradoxically,
helping Irish nationalism would contribute to the unity and
integrity of the British state, whose Ulster Unionist citizens were,
it seemed, becoming British people with a difference: or, perhaps,
were having that difference increasingly recognized.

Some indication of the government's perception was given by
Christopher Patten, parliamentary Under-Secretary of State at
the Northern Ireland Office 1983–5, in the summer of 1985.
Patten had no doubt that the constitutional status of Northern
Ireland as part of the United Kingdom must be upheld as long as
the majority so willed it. But he believed that the government of
the Republic had a 'legitimate interest in Northern Ireland, and a
special part to play in the politics of the minority there'. And
although the Anglo-Irish Inter-Governmental Council had concerned itself with such uncontentious matters as measles and
security fraud, it did provide a permanent means of adjusting
relationships between the two countries. Patten very properly
refused to discuss the talks then in progress between the British
and Irish governments; but he did refer to the value of construct-
ing an 'acceptable basis' for 'deepening the relations between the
United Kingdom and the Republic of Ireland'. And he reminded
his listeners of the considerable contribution made by the taxpayer to Northern Ireland, which (while perfectly justifiable)
exceeded that made to the European Community.[15]

These words were no doubt the kind of generalities offered by parliamentary secretaries in conferences of political and lay figures. And not even the best-informed observer would have predicted that they would lead directly to the Anglo-Irish Agreement of the following November. But the impetus was growing for some kind of tangible result to arise out of the previous years' exploration of the 'unique relationship' between Britain and Ireland, of the 'totality of relations' within the British Isles. 'Positive proposals' were in the air; and in the summer of 1985 several important books were published urging the construction of a permanent Anglo-Irish institution to cement partnership, and offer a way around the Ulster deadlock.[16] Moreover, when British ministers—and British civil servants—were closeted in conference with their Irish counterparts, the belief that they were men of like mind (pondering on the intractable Northern politicians) who ought not to leave the conference room without something to show for their efforts must take root. The British government, despite Mrs Thatcher's declarations about Northern Ireland being as British as Finchley, must, now that it was in its second term of office, either extend its Anglo-Irish strategy, or admit that it was nothing more than shadow-boxing and empty words. In these circumstances, it was virtually impossible for Mrs Thatcher, even had she wished to do otherwise, to refuse to consent to an Anglo-Irish agreement: she must confront the fact that policy was secreted in the interstices of administration. And senior civil servants, for their part, sought to reinforce a process of bipartisanship which could now be transferred from the British domestic political scene to the broader stage of Anglo-Irish relations.

The Anglo-Irish Agreement of November 1985 was thus the outcome of two assumptions: that the feuding parties of Ulster could not be allowed to hold up a process whose momentum had now been created; and that the British and Irish governments must resolve any disagreements occasioned or created by the Northern Ireland problem. Out of these two broad achievements, other achievements of a more specific kind would follow: the improvement of security co-operation between Britain and Ireland, and between their respective forces on either side of the border; the bolstering up of the Social Democratic and Labour Party, representing constitutional nationalism; the isolation of Sinn Fein and the IRA from its supporters; the strengthening of Britain's reputation in Ireland at an international level.

The Hillsborough Agreement declared that the purpose of the two signatories was to promote 'peace and stability in Northern Ireland' and to help reconcile the 'two main traditions in Ireland' (not only in Northern Ireland; which was itself a form of words suggesting a deeper 'Irish dimension'). It was a subtle and clever document, for it held out various possibilities to the contending parties in the North: it was enough of a blow to the Unionists to bring them to acknowledge that they were not as powerful a factor in policy-making as their numerical majority and its 'veto' seemed to suggest; yet it was not 'Irish' enough to provoke them to a blind and suicidal rebellion against the British government. It offered an Irish dimension to the SDLP, especially in its creation of an Anglo-Irish Secretariat and an Inter-Governmental Conference which gave the Republic a consultative role (or, as the Irish Taoiseach put it, 'going beyond a consultative role but necessarily ... falling short of an executive role') but retained British sovereignty (while not however explicitly denying the sovereignty of the Republic, asserted in article 2 of the 1937 constitution). It offered Britain better security co-operation, which Mrs Thatcher returned to again and again in her speech in Parliament in which she explained and defended the agreement. British public and political opinion rallied behind the government as never before, with the agreement carried by 473 votes to 47, one of the largest majorities on a division in parliamentary history.[17]

The Conservative government did not go unscathed through the division lobbies in November 1985. The agreement cost it one minister, Ian Gow, who in a passionate and weighty speech warned the government of the consequences to Northern Ireland of a policy which, in his view, could only further nationalist irredentism and republican violence.[18] His warning seemed to be vindicated in the weeks immediately following the signing of the agreement, as Ulster Unionists mounted a serious challenge to the government and its policy; and, despite the violent behaviour of a minority of Unionists, the significant development was the strong opposition of the Unionist middle ground, the very people who might have been expected to recognize where their 'true' interests lay: in Anglo-Irish co-operation.[19] The province appeared on the edge of anarchy; and the agreement seemed to depend on the resolution of the RUC. Unionist protests were in vain, however, for the government adhered resolutely to its course.

But the three years after the Anglo-Irish Agreement saw the most turbulent period in British–Irish relations, and in Northern Ireland itself, since the dangerous days of 1969–74, with the two governments locked in dispute over a series of issues which, while not destructive of the agreement, certainly seemed to deprive it of much of its purpose; and with an alarming increase in political violence in the North,[20] culminating in the disastrous month of August 1988, which forced the British government to review its whole legal and security procedures, and not always to the liking of Dublin, despite the benefits in co-operation which were supposed to follow from the Hillsborough Agreement.

The Irish government was, apparently, inclined to blame this marked deterioration in Anglo-Irish relations on the change of the Northern Ireland Secretary, with Tom King replacing Douglas Hurd in 1985; and the British could point to the return of Charles Haughey and his Fianna Fáil party to power in February 1988 as problematical, since Haughey had objected to the agreement on the grounds that it derogated from Irish sovereignty over the whole island. But there were perhaps deeper reasons than this, which indicated that not even the ingenious Hillsborough Agreement, backed by a strong Prime Minister and a bipartisan Commons majority, could wipe the slate clean when it came to Anglo-Irish relations. In the Commons debate on 27 November 1985 Tom King promised that the agreement marked 'a real advance in the fight against terrorism';[21] and the government had to demonstrate that this was so, not only to vindicate its policy, but to assure Ulster Unionists that the strategy was one for Unionists' benefit in the long run. But terrorism tends to be a phenomenon that people regard as important in the short, rather than the long, run, especially when they are numbered among its victims. And while the Republic sought to fulfil its side of the bargain, several key decisions on extradition (always a touchy subject in the South) seemed to indicate a lack of will on Dublin's part to deliver the goods; a suspicion increased by the Republic's unsatisfactory (in British eyes) extradition legislation of December 1987 which, Mrs Thatcher declared, made Britain 'the least favoured nation in this matter'.[22]

The problem was compounded by the British necessity to step up its anti-terrorist offensive, if only, again, to demonstrate that the Hillsborough Agreement was not, as Unionists claimed, a surrender to Irish nationalism occasioned by IRA violence. Britain had to show some results; and she must therefore maintain a high security profile. This included continuing the unpopular (in Irish official circles) Prevention of Terrorism Act, retaining the Diplock Courts intact, and showing a passivity over the alleged 'shoot to kill' tactics of some members of the RUC in 1982. All these were perfectly understandable in the light of the British government's definition of what its immediate and overriding concerns in Northern Ireland and in mainland Britain were: to control, curb, and defeat terrorism, while the SDLP enjoyed the political benefits of the agreement, and before Unionist claims that it would worsen the situation could be in any respect vindicated. But this ignored the fact that *any* security improvement, involving British and Irish co-operation across the border, was bound to be only gradual, especially when the British and the Irish differed about what 'co-operation' meant in the first place.

For the question of producing agreement from the agreement was more difficult than the British, and probably the Irish, signatories supposed. And this reflected a weakness in Thatcherite political perception; the lack of a historical sense, the determination of radicals to close down the past, to bring it to its knees. This was to ignore the potentially sensitive nature of the Anglo-Irish relationship, which Hillsborough could not sign away. The anger of Britain at extradition in Ireland was only matched by Irish dismay at what they regarded as a miscarriage of justice in the case of the Birmingham Six. Both governments could react self-defensively to such incidents, and forget how different the issues looked on the other side of the water. Instead of the Anglo-Irish Conference providing the opportunity for mutual understanding, it seemed to supply a venue for the airing of misunderstandings: Dublin could not influence important British decisions; and London could not get what she wanted from the Irish. Thatcherite policy neglected the point that Fianna Fáil, like all Irish political parties, had to live in Ireland.

Nevertheless the government expressed its determination to adhere to the agreement as the best means of achieving its goals. These goals might be obscured in the hectic and frequently mismanaged Anglo-Irish diplomacy since 1985; but they were still discernible: the Conservative Party sought to save constitutional nationalism from destruction, in the well-founded belief that such a fate would pose a crisis for Northern Ireland, the Republic, and the whole British Isles; and it wanted to distance itself from Ulster Unionism, depriving it of any vestigial notion it may have possessed that it had any special claim on a British political party, and especially the British Conservative Party. Thus isolated, the Ulster Unionists might at last accept power-sharing in a devolved government *and* an Irish dimension with (Tom King announced in February 1989) a parliamentary tier. As Ferdinand Mount put it in the *Spectator*, Mrs Thatcher was 'rock-hard for the Union but just as impatient with the Unionists as the rest of her tribe'.[23]

All this must seem odd in the light of a speech made by Mrs Thatcher at a meeting of the Ulster Unionist Council in Belfast in June 1978, when she declared that 'our two parties show one overriding common purpose, the maintenance and strengthening of the Union of Great Britain and Ireland. We shall not consider any plans for the political future of the United Kingdom which could result in the weakening of the Union.'[24] But it all depended on how the 'Union' was defined in the first place, and how best it could be 'strengthened'. The Thatcher government in the end became convinced that only by breaking out of the cockpit of Ulster politics could the continuing problem of Northern Ireland be resolved; and its resolution would indeed be of lasting benefit to the British taxpayers' United Kingdom (as well as Ulster). The Thatcher effect on Northern Ireland was to make it clear that the British government did not see constitutional nationalists, Northern or Southern, as the central difficulty any more. They were part of the solution, while Ulster Unionists were now identified as part of the problem: a perception which was revealed in the fact that Ulster Unionists (and the head of the Northern Ireland Civil Service) were completely ignored in the making of the agreement, whereas the views of the SDLP were put forward by the Dublin government. 'Bipartisanship', and the natural inclinations of the British Parliament and people, would ensure the continuity of that final shift in Conservative perception, and carry it on into the foreseeable future.

Notes

1. *The Government of Northern Ireland: A Working Paper for a Conference*, Cmnd. 7763 (1979); *The Government of Northern Ireland: Proposals for further discussion*, Cmnd. 7950 (1980).
2. Eamon Exley, 'A Critical Analysis of Formal Governmental Proposals to Resolve the Ulster Crisis' (Sheffield City Polytechnic CNAA degree (BA) in Public Administration, 1983), pp. 48–50.
3. Bernard Crick, 'The Concept of Consent and the Agreement', paper read at the University of Keele, Apr. 1986, n. 13. This quotation is included with the kind permission given in his paper by Professor Crick.
4. HL Deb., 5th series, vol. 432, 8 July 1982, col. 901.
5. Exley, op. cit., pp. 52–3.
6. Anthony Kenny, *The Road to Hillsborough* (Pergamon Press, 1986), pp. 33–4.
7. Ibid. p. 38.
8. W. Harvey Cox, 'Managing Northern Ireland Intergovernmentally: An Appraisal of the Anglo-Irish Agreement', in *Parliamentary Affairs*, 40 (1987), 83.
9. HL Deb., 5th series, vol. 432, 8 July 1982, cols. 904–5.
10. *Keesing's Contemporary Archives* (Longman, 1982), vol. xxviii, 9 July 1982, p. 31579.
11. Ibid. 5 Nov. 1982, p. 31790.
12. Kenny, op. cit., ch. 8.
13. HC Deb., 6th series, vol. 63, 2 July 1984, cols. 102–6.
14. Cox, op. cit., p. 86.
15. Christopher Patten, 'The Future: A Contribution from Great Britain', in James McLoone (ed.), *The British-Irish Connection* (Social Study Conference, Galway, 1985), pp. 69–82.
16. Kenny, op. cit., ch. 14.
17. Ibid. p. 117.
18. HC Deb., 6th series, vol. 87, 26 Mar. 1985, cols. 758–63.
19. Cox, op. cit., pp. 92–3.
20. Almost 100 deaths in 1987, double the figure for the last year of 'direct' Direct Rule (Figures supplied by Dr Paul Bew of Queen's University, Belfast).

21. HC Deb., 6th series, vol. 87, 27 Nov. 1985, col. 883.
22. HC Deb., 6th series, vol. 123, 1 Dec. 1987, col. 762.
23. *Spectator*, 23 Nov. 1985, p. 6.
24. HC Deb., 6th series, vol. 87, 26 Nov. 1985, col. 762.

18

Values: The Crusade that Failed

IVOR CREWE

> I was brought up by a Victorian grandmother. We were taught to work jolly hard. We were taught to prove yourself; we were taught self reliance; we were taught to live within our income.
>
> You were taught that cleanliness is next to godliness. You were taught self-respect. You were taught always to give a hand to your neighbour. You were taught tremendous pride in your country. All of these things are Victorian values. They are also perennial values.
>
> You don't hear so much about these things these days but they were good values and they led to tremendous improvements in the standard of living.
>
> (Mrs Thatcher, radio interview on LBC, 15 Apr. 1983)

Newly elected governments in Britain have traditionally confined their ambitions to a few institutional reforms and some changes in the law. The idea of replacing the old public philosophy with a new one, of instigating a cultural revolution, would have struck Mrs Thatcher's predecessors as a deeply foreign notion, as unrealistic as it was undesirable. Even the great reforming governments of 1906 and 1945 saw themselves as working with the grain of public sentiment, bringing forward reforms whose time had come.

As in so much else, the 1979 government was different. For Thatcher and her immediate circle a century of economic decline could not be reversed without a transformation of public attitudes. Paradoxically, the government needed to take on a new role—as economic tutor to the nation—in order to divest itself of its old ones. The public had to be persuaded to lower its expectations of, and dependence upon, the state. The old dependency culture had to be replaced by a new enterprise culture.

Mrs Thatcher was the natural chief preacher of this new doctrine of economic realism. Unlike most politicians, including prime ministers, she has always possessed a political philosophy—a coherent set of core principles which shape her views on specific matters. Quite exceptionally, she has firm convictions on almost every issue under the sun. Not since Gladstone has Britain been led by such an opinionated and evangelical Prime Minister. Most prime ministers see themselves as 'healers'; a few, like Lloyd George and Churchill, as warriors; Thatcher, uniquely, sees herself as a crusader.

Mrs Thatcher has been singularly fortunate in having a full decade in which to stamp her personal vision upon the country. No previous government has enjoyed such a long uninterrupted period to carry through a major programme of reform. The only parallel abroad, dictatorships excluded, is de Gaulle's eleven years at the helm of the fledgeling Fifth Republic.

Will her legacy be as enduring? Airy generalizations about cultural change are the most superficial form of social comment. Take a few casual impressions, add some personal hunches, sprinkle with some selected statistics, and a plausible case can be made for almost any thesis about how the values of the British have changed. Thatcherism's defenders talk of a sea change in attitudes and point to the new mood on the shop-floor; Thatcherism's detractors talk of the 'uncaring society' and point to the growth of begging and homelessness. The common fallacy in both cases is to confuse the distinctive with the representative. The Porsche-driving yuppie, the council tenant-turned-owner, the one-union no-strike deal, and British Gas's Sid are all distinctive to the Thatcher decade. But they are all exceptional too: most council tenants continue to rent; most large companies have a multi-union membership; most people do not own shares, let alone drive Porsches. They symbolize the Thatcher decade, making up its tone and style, but they do not necessarily add up to the cultural revolution that the Thatcherites have sought.

A proper assessment requires hard evidence on actual national trends across the decade, but appropriate data are difficult to find. The attitudes and values of the public reported by the opinion polls are revealing but are subject to fashion and notions of respectability, and do not always translate into how people actually behave. Moreover, most people do not possess a well-worked-out set of values. They get by quite comfortably with a contradictory, loosely held repertoire of principles, attitudes, and habits which legitimizes the mixture of selfishness and decency by which they lead their lives. Alternatively, one can examine changes in actual behaviour. Here the problem is to infer values from what people do. Does the steady growth of single-parent families reflect an increase in permissiveness—or in self-reliance? Does the sharp rise in credit-card debt mark a decline in the Thatcherite values of frugality and self-sufficiency or a spread in the Thatcherite values of self-improvement and acquisition?

These problems of interpretation cannot be entirely avoided. But they matter less than they might because almost all the trend evidence points in the same direction. Quite simply, there has been no Thatcherite transformation of attitudes or behaviour among the British public. If anything, the British have edged further away from Thatcherite positions as the decade has progressed. The Thatcher governments have undoubtedly transformed the British political economy, overturned the political agenda, and permanently altered the social structure. But this has been done without a cultural counter-revolution in the thinking of ordinary people.

This is best demonstrated by the remarkable results of an opinion poll conducted by MORI in June 1988 (Table 18.1).[1] In large to overwhelming proportions the public's perception of the state of Britain is close to the Thatcherite idea. Britain is a mainly capitalist society in which private interests and free enterprise prevail (77 per cent agree), the creation of wealth is more highly rewarded than caring for others (75 per cent), efficiency takes precedence over keeping people in work (68 per cent), individuals are encouraged to look after themselves (66 per cent), and people are permitted to make and keep as much money as they can (73 per cent). But this is a very long way from the public's ideal. Confronted with the choice between a 'Thatcherite' and 'social-ist' society the public opted for the Thatcherite model on only two

TABLE 18.1. *Socialist v. Thatcherist values*

People have different views about the ideal society. This card shows a number of alternatives. Q.(1) Please read each pair of statements and then tell me which one, in each case, comes closest to your ideal—statement A or statement B. Q. (2) Now, for each pair of statements, please tell me whether you think statement A or statement B is most like Britain today?'

	(1)	(2)
A. 'A mainly capitalist society in which private interests and free enterprise are most important'.	43	77
B. 'A mainly socialist society in which public interests and a more controlled economy are most important'.	49	17
A. 'A society which emphasises the social and collective provision of welfare'.	55	27
B. 'A society where the individual is encouraged to look after himself.'	40	66
A. 'A society which emphasises keeping people in work even where this is not very efficient.'	42	25
B. 'A society which emphasises increasing efficiency rather than keeping people in work.'	50	68
A. 'A society which allows people to make and keep as much money as they can.'	53	73
B. 'A society which emphasises similar incomes and rewards for everyone.'	43	19
A. 'A society in which the creation of wealth is more highly rewarded.'	16	75
B. 'A society in which caring for others is more highly rewarded.'	79	19

Source: Market & Opinion Research International, *British Public Opinion*, 10/6 (July–Aug. 1988), p. 4.

out of five dimensions, and then by slender majorities. They preferred a free society 'which allows people to make and keep as much money as they can' (53 per cent) to an egalitarian society which 'emphasizes similar incomes and rewards for everyone' (43 per cent). And they chose efficiency (50 per cent) in preference to 'keeping people in work even where this is not very efficient' (42 per cent). Yet a small majority preferred a 'mainly socialist society in which public interests and a more controlled economy are most important' (49 per cent) to a 'mainly capitalist society' (43 per cent) and a larger majority opted for a society 'which emphasizes the social and collective provision of welfare' (55 per cent) over one in which 'the individual is encouraged to look after himself' (40 per cent)—so much for self-reliance. And by a massive five to one ratio they preferred a society in which 'caring for others' (79 per cent) is more highly rewarded than 'the creation of wealth' (16 per cent). In other words, efficiency is necessary and the inequalities that accompany it acceptable; but untrammelled free enterprise and individual acquisitiveness are not. After nine years of Thatcherism the public remained wedded to the collectivist, welfare ethic of social democracy. No wonder that, according to Gallup, 'Mrs Thatcher's Britain' is regarded as a term of abuse. When people hear others using the phrase, Gallup reports, twice as many assume that an unfavourable view is being taken as assume a favourable view.[2]

We cannot know how the public would have responded to the same questions in 1979; perhaps they were even less Thatcherite then, but it seems unlikely. The evidence from different specific questions for which trend data are available suggests that the public has moved away from some of the central tenets of Thatcherism.

The core principle of Thatcherism is the 'Victorian' value of individual self-reliance. Above all else Mrs Thatcher has wanted to liberate the individual from the stultifying, enfeebling dependency upon the welfare office, local housing department, and union official and to give the individual responsibility and choice. Yet there is no evidence that the ethic of self-reliance has spread. In 1984 Gallup asked voters whether they thought the government's most important job was to provide good opportunities for everyone to get ahead or whether its job was to guarantee everybody steady employment and a decent standard of living. Only 30 per cent said they were content with good opportunities; 65 per cent wanted a government guarantee. The proportion believing in self-reliance was actually higher when the identical question was put, after six years of war, under Attlee's Labour government in 1945.[3]

The ethic of self-reliance easily turns into callousness; but the public is increasingly reluctant to attribute individual misfortune to what the Victorians called fecklessness. In 1977, before Mrs Thatcher came to power, Gallup reported that 35 per cent of voters thought that, if people were poor, their own lack of effort was probably to blame; by 1985 that figure had fallen to 22 per cent and 50 per cent blamed 'circumstances'. Asked in November 1987 whether the unemployed have usually themselves to blame, only 13 per cent agreed; 87 per cent disagreed. So far the doctrines of Samuel Smiles have fallen on deaf ears.

But have people *in fact* become more self-reliant in the past decade? The few measurable indicators available offer a mixed picture. The number of self-employed, having remained constant throughout the 1970s, rose from 1.9 million in 1979 to almost 3.0 million in 1988,[4] a 50 per cent increase as a proportion of the total labour force. The spread of home ownership has been accelerated by the sale of over a million council houses to their tenants. On the other hand, the proportion of the population depending on income support and one-parent benefits grew from 3.4 million in 1981 to 5.6 million in 1988—an even larger rise than that for self-employment.[5] As for frugality, outstanding debt (excluding home loans) grew in real terms by 3 per cent a quarter between the end of 1981 and the first quarter of 1988, rising from 8 per cent of annual household disposable income in 1981 to 14 per cent by 1987. Over the same period, personal savings as a percentage of personal disposable income (excluding life assurance premiums) steadily fell, from 16.3 per cent in 1980 to a mere 1.3 per cent in late 1988—its lowest level for over a quarter century. The low savings ratio can be celebrated as the product of the government's success in bringing down inflation and increasing per capita real wealth, but it is not the economic behaviour of the Japanese or Germans—nor of Mrs Thatcher's Grantham household.

The doctrine of individual self-reliance lies at the heart of four distinctively Thatcherite policies: the defeat of inflation, tax cuts, trade union reform, and privatization. All of these objectives have attracted substantial public support, but less by the end of the decade than at the beginning. Consider the absolute priority Thatcherism gives to eliminating inflation over other macro-economic objectives, such as full employment. A moral as well as economic imperative is at work here. Inflation breeds economic irresponsibility by discouraging savings and thus individual provision for future welfare; sound money is good morality as well as good economics. But as the inflation and unemployment curves crossed each other, the public weakened in its commitment to sound money. In 1980, Gallup reported that 52 per cent wanted the government to give priority to curbing inflation, 42 per cent to cutting unemployment. By mid-1986, however, these priorities were massively rejected, by over six to one, and 75 per cent agreed that the government 'should always keep unemployment as low as possible, *even if this means some inflation with rising prices*'.

The Thatcherite preference for tax cuts over social expenditure has a similar basis in the ethic of self-reliance. Fewer taxes mean more money in the voter's pocket, which means more scope for individual choice and responsibility. The emphasis on consumer choice within the public services has been reinforced by the current government's opt-out provisions in health, education, housing, and pensions. Yet so far the public has not responded. It wants an expansion of social expenditure, and in the traditional mould (see Table 18.2). At regular intervals Gallup asks people whether, if forced to choose, they would prefer tax cuts—even at the expense of some reduction in government services such as health, education, and welfare—or the extension of these services even if this means some tax increases. In May 1979, when Mrs Thatcher entered No 10, there were equal numbers of tax-cutters and service-extenders. By 1983 there were twice as many service-extenders as tax-cutters; by 1987 six times as many. Free-market economists object that these are unpriced trade-offs, and thus almost meaningless questions. Surveys on welfare by the Institute

TABLE 18.2. *Thatcherism's economic priorities: taxes v. social services*

Question: 'People have different views about whether it is more important to reduce taxes or keep up government spending. How about you? Which of these statements comes closest to your view?'

- cut taxes, even if this means some reduction in government services, such as health, education, and welfare;
- things should be left as they are;
- government services such as health, education, and welfare should be extended, even if it means some increases in taxes.

	Cut taxes	No change	Extend services
Oct. 1978 (1979 election)	29	26	45
May 1979	37	26	37
March 1980	25	27	47
March 1981	22	25	53
Feb. 1982	22	27	52
Feb. 1983 (1983 election)	24	23	52
Oct. 1983	18	23	53
May 1984	15	27	58
Nov. 1984	13	26	62
Feb. 1985	17	19	63
Feb. 1986	17	20	63
June 1986	17	14	64
Sept. 1986	9	18	68
May 1987	12	21	61
Oct. 1987	11	19	66

Source: Gallup Political Index.

of Economic Affairs suggest that, when people are offered a threefold choice between universal welfare provision, selective provision for the poor, and the option of contracting out, universal provision has declined in popularity since 1963 and the plurality now opt for contracting out.[6] But the *trend* since 1978, when the survey was last conducted, parallels that in Gallup. Under Mrs Thatcher universal provision has revived in popularity, while contracting out has subsided. Of course, this movement of public opinion may be a response to the government's actual changes in taxation and social spending: a middle-of-the-road elector could be in favour of tax cuts in 1979 and against them in 1987 without altering his view of the right trade-off between taxes and spending. In this sense the swing of public opinion against Thatcherite policies is a reflection of their success. But the figures still suggest that the electorate regarded Thatcherite policies in this field as a matter of modest adjustments, not a crusade.

The reforms of the trade unions in the 1980s—Thatcherism's most conspicuous success—stripped unions of many of their legal immunities and disruptive powers and aimed to shift power within unions from leaders to members. These changes were overwhelmingly supported by the public, including trade union members. But Thatcherism has failed in its more ambitious aim of persuading the electorate that trade unions are undesirable or unnecessary institutions. One set of evidence is provided by Gallup's annual questions of thirty years' standing: 'Generally speaking, and thinking of Britain as a whole, do you think that trade unions are a good thing or a bad thing?' As Table 18.3 shows, throughout the decade a majority have always answered positively, despite the sharp decline in trade union membership, and that majority has increased since 1985. By 1988 the public agreed that most non-management staff 'would be better off belonging to a trade union than not belonging to one' (by 61 to 24 per cent); that trade unions 'ensure fair treatment for workers' (by 71 to 19 per cent) and 'improve wages, working conditions and job security for workers' (by 72 to 17 per cent). And a majority disagreed that 'trade unions may have been needed at one time in Britain but not any longer' (by 67 to 23 per cent) or that 'wages and working conditions would have reached today's level even without the effort of trades unions' (by 66 to 23 per cent). The paradox of Mrs Thatcher's reform is that, by reducing the number of strikes and the unions' grip over their own members, she has restored the legitimacy of trade unions in the eyes of the public. The electorate's response to Thatcherite policies on trade unions has been entirely pragmatic. It has

TABLE 18.3 *The standing of the trade unions*

Q. Generally speaking, and thinking of Britain as a whole, do you think that trade unions are a good thing or a bad thing?

Government	Good thing	Bad thing	Don't know
Eden–Macmillan (1954–9)	62	18	20
Macmillan–Home (1960–4)	62	19	19
Wilson (1965–70)	61	23	16
Heath (1971–3)	59	25	16
Wilson–Callaghan (1974–8)	55	30	15
Thatcher I (1979–82)	56	31	13
Thatcher II (1983–6)	64	25	11
Thatcher III (1987–8)	70	19	11

Note: The question is asked each September. Entries for each period are the average.

Source: Gallup Political Index, 337 (Sept. 1988), p. 14.

welcomed the elimination of obvious abuses without embracing any principled objection to the collectivism of trade unions.

Finally, we turn to privatization. Of the four components in economic Thatcherism, privatization was the one most prompted by purely economic considerations (i.e. reducing the PSBR). None the less, the government has expended a considerable PR budget and much political energy in persuading the public of the virtues of privatization in terms of consumer choice and the spread of property ownership; but to little avail. Mrs Thatcher came to power when the public was firmly in favour of privatization: between 1979 and 1983 the majority preferring privatization to nationalization hovered around 20 per cent, a peak for the post-war period (see Table 18.4). By 1987 the majority was a mere 4 per cent and the proportion believing that nationalized industries are less efficient than private companies has steadily declined during the Thatcher decade.[7] A more recent survey in August 1988, asking a similarly phrased question, reports a net majority in favour of more public ownership rather than more privatization (with a substantial proportion supporting the status

TABLE 18.4. *Nationalization and privatization*

Q. Which of these alternatives comes nearest to your own attitude to
nationalization on the whole?

- all industries should be nationalized
- some more industries should be nationalized
- no more industries should be nationalized
- some of the nationalized industries should be de-nationalized
- all of the nationalized industries should be de-nationalized
- no opinion.

	Net support for nationalization (%)[a]
1973–4	+5
1975–8	−15
1979	−19
1980	−21
1981	−21
1982	−20
1983	−20
1984	−12
1985	−0
1986	−7
1987	−4

[a] i.e. % in favour of nationalizing all or some more industries *minus* % in favour of denationalizing all or some more industries.

Source: Market & Opinion Research International, *British Public Opinion*, 9/8 (Oct. 1987), p. 7.

quo). A majority is as heavily opposed to the privatization of the remaining public industries—electricity, water, coal, and railways—as it was to the previous privatizations.[8] Once again, Thatcherism appears to have paid the price of its own achievements: as loss-making nationalized industries become a thing of the past, public ownership has become more attractive again.

It is tempting to dismiss these attitudinal trends as implausible and immaterial. They do not square easily, it could be argued, with Mrs Thatcher's hat trick of election victories, nor with the remarkable degree to which she has remoulded the British political economy and social structure in her own image. It is true that, irrespective of trends in public values, many of Thatcherism's achievements are probably irreversible: it is difficult to envisage re-nationalization on a large scale, or a return to fixed exchange rates, or a decline in owner-occupation. But that does not make the failure of Thatcher's cultural crusade unimportant. For it reminds us that the Conservatives owe their three election wins not to ideology but to much more pragmatic causes—their economic record, Mrs Thatcher's leadership, and the electoral system. And it reminds us that much of Thatcherism will die with Thatcher. Its permanent legacy at the level of the mass public will be very limited. It will not have killed off popular socialism, at least not in its welfarist forms. A post-Thatcher Labour government will inherit an electorate as friendly to its major objectives as the 1979 electorate was to those of the Conservatives. The values of the ordinary public are beyond the control of government, even when it is a missionary one. They are shaped by experience, not theory, and mutate slowly in response to real change, not to government exhortations.

Notes

1. Market & Opinion Research International, *British Public Opinion*, 10/6 (July–Aug. 1988), 4.
2. *Gallup Political Index*, 329 (Jan. 1988), p. 8. The question was: 'When you hear people talking about "Mrs. Thatcher's Britain", do you think they are taking a favourable or an unfavourable view of how things are going in Britain?' The answers were: Favourable 25%, Unfavourable 53%, Neither/ neutral 12%, Don't know 10%.
3. *The Economist*, 25 May 1985, p. 22.
4. *Social Trends* (1989), p. 74.
5. See *Social Trends* (1989), p. 91, and *Social Trends* (1988), p. 86.
6. Ralph Harris and Arthut Seldon, *Welfare Without the State* (Hobart Paperback No. 26) (London: Institute of Economic Affairs, 1987), p. 21.
7. Market & Opinion Research International, *British Public Opinion*, 9/8 (Oct. 1987), p. 7.
8. *Gallup Political Index*, 337 (Sept. 1988), p. 19.

19

Divisions That Unite Britain

RICHARD ROSE

Like socialist principles, the principles of Margaret Thatcher are meant to be universally valid. Hence, she has a national not a regional policy—and Britain is her nation. The virtues of the market are meant to be as valid in the high streets of the South of England as they were when first identified by Adam Smith in the High Street of Glasgow. And the Prime Minister thinks that it is as wrong for social workers in Southend to blame society for hooliganism and criminal behaviour, as it is for this explanation to be offered in Swansea or Belfast. Just as Labour claims to represent the working class and the have nots from Cornwall to Aberdeen, so Margaret Thatcher claims to stand up for the industrious classes from one end of Britain to the other.

Economic divisions unite what geography separates. Ideology not territory is the primary dividing line in the mental map of Margaret Thatcher, as it is in the mind of another migrant to London, Neil Kinnock. Since 1979 Downing Street has stressed the importance of individuals expecting less from government and doing more for themselves, whether they are unemployed workers in the South of England or Pakistanis building up small businesses in the Hebrides. In a complementary fashion, Labour campaigns for the collective provision of education, health, and social security, from County Durham to Dulwich.

The consequences of actions taken in the national interest can differ greatly from one part of Britain to another. The Channel tunnel is an extreme example, drawing the South-East of England closer to France—and increasing its distance from the North of England and Scotland. Many consequences of Thatcherism have been felt throughout the island, for better (the substantial fall in the rate of inflation since 1979) or worse (the rise in unemployment). And many territorial differences discussed have their origins a generation, or even a century, ago; for example, differences between the industrial North of England and the service centres of the South. In early Victorian times much of the South of England suffered from the effects of agricultural depression while the North boomed. Since the era of Ramsay Macdonald and Stanley Baldwin we think of North–South differences as being to the advantage of the South.

Before examining differences between parts of Great Britain, we should recognize commonalities in all parts of the island. English is the common language; even for four-fifths of Welsh men and women English is their only language. Vestigial Christianity is the common religion, and everywhere Britons are overwhelmingly white. Where racial ghettos exist they are a neighbourhood or a part of a city, not a region unto itself. Northern Ireland, the one part of the United Kingdom that has alien values, has been treated as an object of foreign policy by both Conservative and Labour governments, to be dealt with by London and Dublin, with Ulster voices largely ignored.

Secondly, many divisions in British society exist within nations, regions, and conurbations, as much as or more than between them. The route of the District Line from Wimbledon to the East End of London traverses differences as great as those between the North and South of England. Roy Jenkins's old constituency of Glasgow Hillhead has more in common with Oxford or Cambridge than with Jim Sillars's neighbouring constituency of Glasgow Govan. The 'two nations' that concerned Victorian writers could be found in the contrast between the East End of London and Belgravia, as well as between Sheffield and Bath.

THE ECONOMY

The state of the economy is the standard by which the Thatcher government asks to be judged, and the downs and ups of the economy in the past decade have been felt throughout Britain. In the 1970s inflation affected all parts of Britain and the government's significant success in lowering the inflation rate has affected all parts of Britain. The benefits of greater price stability are felt by people spending Scottish paper pound notes as well as by Londoners reckoning purchases in round metal coins, and the Thatcher government can claim that its economic policies have played a significant role in getting rid of double-digit inflation.

However, the benefits of more stable prices have costs. The economy was contracting instead of expanding in the early 1980s, and the contraction was particularly severe in manufacturing industries. The revival of the economy in the mid-1980s and a rate of growth above the European average since has meant that, in current money terms, the gross domestic product per person has more than doubled since 1979. Even after discounting for the effect of inflation, the living standards of the average person have risen substantially. However, growth in the economy has not been spread evenly—nor should it be, argue free-market economists. The logic of the market is that areas with competitive advantages should benefit more by exploiting their advantages.

Critics of the Thatcher government usually commit the logical fallacy of wanting every region of Britain to be above average in economic growth. Yet it is inevitable that half the regions will be below the median, just as half will be above. Unlike previous Conservative as well as Labour governments, the Thatcher administration has rejected the idea that the government ought to try to use public policies to help poorer regions grow faster than richer regions. It has preferred to trust the market to foster growth everywhere, and to argue that the failure of a region to grow fast may indicate a lack of enterprise and an undesirable dependence upon Whitehall hand-outs, rather than shortcomings in government policy.

Regional variations in national product

When the Conservatives entered office in 1979 there were differences in the Gross Domestic Product (GDP) per head of the nine regions of Britain—but these differences were small (Table 19.1). Seven of the nine regions were within 3 per cent of each other. Because of the dominance of the South-East, where the GDP per head was 15 per cent above the average for the country as a whole, GDP per head in every other region of England was also below the national average. London, rather than Yorkshire or Scotland, is the odd region out. The differences could not be characterized as national differences, for even though Wales was at the bottom of this league table, Scotland was exactly in the middle.

TABLE 19.1.   *Regional differences in GDP per head* (UK=100)

	1979	1986	Change
South-East	115	117	+2
East Midlands	96	96	0
North-West	96	94	−2
West Midlands	95	91	−4
Scotland	95	93	−2
East Anglia	94	101	+7
Yorkshire and Humberside	93	93	0
South-West	93	96	+3
Wales	88	86	−2
UK average per head	£2,964	£5,597	+£2,633

Source: Regional Trends, 23 (1988), Table 11. Excludes North Sea oil revenues.

In the Thatcher years differences in economic performance have widened—but by only a very little. According to latest government statistics, the difference between GDP per head in the South-East of England and for the country overall is now 2 per cent greater than in 1979, and Scotland and Wales have fallen 2 per cent further below average. Yet in the Thatcher years the biggest decline has occurred in the West Midlands, the centre of the declining British motor industry. The West Midlands has historically been reckoned as at the south end of Britain economically as well as geographically. Yet its GDP per head is now the lowest in any English region.

The most dramatic change implicit in the trends of the past decade has been the *detachment* of the South of England from the rest of Britain as it strengthens its links with the Continent and with the rest of the world. This is most dramatically demonstrated in the City of London, as Thatcher-inspired deregulation has been followed by a boom in which financial institutions in the old Square Mile of the City threaten to expand into 10 square kilometres. In many respects the City of London is closer to Frankfurt, New York, or Tokyo than it is to Birmingham or Beckenham.

Another Thatcher achievement, the building of the Channel tunnel linking Kent with France, will intensify this, for it will give this most English, yet isolated, county easier road access to France and Belgium than to Nottingham or Manchester. The integration of parts of the South-East with Europe is also shown by the fact that East Anglia, once below average economically because of its agricultural base, is now above the British average, and the South-West has grown at a faster-than-average rate in the past decade too.

Population movements reflect changes within the South of England and within regions more than between them. People have been moving out of cities to suburbs or what was once considered countryside. Thus, London, Manchester, Liverpool, and Greater Glasgow have lost population, while the remainder of the South-East, the North-West, and the rest of Scotland have gained population. The reshuffling of population reflects a process that has been going on for a generation or more.

When new boundaries are drawn for parliamentary seats in the 1990s Labour will see more than a dozen of its safe seats abolished as a consequence of population movements. The Conservatives (or the heirs of the Alliance parties) hope to benefit from the creation of new seats in suburbs and formerly rural areas, where their vote is above average. But politicians cannot claim to have caused these intra-regional shifts in population, which reflect economic and social processes common throughout Europe.

Housing

House prices show that being top of a regional league table is a mixed blessing. In response to inflation, property values have escalated everywhere in the Western world, as people prefer to hold bricks and mortar rather than paper currency. In 1979 house prices were higher in the South of England than in the

North, but the differences were matters of degree, not kind. The
gap has widened since.

In the past decade house prices in the South-East of England
have risen more than twice as much as the North of England,
Scotland, and Wales. Almost anyone who owned a house in the
South-East before 4 May 1979 could be laughing all the way to
the bank, if the object were to sell up and move to a retirement
home in Portugal with the proceeds. But a Londoner with the
Thatcherite ideal of moving to a better house will find that
achieving this will require a much bigger mortgage, as bigger
houses have increased in value by hundreds of thousands of
pounds. Since interest rates have risen too, monthly mortgage
payments are now much higher.

Younger people and other first-time buyers are now crying all
the way home from the building society, as they realize that a
home of their own within the bounds of the London Under-
ground system may be beyond their reach. Anyone who gets on
his or her bike in the North of England to find a job in the South-
East will pay a big penalty, for the house prices for first-time
buyers in Greater London are more than double those for first-
time buyers in the North, in Wales, or in Scotland.

The availability of cheaper housing in regions distant from
London has added material weight to the claim beloved of
regional planners that the 'quality of life' is better the further one
moves from London. The Thatcher government cannot claim
credit for the fact that access to the sea and to miles of moorlands
is easier in Yorkshire or Scotland or Wales than in London. But
the net effect of changes in house prices in the past decade is that
these 'priceless' amenities are now much easier to afford, for
when one moves north it is possible to buy twice as much house
for the money as a family could afford in London.

In and out of work

During the past decade unemployment has been the Achilles' heel
of the government's management of the economy. In the four
years after the 1979 election the total number out of work
zoomed from 1.3 million to above 3 million. While unemployment has fallen substantially from its peak in 1986, part of the fall

is due to changes in government statistics. By any calculation, the level of unemployment in 1989 is substantially higher than it was on the day Margaret Thatcher entered Downing Street. Nor should this be surprising, for unemployment has increased substantially in nearly every industrial nation in Europe.

In the bygone era of full employment, the South-East and the West Midlands experienced labour shortages, and regions where unemployment was above 4 or 5 per cent were said to be deprived. The rise in unemployment since has affected all parts of the United Kingdom, but the impact has been uneven. Unemployment has gone up to a lesser degree in the North of England, where it was already high, and in the South, where it was low.

If we want to make differences in levels of unemployment appear great we can say that unemployment in the North of England is now more than 50 per cent greater than the national average of 7 per cent, and it is more than a third above the national average in Scotland, the North-West, and Wales. The four parts of Britain where unemployment is below average are closest to London. However the decline in the motor industry has made the West Midlands a region with above-average unemployment today.

Differences are reduced to matters of degree when we look at the proportion of the labour force that is actually in work. It is often forgotten that an unemployment rate of 10 per cent in Scotland shows that 90 per cent of the labour force is in work, just as an unemployment rate of 5 per cent in the South-West indicates that 95 per cent of the labour force there is in work. While higher levels of unemployment cast a shadow over the jobs of some in work, from one end of Britain to the other the great bulk of the labour force is in work. By comparison with a country such as Germany, a larger portion of the population of working age is participating in the labour force, due to the larger number of part-time workers in Britain, and a larger service sector.

PARTY POLITICS

In party politics, the lines along which Britons divide owe less to geography than to class and political principles. Politically, the socio-economic composition of a region is more important than cultural residues of history. If we want to predict the vote in a constituency, it is far more important to know its percentage of home-owners or of manual workers than to know in which region it is located. One reason why the North of England and Scotland return more Labour MPs than the South is that they have a higher proportion of manual workers, council tenants, and unemployed persons. In predicting the behaviour of individual voters, it is much more important to know how they stand on left–right economic issues than where they are located on a North–South geographical axis.

Disproportional representation by region

The only way in which the opposition party can win any seats in the House of Commons is to be stronger in some regions of Britain than in others. If the electorate in every constituency and every region of Britain divided similarly, the Conservatives would have won 633 seats at the last general election, and Labour would have done the same in the 1960s and 1970s. Under the first-past-the-post electoral system, inequalities between regions—or between inner cities and suburbs—are a *necessary* condition of competitive party politics.

When we look at a map there appear to be big disparities between North and South, because seats in the House of Commons are awarded on the first-past-the-post principle rather than by proportional representation. Thus, six of the seven MPs for County Durham are Labour, though Labour takes little more than half the vote there, and 10 of the 11 MPs for Devon are Conservative, though the Tories take less than half the vote there. Disproportionality is great at the regional level. In the South-East, the opposition parties took 44 per cent of the popular vote at the last election, but won only one of its 108 seats. In the Northern region, Labour won three-quarters of the seats with 46 per cent of its vote.

Voting trends

Throughout the post-war era social differences have led to big differences in votes by region and nation. In 1964, when the

Conservative and Labour parties secured an almost equal share of the nation-wide vote, the Conservatives did better than Labour in England, and Labour did better in Scotland and Wales (Table 19.2). The Tories did not issue demands for the creation of a

TABLE 19.2.   *Changes in electoral support in Britain, 1964–1987*

	Conservative	Labour	Liberal/ Alliance	Nationalist
	(% share of vote)			
England				
1964	44·1	43·5	12·1	
1979	47·2	36·7	14·9	not
1987	46·2	29·5	23·9	applicable
Change	+2·1	−14·0	+11·8	
Wales				
1964	29·4	57·4	7·3	4·8
1979	32·1	48·6	10·6	8·1
1987	29·5	45·1	17·9	7·3
Change	+0·1	−12·3	+10·6	+2·5
Scotland				
1964	40·6	48·7	7·6	2·4
1979	31·4	41·5	9·0	17·3
1987	24·0	42·4	19·3	14·0
Change	−16·6	−6·3	+11·7	+11·6

devolved English Assembly to meet in Winchester, on the grounds that Labour was unrepresentative of England. Losers as well as winners accepted that the power of government belonged to the party winning the most seats in Britain overall. In 1979 the Conservatives won virtually the same share of the popular vote as in 1964. Margaret Thatcher became Prime Minister because of divisions in Labour's ranks rather than because of a division between England, Scotland, and Wales.

In the last quarter-century the most striking feature is that Labour support has declined greatly throughout Britain. It is down almost as much in Wales as in England, and it is down in

Scotland too. Moreover, the vote for the centre parties has risen greatly in all parts of Britain.

To denigrate Margaret Thatcher as the voice of England is to undermine democracy, for a party should not have to apologize for winning an absolute majority of seats in the House of Commons—358 seats of a total of 650—in the largest part of the United Kingdom. To criticize the Conservatives for 'failing' to win half the vote in England is a double-edged sword, for Labour has never in its history won half the vote in Scotland.

Scotland is different, for the Conservative vote there has fallen more than the Labour vote, and is now below 25 per cent of the Scottish total. The rash interpret this as the end of the Union or as the loss of Westminster's claim to govern Scotland. Yet such weakness is not unprecedented; in October 1974 the Conservative share of the vote was even less in Wales—and five years later the Welsh referendum overwhelmingly rejected the devolution offered it by the Labour government. In Scotland, the Conservative road to recovery has been complicated by the re-emergence of the Scottish National Party as a threat in rural Tory seats.

If Margaret Thatcher's personality is said to be the cause of Scots' rejection of the Tory Party, this implies that her retirement would lead to a resurgence in Conservative fortunes north of the Border. However, the longer Mrs Thatcher remains in office and the greater the impact of such policies as the poll-tax, then the greater the risk for the government that it could be relegated to third-place status in Scotland for a decade or longer. This would also pose difficulties for Labour, which has found itself competing with Scottish Nationalists for the title of the most effective alternative to Thatcherism. If Labour were to succeed in winning devolution for Scotland, then a future Conservative government could strike a blow for equality and for party advantage by reducing the representation of Scots and Welsh at Westminster to accord with population, and boost the number of Tory seats in England.

Because the Thatcher rhetoric has undoubtedly heightened the rhetoric of conflict, albeit along economic not territorial lines, its impact upon political cohesion in Britain will be easier to discern when that voice is stilled. Meanwhile, if British politicians want to see what *real* political conflict is about, they need look no further than Northern Ireland, where during twenty years of successive Labour and Conservative governments murderous civil war has claimed thousands of lives.

20

The Family

DAVID WILLETTS

1. SOCIAL TRENDS

A few sensational statistics are frequently cited in any discussion of changes in the family:

- only 28 per cent of households consisted in 1987 of a married couple with dependent children as against 31 per cent in 1981 and 38 per cent in 1961;
- a quarter of all households in 1987 consisted of people living on their own as against one-eighth in 1961;
- one in three marriages ends in divorce;
- the number of births outside marriage has risen from 6 per cent in 1961 to 12 per cent in 1981 and 23 per cent in 1987.

The message from these statistics is supposed to be that the nuclear family is breaking up into atomistic individuals. Just as the government's policies are believed to have encouraged egoism and self-aggrandizement in commercial life, so they seem to have weakened the bonds that tie us together in our domestic lives. But, as Robert Chester has convincingly shown ('The Rise of the Neo-Conventional Family', *New Society*, 9 May 1985), reports of the death of the conventional family are much exaggerated. There clearly are some changes in the nature of the family but behind each of the crude statistics above there is a much more subtle and complex story.

Longer periods of our lives are indeed spent outside the nuclear family—people are more likely to live alone before getting married and after the death of a partner. As a result the total number of households has risen and their average size has fallen. But that does not mean that other stages of the life cycle are disappearing—most people still get married and have children. Indeed, if one measures people not households, then the picture is of much more continuity. In the words of *Social Trends*, 'just over 77% of people living in private households in Great Britain in 1987 lived in families headed by a married couple, a proportion which has fallen only slightly since 1961. Within this, the proportion of people in households consisting of a married couple and no children has risen whilst the proportion of married couples with children has fallen' (*Social Trends* (1989), p. 39). Table 20.1 shows the full picture.

TABLE 20.1. *People in households in Great Britain: by type of household and family in which they live* (%)

Type of household	1961	1971	1981	1987
Living alone	3·9	6·3	8·0	9·9
Married couple, no children	17·8	19·3	19·5	21·5
Married couple with dependent children	52·2	51·7	47·4	44·1
Married couple with non-dependent children only	11·6	10·0	10·3	11·8
Lone parent with dependent children	2·5	3·5	5·8	4·7
Other households	12·0	9·3	9·0	8·0
All households	100·0	100·0	100·0	100·0

There has admittedly been a big rise in the divorce rate but this may be picking up the consequences of social mores twenty or thirty years ago, rather than reflecting current marriage habits. Indeed today's marriages may be more robust than those made a generation ago. There are a couple of reliable rules for predicting the fate of a marriage—it is more likely to fail if the bride is young or if she is pregnant. The average age of marriage fell from the 1940s to the beginning of the 1970s. There has since been a shift to later marriage—in 1984 1 in 6 spinsters marrying was a teenager; a decade earlier the ratio was 1 in 3. This shift to later marriage is associated with a dramatic increase in pre-marital sex (it is estimated that in the late 1960s less than 50 per cent of brides had engaged in pre-marital sex as against 80 per cent to 90 per cent by the late 1970s). But with the spread of contraception there are fewer shotgun marriages caused by pregnancy—Kathleen Kiernan reports that during the 1960s 1 in 5 brides were pregnant at marriage as compared with 1 in 8 brides by the 1980s.

These favourable trends—later marriage and fewer pregnant brides—lead this author to forecast that by the year 2000 the divorce rate will be significantly lower than it is today and divorce will be as unusual and unacceptable among the middle classes as cigarette-smoking has already become.

Even the rise in illegitimacy may not be quite as dramatic as it seems. Of all those children born illegitimately between 1978 and 1981, 40 per cent were in a family headed by a married couple by the time of the 1981 Census. So the appeal of marriage and the family unit remains powerful even to those whose behaviour takes them (temporarily) outside it.

Perhaps the people who wish to argue that there has been a dramatic change in the conventional family are looking in the wrong place. Instead of considering the statistics for family breakdown and single households, they should look at changing family roles—the biggest change by far being the increase in the number of working women. Between 1971 and 1987 the proportion of economically inactive married women decreased sharply from 51 per cent to 34 per cent, while the proportion in employment grew from 47 per cent to 60 per cent. Many women therefore enjoy a degree of financial independence, which is behind the powerful pressure during the 1980s to change the tax rules so as to give full independent taxation of husband and wife. Ironically this increased female participation in the work-force is partly caused by the peculiarly favourable tax treatment of the second earner in the British income tax system—deliberately introduced during the Second World War so as to encourage women into the work-force.

There are many other complex reasons for this increase in paid work by women. Women's aspirations now go beyond the home. Women tend not to be unionized and have a good reputation as flexible and diligent workers. The development of household technology has reduced the amount of labour required to run a house. Other household services can now be bought in the market-place, whereas previously they were provided 'unpaid' by women in the home—in the language of economists the household has changed from a unit of production to a unit of consumption.

Even so, there is still a lot of housework to be done! Surveys by Social and Community Planning Research suggest that housework is mainly done by women in 72 per cent of cases where both husband and wife work full time, in 80 per cent of cases where the wife works part time, and in 91 per cent of cases where the man works and the woman does not. As a result women have much less leisure time than men in similar circumstances. This unsatisfactory position may explain why, in England and Wales in 1987, 73 per cent of all divorce decrees were granted to wives, the highest proportion ever recorded, with over half of the decrees because of unreasonable behaviour of husbands.

2. FAMILY POLICY

Conservative politicians proclaim that they are the party of the family and respect the solid domestic aspirations of ordinary citizens—as against the rainbow coalition of eccentric life-styles that comprises the Labour Party. One of the reasons that Conservatives value the family so much is that it is the most powerful social institution outside the political sphere. It is where altruism and civility are first learned and practised. For most individuals it gives their life meaning and purpose, and shapes many of their greatest obligations to others. Indeed Mr Ferdinand Mount, the head of the Prime Minister's Policy Unit 1982–4, wrote a book calling it 'The Subversive Family', because it stands free from state control and direction.

There is a paradox here: Conservatives value the family because of its independence from the state yet they often find themselves tempted to use government policy levers so as to support it, or prop it up, or encourage it. The idea of a 'Minister for the Family' is one example of this desire to politicize and fiddle with an institution which is so valuable because it is unpolitical. There are two obvious routes for resolving this tension. One option is to argue that government ought at least not to act as a threat to family life by policies (notably in taxes and benefits) which create a perverse incentive to be 'married to the state'. This is considered further below.

But the other route forward is to identify ways in which greater power and responsibility can be passed to the family away from the state. This was the approach adopted by the Family Policy Group set up in March 1982, chaired by the Prime Minister, in which Ferdinand Mount played a large part. It is a good example of how policy advisers at No 10, and of course the Prime Minister herself, can successfully raise departments' awareness of an issue hitherto ignored because of Whitehall's inability to see the wood for the trees. The Group deliberately took a broad view of its task—family policy became social policy.

Some of the initial proposals from departments for family policy initiatives were feeble—dusting off long-standing departmental proposals in health or local government and inventing a tenuous link to family policy. Others were bizarre—such as the Treasury's reported desire to encourage the saving of pocket money. But gradually the broad themes emerged which have pervaded government policy on the Welfare State ever since. The main objective was to shift power from producers to consumers and extend as much choice as possible within the framework of the tax-financed Welfare State.

The 1980 Education Act had already given parents a statutory right to express a preference for the school of their choice. Next, parents were brought into partnership with teachers and local authority representatives as governors of schools. Some of the more ambitious ideas for open enrolment and grant-maintained status for schools finally embodied in the 1988 Education Reform Act were first mooted in the Family Policy Group. Headmasters were also given greater power in the day-to-day running of their schools. In the health service, the message was 'putting patients first', though the policies which actually implemented this principle only began to emerge in the Primary Care Green Paper of 1985 and the waiting-list initiative of 1986, culminating in the health review of 1988–9.

In housing, further steps were taken to encourage the right to buy, which led to the commitment in the 1983 manifesto to give larger discounts to potential purchasers.

Pensions were also looked at in the Family Policy Group. The government pursued two objectives—for a higher proportion of pensioners' income to come from the private sector rather than state benefits, and secondly to reduce the role of the big institutions in private pension provision and to encourage individual saving through personal pensions. Linking the state retirement pension simply to prices and not to earnings in 1980 was the first crucial step in this direction. The cutting back of SERPS and the encouragement for personal pensions in the 1986 Social Security Act was the next main step. The impact of these measures is now being felt as, on average, pensioners now only get approximately half of their total income from the state, the rest coming from their buoyant savings and private pension schemes.

There were also measures in the area of law and order which were not so much extending new powers to families as new responsibilities. Parents, for example, were made more responsible for the offences of their children aged under 17 and can now be obliged to pay compensation for damage and injury done by their children.

The striking feature of this family policy agenda is that it largely avoids those areas of sexual behaviour which are the subject of so much prurient interest whenever people talk about morality or family values. The Prime Minister, Norman Tebbit, and others attack 'permissiveness' but have made no attempt to reverse the legalization of homosexuality and abortion associated above all with Roy Jenkins. The modest legal changes which have been introduced are not really part of family policy but by-products of other policies. The clause in the Local Government Act preventing the use of public money to promote homosexuality should be seen rather as part of the 'loony left' council issue. The Obscene Displays Act essentially tidied up the definition of an existing offence of offending public taste and decency. There has still not been any legislation to bring down the age at which a foetus can be aborted, though it has now become accepted practice not to carry out an abortion after twenty-four weeks.

Instead of focusing on homosexuality and abortion, government ministers have taken a much broader and deeper view of permissiveness, as shown in, for example, Norman Tebbit's first Disraeli lecture 'Britain's Future—A Conservative Vision' (1985): 'I believe that by the 1990s we shall see the effects of a revulsion against the valueless values of the permissive society. The public are demanding stiffer sentences for criminals—and in the end—they will get them.' Conservative thinkers argue that the behaviour problems of the 1980s—lager louts to litter—were attributable not to the enterprise culture and individualism but to the permissiveness of the 1960s and 1970s, when figures in authority were afraid to say 'no' and every personal failure was society's fault. That is the context in which the Prime Minister's statement, 'There is no such thing as society', is to be understood. She was arguing that making the society the scapegoat was untenable—people had to accept responsibility for their own behaviour because anything else would infantilize us all.

3. FAMILY INCOMES: EMPLOYMENT, TAXES, AND BENEFITS

Families have become more prosperous since 1979. The real take-home pay (i.e. after direct tax, and after inflation) for a married one-earner couple with two children on average earnings rose by 0.7 per cent between 1973/4 and 1978/9: by contrast it rose by 29.3 per cent between 1978/9 and 1988/9. A man in similar circumstances but on half average earnings saw his income rise by 4.2 per cent from 1973/4 to 1978/9 and by 22.7 per cent between 1978/9 and 1988/9. This shows clearly a move to greater equality of incomes under the last Labour government and to greater inequality since 1979. But absolute incomes have increased much more since 1979.

The statistics on poverty confirm this impression. The best authoritative government figures on households below average income only cover the 1981–5 period so far. Nevertheless, the trends they show are interesting. They measure both 'absolute' and 'relative' poverty. 12 per cent of married couples with children in 1981 had incomes less than half the average. Taking their incomes as determining the bench-mark in absolute terms and applying it to actual incomes in 1985 shows the number of married couples with children with incomes below that absolute level had fallen to 10 per cent. On the other hand, in 1985, 13 per cent of married couples with children had incomes below half of what was the average. So again the picture is of increasing absolute incomes and a widening of the income distribution. Some critics would say that this was too complacent a picture of family incomes over the past ten years. They would point out that there are several other pieces of evidence which show an increasing problem of family poverty.

- The real pay figures only include the effects of direct taxes. The government has deliberately shifted the burden of taxation to indirect taxes and estimates of increases in disposable income after all taxes are therefore not quite as dramatic.
- Average incomes of many families may have fallen during the recession of 1979–81 with high inflation and big increases in unemployment, though since 1981 the position has been getting better for most people.
- Looking at a longer time-scale, there has been a significant change in the composition of the poorest quintile of households. In 1971 16.7 per cent of the poorest 20 per cent of households were couples with children. By 1982 that had risen to 23.3 per cent of the poorest 20 per cent of households, reflecting rising unemployment and the dramatic improvement in pensioners' incomes.

The late 1970s and early 1980s saw external changes—the rise in unemployment and the rapid increase in the number of old people and single parents—combining to put enormous extra strains on the social security budget. Though there were some specific reductions in social security entitlements—such as the abolition of the Earnings Related Supplement for unemployment benefit—the general picture was of the social security safety net taking the strain. This is probably too boring for the rhetoric of politicians from either party. Opposition spokesmen want to convey a sense of appalling cuts in social security while some government supporters claim radical reforms in social security even when their actual record was more modest.

The best way to formulate some overall assessment of the impact of tax and benefit policies on families is to consider those in three different types of circumstance—families without an earner, one-earner families, and two-earner families.

Families without earners are almost certain to be dependent on social security. Indeed, if a husband loses his job and claims benefit, the part-time earnings of his wife are taken into account, so often the wife withdraws from the labour market as well. Research done by the Policy Studies Institute suggested that these people were the group which found it hardest to make ends meet on social security—harder than pensioners, for example. So the government was always under pressure to raise supplementary benefit rates for this group. But the level of benefits paid to unemployed people constitutes their reserve wage. Raising it would exacerbate the 'unemployment trap', so that they would find themselves able to earn little more in work than out of work. Any change in benefits for unemployed families had to take account of the effect on poor working families.

Poor working families are almost exclusively one-earner families. If both the husband and the wife work a family is unlikely to be near the bottom of the income distribution. Family Income Supplement was introduced in 1971 as a means-tested benefit to top up the incomes of low income working families. Unfortunately, it was not aligned with Supplementary Benefit, so that, depending on the age of their children, for example, a poor family might still not find themselves much better off in work than out of work.

The Social Security Act of 1986 established a consistent logical structure for helping both unemployed and poor working families. A new Family Premium was added to income support rates so that unemployed families enjoyed a modest increase in their benefit entitlements. The new Family Credit, which replaced Family Income Supplement, matched the structure of the new income support system so that, whatever a family's circumstances, Family Credit would always ensure that they were better off in work than out of work. These two changes to the benefit structure have enabled the government to target extra money for poor families without exacerbating the unemployment trap.

The government has financed this extra expenditure by not necessarily up-rating the universal Child Benefit in line with inflation. This policy has proved controversial because it is argued that, with the abolition of the Child Tax Allowance, Child Benefit is the mechanism whereby governments should recognize that, in traditional Inland Revenue terminology, families with children have a lower taxable capacity than those with similar incomes and without children. Some people on the radical right have argued against this, that children should now be seen as a consumption good, no more meriting recognition for tax or benefit systems than a consumer durable. This is not the government's philosophy; rather it has pursued a more modest incremental shift in support away from expenditure on Child Benefit (costing about £4 billion to help 12 million children) and towards targeted help for poorer families. The systems targeted on low income working families may also be seen as support for the traditional family life-style, because such families are likely to consist of one earner with a non-working wife.

Two-earner families are particularly well treated in the British tax system. The married man's tax allowance exceeds that of a single person and, in addition, a working wife is entitled to the wife's earned income allowance, which equals a single person's allowance. This means that a two-earner couple enjoys a larger tax allowance in total than two single earners. If a woman goes back into work therefore she will find that approximately the first £2,500 of her earnings are tax free.

The government twice published Green Papers (in 1980 and in 1986) which considered schemes that were 'neutral' between one- and two-earner couples, but they all suffered the problem of penalizing the two-earner couple because they do disproportionately well out of the current structure. But it was increasingly offensive for many women that for tax purposes they were in effect subordinate dependents of their husbands. In the end, the Chancellor announced in his 1988 Budget that he would be introducing independent taxation in 1990, though with a new 'married couple allowance', which ensured two-earner couples did not lose out from his changes. As Macaulay said of the 1689 Act of Toleration, 'It removed a vast mass of evil without shocking a vast mass of prejudice'.

4. CONCLUSION: COULD THINGS HAVE BEEN ANY DIFFERENT?

Many of the deeper trends in family life have also been occurring in other countries and would have happened in Britain regardless of the party in power. One can however speculate about four ways in which things could have gone differently.

First, we might not have seen such a dramatic shift away from old-style manufacturing industry with full-time unionized male labour towards service industries with non-unionized female labour. A Labour government which propped up traditional manufacturing and had close links to male-dominated trade unions might well have presided over a much smaller increase in female participation in the labour force.

Secondly, we might have seen a more dramatic expansion of publicly financed and publicly run services for families such as child care and nursery education. We could have moved closer to a Scandinavian model of the role of the state in providing support for the family or, as others might see it, displacing it.

Thirdly, the pattern of social security benefits could have been rather different. Superficially it may seem odd that it is a right-wing government which wishes to target help on the poor and a left-wing policy to spread benefits universally, however affluent the recipient. But left-wing thinkers argue that services or benefits exclusively for the poor become poor services and benefits. A Labour government would have kept up a larger constituency for social security benefits by spreading them more widely and at higher levels, though might have found the legitimacy of the system threatened by the higher tax rates that would have resulted and the 'why work?' problem.

The final difference is of the greatest significance philosophically, though difficult to pin down in practice. There are two great institutions which above all offer us support and help: the state and the family. No advanced society will ever rely solely on one of these institutions, and indeed, they are not necessarily and always in conflict. But the more the state does to help us on a rainy day, the less we need to do for ourselves through reliance on the extended family or personal saving. The pattern of causation is complicated. An increased role for the Welfare State reduces the need to rely on the resources of the family. Maybe the role of the family in providing its own welfare services is shrinking anyway, and the state comes in to fill a vacuum. Maybe an increased role for the state is simply another example of specialization of labour—we don't bake our own bread, nor do we directly care for our elderly parents as much as we did—both tasks are now done more by outside providers. There are deep philosophical questions here. But it is clear that at the margin a different government with a different philosophy would have had a more ambitious role for the state, both in financing and in providing services, and put less stress on the family's responsibility for providing, or at least choosing, services itself.

21

The Law

GRAHAM ZELLICK

The chill wind of Thatcherism has, until now, gusted well away from the law, sheltered as it has been by the ample bulk of Lord Chancellor Hailsham. Only with the reluctant departure of Hailsham following the 1987 election was the way cleared for the Thatcher revolution to reach the legal profession, which it now threatens to do with the publication in January 1989 of the three Green Papers by Lord Mackay of Clashfern, the first Scottish advocate to sit on the Woolsack.

Strangely, Hailsham saw himself, and wished to be seen, as a notable reformer. It was he after all who implemented the Beeching proposals in the early 1970s on the reform of the higher criminal courts, sweeping away the old assizes and quarter sessions, establishing the Crown Court, and creating the judicial rank of circuit judge, to which even solicitors could aspire. But when it came to the legal profession itself, Hailsham was as staunch a defender as the Bar in particular could hope for, just like his Labour predecessor from 1964 to 1970, Lord Gardiner, a radical reformer on every issue but one—the legal profession.

Time and again when it was suggested, quite modestly, that solicitor circuit judges should be eligible for promotion to the High Court Bench, Hailsham resisted with a firmness that encouraged no reasoned debate. A lifetime's experience of High Court litigation and advocacy was apparently a prerequisite for appointment as a High Court judge which not even superlative performance of the duties of a circuit judge could displace or compensate for. The real reason, however, lay in Hailsham's observation that to permit such appointments would sour relations between the two branches of the profession. In other words, it would displease the Bar; and Hailsham was, as ever, their champion.

In the widest sense, the law is not something which is likely to be susceptible to Mrs Thatcher's philosophy or dogma: the law is merely the vehicle or mechanism through which substantive changes are effected. In another sense, however, by law we mean the administration of justice and the legal system, the legal profession and the delivery of legal services, all of which could fall victim to a thoroughgoing shake-up. It is this aspect of the law which will be considered here.

Another complication in this area is the fragmentation of ministerial responsibility for matters legal: civil law and justice and legal aid fall to the Lord Chancellor; criminal law and justice to the Home Secretary. Throughout this period, there were three Chancellors: Hailsham from 1979 to 1987, resuming the office he held between 1970 and 1974, making him the longest-serving Chancellor this century; there was then the ephemeral tenure of Lord Havers, rewarded, despite poor health, for his loyal services as Attorney-General, particularly over Westland and *Spycatcher*, who came and went (not a little reluctantly, it would seem) within a few months, all of which were bedevilled by illness; and then James Mackay, who has at least until the end of this Parliament to make his mark. At the Home Office, by contrast, there have been three Home Secretaries but none has by length of tenure dominated the scene in the way Hailsham did: Willie Whitelaw served from 1979 to 1983; he was followed by Leon Brittan until 1985; and then came Douglas Hurd, who remains in office.

While Hailsham may plausibly lay claim to some kind of reformer's mantle, he was a Tory of the old school and certainly not in any sense a Thatcher acolyte. Whitelaw, too, was a similar kind of Conservative; and none of the Home Secretaries over the decade has been closely identified with the sharpest of Mrs Thatcher's ideology.

CRIMINAL LAW AND CRIMINAL JUSTICE

This is not to say that nothing innovative has emanated from the Home Office, as part of the government's law and order platform, and there is even talk now of privately owned and run prisons and remand establishments, which bears all the hallmarks of this government's philosophy. But on the whole the Home Office has had to wrestle with all the problems and pressures of crime and a criminal justice and prison system which is barely able to cope, and it has responded neither better nor worse than it has done under previous administrations. For all the rhetoric at party conferences, crime does not readily admit of instant solutions, and party dogma has little to offer. Placating party supporters is one thing: reversing the crime wave is quite another.

The Home Office has given birth to a formidable body of legislation over the period, some of it, like the Police and Criminal Evidence Act 1984 and the Prosecution of Offences Act 1985, of major importance, and much of it intensely controversial, but it derives from no comprehensive philosophy save perhaps an ongoing commitment (in word at any rate) to promoting the efficiency and effectiveness of the criminal justice system.

What distinguishes this government from its predecessors is its determination, often in the face of the fiercest opposition, to press ahead with proposals which other governments might have abandoned. One example is the peremptory challenge to jurors, which has now been abolished. Another—the power of the Attorney-General to refer unduly lenient Crown Court sentences to the Court of Appeal—was indeed dropped in the face of strenuous criticism but only to surface again a year or two later, in stronger form, with the Court of Appeal actually empowered to increase the sentence, rather than just issue guidance for the future. In this form it reached the statute book in 1988.

We shall see something similar with the right to silence, which Douglas Hurd has been questioning aloud for some time now. Despite the depth of feeling its retention evokes, it is unlikely to survive much longer, having already been abolished in Northern Ireland. Other casualties have included the right of a defendant to make an unsworn statement from the dock on which he could not be cross-examined and the right of a defendant remanded in custody to be brought back to court every week. The Roskill Committee recommendation, however, that serious and complex frauds should be withdrawn from a jury and tried by a judge sitting with two assessors expert in financial matters proved too much; another potential victim to have escaped thus far, despite the demands of efficiency, has been the right to elect jury trial in the Crown Court for minor thefts.

Other recommendations from Roskill on fraud trials were implemented, in the Criminal Justice Act 1987, which established the Serious Fraud Office and, in a dramatic departure from the principles of English criminal procedure, provided that any person under investigation or believed to have relevant information may be required, on pain of imprisonment, to answer questions, furnish information, or produce documents. Abolition of trial by jury may have been too much to stomach, but an unprecedented obligation on a suspect to respond to questioning, which is a much greater interference with individual rights, proved quite palatable.

Some of the changes may even be characterized as verging on the liberal or enlightened, such as the abolition of imprisonment for soliciting, the abolition of 'sus' (loitering with intent), the reduction in the period served in prison before parole eligibility, the imposition of criminal liability on men for kerb-crawling and persistent soliciting of women, the abolition of the corroboration requirement in respect of children's unsworn evidence, the introduction of live video links for the evidence of children (and some others), the arrangements for those imprisoned abroad to serve their sentences in the UK, and a right of appeal against reporting restrictions imposed by the Crown Court. However, the Prior Committee recommendations on reforming the prison disciplinary system have been rejected.

Other changes were responses to particular pressures. The penalties for attempted rape, indecent assault on a girl under 13, firearms offences, insider dealing, and cruelty to children have been increased; defendants' anonymity in rape cases has been abolished (without disturbing the victims' right to anonymity); the law on possessing knives and offensive weapons in public has been strengthened; courts must now give reasons for *granting* bail in certain serious cases (because of anxieties that some dangerous offenders are released pending trial); and prisoners may be detained in any place approved by the Home Secretary and even released prematurely (both occasioned by industrial action by prison staff, which has been a recurring problem).

There is much else which is sensible and useful or at least gives rise to no serious objection. In 1982, far-reaching changes were made to the system of custody for those under 21, which were further modified in 1988: the old Borstal sentence was superseded by youth custody and we now have a generic sentence of detention in a young offenders' institution. Those sentenced to imprisonment (even if suspended) or even community service within the last ten years are now excluded from jury service. The Drug Trafficking Offences Act 1986 deals with confiscation orders against persons convicted of drug trafficking and provides stringent enforcement procedures. The Criminal Justice Act 1988 strengthens the law on confiscation and compensation orders, puts the Criminal Injuries Compensation Scheme and compensation for miscarriages of justice on a statutory basis, and gives effect to an international convention on torture by making torture a criminal offence. More controversial was the Act's simplification, or over-simplification, as its critics would say, of the extradition law, making it now largely a matter for executive rather than judicial determination.

Some important changes have been forced on the government by developments elsewhere. Two decisions of the European Court of Justice led to the Sex Discrimination Act 1986, which brought the Sex Discrimination Act of 1975 and the Equal Pay Act 1970 into line with the EEC's Equal Treatment Directive; and decisions of the European Court of Human Rights brought about the Interception of Communications Act 1985 and the Contempt of Court Act 1981.

Repeatedly, the government had refused to legislate on telephone tapping, but the 1985 Act puts it on a statutory basis for the first time; it was hitherto authorized by warrants issued by the Home Secretary which had no legal validity. He is now explicitly empowered to authorize telephone tapping and mail interception, which if done otherwise amounts to a criminal offence. A tribunal handles complaints of authorized taps which have some procedural or other irregularity about them; but completely unauthorized taps—the source of most concern—being 'illegal', are not for the tribunal but for the police to investigate. If there is no warrant, the complainant will simply be told there has been no infringement.

The Contempt of Court Act (which was the Lord Chancellor's Bill) was the culmination of the thalidomide saga, in which the decision of the House of Lords that a series of *Sunday Times* articles on the affair and the liability of the drug company Distillers constituted contempt of court was itself held by the European Court of Human Rights to amount to a violation of the European Convention on Human Rights. The Act was a long time coming, and it makes heavy weather of relatively simple matters, but it responds to the human rights infringement in three ways: it substitutes a new test of 'a *substantial* risk that the course of justice ... will be *seriously* impeded or prejudiced'; the *sub judice* rule applies only to proceedings which are 'active'; and a publication discussing matters of public interest does not become a contempt if the risk of prejudice to the proceedings is merely incidental to that discussion.

The complete revision of the nationality law, bringing it back into congruence with the immigration law, in the British Nationality Act 1981 was an enormous legislative exercise and vigorously opposed by Labour. So, too, was much of the Public Order Act 1986, despite its genesis in a Law Commission report. Apart from replacing all the old common law public order offences by revised statutory ones, the criticism was directed chiefly at the new offence of disorderly behaviour which causes harassment, alarm, or distress and the requirement to give advance notice to the police of public processions. Less controversial, though not regarded as a perfect piece of legislation, was the 1984 Data Protection Act, which established the Data Protection Register and a formidable bureaucracy but which covers only computerized and not manual records.

The two most significant pieces of legislation, however, were the Police and Criminal Evidence Act 1984 (PACE) and the Prosecution of Offences Act 1985, both of which have their provenance in the report of the Royal Commission on Criminal Procedure appointed by the previous Labour government. The commission had proposed a balanced package: the reform and extension of police powers and a system of public prosecution. The 1985 Act established the Crown Prosecution Service under the Director of Public Prosecutions, removing from the police their control of prosecutions and transferring it to a new breed of legal civil servant, the Crown Prosecutor. Chronic staff shortages and underfunding have caused endless problems, but the principle remains of the first importance. England was unique in having no proper public prosecution arrangements; it was not a function lying properly with the police; and the Act may one day come to be seen as the most significant and welcome development in criminal procedure this century.

PACE, on the other hand, continues to be seen as a vile monster by nearly everyone. Even the police deplore the paperwork and record-keeping and have claimed that it obstructs criminal investigation. Much of the obloquy can be traced back to the first version of the Bill introduced by Willie Whitelaw, which owed too little to the Royal Commission report and which understandably provoked strenuous opposition. The Bill to reach the statute book, while not eliminating all cause for concern, was a very much improved measure and does not deserve the universal condemnation to which it has been subject.

Police powers were fragmented, uncertain, unclear, and confused, and in some respects they were unarguably inadequate. Reform was long overdue. That search powers in respect of such serious crimes as murder, rape, and kidnapping did not exist was indefensible. Many provisions perceived as extensions of existing powers were in truth no such thing: they were either limitations or clarifications, such as intimate body searches and warrants of further detention (allowing for detention before charge of up to ninety-six hours, but only after appearances before a magistrates' court with the benefit of legal representation). Criticism and concern was certainly legitimate over some provisions, including the stop and search power, the power to arrest for any offence, however trivial, if one of the 'general arrest conditions' is satisfied, and the definition of 'serious arrestable offence'. But then there are other provisions which represent no small advance—on tape-recording of interrogations, on the right of access to legal assistance before charge and the nation-wide duty solicitor scheme established at a cost approaching £20 million a year, on the role of the custody officer in police stations, and even in the reforms (though they may not go far enough) in handling police complaints.

For its supporters and promoters, it was a crucial plank in the government's 'law and order' platform: for its critics, it was a measurable step along the road to a police state. In truth, it was neither. It has proved workable; the statistics on its operation so far available occasion no alarm; and the trends towards easier access to legal assistance and careful record-taking can only be welcomed.

More notable perhaps than all these changes promoted by the Home Office are the changes which have *not* come about. Despite her commanding position and her strong conviction, Mrs Thatcher has not been able to bring about the restoration of either capital or corporal punishment (indeed, the latter has even had to be abandoned in schools after a decision under the European Convention on Human Rights). It is also noteworthy that the right of individual petition under the European Convention, of which this government is not especially fond, has survived unscathed, although so far the campaign to incorporate the European Convention on Human Rights into British law has been held at bay.

Another area where we might have expected to see considerable change—obscenity—has witnessed only marginal strengthening of the law. Commercial cinema clubs have been brought within local authority licensing control; video films are now subject to a regime of certification; a statutory Broadcasting Standards Council has been established; public displays of indecent material have been prohibited; it is an offence to possess indecent photographs of children; and local authorities have been empowered to control, by way of licensing, 'sex establishments' in their areas. But the law of obscenity itself, despite its many imperfections, has not been touched. The Williams Committee reported in 1979, but their recommendations were unlikely to commend themselves to this, or indeed to any, government. They proposed that there should be no restrictions whatever on the

printed word as opposed to pictorial material; that other offensive matter should be restricted only in the sense that it could not
be publicly displayed; and that the only matter to be prohibited
would be that dealing with the sexual exploitation of children
under 16 or where actual physical harm has been inflicted during
its production.

Nor has there been any major immigration legislation, though
this is because the existing powers are quite sufficient for the
government's purposes. The problem of terrorism in relation to
Northern Ireland called for a revised Prevention of Terrorism Act
in 1984 but this merely re-enacted earlier provisions on pro-
scribed organizations and exclusion orders with modifications
following various reviews. Other actions—like the ban imposed
in 1988 on broadcast interviews with terrorist suspects and their
supporters—are chiefly symbolic.

The Home Secretary is currently embroiled in controversy over
two Bills dealing with national security—one on official secrets
which would replace the 1911 Act and the other, the Security
Service Bill, which would put MI5 (but not MI6) on a statutory
footing. Governments have been trying for nearly two decades to
reform the law on official secrets, but every attempt, even Mrs
Thatcher's earlier effort, has foundered.

Not so this time, although the opposition is surprisingly
ferocious, coming both from the Conservative side (including
Edward Heath) and from Labour. The new Bill is, in fact, a great
improvement on the 1911 Act in that it limits the disclosures
which would be subject to the criminal law and further provides
that in most cases the Crown will have to prove—to the satisfaction of a jury—that some specified harm has been caused. It also
dispenses with any kind of ministerial certification of classified
material, which was a feature of earlier attempts at reform, and
entrusts the decision to a jury instead.

What troubles the critics is that disclosures by former security
personnel, for example, will not need proof of harm and they will
be subject to lifelong confidentiality; that there is no defence of
'prior publication' of the revealed information; and above all that
there is no public interest defence for disclosures which reveal
wrongdoing or impropriety. There is, of course, substance in

these anxieties, but the Bill is nevertheless better than both the existing law and the earlier Bills presented by other governments.

The Security Service Bill has so far attracted less criticism. It was preceded by no public discussion and was wholly unexpected. It is in part modelled on the Interception of Communications Act in that it introduces a tribunal to consider complaints and provides for search warrants to be issued by the Home Secretary. This latter provision is extraordinary and overturns two centuries of English law.

LEGAL AID AND CIVIL PROCEDURE

Back, then, to Lord Hailsham. His last uninterrupted seven years cannot be accounted a notable era of reform. He tantalized us with the prospect of a family court for many years, but it never came. Instead, as an interim measure, we were given the Matrimonial and Family Proceedings Act 1984, which reorganized family business as between the High Court and the county court (it also, on the Law Commission's recommendation, though surprisingly for this government, replaced the discretionary three-year ban on petitioning for divorce after marriage by an absolute one-year bar).

There were half-hearted reforms of the solicitors' complaints system, making punishable for the first time inadequate professional services, and a wholly inadequate incursion into the solicitors' conveyancing monopoly by creating Licensed Conveyancers. The Supreme Court Act 1981 was a huge piece of legislation—153 sections and seven schedules—but it largely consolidated earlier statutes. It did, however, introduce some innovations: two-judge Courts of Appeal and the office of Registrar of Civil Appeals, which is a useful administrative reform. It also put the 1977 procedure for judicial review on a statutory footing, despite the marked lack of enthusiasm which this government has exhibited for this particular form of governmental challenge, now so deeply rooted in the legal-constitutional culture of the country. A particularly ill-judged attempt by Hailsham, on the urging of the Master of the Rolls, Sir John (now Lord) Donaldson, to abolish appeals against High Court refusals of leave to apply for judicial review had to be withdrawn in the face of intense opposition, not least from the judges, who had not been consulted.

The Department's chief preoccupation, particularly towards the end of this period, has undoubtedly been legal aid. It has not been the unrelenting pressure from interest groups and consumer organizations to extend the scheme to tribunals and bring more people within its scope by lowering the financial thresholds; nor even the vigorous complaints of the legal profession of inadequate remuneration—the Bar even took Hailsham to court and secured a better deal—and administrative chaos; but primarily the worries of the Treasury that this demand-led service, which could not be cash-limited, was escalating out of control: in 1976–7, the total expenditure was £50 million; at the beginning of the period under review here (1979–80), it had risen to £78 million; it first topped the hundred million mark the following year and is now running at £500 million a year.

In 1979, a new type of legal aid called 'ABWOR' (assistance by way of representation), together with powers to vary financial eligibility, could be introduced, funded by savings from the withdrawal of legal aid for undefended divorces; in 1982, the recommendation of a joint Bar–Law Society working party on appeal provisions against legal aid refusal in criminal cases could be introduced; but by 1986 one of the infamous efficiency scrutinies was imposed on the legal aid system by the Treasury.

Its report was mostly a disappointing document. Its welcome recognition of the need to provide funds for tribunal representation was offset by its proposal to fund it by withdrawing 'Green Form' advice from certain areas of legal work and further to limit it to those solicitors or agencies which had been specifically awarded contracts for this purpose. Their overall savings, based on the crudest calculations, were in the region of £10 million a year, which doubtless did not impress the Treasury.

The scrutiny report was quickly followed by a White Paper the following year and then by a Bill which it fell to Lord Mackay to steer, not without difficulty, on to the statute book. The Legal Aid Act 1988 itself, apart from removing the administration of legal aid from the Law Society, where it had been since its introduction forty years ago, to a new Legal Aid Board, appointed by the Lord Chancellor and accordingly subject to closer ministerial control, reveals very little of the government's ultimate intentions, for it provides an outline only, with all the detail left to be made by subordinate legislation. The Act runs to just forty-seven sections, but even with its eight schedules is a short measure by today's standards for such an important and complicated social service.

Fears about the future of legal aid have not been assuaged. Apart from contracting out advice services, there is little in the Act which bears the hallmark of this government's ideology, though it purports to give expression to several objectives—containing public expenditure, value for money, and efficiency—as well as evincing the government's hard-nosed attitude to the provision of support from public funds. What is not clear is how the government will administer the legal aid system in the future: what remains clear is that even £500 million a year does not begin to secure decent access to justice for the citizens of this country.

Legal aid problems notwithstanding, early in 1985, Hailsham announced the Civil Justice Review—'To improve the machinery of civil justice . . . by means of reform in jurisdiction, procedure and court administration and in particular to reduce delay, cost and complexity'—heralded as the most far-reaching review of the administration of civil justice since the 1873 Judicature Act. It was Hailsham's last bid to go down as a great reforming Chancellor, which is why he was particularly discontented at not being able to see it through to a conclusion after the 1987 general election.

The Civil Justice Review Body published its report in June 1988. It made little impact. Apart from recommending a transfer of more High Court business to the county court, it deals largely with procedural minutiae. On the big issues—class actions and contingency fees—it does no more than call for further investigation. Despite all the trumpeting, it is not the stuff of which history is made.

THE GREEN PAPERS AND REFORM OF THE LEGAL
PROFESSION

And so to Lord Mackay of Clashfern and of the Green Papers, who in little more than a year in office has undoubtedly secured for himself a place in the legal history books. Not only were his antecedents unusual—the Scottish Bar and no visible political allegiance before his earlier appointment as Lord Advocate—but, with disarming charm and patience, he has, if not declared war, at least taken on the legal profession in a way that no Chancellor has done heretofore. No English lawyer will ever again be able to hear or read the words 'Green Paper', in whatever context, without associating them with Mackay and the future of the legal profession.

Much nervousness was occasioned in the autumn of 1988 when the Lord Chancellor's Department announced the publication of a series of Green Papers in the new year on the legal profession and related matters with a proposed timetable which spoke of legislation in the 1989–90 session. So soon (in legal terms) after the 1979 report of the Royal Commission on Legal Services had applied its stamp of approval to the legal profession, which had attracted Lord Hailsham's endorsement, the spectre of fusion and other gloomy prospects again surfaced, and this despite the publication of the profession's own Marre Report in 1988, which had likewise found virtually everything satisfactory in the legal world, although much heat and barristerial dissent was generated by the majority conclusion that solicitors should be given the right of audience in the Crown Court.

The appearance of the three Green Papers has done nothing to allay these fears. In a singularly ungracious attack on his successor, Lord Hailsham denounced the proposals on the legal profession as 'badly thought out', 'ill-timed', 'divisive', and 'very seriously flawed'; the Lord Chief Justice described the paper on the legal profession 'as one of the most sinister documents ever to emanate from government', a view subsequently endorsed by the Master of the Rolls; a Law Lord accused the government of being 'deluded by dogma'; and the Bar, in total despair, has rushed off to Saatchi and Saatchi for help. Only the solicitors' side has taken it all calmly and quietly, perhaps because they feel they stand to lose little or because they are realistically fatalistic.

The judiciary claims that it threatens the independence of the legal profession, which provides an indispensable foundation for an independent judiciary. The Bar insists that it threatens the existence and certainly the vitality and viability of the Bar and would damage standards of advocacy in the courts.

There are three short papers: *The Work and Organisation of the Legal Profession*, on which most attention has focused (72 pages); *Contingency Fees* (14 pages); and *Conveyancing by Authorised Practitioners* (12 pages).

For years the legal profession, despite the shortcomings of the legal aid system, has refused to take seriously the possibility of finding virtue in some kind of contingency fee arrangements under which lawyers receive payment only if the case is won. The Green Paper questions these assumptions and surveys various forms which a scheme might take.

The conveyancing paper takes off where the Licensed Conveyancer reform ended and proposes the extension of conveyancing powers to the financial institutions—banks and building societies—and estate agents, which Hailsham had previously resisted. These changes are likely to impact heavily on solicitors, many of whom still depend to a large extent on conveyancing income.

The legal profession paper claims to draw its inspiration from notions of free competition which underlie the government's general policy. The main proposal is that the Bar would lose its monopoly of rights of audience in, and judicial appointment to, the higher courts, which would instead be open to any lawyer—barrister or solicitor—who had obtained an 'advocacy certificate', the conduct of such advocates being regulated by the government. Moreover, lawyers could practise in multi-disciplinary practices which might include not just accountants, for example, but even barristers.

It is not at all clear what effect these proposals would have if implemented. At one extreme, the Bar could disappear as solicitors employed their own advocates; at the other, there would be no discernible change, as solicitors evinced no interest in becoming advocates and preferred to instruct counsel from the Bar as and when needed rather than retaining them in-house. It is also not clear what vision, if any, the Lord Chancellor has for the future of the legal profession. It is, however, in line with government policy elsewhere—to pile on the pressure, undermine the foundations, facilitate a free-for-all, and withdraw to watch the resulting consternation.

There are any number of opinions, even from barristers, as to the likely consequences. While many are deeply fearful, others have expressed quiet confidence that the Bar will survive. Parts may wither: the Criminal Bar is probably the most vulnerable as specialist criminal solicitors may want to take on some of the advocacy themselves or at least have advocates within the firm. The specialist Bars, however, are likely to survive. Few solicitors' firms would be able to make the best use of the leading advocates on a full-time basis even if they were willing to join; and even the biggest City firms may prefer to pick and choose the best and most appropriate from the Bar for each particular case. A real danger, however, is that the uncertainty over the Bar's future will dissuade many able graduates from entering the profession, which would itself damage the Bar irreparably within two decades.

It is idle here to speculate on how it will work out. Certainly the Lord Chancellor will have no easy task in implementing these reforms and the timetable is inimical to a full public debate, but it is clear that the Thatcher revolution is finally about to engulf one of the last remaining bastions. Whatever happens, it must be doubted whether the consumer will derive any material benefit from changes in the organization of the legal profession as opposed to changes over conveyancing and contingent fees.

CONCLUSION

The law as a whole has not seen particularly notable changes over the decade, although public law has prospered and flourished. Criminal justice has been tampered with a good deal, but possibly no more than in any other decade in recent times, and certainly not in a way that can be said to have changed its familiar face.

Civil justice has remained fairly resistant to change, though some useful reforms and inquiries have been noted. Only now does the legal profession face an unprecedented shake-up, although the solicitors have themselves, independently of government, experienced cataclysmic changes in recent years. Mergers, specializations, competition from accountants and others, and a burgeoning of commercial work have all brought about major changes from which the Bar has been largely immune. Times have been good for barristers, at least those not dependent on legal aid, but they may now be about to pay the price for a degree of complacency and inertia.

Access to law for the majority of people remains problematic and the wheels of justice continue to turn slowly and expensively. No convincing government assault on these intractable evils is conspicuous.

22

The Mass Media

ALASTAIR HETHERINGTON

Look at the audited daily sales of national newspapers in the early Thatcher days, and compare them with 1989. Because of inability to publish, in the six months January to June 1983 the audited figures discount 26 days for the *Daily Telegraph*, 28 for the *Financial Times*, 21 for the *Guardian*, and 12 for *The Times*. Look at the lists for the late 1980s, and those stoppages have virtually disappeared. The change is due to the Employment Acts of 1980 and 1982, and to the vigour in 1984–6 of Mr Eddie Shah and Mr Rupert Murdoch in breaking the stranglehold of the printing unions and the National Union of Journalists. Look also at the rapid introduction of new technology in newspapers—some of that 'new' technology being thirty years old and of British origin, but not used in the UK until the mid-1980s.

In broadcasting the changes from 1979 to 1989 were less dramatic, though under Mrs Thatcher's own direction the government is preparing for major reform in the 1990s. Her first few years were marked by the arrival of Channel 4 (November 1981), already planned but fully supported from 1979 by the new Home Secretary, William Whitelaw. Sianel Pedwar Cymru (the Welsh fourth channel) came with it, also with the Home Secretary's blessing. Satellite and cable services, much publicized in the early Thatcher years, proved to be a disappointment—though for satellite channels a rapid increase is likely in the 1990s. On the downside, Mrs Thatcher's dislike of the BBC, the IBA, and the ITV companies became increasingly evident and its consequences will be felt in the 1990s.

The Prime Minister summed up her own thoughts in an address to the Press Association—a newspaper body, though also serving broadcasters—in June 1988. We needed more television channels, she said, because 'the free movement and expression of ideas is guaranteed far better by numbers and variety than it ever can be by charters and specific statutes'. To the criticism that multiple channels might lower the standards of British broadcasting she said, 'I have always believed that there is a market for the best . . . and I do not believe that it is necessarily true that television goes downmarket'. New channels and subscription channels, she said, 'will perhaps enable us to have some very upmarket television'. She went on to urge journalists themselves to uphold standards. 'I believe basically that you can do far more to uphold, retain and improve your own standards than any outside body can'. There was a need to protect families from 'the kind of thing that you would not like to see on your living-room table or the screen in your living-room'. She would 'strain everything', she said, 'to protect our young people from some of the violence and pornography that they would otherwise see'. She was delighted that the debate about standards and the values of journalists was taking place. 'That is really all I am going to say about the media.' There was no direct mention of the popular press.

Having outlined the broad themes, let us look more closely at newspaper developments in the 1979–89 years, and at the changes in broadcasting, past and coming.

The 1980 and 1982 Employment Acts were not particularly directed at Fleet Street or the press elsewhere, but the 1980 Act restricted 'closed shops' and lawful picketing, and the 1982 Act tightened the provisions. They were a powerful aid for anyone who wanted to challenge the 'closed shops' of the NGA, Sogat, the National Union of Journalists and others in the newspaper industry. Eddie Shah, then proprietor of a series of six 'free' papers based at Warrington, saw in early 1983 that the new legislation would give him legal protection in challenging the closed shop and the restrictive practices imposed by the unions. He was popular with most of his staff, and he embarked on a struggle which few other newspaper managements, large or small, thought he could win. That autumn the riotous scenes outside his Warrington plant—with mass pickets trying to prevent his delivery vans from setting out—received nightly television cover. Shah won. After that success he went on to plan a new technology national newspaper, to be based in London. *Today* began publication in 1986, but it was not well planned and eventually had to be sold. Nevertheless, the debt of the whole newspaper industry to Eddie Shah remains great.

An even more spectacular coup was brought off in January 1986 by Rupert Murdoch—the Australian (now naturalized American) proprietor of the *Sun*, the *News of the World*, *The Times*, and the *Sunday Times*. After negotiation over a long period to secure a sensible level of manning and the introduction of new technology, the talks finally broke down in late January, and the printing unions called on their members to strike. They knew that for some time Murdoch had been preparing a new printing plant at Wapping, far away in east London, but they believed it was only for the *Sun* and the *News of the World*. What they did not know, for it was an extraordinarily well-kept secret, was that the plant was now ready also for *The Times* and the *Sunday Times* and that a new technical staff, much of it recruited from the electricians' union, was ready to operate the electronic equipment.

Not only that, but Murdoch's News International company had organized road delivery throughout Britain, using Murdoch's TNT van company. Previously the printing unions could count on the railway unions to prevent delivery during a major strike. That threat had been removed, not only for News International. And Murdoch had also prepared a new, high-technology printing plant in Glasgow for his four papers, with overnight road delivery as far south as Yorkshire and Lancashire. It was a brilliant action; but it meant that many reasonable printers who had tried to be loyal both to their unions and to *The Times* and *Sunday Times* lost their jobs, and both papers also lost a number of talented journalists who did not like the style and attitudes of their papers' top editorial and management tiers.

With News International's production costs halved and the obstacles to computer setting and direct input removed, the other national newspapers had to cheer and cry: cheer because the way was open for them to follow, and cry because, being unable to use Murdoch's ruthless methods, they could not cut their production costs quickly. All, however, moved as quickly as they could. The

Daily Telegraph was to some extent a casualty, having to sell out to the Canadian Conrad Black; but, under its new management, it soon became a stronger and less overtly Conservative newspaper. And, nine months after Wapping, a new high-quality national daily was launched in October 1986—the *Independent*—making full use of electronic publishing free of union restrictions. The movement of daily sales is shown in Figs. 22.1 and 22.2.

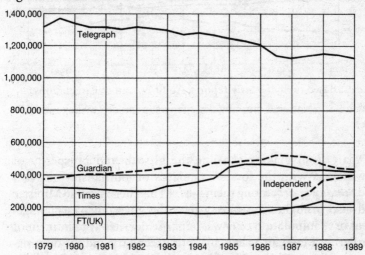

Source: Based on half-yearly reports, Audit Bureau of Circulations.

FIG. 22.1. National morning newspapers (quality): average daily sales

In the regions, too, the introduction of new printing was accelerated. The regional and local newspapers had rarely been subjected to the degree of disruption or the 'Spanish practices' of Fleet Street (such as paying for men who do not turn up for work) but they now had a new incentive to improvement. Altogether, the consequences of the two Employment Acts brought a long-overdue and very welcome reform to British newspapers. Which is not to say that newspapers such as the *Sun*, the *Star*, or the *Daily Express* became any less sexist, vulgar, or irresponsible; if anything, in the late 1980s they became worse. But at elections Mrs Thatcher could count on their support.

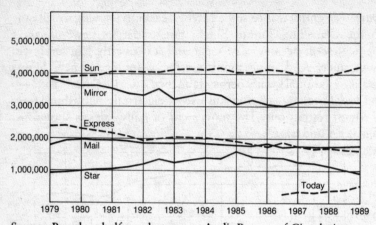

Source: Based on half-yearly reports, Audit Bureau of Circulations.

FIG. 22.2.   National morning newspapers (popular): average daily sales

Apart from making possible the growth and prosperity of newspapers with the lowest standards of journalism—the *Sun* and *Sunday Sport* among them—Mrs Thatcher as Prime Minister had also brought controversy over the government's management or manipulation of news. In particular, her appointment of Mr Bernard Ingham as her chief press secretary and the domination that he quickly achieved over the 'Lobby' journalists have drawn much criticism. The *Guardian* and the *Independent* withdrew their parliamentary staff from the 'Lobby' system in 1986, followed later by the *Scotsman*, because Lobby briefings were unattributable and in their view at times misleading. To Mr Ingham's briefings are attributed the downfall of such ministers as Mr John Biffen, Lord (Francis) Pym, and Lord (Patrick) Jenkin; and he was much involved in the Westland Affair, leading to the resignations of Mr Michael Heseltine and Mr Leon Brittan. Mr Heath, the previous Conservative Prime Minister, went so far as to say (2 February 1989) that the No 10 Press Office was 'corrupt' and the source of a series of leaks. In his time—though Mr Heath did not say this—the Press Office was run by Sir Donald Maitland, a senior Foreign Office man and one who had the total respect of journalists of every kind. Mr Ingham, nevertheless, must be seen as a highly articulate spokesman who accurately reflects the Prime Minister's view.

In another area the media have come into increasing conflict with the government during the decade. It is an area of common interest to the newspapers and the broadcasters—freedom of speech, freedom of information, and the Official Secrets Act. As early as 1980 Mrs Thatcher instigated the 'Protection of Government Information' Bill, but it had to be abandoned when shown to be too restrictive. Then there was friction over the reporting of the Falklands War. In 1984 Sarah Tisdall went to prison for having divulged to the *Guardian* the Defence Minister's intention to withhold from the Commons information about the arrival of US cruise missiles at Greenham Common; and some months later Clive Ponting was acquitted by a jury—perhaps because of public anger over the sentencing of Tisdall—after he had given an MP, Tom Dalyell, information that conflicted with the government line on the sinking of the *Belgrano*. Some time later two distinguished retired Permanent Secretaries, Sir Douglas Wass and Sir Frank Cooper, spoke of the need for a safety net or system of appeal within the Civil Service.

Then in 1985–6 there came a sequence of conflicts. Home Secretary Leon Brittan's request to the BBC for withdrawal of a 'Real Lives' programme on Northern Ireland which neither he nor anyone else outside the BBC had seen; the further dispute over 'Zircon' and the police raid on the BBC's Glasgow studios; at the same time the *Observer*'s revelation that BBC staff were being vetted by MI5; also *Spycatcher* and the long-running legal conflict to prevent newspaper or other publication in the UK; and in December 1987 the government's injunction to prevent broadcasting of the Radio 4 series 'My Country, Right or Wrong'. (The irony of the last was that it had been cleared by the government-appointed secretary to the D-Notice Committee, and in the end was broadcast unchanged.) In November 1988, the Home Secretary used his powers under the 1981 Broadcasting Act and the BBC's Licence and Agreement to ban all radio or television interviews with members of Sinn Fein and ten other paramilitary or political organizations in Ireland—a decree resented by many journalists as a breach of free speech and responsible reporting.

And in January 1989, after a prolonged controversy over a Thames Television programme, 'Death on the Rock', about the shooting in Gibraltar of three IRA members, Mrs Thatcher brusquely repudiated the findings of a long independent inquiry; that was the culmination of a sustained government attack on the IBA and Thames Television because of their decision to broadcast the programme.

It was against this background that the government's long-promised reform of the Official Secrets Act came before the Commons in the winter of 1988 and spring of 1989. It is a complex reform, wiping out the old 'blunderbuss' Section 2 but replacing it with tighter provisions on defence, international relations, aspects of crime, and some security service operations. It frees from prosecution leaks or publication on such matters as education, health, housing, social security, the Budget, or the nuclear fuel industry. 'That's worth at least one cheer, isn't it?' Mr Hurd asked in the *UK Press Gazette*. Yes, indeed, for it is an important relief after the old Section 2. But it leaves newspaper editors and broadcasting executives unhappy, to say the least, that they will have no defence of 'public interest' in military, diplomatic, crime, or security disclosures. The Home Secretary replies that no such statutory defence has existed hitherto, and that in most cases the prosecution would have to prove 'beyond reasonable doubt' that damage has been done to the security or other service by the disclosure. It remains to be seen how the courts will react. The new law, however, will certainly make some forms of investigative journalism more hazardous. To take a distant example, in 1970–1 *The Times* and the *Guardian* separately uncovered corruption in the Metropolitan Police, including the CID. That involved 'damage' to the CID; but the disclosures were also in the public interest. It may be noted, too, that the Thames programme 'Death on the Rock' could not have been made once the revised Section 2 was in force, since it involved inquiry into a security operation.

On, then, to Mrs Thatcher and the broadcasters. In the early 1980s satellite and cable seemed to promise a multitude of new channels and new programmes, but both proved slow in their development. Cable had grown rapidly in North America, partly because the transmission standards of terrestrial television were so poor. Big cities might have nine, ten, or twelve channels, but the pictures were (and are) often blurred and fuzzy and the sound grating. To get a decent picture and clear sound, in many places cable was the way; and it quickly developed a wide choice of programmes, including specialist interests. In the UK, however, transmission standards were among the highest in the world, with effective co-operation between the BBC and IBA bringing a good picture even to the smallest of communities. Consequently cable in the UK grew only slowly, and with revenue inadequate to build specialized programme series.

As to satellite, it has been coming 'next year' ever since the mid-1980s. A Home Office document 'Direct Broadcasting by Satellite' first proclaimed the government's enthusiasm in May 1981. Satellite really arrived, however, only at the end of the decade—though still with a shortage of small dish receivers and decoders, and with three or more conflicting systems which put up the cost to prospective viewers. If one wanted both the Sky channels and BSB (British Satellite Broadcasting, with three to five channels) the extra equipment cost at least £500, or more probably about £1,000. It is reasonable to assume that there will be at least twelve to sixteen direct satellite channels by 1991, but it would be unwise to expect large audiences before the mid-1990s. The government has, of course, refrained from offering any subsidy to satellite or cable, though ready to help them in other ways—such as Mrs Thatcher's willingness to be interviewed by Sky channel on its opening day, though to a minimal audience.

For the great majority of viewers, therefore, the terrestrial Channels 1 to 4 remained the prime source, with the government's promise of a fifth channel (commercially financed) in 1993 and after that possibly a sixth channel in the less hilly parts of the UK (not Wales, the Pennine areas, or the Highlands). A further possibility is the development of local channels in limited areas, using short-range microwave (MVDS). The big upheaval, though, will be in the character and operation of Channels 1 to 4—and possibly in radio. To trace the evolution of Mrs Thatcher's strategy—it came from her rather than anyone else, judging by the many sessions at 10 Downing Street—we have to go back to the Peacock Committee of 1985–6. That is, to 'The Committee on the Financing of the BBC', whose remit also extended to ITV and newspaper finance.

Although the committee was told that there were no presumptions about what it might recommend, there can be little doubt that the Prime Minister hoped for advertising as the way to finance the BBC in future. The committee rejected that option, for reasons that I believe none of the seven members at first foresaw (I was one of the seven). The reasons were (1) the results of five or six economics research studies, two commissioned by the committee and others by the BBC, ITCA, and other interests, and (2) the results of a study of the range and quality of television services in the UK, North America, Australia, and five European countries, commissioned by the committee and carried out by Leeds University.

The economic studies—by Cave and Swann, NERA (National Economics Research Associates), Brown Shipley & Co., and others—reached the staggering conclusion, almost unanimously, that even limited advertising on BBC 1 would cripple the finances of the ITV companies. One study projected a 7.5 per cent drop in profits, with five of the fifteen regional companies going out of business. (Professor Peacock at first took the robust view that that would be only 'a temporary hiccup'.) The 'range and quality' study concluded that with their four channels UK viewers were receiving 'among the most extensive' programming provided by the major broadcasting systems throughout the world; and that on quality, while judgements must often be subjective, BBC and ITV output was regarded 'with high respect' by professional broadcasters in other countries. The effect of a high proportion of advertising in peak time on the major channels in Australia, Italy, and the US was also noted.

The Peacock Report rejected advertising on BBC television, preferring the option of preparing for subscription by the late 1990s and an indexed TV licence fee to finance the BBC meanwhile. That was accepted by the government, though with the indexed licence fee guaranteed only until 1991. Of the eighteen recommendations of the committee, eight were accepted, three rejected, three partly accepted and partly rejected, and four were still undetermined (spring 1989). On the key question of subscription, the government commissioned two further studies, neither of which reached a clear conclusion. Subscription television was found to be technically possible, but the likely degree of take-up by the public was uncertain. In the summer of 1988 the Home Affairs Committee of the House of Commons—an all-party group, chaired by the Conservative MP John Wheeler—published a report which endorsed much of Peacock but carried some proposals further. It warned the government not to destroy the best of British television in its drive for competition and new commercial channels. It saw the BBC as remaining 'the cornerstone of British broadcasting', to be financed by the licence fee in the medium term, and it called for a fifth channel to be based on a 'network of local stations'.

In November 1988 the Home Office presented to Parliament the White Paper, *Broadcasting in the '90s: Competition, Choice and Quality*. It was the fruit of Mrs Thatcher's Downing Street discussions, together with the sometimes conflicting views of Mr Douglas Hurd (Home Secretary) and Lord Young (Trade and Industry). It went further than the Home Affairs Committee had recommended, and it was to be followed by the Broadcasting Bill, to go before Parliament in the 1989–90 session. The salient features and reactions to them follow.

- For the *BBC*, 'a special role', though it need not 'involve itself in every aspect of broadcasting'. Progressive introduction of subscription, the licence fee to be frozen or reduced from 1991, and the night hours on one BBC channel to be 'sold for use to provide new services by the highest bidder'. (The night-time provision is in line with Peacock, but the rundown of the licence fee comes five years earlier than Peacock ever conceived and appears contrary to the Home Affairs Committee's view.)
- For *ITV*, a more competitive environment. From 1992–3, competitive tendering for regional franchises in the renamed Channel 3. Applicants must satisfy the Authority (the Independent Television Commission, replacing the IBA) of their professional and financial competence; thereafter, the highest bidder wins. The franchise areas to be determined by

the ITC; no group may have control over or an interest in more than two licences, but, apart from that, the ITC will no longer be able to block take-overs. (The franchise proposals are as the majority of Peacock recommended, except for one important point: Peacock said that the IBA/ITC should have the option of appointing a company that had offered a lower price, when that company was likely to give 'more "value for money" in terms of public service'—but in doing so the Authority must 'make a full, public and detailed statement of the reasons'. The omission of that provision seems a serious flaw, if British broadcasting standards are to be maintained.)

- For *Channel 4* and the Welsh fourth channel, no structural change but C4 probably to sell its own advertising time and possibly to be privatized. S4C (Wales) to be financed by a levy on the C3, 4, and 5 companies.
- The new *Channel 5* to be national, not regionally based, but probably with three licences covering different hours of day and night. (Because of the shortage of frequencies, it is likely to reach no more than 70 per cent of the country; it was because of frequency problems that Peacock abandoned any recommendation of fifth and sixth channels.) A Channel 6 may follow if it proves technically feasible.
- *Independent producers* to supply 25 per cent or more of BBC and Channels 3–6 programmes. (A revision of Peacock.)
- *Independent radio* to be largely deregulated, probably with three new national channels and encouragement of local and community radio. To be handled by a 'slim' new Radio Authority.
- The *Broadcasting Standards Council* to reinforce 'taste and decency'. (The Home Affairs Committee said that it should base its findings on proper research, not hearsay or views of special interest groups.)
- Transmitters (TV and radio) to be privatized in 1996 or later (which, unless in some way subsidized, will cripple the services in Wales, the Pennine area and much of Scotland).

These, then, are the changes that lie ahead. It is the Prime Minister, above all, who has driven for these reforms. The upheaval in television is bound to be great. Already, with competitive tendering in the offing, ITV companies are pulling back both from the more expensive drama and documentary programmes and from the more hard-hitting current affairs—as indeed they had told Peacock would inevitably happen if the price offered was to become the only basis for future franchising. The BBC, battered by government criticism, now tends to 'play safe' in controversial areas. It has adopted a policy of not challenging government decisions about the future of broadcasting; and in its higher ranks there are those who believe that Mrs Thatcher's unstated strategy is to squeeze its resources so that it is forced into a gradual withering away. Which may or may not be correct.

One certainty is that, during the ten years, the Prime Minister secured the appointment of BBC Governors who were or are 'one of us' as she saw it. That, too, contributed to the demoralizing of senior BBC executives. Of the eighteen appointments between 1979 and 1988, eleven were of individuals presumed to be in Mrs Thatcher's camp. The fifty-year-old tradition of appointing people representative of a wide variety of British interests has been broken. As to chairmen, George Howard (latterly Lord Howard of Henderskelfe, chairman 1980–3), Stuart Young (1983–6), and Marmaduke Hussey (1986–) were all reliable Conservatives but also men of strong individual approach; and both Young and Hussey did what they could to protect the best of the BBC. Independent Television, in contrast to the BBC, came off easily in Mrs Thatcher's early days. From 1981 to 1988 the IBA's chairman was Lord Thomson of Monifieth, former Labour Cabinet minister and an EEC Commissioner from 1973 to 1977; and his board, though predominantly to the right, was of a broad character. The Prime Minister's distaste for the ITV sector seems to have grown only from the mid-1980s onwards, culminating in her attacks on 'Death on the Rock'. Even so, she appointed as successor to Lord Thomson and to be the first chairman of the new ITC, replacing the IBA, a northern businessman, George Russell, with no evident political commitment—but then added the controversial Lord Chalfont as his deputy.

The concluding section of the Leeds University study for Peacock drew attention to the US and European tendency towards programme structure and content 'increasingly determined' by marketing criteria—a big increase in entertainment programmes in Italy, a more 'commercial' spirit in Holland, and French television moving closer to the American model (even before the privatizing of the French first channel). The study, written in the winter of 1985–6, noted that the range of programming available to *all* the population in the UK was probably the most extensive of any of the main broadcasting systems; but already, over the preceding ten years, the schedules had narrowed.

It may be said that in broadcasting Mrs Thatcher's Britain moved more slowly than France or Italy. There was, of course, the disappointment over the slow development of the cable and satellite systems. That apart, the more cautious approach in the UK appears to have been wise. In both France and Italy the development was chaotic. 'A state of anarchy and confusion' was one phrase used in the Leeds University report to Peacock, and committee members witnessed some of it in Rome. Italian governments had poor control over events, and primary credit for change should go to Avocat Berlusconi for his skill in finding ways round the law. As to France, there are widely differing views about the ways the three governments of the 1980s chopped and changed their three main channels; and in 1989 there were still substantial parts of France where television transmission was of a standard unacceptable in the UK. The one real success in France is its first subscription channel, Canal Plus.

Overall Britain has maintained high standards in its broadcasting. Whether Mrs Thatcher's revolution will bring a lowering of standards in the 1990s remains an open question. The Commons Home Affairs Committee—all party—has recommended caution. Beyond doubt, the Prime Minister can justly claim to have brought major changes and great technical improvements in the newspaper industry, and to some extent in magazines. It is easier for new publications to start, though still at high costs, and the quality of printing is much improved. At the same time, though, the standards of journalism in parts of the popular press have visibly declined—a matter on which Mrs Thatcher does not choose to comment.

In broadcasting my own view is that the greatest safeguard lies in the fact that British audiences have become accustomed to a rich diet in broadcasting. They will continue to want a wide range of programmes, and advertisers will continue to buy time besides a varied schedule—at least for a few years ahead. Among others, Channel 4's survival will depend on that. There is also the remote possibility of an 'Arts Council of the Air'. But the upheaval is bound to be great. Sir Alan Peacock may have been right in speaking of a 'temporary hiccup', committed as he is to the Adam Smith free-market philosophy; but to other observers the upheaval carries great dangers. The ultimate test will be whether in the 1990s British broadcasting maintains its standards. Gresham's law is as relevant as Adam Smith's.

Television Audiences, 1979–1988

The measuring of television audiences is a well-developed science, though with differences of interpretation among the researchers. A study of audiences was, for example, published by the IBA in 1982 showing that in 1981–2 ITV had had a 49 per cent 'share' of the national audience, while BBC 1 had 38 per cent and BBC 2 only 12 per cent. This was warmly disputed by the BBC, who believed that in aggregate they had a greater lead than the IBA figures showed.

Since 1984–5, however, joint research for BBC and ITV has been carried out by BARB, the Broadcasters' Audience Research Board. Its 1985–6 report showed ITV a fraction ahead of BBC 1 on a daily basis and a fraction behind on a weekly basis. Overall its figures are given in Table 22.1.

Looking at the popularity of programme groups, the variations over the years are not great. Thus, taking the top individual programmes in some categories, we find audience figures such as light entertainment, 1980–1, at 20m., 1984–5 at 17m., and 1988–9 at 22m. Then drama at 17m., 14.4m., and 16m.; or children's programmes at 14m., 11m., and 12m. News and current affairs programmes hold good ratings, both on BBC and on ITV, with four or five in the weekly top twenty places. It must be remembered, however, that there are marked differences region by region. Broadly speaking, these appear to be healthy figures.

References

The 1980 Employment Act, in *Keesing's Contemporary Archives*, 7 Nov. 1980, pp. 30553–5.

TABLE 22.1.   *TV audiences: average reach and viewing*

	Reach (% of population, aged 4+)		Viewing per head weekly (hrs. & mins.)	Share of viewing (%)
	Daily	Weekly		
BBC 1	64·6	92·0	9·22	36
BBC 2	35·3	80·6	2·57	11
Any or all BBC	69·1	93·0	12·19	47
ITV	65·2	91·5	12·04	46
C4/S4C	28·5	72·8	1·54	7
Any or all commercial	69·2	92·6	14·02	53
Any or all TV	79·3	94·3	26·21	100

The 1982 Employment Act, in *Keesing's*, Mar. 1983, pp. 32014–5.

Report of the Committee on Financing the BBC, Cmnd. 9824 (1986).

Research on the Range and Quality of Broadcasting Services (HMSO, 1986).

Subscription Television: A Study for the Home Office (HMSO, 1987).

Hansard, 19 Oct. 1988, or newspapers of Thursday 20th, for the Home Secretary's ban on Sinn Fein and other interviews.

The Future of Broadcasting, Report by the Home Affairs Committee of the House of Commons (HMSO, HC 262-1, 1988).

Broadcasting in the '90s: Competition, Choice and Quality, Cm. 517 (1988).

BALDWIN, PETER, 'The Hurd Instinct', in *Listener*, 12 May 1988.

CROZIER, MICHAEL, *The Making of the 'Independent'* (Gordon Fraser, 1988).

FRASER, NICHOLAS, 'Mrs Thatcher and Broadcasting', in *IPPA Bulletin* (July–Aug. 1988).

GOLDING, P., MURDOCK, G. and SCHLESINGER, P., *Communicating Politics* (Leicester University Press, 1986) (in particular, the chapters by S. Hood and R. Bolton).

TUNSTALL, JEREMY, 'The Media Portfolio under Thatcher', in *Contemporary Record* (Spring 1989).

WOFFINDEN, BOB, 'Vision of the Future', in *Listener*, 19 Jan. 1989.

23

The Arts

BRYAN APPLEYARD

'The arts' is, on the one hand, a public policy category and, on the other, a term that covers all the higher levels of free creativity within society. The first sense is, of course, comparatively modern. In spite of certain developments in the nineteenth century, the arts were not systematically integrated into public policy until 1945, with the founding of the Arts Council. The second sense is traditional and embodies all the values of enlightenment and spiritual enrichment usually attached to art—the very values which finally inspired the belief that the arts should indeed become a concern of government.

In 1945 this acceptance of the public virtue of aesthetic values appeared unarguable to the upholders of the incoming socialist orthodoxy. The arts were like health or good housing in that they represented a socially desirable service which was of absolute value in itself and of relative value as a means of improving national unity and self-esteem. The irony was that the institutional realization of this view had come 100 years too late. The 'improving' view of art was, in essence, that of the Victorian progressives and was profoundly at odds with the radical and, finally, anti-humanist redefinitions of art that had taken place in the twentieth century.

Nevertheless, in a secular society progressive humanist values were all that was immediately available and the socialists needed art as one of the highest aspirations of the new society they wished to construct. Over the years the initial crusading zeal was predictably diluted, but the underlying ideology remained unquestioned. The weakening of enthusiasm combined with the practical impossibility of deciding how much money the arts actually needed produced a continuing friction between consumers of subsidy, Arts Council, and government. But, those difficulties apart, post-war administrations accepted their role as the modern successors of the private patrons of the past.

Perhaps the sums were so small that a certain creative lassitude about their function was inevitable. Or, perhaps, the essence of the post-war welfare consensus lived on in every administration until that of Mrs Thatcher. Either way, with the Tory victory of 1979, the arts suddenly became one more brick in the edifice of socialism which she was determined to tear down.

The argument was clear enough: subsidy was a denial of the new Tory anti-welfare ideal of self-help, it removed the discipline of demand from the providers of art. Some right-wing thinkers—notably Paul Johnson—took this to be a complete argument against any form of subsidy. The government, however, accepted its role as a patron, but insisted that money would be more tightly controlled and the arts would be expected to reform themselves as comprehensively as other institutions under Mrs Thatcher. Increasingly in the later years of the administration that has been combined with an enthusiasm for private sponsorship. Arts organizations had to fight in a bracing, Thatcherite way for funds from companies as the only means of ensuring growth against a background of stagnant government funding. This neatly implied the kind of discipline the New Right would wish to see—perhaps not the simple discipline of the box office, but certainly one that would guarantee a degree of public responsibility.

There is, of course, beneath all this a subtext of simple prejudice on both sides of the argument. The subsidized arts establishment as well as artists themselves, particularly in the theatre, have always been broadly left-wing. In many cases—say, the plays of David Edgar or Edward Bond—almost the sole role of the art has been to advance the cause of socialist revolution. But, even in less committed circles, the very narrow view of art as a part of the mechanism of social change was embedded deep within the culture. To back such views with public money would clearly be anathema to the new government. Equally, specifically *not* to back such views would represent censorship and repression to the old left. And obviously, for the left, private sponsorship could only be a means of neutralizing art's radical aspirations.

The first point to make about the decade since the election that established these polarities is that Mrs Thatcher has succeeded. It is now commonplace for the left, even the hard left, in the arts to be found seeking and advocating corporate sponsorship. Whether this amounts to a victory for sheer electoral longevity or there has been a genuine change of attitudes cannot, for the moment, be known. Either way there can be little doubt that most arts companies have adjusted to a new climate in which they must understand both the market-place and the promotional values of their products.

The government's role in this has been to smile benignly on the growing enthusiasm for corporate funding and to indicate its willingness to reward effort in this area. The Arts Council, meanwhile, has been through a long and complex process of attempting to redefine itself. Under the chairmanship of Lord Rees-Mogg this began with its policy document *The Glory of the Garden* in 1984. The main thrust of this was regionalization of the arts by correcting the heavy funding bias towards London. The slightly unfocused nature of this idea clears a little when it is compared to the government's commitment to more precise 'targeting' of funds in other areas of public spending. The council was attempting to display a concern for better value for money by serving a wider population with existing funds. Over the ensuing years the redefinition process continued with an increased emphasis on the council's role as consultant and manager rather than simply as the paymaster and aesthetic scrutineer. The latest statement came in the Three-Year Plan covering the years 1988–91, which outlined four tasks for the council: to enable as many people as possible to enjoy the arts, to demand the highest possible creative standards, to expand the arts economy, and to speak for the arts. This clearly emphasizes a functional, entrepreneurial role for the council at the expense of the old, rather more mandarin posture adopted during the high growth years of government funding under ministers like Jennie Lee and chairmen like Lord Goodman.

So the effect of government policy has not been simply to persuade arts companies to find private money, it has also been to force a more dynamic definition of the role of subsidy as a provider of management skills and incentive funding. With this redefinition subsidy becomes a more acceptable Tory policy and allows a more positive view of the arts as a part of the economic fabric. This positive view was first outlined in the report of the Select Committee on the Arts but did not take on real policy significance until the publication by the Policy Studies Institute of John Myerscough's *The Economic Importance of the Arts in Britain* in 1988, a document which put precise and remarkably high numbers on the kind of economic benefits provided by specific arts investments. By the end of last year some startlingly enthusiastic speeches about the arts by Mrs Thatcher had begun to raise hopes that they were about to join the environment as one policy area for the new 'citizenship' style of Toryism. The positive, economically valuable view of the arts appeared to be about to triumph. Such hopes, at the time of writing, are still waiting to be fulfilled.

There remains, however, a degree of abstraction about all this in that government policy and, indeed, all such debates about arts funding tend to be conducted around an unacknowledged vacuum. What should be there is a clear notion of art itself. Instead there is little more than a foggy glow towards which most people can agree they are well disposed. Encompassed by this glow are, for example, a production of *Madama Butterfly* at the Royal Opera House and Gay Sweatshop Limited, Henry Moore and the Flamboyan Carnival Club. The view has to be that such a plurality is fundamental to the nature of creativity itself and all such activities are related by the common, human, expressive impulse. Unfortunately that is an impossible basis for a public policy decision—the complete acceptance of the view would mean that anything people chose to call art would have to be funded. Tory policy has nothing to say on this, perhaps surprisingly given government enthusiasm for the 'targeting' of funds. Lord Rees-Mogg implicitly referred to the problem in the last Arts Council annual report by stressing the need for 'excellence' alongside the other goal he had established—'increasing the accessibility of the arts to all sorts and conditions of men and women'. 'Excellence', of course, is a fairly transparent way of shirking the question—though one has to accept that, for any public servant in such a position, shirking on the matter of the nature of art is the only available option.

The reason for the problem is the extent to which in this century art has consciously made itself indefinable. Its nature has seemed to change with every artist. In order to create at all, it has been necessary to rewrite all the rules from scratch. As I remarked above, the advent of the state as the main national patron in 1945 was based upon an essentially nineteenth-century view of art as a relatively stable and recognizable commodity with definable social benefits. This was also the view that informed the mainstream of educational thinking in this country—the most obvious example being the development of Cambridge English teaching inspired by F. R. Leavis's insistence on moral rigour and the centrality of a single tradition. The problem was that twentieth-century modernism in all its multiplicity of forms had tended to undermine any such certainties. Art became overwhelmingly conscious of its own form and, in doing so, created a problem of definition that would not go away. Thus Marcel Duchamp's celebrated urinal, which was art because it was installed in a gallery by an artist, had its precise correlative in Carl Andre's collection of bricks bought by the Tate Gallery. The difference was that, in the latter case, British public money was involved and the people could feel righteously indignant that this was not 'really' art.

The public funding argument survives this problem of definition primarily by the application of the 'arm's-length' policy. The Arts Council as intermediary both politically neutralizes government subsidy and applies external expertise to deciding what kind of art qualifies. Clearly such a structure would tend to insulate aesthetic decisions from either an audience or a marketplace and induce the kind of mandarin mentality which would patiently explain that Andre's bricks were indeed just bricks, but that was not the point. So the pressure on the product from such a structure tends to be towards a hermetic obscurity or to a specialized proselytizing—as in the highly charged political theatre of the 1960s and 1970s. Subsidy, therefore, in spite of what purists might claim, does to some extent condition the art that is produced.

Equally, however, so does the mix of highly targeted subsidy, private sponsorship, and more aggressive marketing. The pressure in this climate will be towards accessibility and the kind of 'excellence' to which a general audience can subscribe. In the event the pressure was hardly necessary. British arts had been moving into a more accessible 'post-modernist' phase ever since David Hockney abandoned modernist abstraction at the Royal College of Art in the early 1960s.[1] Pop art, the youth culture of the 1960s, the return of decoration in architecture, and many other manifestations had all represented a reaction against arid, late modernism. The latter seemed to have wandered into a content-less desert of formalism and the reaction involved a return to figuration, meaning and narrative.

In the 1980s the process accelerated to become the overwhelming orthodoxy. The emphasis was now on inclusiveness, on art that grew to include the world and its contingencies. So *The Penguin Book of Contemporary British Poetry*, published in 1982, defined the aim of all the poets included as being 'to extend the imaginative franchise'[2] Meanwhile, the Royal Academy's 'A New Spirit in Painting' exhibition in 1981 was introduced specifically as a reaction to the 'positivistic, onetrack reading of art history'[3] represented by the austere, exclusive demands of strict modernism.

The clearest and most characteristically British expression of this development was in the novel. From the late 1970s onwards fiction underwent an extraordinary renaissance. A revived realism had dominated the art in the post-war period with the deliberate intention of rejecting the 'difficult' modernist texts. There was a thin trickle of more adventurous fiction—notably in the work of William Golding, Iris Murdoch, and Angus Wilson—as well as avant-gardists like B. S. Johnson and Brigid Brophy. But, as a whole, the form could not be seen as a centre of artistic debate and excitement. Instead, interest in Britain had shifted to theatre, painting, and sculpture.

The renaissance of the late 1970s and 1980s was led by writers who were more or less coevals—Martin Amis, Peter Ackroyd, Salman Rushdie, Julian Barnes, and so on. Their influences were international—notably the 'magic realism' of South American fiction, the hard urban imagery of the United States, and the cosmopolitan air of European writers like Günter Grass. Their books were not bound by the obligations of realism: the language tended to be active in the sense that it functioned as an entity itself rather than as a transparent window on the world and the themes tended to range far beyond the minutiae of human relationships.

These novels also displayed a revived interest in the nature of narrative. In realism narrative tends to be a passive tool while in modernism its value was undermined. But, for these writers, the value of the story was reinstated. Narrative was found to be necessary, though it could never quite regain its innocence. Cinema and television had, to the discerning writer, annexed the linear forms of realism so the novelist was obliged to produce something new. Narratives became deformed, layered, and counterpointed and, to a surprising degree, the new, younger audience for 'literary' novels stayed with the trend. Sales of what would once have been called 'difficult' novels were unprecedentedly high.

One rather prosaic reason for this was that there was a new commercial background. The appearance of this new, more expansive, more experimental fiction was matched and encouraged by significant changes in the market. British publishing houses became subsidiaries of multi-national corporations who were more interested in cosmopolitan experiment than parochial realism; against the background of a stagnant and even declining book market in general, literary fiction was proving one of the few growth areas; book marketing and promotion were transformed by the sudden success of a number of literary prizes, most notably the Booker; and finally, led by the Waterstones chain, book retailing was revitalized in the 1980s—small independents began to disappear to be replaced by companies with the clear objective of selling to the newly affluent young middle classes.

But, irrespective of whether the inspiration or the market came first, the net effect was a double process of rejection by the new novelists. On the one hand they were turning against the formalistic dead end of late modernism and, on the other, they were rejecting the parochial themes and relentless empiricism of post-war British realism. Above all, they required the novel to take on the broadest possible preoccupations of the age. This can, in effect, be seen as a demand for content, a demand that surfaced most dramatically in sculpture, perhaps the one art in which Britain can genuinely be seen as a world leader over the past forty years.

World leadership had been established by Henry Moore—the artist about whom Mrs Thatcher has waxed most passionate in her recent pro-arts speeches—and subsequently by his pupil Anthony Caro. In Moore's old age Caro came to dominate the teaching of sculpture through his own austere and exquisitely balanced constructions in metal. But abstraction, as it had in painting, inevitably produced a reaction. The artist Bruce McLean memorably described the process of the judging of a work at St Martin's School of Art, where Caro taught: 'Twelve adult men with pipes would walk for hours around a sculpture and mumble.'[4] Suddenly the activity seemed too remote from the concerns of the world.

The result of the sense of impatience expressed by McLean was a development comparable to the changes in fiction. Another new generation began to produce sculpture with the equivalent of a new 'narrative' content. Thus Tony Cragg began with abstract organizations of 'found' objects and then moved on to figurative organizations—bits of discarded plastic, for example, being shaped into a map of Britain. Similarly Bill Woodrow dissected manufactured products and turned them into new figurative images—so a washing machine was half transformed into an electric guitar.

Overwhelmingly the dominant theme in this new sculptural content was the environment. This was, in any case, a theme for which the art was evidently suited. Sculptures are direct interventions in the world, unmediated by processes such as printing, technology or performance. They have an imaginative reality as unarguable as that of the planet itself. But the planet was being destroyed by commercial forces that were polluting its atmosphere and threatening to destabilize the systems whereby it supported life. In the work of Richard Long the theme found its clearest and most formally complete expression.

'To walk in the Himalayas,' Long has said, 'is to touch the earth lightly. ... I prefer to be a custodian of nature, not an exploiter of it. My position is that of the Greens. I want to do away with nuclear weapons, not make art that can withstand them.'[5]

Long's work may consist of a line of stones he has assembled on a remote mountain which he then photographs and exhibits. Or he may bring stones or mud into the gallery and arrange them into arbitrary lines or circles. Art is being returned to the most elementary organizing principle—in effect, the principle of narrative—and being made humble before the facts of the planet itself. Yet also an ancient magic is being restored to the role of the artist. Once again he is a transformer of reality as a way of embodying spiritual values of integration and harmony.

So, in the spheres of public policy and of art itself, developments have taken place which can be seen to be parallel. Art in the past ten years has made renewed efforts to reach its audience, to adopt a new plurality, and to shake off certain ideologies which had become repressive. In some areas—notably in architecture with its frenzied adaptation of 'post-modern' decorative devices—the result can be seen to be a rather pallid transitional style; in others—sculpture and the novel—genuinely new forms have been found which appear to engage more closely with the preoccupations of the age. Meanwhile, the government has successfully obliged the arts mandarins to shake off the old welfare ideology, to adopt a new plurality in methods of funding, and to cater more directly to audiences.

The implications of such parallels is that similar cultural forces are at work behind the success of Mrs Thatcher and developments in the arts—a possibility that would horrify most of the artists involved. In certain senses, however, it is obviously true. There was, in the 1970s, a perception both in the arts and in government that the country was in danger of collapsing altogether, that we had become ungovernable to the point where we might actually begin to regress to the status of a Third World nation. The image of the machine stopping became part of the imaginative vernacular and inspired the whole range of environmental concerns which are so dominant today. The belief in the necessity for change both swept Margaret Thatcher into power and generated new energies within the arts. There is a further, important parallel: Thatcherism represents a particular type of economic internationalism which rejects protectionism and insists on our ineluctable involvement with world markets. Similarly, these changes in the arts are all characterized by a turning away from the obsessions of Little England and the desire to produce internationally comprehensible and acclaimed art.

Of course, any such parallels are bound to have glaring weaknesses. There has, for example, been the enormous recent success of Philip Larkin, a poet who represented the very essence of Little Englishness. And certain utterly local traditions of art will always persist. But the point can be made that, in reacting to various perceived problems of our recent past, politics and art have advanced along broadly similar paths. This is a conclusion that undermines the fashionably 'dissident' view of art usually expressed within the business and from which many artists derive their identities. And it also raises one final and, for the moment, unanswerable question: can we still claim to be the possessors of a characteristically national culture? If American domination or a bland Euro-art are the alternatives, it is to be hoped that the answer is yes and that its outlines will become clearer in the best work of the new artists who have emerged in the past decade. Certainly among some of them—notably the writer Peter Ackroyd—a novel redefinition of British history seems to be taking place. But such a redefinition *is* new and profoundly alien to the traditions we have been taught to accept. Perhaps this means that the real artistic crisis for the future will be our confrontation with the discovery that we have long been strangers in a strange land.

Notes

1. For his own description of his rejection of abstraction see David Hockney, *David Hockney* (Thames and Hudson, 1976), p. 41.
2. Blake Morrison and Andrew Motion (eds.), *The Penguin Book of Contemporary British Poetry* (Penguin, 1982), p. 20.

3. Christos Joachimides *et al. A New Spirit in Painting* (Royal Academy of Arts, 1981), p. 12.
4. Quoted in Terry A. Neff (ed.), *A Quiet Revolution: British Sculpture since 1945* (Thames and Hudson, 1987), p. 16.
5. Quoted in ibid. p. 112.

24

The Thatcher Effect in Science

TOM WILKIE

The way science has been done in Britain for most of this century is coming to an end. In particular, the post-war dispensation and the research system built up in the 1960s are being dismantled.

And yet, the evidence suggests that this change was not intended by Mrs Thatcher's government. It was an unhappy accident, accentuated by trends and pressures that pre-dated the Thatcher administration.

The government's policy towards science has been characterized by a curious compound of ideology and ignorance. The ignorance was not that of the nature of science itself—regrettable though the fact may be, government ministers of all parties have always been ignorant of basic time-scales of research, of how easy it is to destroy a creative team of scientists, and of how difficult and painstaking the effort needed to build up world-class research groups.

It appears that, when it first took office, the government was surprisingly ignorant of its own machinery for supporting science—machinery that had developed gradually since the recognition, during the First World War, that modern states had to support scientific research if they were to survive. There was also profound ignorance of the interdisciplinary nature of science—of how decisions taken by one department of state could affect the scientific interests of others.

Even within a single department, that of Education and Science, ministers were unaware that their determination to reduce public expenditure on the universities—the ideological element to the policy—would conflict with their desire to maintain level funding for science. In effect, ministers had not heard of, or did not sufficiently understand, the so-called 'dual-support system' for the funding of basic scientific research. The consequences of that ignorance and the careless way in which a major plank of British science policy was discarded are still being worked through the system today.

The science vote—the money granted by Parliament to the Department of Education and Science to support basic science—is distributed among five independent statutory bodies who conduct or commission research: the Medical Research Council; the Science and Engineering Research Council; the Natural Environment Research Council; the Agriculture and Food Research Council; and the Economic and Social Research Council. But the science vote, which in 1987/8 was around £612 million, actually accounts for only a small proportion of the money that the state spends on science (Table 24.1). In this has lain one of the secrets of the productivity and creativity peculiar to British science.

In 1987/8, the University Grants Committee (UGC) contributed £750 million to funding science. The UGC contribution is the second and greater part of the dual-support system. Its money is supposed to pay the salaries of the tenured research scientists in universities and of their laboratory technicians (who are vital members of a research team in these days of complex sophisticated apparatus). The UGC money also goes to the provision of small items of equipment and 'consumables'—straightforward laboratory chemicals for example. The UGC contribution was intended to provide a 'well-found laboratory'. Thus, a scientist who had an unorthodox idea that he wished to explore informally to see if it was promising could do so using the facilities of the well-found laboratory funded by the UGC. If the idea did turn out to have promise, the scientist could then apply to the appropriate research council for a project grant to pursue the research further, to purchase large items of capital equipment, and perhaps a couple of research studentships so that he could take on students to help him with the research project.

This flexible system—unique to Britain—grew up almost by accident in the years after the First World War when the government started directly to finance science on a large scale for the first time. It is difficult to find a scientist or scientific administrator

TABLE 24.1. *Expenditure on R. & D. by departments*

Department	Out-turn		Estimate
	1985/6	1986/7	1987/8
Civil departments			
MAFF	122·3	118·3	109·0
DES	73·0	72·8	75·0
DEn	33·4	192·4	168·6
UKAEA	195·8		
DoE	47·2	59·0	60·8
DHSS	28·1	49·4	48·5
HSC	5·5	5·4	4·9
Home Office	14·2	13·3	15·0
ODA	24·3	27·0	31·0
DTI	386·7	362·9	308·9
DTp	25·8	24·6	24·8
NI Depts.	14·2	17·0	17·3
Scottish Depts.	55·6	53·4	51·0
Welsh Office	2·7	3·5	1·8
DEmp	1·3	1·5	1·9
MSC	14·1	18·4	24·1
Other depts.	27·8	28·5	29·7
Total civil departments	1,071·8	1,047·2	971·2
Research councils			
AFRC	46·2	46·3	45·7
ESRC	19·0	20·0	20·0
MRC	125·3	127·6	132·4
NERC	68·3	68·0	68·1
SERC	286·5	295·9	317·1
Unallocated			
Total research councils	545·2	557·7	583·3
UGC	690·8	720·0	714·3
Total civil R. & D.	2,307·8	2,324·9	2,268·8
Ministry of Defence			
Research	412·3	407·8	382·1
Development	1,927·9	1,778·3	1,852·3
Staff & superannuation	77·0	78·2	76·5
Total defence	2,417·3	2,264·2	2,310·8
TOTAL	4,725·1	4,589·2	4,579·7

Note: Amounts, in constant £million (base year 1986/7), have been rounded off. Figures quoted in the main text refer to cash in year of expenditure and so will not correspond exactly.

Source: Annual Review of Government Funded Research and Development, 1988.

who does not believe that the dual-support system was an excellent and a successful way of providing 'risk capital'. Its passing has been universally mourned.

The effect of the government's 1981 cut in UGC funding has been to cut the state's support of basic science by more than 11 per cent. Civil servants within the Department of Education and Science recall that 'it came as a surprise to ministers' to learn that their planned UGC cuts would affect science in this way. The confidentiality with which the decision was made—to prevent leaks to the press among other things—meant that the decision process was so compartmentalized that no one was able to gauge the impact until it was too late.

The science vote and the UGC contribution to the dual-support system are the principal means whereby the state supports basic and strategic scientific research in the universities and in research institutes. But such 'blue skies' research represents only a fraction of the research and development of interest to government departments. In all, the government spends nearly £5 billion on scientific research and development, with fourteen major departments of state, and several statutory bodies, commissioning work. The system by which this government money is distributed is complex and not always well co-ordinated. Only in 1983, under pressure from a highly critical report by the House of Lords Select Committee on Science and Technology, did the government first institute an annual review of the research being undertaken by all departments. The most recent review revealed that in 1987/8 the civil departments funded just over £1 billion worth of research, roughly comparable with the £1,362 million that went direct to the research councils and the UGC. The Ministry of Defence spent £2,426 million, more than the entire civil research budget.

Over the years since Mrs Thatcher took office, the government has been devoting proportionately less of the nation's wealth to civil research and development (Table 24.2). Total spending has fallen from 0.72 per cent of GDP in 1981 to 0.62 per cent in 1986. In proportion to GDP, the governments of Italy, France, West Germany, and Sweden now spend more than does the British government in support of civil science. Of our major interna-

TABLE 24.2. *Government funding of R. & D. as a percentage of GDP*

	1981	1982	1983	1984	1985	1986
France	0·81	0·85	0·95	0·97	1·01	0·95
Germany	1·05	1·11	1·03	1·00	1·00	0·97
Italy	0·61	0·61	0·66	0·69	0·70	0·67
Sweden	1·01	1·02	1·04	1·03	0·96	0·90
UK	0·72	0·70	0·67	0·66	0·62	0·62
USA	0·51	0·45	0·41	0·40	0·41	0·39

Source: Annual Review of Government Funded Research and Development, 1988.

tional competitors, only the government of the USA spends less than the UK.

However, science in Britain was under stress long before Mrs Thatcher's government took office. Since the early 1970s, the science vote has remained roughly constant in real terms. The 'level funding' of the past decade and a half contrasts sharply with the situation after the end of the Second World War, when the money for science, and the supply of scientists able and equipped to do research, increased exponentially. It was Mrs Shirley Williams, the Secretary of State for Education and Science, in the Labour government of 1974–9, who confirmed the end of the era of rising budgets with her remark that 'the party is over for the scientists'.

While the science vote has been at a standstill, there has been a second inadvertent and unplanned decline in the total government resources going to support civil science. This time, the decline was the unforeseen and unintended consequence of an ideological decision taken in 1972 by the Heath government. One of the few lasting changes effected by Lord Rothschild and the Central Policy Review Staff was to introduce the 'customer-contractor' principle into government dealings with the research councils. Instead of the research councils getting their money as a block grant from the science vote and deciding themselves on what to spend the funds, Lord Rothschild proposed that government departments should contract with the councils (or indeed with other organizations if they wished) for the performance of a specified piece of research. The virtue claimed for this system was that there would be closer government scrutiny of what the councils actually did with the taxpayers' money. To facilitate this, the MRC, AFRC, and NERC lost substantial proportions of their science vote income: these moneys were distributed to the commissioning departments and the research councils were to try and win the money back as research contracts.

The idea was highly controversial at the time, and represented a clear and abrupt break with the philosophy of the previous fifty years, but the relevant point, in assessing the science policies of Mrs Thatcher's government, is that the commissioning departments have proved careless in their stewardship of the research that it became their duty to commission. The Agriculture and Food Research Council, for example, now estimates that its annual income—just over £100 million in 1987/8—would be some £30 million higher if the Ministry of Agriculture, Fisheries and Food had maintained a proper level of research contracts. Instead, as was almost inevitable, when the Ministry was faced with constraints on its public expenditure, one of the first things to be squeezed was its long-term commitment to the funding of scientific research. A similar situation obtains between the NERC—whose income is also at the £100 million mark—and the Department of the Environment.

The Medical Research Council managed to reverse the Rothschild arrangements early in the term of this government and obtained a refund from the Health Department of the moneys that had been taken away from it. The council maintains that it welcomes research contract work, but only so long as it is in addition to the core programme of research that the Council's own assessment of scientific priorities indicates to be the correct choice. It is perhaps no surprise that morale among the scientists who obtain funds from the MRC is much higher than that of their peers supported by the other research councils.

Of course, the problems caused by the Rothschild reorganization affected not only the research councils, which to some extent were able to protect their programmes of core research by using money from their science vote grant. The in-house research laboratories run by the individual government departments were in a more difficult position and, over the decade and a half since Rothschild, the contracts placed by the commissioning departments have changed the character of the work done so that the emphasis has been more and more on short-term applied research whose benefits could be seen immediately. This has inevitably led research to stray into commercially applicable areas.

In the industrially related sector, one of the main initiatives early in the Thatcher government was the Department of Trade and Industry's 'Alvey programme', intended to help Britain catch up with its competitors in the new generation of 'information technology' industries. To encourage industry, which has a dismal record of investing in research and development, the government announced that it was willing to match, pound for pound, the spending of companies in information technology research. The benefits have been questionable: cynics have argued that most of the government money went to large electronics companies who then simply cut back on their own in-house research budget because work that they would have done in any case was being subsidized by the state. Because the Alvey programme was not intended to produce tangible marketable products, there are intrinsic difficulties in measuring its success.

In 1988, the government suddenly announced that it would no longer fund 'near-market' research. The announcement caused great confusion, not least because no one in any previous discussion of science policy had ever used the term 'near-market' research. A further source of confusion is that the only written policy statement about near-market research comes in the DTI's 1988 White Paper *The Department for Enterprise* and refers only to an internal review of the research financed by the DTI itself. The DTI review spelled the end for the Alvey programme and its successor which had been proposed in 1986. But it was not apparent at the time that the DTI's internal review of its research was to be the blueprint for a new government policy for research funded by all departments. The result—confusing to outside observers and to research scientists alike—has been the apparent invention of a category of research solely for the purposes of stopping government funding of it.

The effects of this apparently sudden policy shift have been most apparent in the fields of energy research and agricultural research. The Department of Energy announced that it would no longer fund anything other than a token programme of research into fast breeder nuclear reactors and that the establishment at Dounreay in Scotland would shut some five years before the end of the design lifetime of the existing reactor there. This, together with a decrease in support for research into nuclear fusion, leaves a considerable question mark over the future of the UK Atomic Energy Authority, a statutory body set up in the 1950s to provide advice to government and to conduct research into nuclear power. The Authority remains the largest single scientific research organization in Western Europe, but it is now a body of scientists and engineers without a role. In the agricultural sector, the decision will deprive the hard-pressed AFRC of £9 million in 1989/90 and will have a much more severe effect on the Ministry of Agriculture, Fisheries and Food's own research laboratories.

In February 1989, a short report from the House of Lords Select Committee on Science and Technology questioned whether British industry was willing or able to fill the vacuum that will be created by the government's withdrawal from near-market research.

British science has been creative commercially as well as intellectually: in a survey of US patents of British origin, commissioned by the Department of Trade and Industry, the top-ranking patent by far was not granted to a British company, but resulted from publicly funded research done by scientists from the Agriculture and Food Research Council into synthetic pyrethrin insecticides. The second most frequently cited patent was for work on liquid crystals carried out at Hull University.

British industry on the other hand has had a poor record of investing in research and development. According to Professor Keith Pavitt of Sussex University's Science Policy Research Unit, since the late 1960s R. & D. funded by British companies themselves has grown more slowly than in most major OECD countries until, by the 1980s, it lagged well behind that of its main competitors. In his contribution to the book *The Evaluation of Scientific Research* (Wiley, 1989) Professor Pavitt warns that this cannot be attributed to an unfavourable economic climate, but to the inability or unwillingness of firms in Britain to commit an increasing share of profits or output to R. & D. at the same rate as their main foreign competitors. Yet Professor Pavitt's studies have shown a clear correlation between a company's investment in R. & D. and its economic and market performance.

The post-war trends in British science could not have continued: exponential growth in men and money was clearly unsustainable. Scientists in other countries have also had to go through periods of retrenchment. But the combination of the standstill in the science budget and the actual reduction consequent upon UGC funding and the Rothschild reforms has precipitated a collapse of morale among the scientific community in Britain.

It is much easier to measure the inputs to scientific research than to assess the quality of the output. Money and manpower (Table 24.3) are easy to count. But simply measuring the numbers of scientific papers produced by the British scientific community is no measure of the quality of the science contained in them. In fact, almost no work has been done to try and assess relative national performance in science. In 1986, the Advisory Board for the Research Councils, which advises the Secretary of State for Education and Science on the size and distribution of the science vote money, published the first serious study, covering the period 1960 to 1984. But events occurring after 1980 would not show up in the data, the study concluded.

At the beginning of 1987, a report from the House of Lords Select Committee on Science and Technology gave a reasonably synoptic assessment. The report was pessimistic: 'During the last five years, the general state of science and technology in the United Kingdom has not improved. In some areas it has even become worse. In spite of valiant efforts of individuals to make the present system work, and in spite of a few success stories in branches of science and technology, the overall picture conveys an impression of turmoil and frustration.' Their Lordships went on to warn, 'morale is low in the scientific community. A gap is growing between the potential of science and the resources

TABLE 24.3. *Manpower engaged on R. & D. (degree or equivalent)*

Department	Out-turn		Estimate
	1985/6	1986/7	1987/8
Civil departments			
MAFF	913	849	815
DES	6	5	6
DEn	38	34	37
UKAEA	3,376		
DoE	375	393	370
DHSS	58		
HSC	77	71	62
Home Office	195	192	198
ODA	176	169	159
DTI	573	591	586
DTp	343	350	357
NI Depts.	134	162	162
Scottish Depts.	175	159	158
Welsh Office	7	7	6
DEmp	15	14	36
MSC	31	36	30
Other depts.	341	373	358
Total civil departments	6,833	3,405	3,340
Research councils			
AFRC[a]	1,056	2,399	1,974
ESRC	59	51	51
MRC	1,504	1,479	1,492
NERC	1,377	1,344	1,343
SERC	1,108	1,099	1 086
Total research councils	5,104	6,372	5,946
Total civil R. & D.	11,937	9,777	9,286
Ministry of Defence	5,037	4,968	4,964
TOTAL	16,974	14,745	14,250

[a] From 1986/7 staff of grant-aided institutes were reported and costed as AFRC employees.

Source: Annual Review of Government Funded Research and Development, 1988.

available to scientists. The academic community is held back from breaking new ground or enthusing its pupils. A brain drain among the best graduates is again evident.'

One of the most public signs of this frustration and turmoil of which the Lords spoke was the formation, in January 1986, of the Save British Science Movement. The formation of such a group of scientists trying to defend research in the face of government cut-backs is essentially without precedent in the post-war period. It is only the third such grouping to be formed this century: similar groups came into existence during the other two periods of reform or crisis for science—in the early years of the century, when the necessity for state support of science was being recognized for the first time, and before the Second World War, when the need for reform of the system became apparent. In less than three years since its foundation, Save British Science has transformed itself, and the government's perception of it, from a body of 'whingeing scientists' to one of the most effective and persuasive groups attempting to influence government policy.

The indications are that the loss of morale affecting the country's research scientists has filtered down to prospective students and is affecting their choice of university undergraduate course. Over the past three years, the numbers of students studying humanities, business and finance, and social sciences have increased sharply, whereas there has been a fall in the numbers taking physical sciences and medicine. Social science undergraduates are up from 34,100 in 1985/6 to 36,100 in 1987/8, an increase of 5.9 per cent. Physical science undergraduates are down from 20,500 to 19,900, a 2.9 per cent fall. The biggest rise, of 16.1 per cent, was in those studying business and finance: from 9,300 to 10,800.

There have been some changes in government policy recently. In response to the 1986 House of Lords report, the government announced in 1987—using the customary coded language—that it was setting up a Cabinet committee on science, chaired by the Prime Minister, and that it was strengthening its advisory com-mittee, now known as the Advisory Council on Science and Technology (ACOST). But ACOST meets in secret and it is difficult to assess its effect. Early this year, the present Secretary of

State for Education and Science, Mr Kenneth Baker, announced a £300 million increase in the science vote over the next three years. The allocation for 1989/90 will be £825 million. Although much of this money is 'earmarked' for specific projects close to the government's heart, rather than being freely available to the research councils for the support of what they judge to be important science, it represents a significant shift in policy. However, even this increase will not allow the science budget to keep pace with inflation. The Advisory Board for the Research Councils warned that, after an initial 13 per cent uplift in the baseline of the science budget, the figures 'imply a 3% reduction in real terms over two years after allowing for inflation'.

The new shape of British science in the universities and the research council institutes is gradually beginning to emerge from this period of painful readjustment. The catalyst was the publication in 1987 of a blueprint for the future of science, entitled *A Strategy for the Science Base*. This document, published by the Advisory Board for the Research Councils, was the first serious attempt to come to terms with the facts of life: a science budget that would at best stay constant in real terms, a scientific establishment that had been conditioned to believe that its income would always grow and that recent history was but a temporary aberration, and a university system in disarray. The document envisaged a complete transformation of the British university scene, suggesting that in future there would be three classes of universities: some, designated 'T', would do essentially no research whatsoever but would concentrate on teaching undergraduates; others, category 'X', would specialize in a few areas of research and teaching postgraduate students; while only a few universities, class 'R', would be designated as fit to do research over a wide area of science and only these institutions would be funded accordingly. The 'binary divide' in British higher education, the distinction between universities and polytechnics, would also be weakened, as an increasing number of polytechnics undertook research.

In addition, the document presaged a move away from research based in university departments in favour of a research institute system akin in some respects to the West German Max

Planck Gesellschaft. The UK role-model for such research institutes was the world-famous Laboratory of Molecular Biology at Cambridge, an institute run by the Medical Research Council, which has consistently remained at the forefront of molecular biology since it was set up after the war. (The double helix structure of DNA; haemoglobin and myoglobin; monoclonal antibodies; are among this laboratory's Nobel-prizewinning successes.)

Not surprisingly, the Board's implicit criticism of the standards of research at the universities provoked a barrage of furious criticism. The explicit proposals for classifying universities as 'R, T, X' have been gently dropped, but the other initiative, the setting up of interdisciplinary research centres—in effect, MRC-style institutes but more loosely managed and more closely tied to universities—has become fashionable. But the underlying imperative of the analysis remains: faced with shortage of resources, there must be selectivity and concentration of resources on a few centres of excellence.

Although this idea has been most clearly articulated by the Advisory Board, it has been put into action principally by the University Grants Committee. It has been reviewing the future of physics, chemistry, and earth sciences within the universities, taking account not only of likely student numbers and departmental teaching size—things which are within its traditional remit—but also assessing the research record of individual departments. The latter, in the view of many, is a task for which the UGC is not properly equipped.

There are signs also that the future of the five separate research councils may be in doubt. Much of the work of the Agriculture Research Council overlaps with that of the Environment, while both these councils sponsor work in biology that overlaps with some of the research funded by the Science Research Council. It is possible that Britain may move over to a system closer to the US model, which has the National Institutes of Health (the equivalent of our Medical Research Council) and the National Science Foundation (a single research council covering all non-clinical sciences).

The story of the Thatcher decade is largely of confusion,

leading to loss of morale among the scientists. That morale will take a long time to rebuild. And the confusion has not yet cleared. For nine years, the government urged its scientists to do more applied, commercially orientated work—to contribute to the creation of wealth. Suddenly, and without warning, it has changed its mind, without taking care to ensure that industry is ready and willing to fill the vacuum. Pure not-for-profit research is once again what the government is willing to pay for. Yet, the University Grants Committee is slashing and burning its way through university departments without an overall plan or design of how the higher education system will look at the end. It seems likely that nearly half the universities will lose their physics or chemistry departments as a result of the UGC action. Large, difficult to manage, and completely unproven interdisciplinary research centres are being set up as scientists scramble desperately for the funds that are available. There is no plan, no overall scheme: above all, there is no confidence for the future. And all the while, our major economic competitors are investing a greater proportion of their national wealth in the support of civil research and development.

25

The Churches: Pink Bishops and the Iron Lady

DAVID MARTIN

Anyone observing the media at the beginning of 1989 would have been struck by the increased salience of news about religion in Britain as contrasted with the decreased salience of religion in the beliefs and practice of ordinary people. A left-wing Sinhalese atheist was ousted from his chosen sanctuary in the Church of the Ascension, Manchester, by a hundred immigration officers and policemen and dispatched to an unknown fate in his homeland. The two years' captivity in Lebanon of the archbishop of Canterbury's special envoy Terry Waite was duly remarked upon and rightly lamented. A lot of comment focused on the choice of a divorced black lady by American Episcopalians as the first woman bishop in world-wide Anglicanism, an event which threw into further odd relief the undigested issue of women's ordination in Britain. And Salman Rushdie's *Satanic Verses* was attacked by leaders of the Muslim community in terms likely to give liberal multiculturalists a heart attack. They made it appallingly clear that in crucial respects they had *not* been assimilated to the liberal consensus or the norms of British society.

Such continuous coverage might lead anyone to think that religion had become a kind of media event: a matter of public pronouncement rather than a matter of love of God and your neighbour. At any rate the figures for belief and practice published about the same time all too plainly suggested a slow withering at the grass roots. This includes even the rites of passage, which are usually the most resilient aspect of religion. For example, at the beginning of this century two out of three babies were baptized at the fonts of the Church of England. Now it is one in three. Between 1930 and 1985 the proportion of the adult population receiving Anglican communion at Easter drop-ped by a half to 4.2 per cent. Between 1970 and 1985 attendance on the average Sunday dropped from 3.3 per cent to 2.5 per cent. All Anglican indices drifted gently downward in the decade 1979–89.

This erosion affected all the branches of more or less liberal Christianity. Thus the age profile of the liberal free Churches tilts ominously to the older age groups. Between 1970 and 1987 membership of the Methodist Church in the UK dropped from 694,333 to 516,739 and of the Presbyterian Church from 1,806,736 to 1,346,366. Those who have resisted erosion best have been the Roman Catholics and evangelicals. Perhaps half of all worshippers on a given Sunday are Roman Catholics. Certainly the evangelicals are the lively sector, just as they are world-wide from Seoul to São Paulo and Uppsala to Sydney. They bid fair to be the largest single party in the Church of England and flourish vigorously in the 'free enterprise' market of Pentecostals, house churches and independent churches, and black religion. The nationalized faith slips; the free market expands.

However, people's private beliefs have seemed to stay more stable than their practice, at least till quite recently. In 1979 about three in four believed in God and prayed to him; and nearly one in two believed in Jesus Christ and an 'after-life' of *some* kind. Many ordinary Anglicans sit quite loose to orthodoxy, certainly more so than most Roman Catholics, but even among the Romans there is a growing margin of deviant belief. For example, one in three of those calling themselves Catholics do not accept papal infallibility or the obligation of weekly mass. Most interest-ing are the big differences between the oldest and the youngest generation of Catholics, which run dramatically parallel to the differences found in Western Europe as a whole. Many young Catholics have strong reservations about traditional teaching on euthanasia, birth control, premarital sex and divorce, though these reservations are not so evident regarding teaching on abortion and homosexuality.

Belief is at its lowest among the young, the male, and the poorly off. Thus the nadir of Christian belief and practice is found among unemployed young males. Investigations by Leslie Francis seem to show a marked decline of belief among young adolescents. Of 1,000 secondary school pupils questioned in 1974 a third found it 'difficult' to believe in God; by 1986 it was a half. According to another study by Francis, in 1974, 42 per cent found God helped in their personal life, in 1986, 25 per cent.

With regard to morals it seems that exhortations about supposed 'Victorian values' have fallen on deaf ears. Perhaps it is difficult to encourage the survival of the fittest and, at the same time, preach respect for moral absolutes. The old are much more morally conservative than the young, about sexuality as well as about work, lying, and stealing. And the young differ from the old in the way they reason about morals, taking up positions largely in terms of their likely consequences. The one secure point in the moral universe is repugnance at the abuse of animals. As G. K. Chesterton once remarked, 'the Englishman's God is spelt backwards'. However, there may be a harbinger of change in one or two respects. A report in *Social Trends* (1989) showed on the one hand an increase from 37 per cent to 54 per cent since 1983 of those supporting a woman's right to choose to have a baby or not, but on the other hand tougher attitudes to homosexuality, extra-marital sex, and the availability of contraception to the under-16s. It is to be feared that the consequence of AIDS have more to do with this than renewed attachment to Kantian morality.

Traditionally morals have been related to education, and there has been growing concern that the 'neutrality' about values propagated by some teachers leads to moral indifference. Clearly, the kind of provisions about Christianity, about daily acts of worship, and about education in religion embodied in the 1944 Education Act have more and more been quietly ignored, even in quite a number of church schools. In some areas the existence of large minorities or even majorities of people of non-Christian religions has led to a kind of celebration of all festivals, without so much as a hint being given that these involve very different beliefs.

This has led to various reactions coming to a head in the 1980s. One reaction aims to remove religion from the schools; another aims to restore some serious content to religious education, including at least some minimum understanding as to what the historic faith of Britain is actually about. A further reaction is to bring children up outside the state system. This is a widespread trend in Australia and the USA, and is evident today in Britain among both Christians and Muslims. These various pressures resulted initially in governmental avoidance of the religious issue in the Education Reform Bill of 1988, but in the event the nettle was grasped and provisions for religious education, and for increased understanding of Christianity, firmed up, at least in law. Significantly the firmest pressure for these provisions came from lay politicians, led by Baroness Cox.

An issue which has come up with increasing persistence is how far Britain is 'multicultural' and how far 'multiculturalism' should be pursued. Since religious minorities do not, in fact, account for more than 4 per cent of the population there is presumably some support for Mrs Thatcher's emphasis on the majority community and Baroness Cox's initiative in securing an emphasis on Christianity in the religious education provisions of the Education Reform Act of 1988. In any case, one major community—the Jewish—has in some important ways become assimilated, meaning that it is culturally very British.

The politics of religion (and race) turn to some extent on social geography. Taking first the original deposits of post-Reformation Christianity, the Church of England is strong in a conservative belt from Dorset to the Wash—and in the conservative suburbs. Old Puritan dissent still has a discernible presence in the East Midlands and East Anglia and evangelical nonconformity retains redoubts in the North-East, the West, and Wales. Significantly sentiment hostile to Mrs Thatcher is concentrated in the non-English areas once strongholds of evangelical Protestantism: Wales and Scotland. At the same time there has been a drift of English nonconformity from North to South, and maybe also in a more conservative direction.

Later religious deposits derive from migration and have concentrated in the cities: Irish Catholics in West Lancashire, Birmingham, Glasgow, and London; Jews in Glasgow, Leeds, Manchester, and London; Christian West Indians in Bristol and London; Pakistani Muslims in Bradford and the West Midlands;

Bangladeshi Muslims in London's East End; Hindus in Greater London (Harrow, Wembley) and Midland cities; and Sikhs in Southall and Gravesend. Social mobility has often brought with it shifting locations, so that Jews have shifted from east to north London, and Catholics from inner London to the peripheries and Home Counties. There is also a social geography of apathy so far as Christianity is concerned, which is concentrated within the cultural radiation of London and Birmingham, but also in depressed areas like Hull.

For religious minorities the situation is in some ways easier than for established religion, since corrosion of commitment can go on inside the outer framework of establishment without being immediately noticed. A minority, by contrast, knows that it has to provide a distinctive home and educational environment if it is to survive. Fail to do that and mobility and marriage will nibble away ceaselessly, as they have in the case of the Jewish community. Undoubtedly, the million or so Muslims are the most resistant minority, though on issues like tolerance and the position of women the price of their resistance has to be segregation and hostility. Yet the 'Islamic ethic' is one that produces solid citizens anxious to better themselves through education and through commerce. Though Muslims currently vote for Labour they are, as Jews have been, potential converts to Conservatism.

Inside the more explicitly Christian sector of the majority community, the major matter has been the clash between traditionalism in all its forms and progressivism. Latterly this has become focused on female ordination and the issue of the status of women. This is a peculiarly vexing issue because the Church of England is an (almost) Catholic Church in what is (mostly) a Protestant country. Its priests have beliefs in common more with Catholics than with their own laity, and that means that a fairly large minority reject the ordination of women either in principle or because it interferes with relations with Rome. Given this overall stance the pressure from liberals and feminists has looked like driving the Catholic party into open rebellion. That still remains a possibility, even though the net result of pressure and resistance is a temporary stalemate in which women are still confined to the diaconate—and therefore denied proper access to a career. One of the problems is that while various traditionalist groups concerned about liturgy or doctrine or morals or politicization or the nature of the priesthood can be countered one by one, they may actually congeal into a critical mass. Something like this occurred with the publication of the Preface to Crockford's *Clerical Directory* in December 1987. In spite of the misleading newspaper headlines, the Preface was only marginally an attack on the style of the archbishop and on the (unsubstantiated) selectivity of his senior appointments. The author was concerned rather about the overt deposition of the historic liturgy and the covert deposition of historic doctrine, and also with the way a centralized and expensive bureaucracy was trying to remould the Church in a novel image. An obvious flashpoint for traditionalists is provided by the pronouncements of the bishop of Durham. Many people feel that he fails to recognize the difference between the proper freedoms of a university chair and the responsibilities of anyone willingly accepting the office of guardian of the faith.

Of course, the main issue agitating the public forum has been the political clash between Mrs Thatcher's government and the leaders of the Church. The government has shown more interest in religious matters than almost any since Gladstone's. Mrs Thatcher has herself addressed the General Assembly of the Church of Scotland, roughly along the lines of St Paul to the Thessalonians, claiming *inter alia* that he that does not work should not eat. Douglas Hurd, the Home Secretary, has adjured the General Synod to concentrate its attention on the proper integration of society and the family. To understand this remarkable clash some historical retrospect is required.

Since the 1920s the association of religious affiliation with particular parties has largely broken up. No longer is the Liberal Party a vehicle for the civil rights of dissenters and for the mobilization of serious artisans and the 'respectable' working class. No longer is the Conservative Party allied with the Church of England and the traditional strata who tended to comprise it. No longer are Roman Catholics quite so strongly identified with the Labour Party and mobilized around the interests of immigrants, above all the Irish.

Of course, there are elements remaining from these ancient alliances. What is interesting, however, is the way the *clergy* of all three mainstream traditions have converged toward the left-liberal consensus view. This change was in train at the time of the Second World War and has surfaced dramatically since the political consensus broke up into radical right and radical left in the mid-1970s. In short, the Churches are now conserving the established left-liberal view, which dominated the intelligentsia and the BBC.

The break-up of the left-liberal consensus has occurred in the political realm, not the cultural realm, where such institutions as the universities, the BBC and the Churches remain influential. This break-up involves the agony of the Labour Party as it strives to find the middle ground and check the power of the far left. The same break-up also involves the demise of the Disraelian tradition of 'One Nation' promoted by aristocratic Toryism. The new Tories are not in the aristocratic mould, but are hungry men—and women—preaching a kind of populism. Broadly they seek the Americanization of English culture.

Supporters of the old consensus have been dismayed at the new divisiveness and at the costs incurred in the attempt to curb trade union power and control inflation. They have been equally dismayed, however, by Mr Scargill and do not want to return to massive inflation and rule by trade unions. For a while they shifted towards the new Social Democratic–Liberal Alliance, and they would still be there had not the Alliance broken up in bitterness and confusion. All the same, the splintered middle parties do have a distinct Christian presence in people like Shirley Williams (Roman Catholic), David Owen (Anglican), Alan Beith (Methodist), and David Steel (Presbyterian).

In the mid-1980s more than half the clergy of all the major denominations supported the Alliance, whereas only one quarter of the electorate did so. Studies of the Anglican clergy in particular showed them holding:

(a) that the Church should be politically involved;
(b) that the national priorities are in education, social services, and health, not in defence and the reduction of inflation.

These views have remained strongly entrenched in the Anglican General Synod, which is an overwhelmingly upper-middle class and liberal body, and which has a membership with qualifications concentraied in theology, arts, and classics. (It may be added that the members of the Roman Catholic Pastoral Congress have similar views, and these are propagated most strongly by teachers and by female religious.)

These dispositions of 'force' have led to dramatic social confrontations. Indeed, the Conservative government has clashed with all the major bastions of the established consensus: the Church, the intelligentsia (including the teachers), the universities, and the BBC. One bishop (Winchester) even claimed that the Church was the real opposition to the government, given that the Labour Party was so crippled as a viable opposition and given the defects of the electoral system as a means of reflecting the public will. Actually, in terms of attitudes, for example towards privatization and welfare, the Church was almost certainly closer to the people than the government.

A minor confrontation, reflecting the wider conflict, has been between the clergy and the laity. While many of the clergy, especially those in the key bureaucratic positions, have aligned themselves with the liberal intelligentsia, Anglican lay people have mostly remained moderately conservative in the old pre-1979 style. They do not see the Church's mission as extending to politics. Indeed, the articulate members of the Anglican laity now include vigorous critics of the Church leadership. These were given their first lead back in the 1970s when Dr Edward Norman was somehow smuggled into the BBC liberal fortress as Reith lecturer and claimed that the political commentary of the Church(es) was secular liberalism glossed with a Christian vocabulary.

The new lay critique of the clergy now comes from Christian journalists on the *Spectator*, the *Daily Telegraph*, the *Daily Mail* (which has very close links with Mrs Thatcher), and—in a more opaque way—*The Times*, since it was taken over. It has included noted Conservative politicians like John Selwyn Gummer. Also involved as critics are ex-nonconformists like Ralph Harris and Rhodes Boyson who have been associated with a key think-tank, the Institute of Economic Affairs (IEA). These people, together with Professor Sir Bryan Griffiths, another ex-nonconformist and personal adviser to Mrs Thatcher (herself after all an ex-nonconformist), have developed a Christian defence of capitalism. Ex-nonconformists can, it seems, deliver a last powerful kick. This Christian capitalism resembles the position taken in the USA by people like Michael Novak, Richard Neuhaus, and Peter Berger. Neo-conservative views are also expressed in the Salisbury Review, which adds in Jewish and conservative Roman Catholic criticism, with a touch of the Hegelian right, and shows unusual interest in religious issues. However, most Christians do not involve themselves in these high ideological battles. Their Christianity is local, moral, and personal, rather than political or doctrinal. Many of them are theologically liberal *and* politically conservative (whereas some clergy are just the reverse!).

The tension between Church and government has been dramatized in several incidents. There was first of all the row over the service of reconciliation with the Argentine which the Church devised after the Falklands War. There was also the archbishop of Canterbury's interview for *The Times* of 28 September 1984 criticizing divisive policies, the erosion of the middle ground, and vituperative politics. Two major publications also generated a great deal of heat. One was the report of a Committee of the General Synod on *The Church and the Bomb*, the other, the archbishop's report *Faith in the Inner City*. The latter was even labelled 'Marxist' by some government sources.

Criticism of the government was fairly uniform throughout the Anglican episcopate as well as the Catholic episcopate, and the leadership of the Free Churches and the Church of Scotland. Perhaps the greatest degree of unity was shown over the Local Government Bill, which stirred many bishops to a defence of locality. Broadly they were for the idea of the locality, for the idea of One Nation, and against the North–South divide. David Sheppard, bishop of Liverpool, used his Dimbleby lecture to defend the corporate sense of the community against utilitarian individualism, and Bishop Newbigin did the same in his Gore lectures. Mark Santer (Birmingham) and J. Austin Baker (Salisbury) emerged as strong critics in the sphere of defence. The bishop of Sheffield was a strong critic of the North–South divide. And the bishops of Durham and Stepney were strong critics about most matters. The bishops of Peterborough and London, however, were more conservatively inclined and the newly appointed bishop of Oxford (1988) has always been a keen opponent of the Campaign for Nuclear Disarmament. The views of the Methodist Conference may be inferred from critical resolutions on health, unemployment, and defence.

This tension was further lighted up by interventions from above. First, a fireball landed on a transept of York Minster, immediately after the consecration of David Jenkins as bishop of Durham. Second, the Queen was 'reported' to share the view of the old high Tories and the Church to the effect that Mrs Thatcher was uncaring and her policies divisive. (It is, indeed, quite likely that the Queen was especially worried by the impact of government policies toward South Africa on Commonwealth opinion.) Third, the University of Oxford refused an honorary degree to Mrs Thatcher on the grounds that she was ill disposed towards higher education. All this is very confusing for the average old-fashioned Anglican who expects God, the Queen, the Church, and Oxford University—and the Conservative Party— to act together in reasonable harmony.

A further aspect of these events has been provided by over a decade of public argument over the devising of a new liturgy eventually embodied in *The Alternative Service Book* (1980). Some conservative papers found this an issue to be included in the list of current ecclesiastical misdoings. Broadly, what happened was that the clergy tried to modernize their image and to push forward the politics of ecumenism only to find themselves criticized by much of the literate intelligentsia, left and right, atheistic and believing, supported by symbolic votes in Parliament and by most of the serious press. (It is only proper for me to confess that I myself spent a great deal of time trying to bring this criticism about.)

One element worth emphasizing again is the rise of conservative evangelicalism parallel to the rise of religious conservatism the world over. As the World Council of Churches has gone one way many Christians have gone another. Evangelicals are now so successful they have even been admitted to the Anglican episcopate. They are not, however, in the main, political Conservatives. Evangelicalism is likely to make another break-through in the media once the state duopoly of television (ITV–BBC) is broken up. At that point, versions of the Electronic Church are bound to appear. Evangelicalism is even present in the government to some extent, alongside the hungry yuppies, the atheists, and several prominent members of the Jewish com-munity. The net effect of this growth of evangelical religion may well be to assist Americanization at the level of cultural attitudes and motivations. Certainly, the emergence of a British equivalent of the Moral Majority is to be expected.

What then does all this amount to? It means that the Church(es), the universities, and the BBC stand for the old left-liberal consensus and the politics of welfare. In this, they are joined by the ousted grandees of the old Tory Party and all those attached to the idea of 'One Nation'. These institutions have always managed to keep any extremism in check and have usually tamed any signs of ideological dogmatism or intense religiosity. They are for the values of liberal education and against the technologization propagated by the government. The clergy, the teachers, and the social/administrative professions are aligned together in the support groups of the upper-middle-class liberal establishment. This establishment and the government are now fighting it out for control.

If one tries to estimate the precise contribution of Mrs Thatcher and her government to the picture just provided it has to be stressed that both 'Thatcherism' and social welfare Christianity are of much wider provenance than Britain. They are persistent currents meeting in turbulent confluence. So far as social welfare Christianity is concerned, it is dominant in the whole of north-west Europe and it is quite difficult to say if it is helped forward by corrosions of religious practice or itself increases them—or neither of these. There are certainly those who see the stress on welfare as related to a loosening of roots in religious practice and conventional social structures. The universal decline of practice itself is undoubted and affects Catholic France and even Catholic Flanders, as well as Protestant north-west Europe. Holland provides the most dramatic instance of the decline.

The evangelical counterflow observed in England is also common to north-west Europe and to the United States and Latin America. This is where to place the specific contribution of Margaret Thatcher. She comes out of an older individualistic version of Methodism, stressing self-help, prudence, discipline, and personal responsibility, and now she finds a new version of evangelicalism making successful inroads which fits in well with her social and religious instincts. Certainly in so far as it stresses health and wealth she and the new evangelicalism are at one. Maybe she gives it a boost and vice versa.

Faced by an aggressive Mrs Thatcher and an aggressive evangelicalism, the traditions of Anglican paternal conservatism and of Liberal Protestant social gospel have been pricked and jarred into self-consciousness. Previously they had consigned all *that*, along with Mrs Whitehouse, to the movement of history. Now, with history turned whimsical, they have to look to their defences and foundations.

INDEX

abortion 267
abstraction in art 309, 310
academic tenure 204
acid rain 223
Ackroyd, Peter 310, 314
Act of Toleration (1689) 271–2
'active citizen' 141
Advisory Board for the Research
    Councils 324, 327–8
Advisory Conciliation and
    Arbitration Service (ACAS) 66
Advisory Council on Science and
    Technology (ACOST) 326
Afghanistan 145, 146, 158
Agriculture and Food Research
    Council (AFRC) 317, 321, 323,
    328
Alliance parties 91, 92, 95, 97, 99,
    336
Americanization of Britain,
    Thatcherite drive towards 336,
    340
Amis, Martin 310
Andre, Carl 309
Anglican churches 330–1, 333,
    334–5, 336–7
Anglo-Irish Agreement 232–6
Anglo-Irish Inter-Governmental
    Council 228, 230, 231
animals, concern for 332
anti-terrorist offensive in Northern
    Ireland 234–5
'anti-Thatcherite majority' 98–100
apartheid 164
architecture 313
Argentina 157–8, 159, 160, 228
arms control negotiations 145,
    148–9
arts 305–14
    developments in 309–14
    and market values of Thatcherism
        306–10
    underfunding of 306–8, 310
Arts Council 305, 306, 307, 308,
    309

Ashdown, Paddy 99–100
Asquith, Herbert 123
Atkins, Humphrey 227
Atomic Energy Authority 323
Attlee government 74
audiences for TV 304
Audit Commission 127
Australia 96
Austria 96
authoritarianism, Thatcherite 3–4,
    102–3, 105–6, 107, 113, 122,
    133–4, 136–40, 141–2, 268,
    296

back-bench MPs 110–12
bail 277
Baker, J. Austin 338
Baker, Kenneth 106, 190, 201, 203,
    204, 206, 208, 327
balance of payments 13–17, 18, 78
Baldwin, Stanley 252
Bancroft, Lord 121
Bandaranaika, Sirimavo 160
Bank of England 50, 54, 55, 57–60,
    82
Banking Act (1979) 58
bankruptcy 46–7
banks 52–3, 55, 62
baptism 330
Bar 274, 284, 286–8, 289
Barber, David 176
Barnes, Julian 310
Barnett, Joel 103
BBC 295, 297, 298, 299, 301, 303,
    336, 337
behaviour, changes in 241
Beith, Alan 336
Belize 157
benefits 24, 35, 270, 272
Benn, Tony 93
Berger, Peter 338
Berlusconi 302
Bevan, Aneurin 166
Beveridge, William 123
Biffen, John 106, 294

'Big Bang' 49, 52, 54–6
Biggs-Davison, Sir John 231
Bill of Rights 139
'Birmingham Six' 235
Black, Conrad 293
Blair, Tony 93, 113
Blunden, Sir George 59, 60, 61
Board of Banking Supervision 59
Bond, Edward 306
books 310–12
Booth, Albert 93
Borrie, Sir Gordon 55
borrowing, government 9
Boyson, Dr Rhodes 107, 198, 337
British Airways 44
British Gas 43
British Medical Association (BMA)
    176
British Nationality Act (1981) 279
British Rover 27
British Satellite Broadcasting 297
British Steel 42
Brittan, Leon 275, 294, 295
broadcasting 290–1, 295–303
Broadcasting Bill 299–300
Brooke, Henry 136
Brophy, Brigid 310
Brown, Gordon 93, 113
building societies 52
Burke, Edmund 140
Butler, David 90
Butler, R. A. 98

Cabinet 102–7
cable television 296–7
Callaghan, James/Callaghan
    government 7, 25, 64, 92, 103,
    117, 125, 146, 147, 183
Campaign for Nuclear Disarmament
    (CND) 145–6
cancer screening 168, 173–4
Carlisle, Mark 103, 189, 198, 199
Caro, Anthony 312
Carrington, Lord 157, 160
censorship 267, 281–3, 291, 295–6
Central Policy Review Staff 102,
    104, 122
centralization of state power 4
    see also authoritarianism,
        Thatcherite

Chalfont, Lord 301
Chamberlain, Joseph 106
Channel 4 290, 300, 303
Channel tunnel 251, 255
Charter 88 movement 92, 136
Chester, Robert 262
Chesterton, G. K. 332
Child Benefit 35, 271
child care 272
children's evidence in court 277
Chilver, Lord 204–5
China 158, 159
Church and the Bomb, The 338
church attendance 330–2, 340–1
Churches 192, 330–41
Churchill, Sir Winston 154, 240
CID 296
City of London 49–63
Civil Justice Review 285
civil liberties, destruction of 136,
    276–7, 280, 281, 296
civil procedure 283–5
Civil Service 114–23
    loss of morale in 122–3
    politicization of 120–1
    problems in 114
    reforms of 115–20
    trade unions in 121–2
Civil Service Commission 122–3
Clarke, Kenneth 106, 177
'Clause 28' 267
Clegg Commission 20
Clerical Directory 335
closed shop 71
cohesion/conflict, political 260–1
collective bargaining 2, 77
collectivism 137
Common Agricultural Policy (CAP)
    27, 45
Commonwealth 154, 155, 156–7,
    163, 165
community care 174–5, 181
'community charge' see poll tax
    ('community charge')
Community Health Councils 178
competition 42–3, 44–6, 55
competitive relationships, supremacy
    of 135–7, 140
competitive tendering, compulsory
    127–8, 131

consensus, break-up of 5, 336, 337, 338–9, 340
Conservative Party 80–8
  and Europe 85–6
  and exchange rates 81–2
  and industrial relations 82–3
  and privatization 84–5
  and USA 86–8
  attachment to 'family' 265–6
  City contributions to funds of 49
  percentage of vote 89
  periods in office 89–90
Constitution 133–42
  and 'freedom' 140–1
  and social pluralism 138–9
  and supremacy of market 135–7
  and Thatcherite authoritarianism 133–4, 137–40, 141–2
  and trade unions 134
  reform of 139–40
Contempt of Court Act (1981) 278, 279
contingency fee arrangements 287
conveyancing 44, 283, 287
Cook, Robin 93, 99, 113
Cooper, Sir Frank 295
corporal punishment 281
corporation tax 29, 41
corruption in police 296
'corset' control of banks 52
council house sales 42, 214, 216, 218–21
Courts of Appeal 276, 283–4
Cox, Baroness 333
Cradock, Sir Percy 101
Craft, Nick 1
Cragg, Tony 312
creativity/excellence in art 308–9
credit, expansion of 31
credit cards 52, 241
Criminal Injuries Compensation Scheme 278
Criminal Justice Act (1987) 277
Criminal Justice Act (1988) 278
criminal justice system 275–7, 279–81
Crosland, Anthony 198, 213
cruise missiles 145–6, 147
Cuellar, Perez de 158
cultural change 240, 241, 249–50

Cunningham, John 93, 99, 113, 121
curriculum in schools 183, 184, 187–8, 189, 191, 192
cuts in spending 25
  see also underfunding

Daily Express 293
Daily Mail 190, 337
Daily Telegraph 167, 290, 293, 337
Dalyell, Tom 295
Darwinism, social 195
Data Protection Act (1984) 279
'Death on the Rock' 296, 301
debt 241, 244
defeats, government 107–9
defence 86, 143–53
  and Falklands War 150–1
  and MoD 151–2
  and nuclear deterrence 144, 145–6, 147–9
  and Thatcher–Reagan 'love affair' 143
  spending on 144, 147–8, 149–50, 151–2
Delors' proposals 77
Denham, Lord 108
dental/eyesight check charges 176
Department of Education and Science (DES) 183, 184, 191, 200–1, 207, 316–17, 319
Department of Energy 323
Department of Trade and Industry (DTI) 46, 322
deregulation 3, 28–9, 44, 46, 49, 52, 56
Dewar, Donald 113
DHSS 172, 174, 176, 177
Dicey, Albert 137
Distillers Company 279
  take-over of 51
divorce rate 263–4
docklands 129
doctors 175, 178
Donaldson, Sir John 283
Donoughue, Bernard 134
Donovan Commission 77
Drug Trafficking Offences Act (1986) 278
'dual-support system' 316–17, 319
Duchamp, Marcel 309

earnings 20
economic policy 1–37
  and industry 38–48
  and regional variations 252–7
  balance of payments 13–17
  exchange rates 21–3, 32–4
  growth record 11–13, 18–20
  inflation 23, 31, 33
  international context of 2–4, 9–11
  leading ideas in 4–7
  macro-economic policies 7–9
  North Sea oil 17–18
  poverty growth 34–6
  privatization 28, 42–4
  public expenditure 25
  taxation 23, 26, 27, 32
  unemployment 24
  union reforms 30
Economist, The 138
economy, problems of 1
Eden, Sir Anthony 160, 219
Edgar, David 306
education see higher education;
  schools
Education Act (1980) 190, 266
'Education for Capability' 188
Education Reform Act (1988) 128,
  183, 184, 185, 186, 187, 190,
  192, 203–4, 209, 266, 333
EEC 44, 45, 77, 85–6, 92, 154, 155,
  159, 162–4, 222, 223
EETPU 72, 73–4
Eire, cooperation/quarrels with
  Britain 228, 229–30, 232–3,
  234–6
elderly 166
elective dictatorship, Thatcherite
  133, 135, 137–40, 141–2
electoral pacts, impetus towards 92,
  99
electoral reform 92
electoral system, first-past-the-post
  96, 137–8, 258
electricity industry 224
  privatization of 44
Elizabeth II, Queen 339
employers, and unions 71, 77
employment, pattern of 70
Employment Act (1980) 66, 291
Employment Act (1982) 67

Employment Act (1984) 68
Employment Bill (1989) 71
Employment Protection Act 66
enterprise, encouragement of 46
environment 222–5
European Convention on Human
  Rights 281
European Court of Human Rights
  278, 279, 281
European Court of Justice 278
European defence co-operation 143
European Monetary System (EMS)
  33–4, 82
evangelicals 331, 339–40, 341
exchange controls 29, 50
exchange rates 21–3, 32–4, 81–2
expenditure, public 25, 81, 83,
  245–6
  see also underfunding
exports 16–17
extradition law 278
  in Ireland 235

Faith in the Inner City 338
Falklands War 103, 105, 144,
  150–1, 157–8, 160, 228, 338
family 262–73
  and party politics 265–6, 272–3
  incomes 268–72
  policies on 265–8
  social trends in 262–5
Family Credit 270
Family Income Supplement 270
Family Policy Group 266–7
Family Practitioner Service (FPS)
  171, 172, 178
Farley's baby food factory 168
Fianna Fail party 234, 236
fiction writing 310–12
Field, Frank 110
financial/capital markets 3, 15,
  29–30, 31, 45
Financial Services Act (1986) 52, 56,
  57
Financial Times 290
Finer, Herman 138
Fitzgerald, Dr Garret 230
'floating pound' 81–2
food prices 27
food safety 168–9

Foot, Michael 92, 94, 97, 113
Foreign Office 105, 159–60
Fowler, Norman 175–6, 178–9, 180
France 19, 20, 31, 96, 154, 165,
    302
Francis, Leslie 332
Franks Report 105
fraud cases 277
freedom:
    as power sharing 141–2
    Thatcherite view of 140, 194–5
Friedman, Milton 65

Gaitskell, Hugh 91, 93
Gallup polls 243–4, 245, 247
Gamble, Andrew 136
Gandhi, Indira 160
Gardiner, Lord 274
Gaulle, Charles de 240
GCHQ (Government Communi-
    cations Headquarters) 122
GCSE exam 184
General Synod 337, 338
George, Eddie 61
Germany 11, 19, 20, 39, 40, 47, 48,
    96, 135, 149, 174
'ghettoization' of schools 192–3
ghettos, racial 252
Gibraltar 159
Gilmour, Sir Ian 103, 157
Giscard d'Estaing, Valery 10
Gladstone, William Ewart 106, 114,
    119, 240
Golding, William 310
Goodison, Sir Nicholas 55
Goodman, Lord 307
Gorbachev, Mikhail 145, 148, 149,
    154, 162
Gould, Bryan 98, 113
Gow, Ian 231, 233
Gowrie, Lord 227–8, 229
Grass, Günter 311
Greater London Council (GLC),
    abolition of 27, 108–9, 130,
    131
'green issue' 222–3
Greenham Common 146, 295
Griffiths, Roy 179
Griffiths, Sir Bryan 338
Griffiths reforms 179–80

Gross Domestic Product (GDP)
    253–4
growth, economic 1–2, 8, 9–10,
    11–13, 14, 19, 253
Guardian 175, 290, 294, 295, 296
Gummer, John Selwyn 337
Gunn, John 61
gutter press 293–4

Haig, Alexander 158
Hailsham, Lord 133, 273–5, 283–4,
    285, 286
Harris, Ralph 337
Hattersley, Roy 93, 98, 113
Haughey, Charles 234
Havers, Lord 275
Hayek, F. A. 133–4, 135, 138
Healey, Denis 7, 93, 113
Health Department 177, 179
health insurance 180
health review (1988–9) 104
health service 166–82, 266
    attacks on 167, 171, 175–7,
        180–2
    collapse of confidence in 167–9,
        176–7, 180–1
    reorganizations of 178–81
    underfunding of 166, 169–71,
        172–3, 175–7, 180–1
    White Paper on 180–1, 182
Heath, Edward/Heath government 5,
    10, 30, 65, 80, 83, 85, 114,
    134, 139, 143, 155, 160, 163,
    165, 226, 282
Heffer, Hugh 93
Heister, Sir Terence 121
Henderson, David 2–3, 4
Heseltine, Michael 105–6, 116, 120,
    125, 127, 129, 143, 146, 151,
    294
Hicks, Sir William Joynson 136
Higgins, Terence 110
High Court 274, 285
higher education 198–211
    and polytechnics 100–1, 202, 207,
        209, 210
    philistinism towards universities
        199, 200, 201–2, 203, 204,
        205–6, 208–9, 316–17,
        327–8, 329

higher education *cont.*
  underfunding of 199–200, 201,
    204–6
Hillsborough Agreement *see* Anglo-
  Irish Agreement
Hobbs, Thomas 138
Hockney, David 310
Holland 302, 340–1
Home, Sir Alec 80
home improvement grants 218
Home Office 275–6
home ownership 27, 213, 214,
  219–20, 225, 244, 250
homelessness 213, 225, 240
homophobia, growth of 267, 332
Hong Kong 158, 159
Honours lists 62
Hoskyns, Sir John 45, 123
Hospital and Community Health
  Services (HCHS) 170–1
hospitals 168–9, 171, 175, 180, 181
House of Lords 102, 107–9, 139
  Select Committee on Science and
    Technology 319, 323, 324,
    326
households, composition of 262–3
housework 265
housing 4, 213–22, 267
  council house sales 42, 214, 216,
    218–21
  finance for 213, 215–18
  legislation on 214–15
  new agencies in 221–2
  policy intentions 214–15
  regional variations in 255–6
  underfunding of 215
Housing Act (1980) 214, 221
Housing Act (1988) 128, 221
Housing Action Trusts 216, 221
housing associations 217
housing market 225, 255–6
Howard, George 301
Howe, Sir Geoffrey 8, 103, 145, 160
'human resource management' 73
humanist values 305
hunger strikes by IRA 228, 229
Hurd, Douglas 106, 141, 195, 234,
  275, 276, 296, 299, 335
Hussein, King 164
Hussey, Marmaduke 301

IBA (Independent Broadcasting
  Association) 296, 297, 301, 303
Ibbs, Sir Robin 117–18
'ideal society', public perceptions of
  242
illegitimacy 264
immigration legislation 282
immunities of unions 30, 66, 67, 247
imports 18, 27
income tax 83–4
incomes, family 268–72
incomes policy 5, 83, 85
Independent 293, 294
independent schools 193, 194
individualism, Thatcherite 194–5,
  251
Industrial Relations Act (1971) 82
industrial relations system 64
industry-wide bargaining 77
inequality, growth in 34–6
inflation 2, 8, 10, 11, 16, 17, 20,
  21, 23, 31, 32, 33, 65, 70, 78,
  81, 82, 83, 245, 253
information technology 322
infrastructure, decline of 224–5
Ingham, Bernard 294–5
inner cities 222
insider trading 56
Inspectorate of Pollution 223–4
Institute of Economic Affairs 84,
  245–6, 338
Interception of Communications Act
  (1985) 278–9
interest rates 16, 24, 32, 33
International Monetary Fund (IMF)
  7, 15, 103
investment 16, 29, 31, 78
IRA 226, 227, 228, 230, 233, 235
Iran 158
Israel 158, 160, 164
Italy 96, 302
ITV 298, 299–300, 301, 303

Jackson, Robert 206
Japan 10, 11, 39, 40, 47, 48, 136,
  155
  Japanese companies 72–3
Jay, Peter 7
Jenkin, Patrick 125, 174, 175, 178,
  294

Jenkins, David, Bishop of Durham 335, 339
Jenkins, Peter 97
Jenkins, Roy 252, 267
Jewish community 333, 334
Johnson, B. S. 310
Johnson, Paul 306
Johnson Matthey Bankers (JMB) 58–9
Joseph, Sir Keith 6, 98, 185, 190, 193, 198, 203, 206, 208

Kant, Immanuel 195
Kemp, Peter 119
Keynes, Maynard 123
Kiernan, Kathleen 264
King, Tom 125, 234, 236
Kinnock, Neil 76, 91, 92–3, 97, 113, 251
Kleinworts merchant bank 53
Knight, Dame Jill 176
Kristol, Irving 97

Laboratory of Molecular Biology 328
labour markets 3, 21, 24, 34
Labour Party 7
    and other non-Thatcherite parties 98–100
    and regional variations 258
    and unions 69, 76, 83
    decline of 93–5, 97, 100
    leadership of 91, 92–3
    new generation in 93
    percentage of vote 89, 93–5, 259–60
    periods in office 89–90
    policy changes in 92, 97–8
    problems in Commons 112–13
    reaction against 90
    turbulence in 91–2
Laing, Sir Hector 61
laissez-faire 48, 136
Lancaster House Conference 156–7
Land Rover, sale of 106
Larkin, Philip 314
law 274–89
    civil procedure 283–5
    criminal justice system 275–7, 279–81

important changes in 277–81
    reform of legal profession 274, 283, 286–8, 289
    successes/failures of right-wing extremism 276–7, 278–9, 280–3
Lawson, Nigel 6, 7–9, 57, 58, 59, 103
lead pollution 223
LEAs (local education authorities) 184, 185, 186, 188, 189, 191–2
Leavis, F. R. 309
Lebanon 158
Lee, Jennie 307
Leeds University 301–2
legal aid 284–5, 287
Legal Aid Act (1988) 284–5
legal profession, reform of 44, 274, 283, 286–8
Leigh-Pemberton, Robin 50–1, 58, 59, 60, 61
'level funding' of universities, broken promises on 199–200
Levene, Sir Peter 120
Leverhulme inquiry 202
liberal consensus view, in Churches 336–7, 338–9, 340, 341
liturgy 335, 339
Livingstone, Ken, 93, 130
Lloyd George, David 240
Lloyd's 49, 51, 62
'Lobby' system 294–5
local government 91, 100, 101, 113, 124–32
    and 'efficiency'/service cuts 127–8
    and housing 213–14, 217, 218, 221, 222
    and poll tax 126–7, 131
    destruction of 124, 125–6, 127–8, 129, 130, 132, 137, 185, 191, 338
    long-term trends in 130–2
    underfunding of 125–6
London 252, 254, 255, 256
Long, Richard 312–13

Macaulay, Thomas 271–2
McCracken Group 10
Macdonald, Ramsay 252
Macgregor, Sir Ian 67

Mackay of Clashfern, Lord 274, 275, 286
McLean, Bruce 312
Macleod, Iain 80
McMahon, Sir Kit 61
Maitland, Sir Donald 294
manipulation of news, Thatcherite 294–5
Manpower Services Commission (MSC) 188
manufacturing industry 11, 21, 38–40, 46, 272
marginal tax rates 26, 34, 36
market, subordination of all other values to 135–7, 140, 192–5
Marks and Spencer 117
marriage, age of 263–4
Marxism Today 128
Mason, Roy 93
Matrimonial and Family Proceedings Act (1984) 283
Maynard, Geoffrey 23
media 290–304
   and Thatcherite news manipulation 294–5
   and trade unions 290, 291–3
   Thatcherite drive towards repression/vulgarization of 294, 295–303
Medical Research Council 317, 321, 328
Medium Term Financial Strategy (1980) 7, 9
Meir, Golda 160
Methodism 331, 339, 341
Middle East 164
Middleton, Sir Peter 58, 61
Militant Tendency 93
Mill, John Stuart 141
Miller, Sir Peter 62
miners' strikes:
   (1974) 65
   (1984–5) 30, 67–8
Minford, Patrick 5
minimum wages 69
Ministry of Agriculture, Fisheries and Food (MAFF) 321, 323
Ministry of Defence (MoD) 151–2, 319
Mitterrand, François 7

monetarism 8–9, 31–2, 65, 81, 82, 83, 84, 85
Monopolies Commission 44
Moore, Henry 312
Moore, John 176, 177
Morgan Grenfell merchant bank 51–2
MORI polls 241–3
Morrison, Herbert 42
Morse, Sir Jeremy 61
mortgage rates 31, 214, 216–17
Mount, Ferdinand 236, 265, 266
Mountbatten, Earl Louis 227
'multiculturalism' 333
Murdoch, Iris 310
Murdoch, Rupert 30, 290, 292
Muslim community 330, 334
mutuality of interest, industrial 72
Muzorewa, Bishop 156
'My Country, Right or Wrong' 295
Mysercough, John 308

N. M. Rothschild merchant bank 53, 61
National Advisory Body (NAB) 201, 202, 209–10
National Association of Health Authorities (NAHA) 170
National Audit Office 107
National Debt 53, 61
National Economic Development Office 20
National Institute of Economic and Social Research 40
'national security' 282–3
National Union of Journalists (NUJ) 290, 291
nationality law 279
nationalization/nationalized industries 28, 42, 67, 248–9
NATO 144, 145, 146, 147, 162
Natural Environment Research Council (NERC) 317, 321
'near-market' research 322–3
Neave, Airey 227
Neuhaus, Richard 338
New Ireland Forum 230
New Society 262
New York Times 227
New Zealand 96

Newbigin, Lesslie, Bishop 338
newly industrializing countries
    (NICs) 14–15
News International 292
News of the World 292
newspaper industry 290, 291–5
Next Steps, The 118–19
Nimrod Early Warning aircraft 144
Norman, Edward 337
North of England 252, 256, 257
North Sea oil 13, 17–18, 21, 39,
    155
Northcote–Trevelyan
    recommendations 119
Northern Ireland 163, 226–37, 252,
    261, 276, 282
Nott, John 144, 146, 150
Novak, Michael 338
Nozick, Robert 135
nuclear accidents 223
nuclear deterrence 144, 145–6,
    147–9
NUM (National Union of
    Mineworkers) 67, 68, 74, 83
nurses 175, 177

Oakes, Gordon 199
'obscenity' 267, 281–2
Office of Fair Trading 44
official secrets 282–3, 295–6
oil price explosion 9–10, 11, 31
Olson, Mancur 38
'One Nation' 336, 340
OPEC 9
opinion polls 167, 241–4, 245–9
opposition parties 89–100
    and 'anti-Thatcherite majority'
        98–100
    and constitutional reforms 139–40
    and left in Western Europe 95–6
    decline of 93–5, 97, 100
    new opportunities for 97–9
    percentage of vote 89, 93–5
    turbulence of 90–3, 99–100
Organisation for Economic Co-
    operation and Development
    (OECD) 2, 10, 25, 28–9
Orme, Stanley 93
overseas assets 15–16
overseas students 199

Owen, David 93, 97, 99, 147, 156
Oxford University 203, 339

Parkes, Sir Edward 201
Parkinson, Cecil 43–4, 55, 103
Parliament 102, 107–13
    and back-bench behaviour 110–12
    and select committees 109–10
    government defeats in 107–9, 111
    opposition parties in 112–13
Parsons, Sir Anthony 101
Patriotic Front 155–6
Pattie, Sir Geoffrey 107
Patton, Christopher 231
Pavitt, Keith 323–4
Peacock, Sir Alan 303
Peacock Committee 298–9, 300
pensions 267
Percy Report 209
Peres, Shimon 164
'permissiveness' 267–8
philistinism towards universities,
    Thatcherite 199, 200, 201–2,
    203, 204, 205–6, 208–9,
    316–17, 327–8, 329
planning issues 222
pluralism, social 138
poetry 314
Poland 145, 162
Polaris 146, 147
Police:
    anti-trade union activities 67–8
    corruption in 296
    powers of 277, 280–1
Police and Criminal Evidence Act
    (1984) 276, 279, 280
Policy Studies Institute 270, 308
Policy Unit 101, 104, 122, 185, 265
political funds 49, 69
politicization of Civil Service 120–1
poll tax ('community charge') 108,
    126–7, 131, 191
pollution 223–4
polytechnics 200–1, 202, 207, 209,
    210
Polytechnics and Colleges Funding
    Council 204
Ponting, Clive 121, 295
population movements 255
'post-materialist' issues 98

'post-modernism' in arts 310–13
poverty, explosion of 35, 268–9
poverty trap 26, 270
Powell, Enoch 174
power, accountability of 141
power-sharing in Northern Ireland 226, 227
Presbyterian Church 331
Press Association 290
Prevention of Terrorism Act 235
prices and incomes policy 83, 85
Prior, James 65, 66, 103, 227, 228, 229, 230
privatization 3, 6, 28, 42–4, 53, 61, 84–5, 109, 219, 224, 225, 248–9
productivity growth 12–13, 18–20, 29, 39–40, 42, 48, 78
profits 41
Prosecution of Offences Act (1985) 276, 279, 280
protectionist measures 4
public expenditure see expenditure, public; underfunding
public good, notion of 140
public health 168–9, 181
Public Health Laboratory Service 169
Public Order Act (1986) 279
public service ethic, loss of 123
publishing houses 311
pupil–teacher ratio 191
Pym, Francis 109, 144, 294

quotas on imports 27

radio 300
rape cases 277
ratecapping 125–6
Rayner, Sir Derek 102, 115–16
Reagan, Ronald/Reagan administration 7, 48, 143, 148, 149, 161
'Real Lives' programme on Northern Ireland 295
Rees, Merlyn 93
Rees-Mogg, Lord 307, 308
regional variations 251–61
  in economy 252–7

  in party politics 257–61
  in religious belief 333–4
religious belief 330, 331–2, 333–4, 340–1
religious minorities 330, 333–4
renal failure 174
rented housing/rents 27, 29, 217, 221
repression/vulgarization of media, Thatcherite drive towards 294, 295–303
research 203, 205, 316–29
restrictive practices 29, 30, 44
Retail Price Index (RPI) 31
Reykjavik summit 149, 161
Rhodesia 155–7
Richardson, Lord 58
Richardson, Michael 61
Ridley, Nicholas 128
Rifkind, Malcolm 106
'right to silence' 276
road vehicles, private 223, 224
Robbins Committee 198
Rodgers, William 93
rolls, falling 190–1
Roman Catholic Pastoral Congress 337
Roman Catholics 331, 334, 335
Rothschild, Lord 320–1
Royal Academy 310
Royal Air Force (RAF) 151
Royal College of Nurses 70
Royal Commission on Environmental Pollution 224
Royal Navy 150–1
RUC (Royal Ulster Constabulary) 234, 235
Rushdie, Salman 310, 330
Ruskin speech (1976) 183, 187
Russell, George 301

S. G. Warburg investment bank 61
Salisbury, Robert Cecil, Lord 124, 136
Salisbury Review 338
Salmonella poisoning 168
sanctuary, government violation of 330
Santer, Mark 338
satellite television 297

Save British Science Movement 326
savings 16, 31, 244, 245
Scargill, Arthur 30, 67–8, 83, 93,
    134, 336
Scholey, Sir David 61
school governing bodies 187
schools 183–95, 266
    and curriculum 183, 184, 187–8,
        189, 191, 192
    and Education Reform Act (1988)
        183, 184, 185, 186, 187,
        190, 192
    religion in 332–3
    Thatcherite philistinism towards
        192–5
    underfunding of 190, 193
science, underfunding of 316–29
'science vote' 317, 319, 320, 327
Scotland 97, 132, 137, 138, 254,
    257, 258, 260, 333
Scotsman 294
Scott, Nicholas 230
Scottish National Party 260
'scrutinies' of Civil Service 115–16,
    117
sculpture 312–13
secondary picketing 66
secret ballots 66
Securities and Investments Board 56,
    57
securities market 54
Security Service Bill 282, 283
select committees 109–10, 207
self-employment 244
self-reliance, ethic of 243–4, 245
Senior Appointments Selection
    Committee 120
SERPS 267
Sex Discrimination Act (1986) 278
sexual morals 267, 332
Shah, Eddie 290, 291–2
share ownership 53
Sheppard, David, Bishop of
    Liverpool 338
shop stewards 71, 72
Silkin, John 93
Sillars, Jim 252
Single European Market 13, 44,
    45–6
single-parent families 241

Sinn Fein 226, 229, 231, 233
Sky channel 297
small firms 46
Smiles, Samuel 244
Smith, Adam 251
Smith, John 93, 113
Soames, Lord 103, 157
Social and Community Planning
    Research 265
Social and Liberal Democrats
    (SLDP) 91, 95, 97, 99–100
Social Democratic and Labour Party
    233, 235, 237
Social Democratic Party (SDP) 97,
    99
social security 3, 34, 35, 269–70
Social Security Act (1986) 267, 270
Social Trends 263, 332
social trends 262–5
socialist v. Thatcherite values 242,
    246, 247, 249, 250
solicitors 44, 283, 287–8
    as judges 274
South Africa 154, 156, 164
South of England 251, 252, 253,
    254–5, 256
Soviet Union 145, 158, 162
Spain 96, 159
Spectator 236, 337
sponsorship of arts, private 306–7
Sprinkel, Beryl 6
Spycatcher fiasco 121, 275, 295
squalor, public, growth of 224
St John-Stevas, Norman 109
St Martin's School of Art 312
'stagflation' 10, 11
Stanbrook, Ivor 231
Stanley Royd affair 168
Star 293
statistical sleight-of-hand,
    Thatcherite 206
Steel, David 336
sterling 20–4
    depreciation of 17, 18, 33
Stock Exchange 41, 54–6
Stockton, Harold Macmillan, Earl of
    108
Stormont Parliament 226
Strategic Defence Initiative (SDI or
    'star wars') 148

Strauss, Norman 123
Straw, Jack 93, 113
student fees/loans 204–5
subsidies, industrial 3, 29
Sun 292, 293, 294
Sunday Sport 294
Sunday Times 279, 292
Sunday trading 111
Sunningdale Agreement 226
supply-side policies 27–30
Supreme Court Act (1981) 283
Swinnerton-Dyer, Sir Peter 201

Tate Gallery 309
taxation:
    and women 264, 271
    cuts in 25, 26, 245, 247
    rates of 26
    reliefs on 26, 27, 216–17
    total burden of 26
Taylor Committee 187
teachers 184, 185, 186, 188,
    189–90, 191, 193–4
Tebbit, Norman 66, 103, 267, 268
Technical and Vocational Education
    Initiative (TVEI) 184, 188–9
technological revolution 52
telephone tapping 278–9
Thames Television 296
Thatcher, Denis 51
Thatcher, Margaret
    and Cabinet 102–7
    and Civil Service 115, 116,
        120–1, 122, 123
    and 'Victorian values' 239
    attitude to City 49, 50–2, 56,
        60–2
    attitude to EMS 33–4
    authoritarianism of 102–3, 105–6,
        107, 113, 122, 133–4, 136–7,
        138–9, 141–2, 268, 296
    dislike of media independence
        290–1, 295–6, 301
    ideological obsessions of 27,
        126–7, 130, 240
    'love affair' with Reagan 143, 161
    militarism of 143–4, 149
    philistinism towards universities
        203, 339
    religious pronouncements by 335

    reported attitude of Queen
        towards 339
Thomson of Monifieth, Lord 301
Thorneycroft, Peter 81
Three Day Week 10
Times, The 290, 292, 296, 337, 338
Tisdall, Sarah 295
Tocqueville, Alexis de 139
Today 292
Tower Commission 143
trade regimes 4
Trade Union Act (1927) 69
trade unions 64–78
    and miners' strikes 30, 65, 67–8
    decline of membership 69–71
    democratization of 68–9, 247
    historical position 5, 64–5, 82,
        134
    in Civil Service 121–2
    in newspaper industry 290, 291–3
    lack of opposition to Thatcherism
        91
    new laws on 30, 65–7, 68
    new patterns in 71–4
    permanent changes in status of
        28, 30, 75–7, 83, 134
    public opinion in 247–8
training programmes 7, 47, 74
Treasury 15, 32, 33, 117, 118, 119,
    200, 266, 284
Tribune Group 111
Trident 146, 147, 148, 149, 150
TUC 68, 72, 73, 74–5
'two nations' 252
two-earner families 271

Ulster Unionists 228–9, 230–1,
    233–4, 236, 237
underfunding:
    of arts 306–8, 310
    of health service 166, 169–71,
        172–3, 175–7, 180–1
    of higher education 199–200,
        201, 204–6
    of housing 215
    of local government 125–6
    of schools 190, 193
    of science 316–29
unemployment 2, 5, 7, 11, 12, 21,

23, 24, 37, 70, 71, 78, 199, 244, 245, 256–7, 269, 270–1
United Nations 156, 157, 162
  UN Security Council 155
universities 200, 201–2, 203, 204, 205–6, 208–9
  and research 203, 205, 316, 327–8, 329
Universities Funding Council 203–4
University Grants Committee (UGC) 199, 200, 201–2, 207, 208, 317, 319, 328, 329
Urban Development Corporations (UDCs) 129, 221
USA 47, 74, 81–2, 86–7, 96, 143–4, 145, 146–7, 148–9, 154, 161, 163, 186, 208

values, social, resistance to Thatcherism 239–50
Vance, Cyrus 156
Varley, Eric 93
'Victorian values' 239, 332
vouchers, educational 197, 198

wage explosion 20–1
Wages Act (1986) 69
Wages Councils 69
Waite, Terry 330
Wales 254, 260, 333
Walker, David 57
Walker, Peter 43, 131
Walters, Sir Alan 50, 60, 101
Wass, Sir Douglas 113, 295
water pollution 223, 224
Waterstone's bookshops 311
Weatherill, Bernard 107

Weinberger, Caspar 144
Welfare State 135, 266, 273
  see also health service; social security
West Germany see Germany
West Midlands 254, 257
Westland affair 103, 105–6, 143, 151
Wheeler, John 299
Whitelaw, William 106, 107, 275, 280, 290
Wilde, Oscar 140
Williams, Shirley 92, 199, 320, 336
Williams Committee 281–2
Wilson, Angus 310
Wilson, Harold/Wilson government 34, 64, 91, 94, 103, 114, 122, 134, 160, 226
'Winter of Discontent' 5, 10–11, 64, 90, 94
women:
  and taxation 264, 271
  ordination of 330, 334–5
  relative emancipation of 264–5
Woodrow, Bill 312
working class 94, 95
world affairs 154–65
World Council of Churches 339

Young, David 188
Young, Lord 44, 46, 299
Young, Stuart 301
Younger, George 151
youth custody 278

Index compiled by Peva Keene

OXFORD

MORE OXFORD PAPERBACKS

Details of a selection of other Oxford Paperbacks follow. A complete list of Oxford Paperbacks, including The World's Classics, Twentieth-Century Classics, OPUS, Past Masters, Oxford Authors, Oxford Shakespeare, and Oxford Paperback Reference, is available in the UK from the General Publicity Department, Oxford University Press (RS), Walton Street, Oxford, OX2 6DP.

In the USA, complete lists are available from the Paperbacks Marketing Manager, Oxford University Press, 200 Madison Avenue, New York, NY 10016.

Oxford Paperbacks are available from all good bookshops. In case of difficulty, customers in the UK can order direct from Oxford University Press Bookshop, 116 High Street, Oxford, Freepost, OX1 4BR, enclosing full payment. Please add 10 per cent of the published price for postage and packing.

THATCHERISM AND BRITISH POLITICS
The End of Consensus?
Dennis Kavanagh

Mrs Thatcher has cited the breaking of the post-war political consensus, established with the support of dominant groups in the Conservative and Labour parties, as one of her objectives. In this penetrating study of her style and performance, she emerges both as the midwife of the collapse of consensus and also as its product.

LABOUR IN POWER 1945–1951
Kenneth O. Morgan

Kenneth O. Morgan's book is a uniquely detailed and comprehensive account of the Attlee government. It is the first study to be based on the vast range of unpublished material from the period, and draws on numerous personal papers as well as public records.

'a remarkable achievement of political history' A. J. P. Taylor, *London Review of Books*

'history at its very best' *New Society*

'A considerable achievement . . . it will be required reading for students of modern history for at least a generation to come.' *The Economist*

'a marvellous account of how this most gifted, intelligent and idealistic Cabinet applied its collective mind to the great questions of the age' Michael Foot, *Observer*

THE REAL WORLD OF DEMOCRACY

C. B. Macpherson

In the Massey Lectures, delivered over the Canadian Broadcasting Corporation in 1965, Professor Macpherson examines what he considers to be three legitimate forms of democracy: the liberal democracy of the West, the kind of democracy practised in the Soviet block countries, and the mass democracy of the newly independent states of Africa and Asia. The work is attractively written and the argument is provocative: it should stimulate discussion on an important subject. At another level it seeks to question the validity of all the acquisitive and competitive motives that have characterized human survival and progress in the past.

THE RISE AND FALL OF ECONOMIC JUSTICE AND OTHER PAPERS

C. B. Macpherson

Aspects of twentieth-century democracy such as economic justice, human rights, industrial democracy, property, pluralism, and the roots of liberalism are explored in this book, which carries further the analyses made in C. B. Macpherson's previous two books. The essays contained in this volume are at once comparative and historical, and their subject-matter is wide-ranging.

'The book is wide in scope . . . For those concerned with the notion of property and its role in society this is a valuable addition.' *British Book News*

WAR AND THE LIBERAL CONSCIENCE

The George Trevelyan Lectures in the University of Cambridge, 1977

Michael Howard

Isn't war rooted in the vested interests of the ruling classes? (But have not democracies proved as bellicose as other states?) Should not political disputes be settled by civilized negotiations? (But what if the adversary is not, by your standards, 'civilized'?) Ought states to steer clear of other states' internal conflict? (Or should they help liberate oppressed peoples?) Which is better, appeasement or a war to end war? Such questions reflect the confusion that still besets liberal-minded people in the face of war, despite centuries of trying to discover its causes and secure its abolition.

Michael Howard traces the pattern in attitudes from Erasmus to the Americans after Vietnam, and concludes that peacemaking 'is a task which has to be tackled afresh every day of our lives.'

'So well written that it could be read as a novel—except few novels are so interesting. To take one strand of history and unravel it in this way is not only a service to historians but to the ordinary bus-riding liberal anxious to clarify his own thought.' Jo Grimond, *Books and Bookmen*

HOW TO BEAT UNEMPLOYMENT

Richard Layard

Unemployment is the major social problem of our time. In Britain it is now as high as it was in the 1930s; many people doubt whether it can be reduced. The obvious remedy of increasing public spending appears to cause an undesirable increase in inflation as well. This book investigates the causes of unemployment and makes strong and detailed recommendations for reducing it, expanding output, and containing inflation. The strategy includes creating jobs to suit the abilities of the unemployed, training the less skilled, reintroducing an incomes policy, and defending the value of the pound.

TOWN, CITY & NATION

England 1850–1914

P. J. Waller

By the outbreak of the First World War England had become the world's first mass urban society. In just over sixty years, the proportion of urban dwellers had risen from fifty to eighty per cent, and during this period many of the most crucial developments in English urban society had taken place.

This book provides a uniquely comprehensive analysis of those developments—conurbations, suburbs, satellite towns, garden cities, and seaside resorts—which so fascinated the rest of the world. Nevertheless, while proper recognition is given to the importance of London, the provincial cities, and manufacturing centres, the author emphasizes the continuing influence of the small country town and 'rural' England on political, economic, and cultural growth. In many respects, P. J. Waller's book is a general social history of late nineteenth- and early twentieth-century England, seen from an urban perspective. Vividly written, it will appeal both to the student and to the general reader who is keen to understand the exuberant and melancholy features of modern English towns and cities.

An OPUS book

SOVIET FOREIGN POLICY

The Brezhnev Years

Robin Edmonds

In this book Robin Edmonds, a former minister at the British Embassy in Moscow, presents a dispassionate view of the foreign policy pursued by the Soviet Union during Leonid Brezhnev's eighteen years as General Secretary of the Soviet Communist Party. Taking as its point of departure the Cuban missile crisis of 1962, the book analyses the Soviet Union's ascent to super-power status, the complex negotiations of the *détente* period, and the evolution and subsequent erosion of the relationship between the Soviet Union and the USA.

SOCIALISMS

Anthony Wright

'an attractive starting point for anyone who has to teach about socialist politics' John Dunn, *Times Higher Educational Supplement*

One third of the world's population now lives under a regime which describes itself as socialist. But what precisely is socialism? Marxists claim that they are the only true socialists, but this is hotly denied by Trotskyists, Anarchists, Fabians, Collectivists, Syndicalists, Social Democrats and members of the many other 'socialist' movements.

In this lucid and unitimidating introduction to the subject Anthony Wright argues that the contradictions, rivalries, and antagonisms within socialism arise from the absence of a single socialist tradition. The very word 'socialism' has (as R. H. Tawney put it) 'radiant ambiguities'.

Socialisms develops this theme throughout a wide-ranging analysis of socialist theories and practices, and concludes, provocatively, with a look at the future prospects of contemporary socialisms.

An OPUS book

THINKING ABOUT PEACE AND WAR

Martin Ceadel

In the nuclear age the ethics of war, and the policies of pacifism have become matters of increasingly urgent concern. Martin Ceadel analyses the various arguments and describes, rather than prescribes, the standpoints, of the twentieth century's most crucial debate.

The author is Tutor in Politics and a Fellow of New College, Oxford.

'a masterly analysis' *Reconciliation Quarterly*

'The book sets out to remedy what the author rightly describes as "an astonishing deficiency in popular or international-relations theory". It does this in a lively and perceptive manner . . . an admirable book.' Adam Roberts, *New Society*

An OPUS book

POLICING LIBERAL SOCIETY

Steve Uglow

In recent years we have seen the British police involved in pitched battles with miners, youths, even hippies. All this is a long way from the comforting image of George Dixon and of the 'friend in blue' of the 1960s.

Steve Uglow argues that our expectations of our police are no longer realistic: they are presented as crime fighters when their ability to affect crime rates is only marginal. Although the police portray themselves as acting within, and accountable to the 'the rule of law', their relationship with the State is complex and ill-defined. Under the guise of the 'public interest', the police can—and do—involve themselves in all areas of life. What then is the proper province of the police within a liberal· society? Are they crime-fighters, social workers, maintainers of public order, or even definers of the 'moral' or 'normal'?

The author suggests that the police have become vulnerable to the authoritarianism of governments. What is needed is a proper constitutional status for the force, protecting its independence, giving substance to its neutrality, and extending its accountability.

An OPUS book

THE LIFE AND TIMES OF LIBERAL DEMOCRACY

C. B. Macpherson

This is a concise and lucid analysis of the changing interpretation of democracy and the accompanying changes in the ways it can be achieved. In tracing the background of current liberal–democratic theory, Professor Macpherson rejects the claims commonly made for the seventeenth-century Puritans, Jefferson and Rousseau, as liberal democrats, and argues that liberal–democratic theory begins (and begins badly) with Bentham and James Mill. He explains how the concept of democracy became both embedded in the shifting ideas of social equality and increasingly dependent on the mechanism of capitalism, and points the way to a more participatory democracy which would give the ordinary man a self-fulfilling role.

CHANGE IN BRITISH SOCIETY

Third Edition

A. H. Halsey

This book was first published in 1978 as an expanded version of that year's Reith Lectures; it has been continually updated, and this third edition constitutes a substantial revision of the original, with the inclusion of important new material. The author is a distinguished sociologist who here analyses the direction British society has taken in this century. He points to changes involving class and status, social and geographical mobility, standards of living and family life, and explains how these changes have been affected by patterns of economic growth, liberal and Marxist political theories, and the power of the State. An additional chapter is devoted to changes in the accessibility, ideals, and practice of education.

This lucidly argued, honest book offers a provocative analysis of British society. It raises questions of importance to us all and proposes solutions which are at once sane and radical.

SPEAK FOR YOURSELF

A Mass-Observation Anthology, 1937–1949

Edited by Angus Calder and Dorothy Sheridan

It would be hard to find more realistic glimpses of British life in the 1930s and 1940s than are provided in this selection from the remarkable Mass-Observation Archive at Brighton. One of the main projects Tom Harrisson established was the investigation into 'Worktown'—in fact, Bolton—and this material is represented here with special attention to pubs and drinking. 'The Blitz and its Aftermath' gives first-hand reports of air-raids, tube-dwellers, and pin-up girls; 'Women 1937–45' covers subjects as diverse as cotton-winding and the intimacies of marriage; and 'Aspects of Politics 1940–49' includes everything from the Eddisbury by-election to an interview with the King of Poland.

Incidents from everyday life suddenly come into focus, incidents too inconspicuous to have reached the newspapers, far more vivid than memory could supply them—some hilarious, some poignant—all fascinating because they aim to be 'objective' truth.

THE INDUSTRIAL REVOLUTION
1760–1830

T. S. Ashton

The Industrial Revolution has sometimes been regarded as a catastrophe which desecrated the English landscape and brought social oppression and appalling physical hardship to the workers. In this book, however, it is presented as an important and beneficial mark of progress. In spite of destructive wars and a rapid growth of population, the material living standards of most of the British people improved, and the technical innovations not only brought economic rewards but also provoked greater intellectual ingenuity. Lucidly argued and authoritative, this book places the phenomenon of the Industrial Revolution in a stimulating perspective.

An OPUS book

THE AGE OF ILLUSION

Ronald Blythe

'*The Age of Illusion* accomplishes more than any orthodox history . . . a moving and stimulating study.' *Sunday Times*

In this brilliant reconstruction of Britain between the wars Ronald Blythe highlights a number of key episodes and personalities which characterize those two extraordinary decades. The period abounds in astonishing figures: the Home Secretary, Joynson-Hicks, cleaning up London's morals while defending General Dyer for the massacre of 379 Indians at Amritsar; Mrs Meyrick, the night-club queen, being regularly raided at the '43'; John Reith putting the BBC on its feet and the public in its place; headline stealers such as Amy Johnson, T. E. Lawrence and the body-line bowling controversy. And behind this garish façade we are shown the new writers emerging from their embarrassingly middle-class backgrounds, and the birth of Britain's first radical intelligentsia.

Ronald Blythe writes with perception, humour and conviction and provides a vivid and compelling portrait of Britain over twenty turbulent years.

A THEORY OF ECONOMIC HISTORY

John Hicks

Economists are inclined to think of the market economy as always existing, just developing or 'growing'; historians (and anthropologists) know very well that this is not the case. An attempt is made in this book to build a bridge between their opposing views. Its subject is the evolution of the market economy, its forms and institutions; an evolution which has great things to its credit, but has many darker sides. Some of the dark sides—slavery, usury, and the grimmer aspects of colonization—are given considerable attention. The discussion culminates in an analysis of the Industrial Revolution. Examples drawn from four thousand years of history illustrate this celebrated study.

THE IMPACT OF ENGLISH TOWNS, 1700–1800

P. J. Corfield

English towns in the eighteenth century displayed great vitality and diversity. While elegant social life was in its heyday in Bath, Hogarth was painting the horrors of London's Gin Lane, and the first Liverpool Docks were opened in an atmosphere of confidence. The book examines both the impact of English towns and their collective influence on the wider economy and society. The towns were a powerful force for change, but urban growth is not presented as the 'first cause' of industrialization. Drawing upon much new material, what Dr Corfield's synthesis reveals is the complexity of the transformation that eighteenth-century towns were themselves undergoing.

'Penelope Corfield looks back on eighteenth-century England from a refreshingly new vantage point . . . All in all, the work succeeds admirably in fulfilling its primary objective of providing an account for the "general reader as well as for students". Among professional historians it is certain to stimulate a new appreciation of that hitherto neglected urban terrain that lies between the early modern town and the Victorian city.' *Journal of Economic History*

An OPUS book